*Building on the Foundations
of Evangelical Theology*

BUILDING ON THE FOUNDATIONS OF EVANGELICAL THEOLOGY

Essays in Honor of John S. Feinberg

Edited by Gregg R. Allison
and Stephen J. Wellum

CROSSWAY
WHEATON, ILLINOIS

Building on the Foundations of Evangelical Theology: Essays in Honor of John S. Feinberg
Copyright © 2015 by Gregg R. Allison and Stephen J. Wellum
Published by Crossway
    1300 Crescent Street
    Wheaton, Illinois 60187

All rights reserved. No part of this publication may be reproduced, stored in a retrieval system, or transmitted in any form by any means, electronic, mechanical, photocopy, recording, or otherwise, without the prior permission of the publisher, except as provided for by USA copyright law.

Cover design: Studio Gearbox

First printing 2015

Printed in the United States of America

Unless otherwise indicated, Scripture quotations are from the ESV® Bible (The Holy Bible, English Standard Version®), copyright © 2001 by Crossway, a publishing ministry of Good News Publishers. Used by permission. All rights reserved.

Scripture references marked NIV are taken from The Holy Bible, New International Version®, NIV®. Copyright © 1973, 1978, 1984, 2011 by Biblica, Inc.™ Used by permission. All rights reserved worldwide.

Scripture references marked NIV 1984 are taken from The Holy Bible, New International Version®, NIV®. Copyright © 1973, 1978, 1984 by Biblica, Inc.™ Used by permission. All rights reserved worldwide.

Scripture quotations marked NASB are from *The New American Standard Bible*®. Copyright © The Lockman Foundation 1960, 1962, 1963, 1968, 1971, 1972, 1973, 1975, 1977, 1995. Used by permission.

The Scripture reference marked RSV is from *The Revised Standard Version*. Copyright ©1946, 1952, 1971, 1973 by the Division of Christian Education of the National Council of the Churches of Christ in the U.S.A.

The Scripture quotation marked KJV is from the *King James Version* of the Bible.

All emphases in Scripture quotations have been added by the authors.

The following Bible versions were cited but not quoted: American Standard Version (ASV), Common English Bible (CEB), Holman Christian Standard Bible (HCSB), New King James Version (NKJV), New Revised Standard Version (NRSV), and Today's New International Version (TNIV).

Hardcover ISBN: 978-1-4335-3817-9
ePub ISBN: 978-1-4335-3820-9
PDF ISBN: 978-1-4335-3818-6
Mobipocket ISBN: 978-1-4335-3819-3

Library of Congress Cataloging-in-Publication Data

Building on the foundations of evangelical theology : essays in honor of John S. Feinberg / edited by Gregg R. Allison and Stephen J. Wellum.
    pages cm
    Includes bibliographical references and index.
    ISBN 978-1-4335-3817-9 (hc)
    1. Evangelicalism. 2. Theology, Doctrinal. I. Feinberg, John S., 1946- honoree. II. Allison, Gregg R., editor.
BR1640.B85 2015
230'.04624—dc23   2014044881

Crossway is a publishing ministry of Good News Publishers.

TS		25	24	23	22	21	20	19	18	17	16	15
15	14	13	12	11	10	9	8	7	6	5	4	3	2	1

Contents

Introduction 7
Contributors 11

I
DESIGNING THE ARCHITECTURE OF EVANGELICAL THEOLOGY

1. Improvising Theology according to the Scriptures: An Evangelical Account of the Development of Doctrine (Kevin J. Vanhoozer) 15

2. Hermeneutics and Evangelical Theology (Walter C. Kaiser, Jr.) 51

3. Does the Apostle Paul Reverse the Prophetic Tradition of the Salvation of Israel and the Nations? (Robert L. Saucy) 66

4. Epistemic Eucatastrophe: The Favorable Turn of the Evidence (Thomas A. Provenzola) 91

5. Christian Miracle Claims and Supernatural Causation: Representative Cases from the Synoptic Gospels and Contemporary Accounts (Gary R. Habermas) 114

II
SETTING THE FOUNDATIONS OF EVANGELICAL THEOLOGY

6. The Glory of God in the Doctrine of God (Bruce A. Ware) 135

7. The Doctrine of the Trinity: Consistent and Coherent (Keith E. Yandell) 151

8. By What Authority Do We Say These Things? Enlightenment Dualism and the Modern Rejection of Biblical Authority (John Douglas Morrison) 168

9 The Many "Yes, buts . . ." of Theodicy: Revisiting John
   Feinberg's Account of Moral Evil (Thomas H. McCall) 189

10 Evangelical Christology and Kenotic Influences:
   A "New" and "Better" Way? (Stephen J. Wellum) 206

11 Holy God and Holy People: Pneumatology and Ecclesiology
   in Intersection (Gregg R. Allison) 235

12 God's Faithfulness, Human Suffering, and the Concluding
   Hallel Psalms (146–150): A Canonical Study
   (Willem VanGemeren) 263

III

ERECTING THE SUPERSTRUCTURE
OF EVANGELICAL THEOLOGY

13 Thinking Theologically in Public about Bioethics: Theological
   Formulation and Cultural Translation (John F. Kilner) 287

14 The Trinity, Imitation, and the Christian Moral Life
   (Graham A. Cole) 312

15 Christian Apologetics in a Globalizing and Religiously
   Diverse World (Harold A. Netland) 329

16 Ethics from the Margins: A Conversation with
   Womanist Thought (Bruce L. Fields) 353

Response by John Feinberg 374
Chronological List of John Feinberg's Publications 379
General Index 384
Scripture Index 392

Introduction

John Samuel Feinberg was born April 2, 1946, in Dallas, Texas, the third child and second son of Charles Lee and Anne Priscilla (Fraiman) Feinberg. When Charles became the founding dean of Talbot Theological Seminary in 1948, the family moved to Los Angeles, California. John did his undergraduate studies at UCLA, graduating in 1968 with a BA in English. In 1969–1970, as an instructor in doctrine at the Los Angeles Bible Training School, he began what would eventually become nearly a half-century teaching career.

John remained in California to pursue the MDiv, graduating from Talbot Theological Seminary in 1971. The following year he completed the ThM in systematic theology from Trinity Evangelical Divinity School. On August 19, 1972, John and Patricia Buecher were married. He began his PhD studies in historical theology and philosophy in the School of Religion at the University of Iowa, but his program was interrupted in 1973; subsequently, he concentrated on metaphysics and epistemology for his MA at the University of Chicago in 1974. He stayed there for his final studies in philosophy and his dissertation (*Theologies and Evil*), earning the PhD from the University of Chicago in 1978. At this time, John and Pat celebrated the birth of their first son, Josiah (1976); two other boys—Jonathan (1979) and Jeremy (1982)—were later added to the Feinberg family.

While pursuing his theological, pastoral, and philosophical training, John was involved in local ministry in a variety of capacities. As a staff member of the American Board of Missions to the Jews, he engaged in mission work in Los Angeles in 1970–1971 and in the U.S. Midwestern region from 1971 to 1974. He was ordained to the ministry in 1971 and served as the pastor of Elmwood Park Bible Church in Illinois from 1974 to 1976.

In God's providence, however, it was to a teaching career that God graciously called John to use his gifts and abilities to serve the larger evangelical church. John served as assistant professor of systematic theology at Western Conservative Baptist Seminary from 1976 to 1981. He then became professor of systematic theology and philosophy, as well as chairman of the Department of Theological Studies, at Liberty Baptist Seminary and College from 1981 to 1983. John's alma mater sought him out, so he became, first, associate professor (1983–1990), then professor of biblical and systematic theology at Trinity Evangelical Divinity School, the faculty position that he has held from 1991 to the present. He has twice served as the chairman of the Division of Biblical and Systematic Theology (1985–1992, 1999–2012).

In addition to these institutions, John has taught around the world. He has served as visiting professor or guest lecturer at numerous other venues, including Bethel Theological Seminary (St. Paul, Minnesota), Freie Theologische Akademie (Giessen, West Germany), Tyndale Theological Seminary (Badhoevedorp, Netherlands), Italian Bible Institute (Finocchio, Italy), Seminario Teologico Centro Americano (Guatemala City, Guatemala), Multnomah Biblical Seminary (Portland, Oregon), Emmaus Bible College (Sydney, Australia), Campus Crusade staff training (Split, Croatia), Greek Bible Institute (Pikermi, Greece), Odessa Theological Seminary (Odessa, Ukraine), University of Zimbabwe (Harare, Zimbabwe), Northern Province Bible Institute (Pietersburg, South Africa), Evangelical Reformed Baptist Seminary (Heidelberg, South Africa), Torch Trinity Institute of Lay Education (Norwood, New Jersey), Trinity Bible College and Equipping Center (Kursk, Russia), Talbot School of Theology: Feinberg Center for Messianic Jewish Studies (New York, New York), and The Master's Seminary (Sun Valley, California).

Having spent the majority of his teaching career at Trinity Evangelical Divinity School, John is a fixture at TEDS and has mentored hundreds of students who are now working as pastors, teachers, professors, staff in churches and parachurch movements, missionaries, philosophers, ethicists, apologists, evangelists, denominational leaders, and much more. Because of his research and writing on, and experience with, evil and suffering, John has also encouraged these students to rely on God's inscrutable providence and loving care as they encounter the trials of life. Trinity has also been the community of faith that has walked alongside John and Pat as Huntington's Chorea has slowly whittled away her life. As an outstanding example of grace and solidarity, Trinity has never questioned the advisability of John's ongoing teaching there in light of the demands that Pat's suffering has placed on him and his career.

Throughout his teaching career, John has established himself as a brilliant thinker, a prodigious scholar and author, an impassioned apologist for the faith, a demanding and fair instructor, a champion of clear and rational thinking, a giving friend, and a supportive mentor. John is well known in the classroom for his preparation and attention to detail, his careful analysis and critique of theological and philosophical positions and ideas, and his desire to see his students grow in the knowledge of Scripture and theological thinking. The same may also be found in all of his writing projects—detailed analysis, precision, and incisive biblical and theological exposition and critique. Besides teaching and writing, John has cultivated other interests and is always ready to discuss sports, show slides from his many travels, share the beautiful music of Andrea Bocelli, and wax eloquent about his wonderful wife and her suffering-proven faith.

John is well known for his many books, including *Ethics for a Brave New World*, coauthored with his brother Paul (Crossway, 1993; 2nd ed., rev. and expanded, 2010); *The Many Faces of Evil: Theological Systems and the Problems of Evil* (Zondervan, 1994; rev. and expanded, Crossway, 2004); *Deceived by God? A Journey through Suffering* (Crossway, 1997); his monumental *No One Like Him: The Doctrine of God*, part of the Foundations of Evangelical Theology series (Crossway, 2001); *Where Is God? A Personal Story of Finding God in Grief and Suffering* (B&H, 2004); and *Can You Believe It's True? Christian Apologetics in a Modern and Postmodern Era* (Crossway, 2013).[1]

Another major activity in which John has been engaged for more than two decades is serving as general editor of the aforementioned series on eleven major areas of evangelical systematic theology, entitled Foundations of Evangelical Theology and published by Crossway. Because Gregg Allison and Steve Wellum, two of John's former students, are contributors to this series, the idea for this Festschrift in John's honor was born. This volume therefore takes its name from it: *Building on the Foundations of Evangelical Theology*. The contributors are John's friends, colleagues, former students, and/or contributors to the Foundations series.

This book consists of three sections that are organized around the

---

[1] A complete list of John's writings may be found at the end of this book.

metaphor of building. Section 1, entitled "Designing the Architecture of Evangelical Theology," provides essays that discuss the areas of theological method (Kevin Vanhoozer), hermeneutics (Walter Kaiser, Jr.), continuity and discontinuity between the Testaments (Robert Saucy), philosophy (Thom Provenzola), and apologetics (Gary Habermas). The second section, "Setting the Foundations of Evangelical Theology," offers essays covering a wide range of biblical and theological topics such as: theology proper (Bruce Ware), Trinitarianism (Keith Yandell), bibliology (John Morrison), the problem of evil (Thomas McCall), Christology (Stephen Wellum), ecclesiology and pneumatology (Gregg Allison), and biblical reflections from Psalms 146–150 on God's faithfulness and human suffering (Willem VanGemeren). Section 3, "Erecting the Superstructure of Evangelical Theology," features essays on bioethics (John Kilner), Christian living (Graham Cole), globalization and mission in the midst of a rising religious pluralism (Harold Netland), and Womanist theology (Bruce Fields).

One of the great concerns of Crossway and all the contributors to this volume is how to honor not only John but his wonderful wife, Pat, as well. We know that heavy on their hearts, and on our hearts as well, is the debilitating illness, Huntington's Chorea, from which Pat suffers. All who know John and Pat are deeply saddened by this reality and have prayed for them and suffered with them. *Building on the Foundations of Evangelical Theology* intends to take this concern one step further. Instead of the royalties from this book going to the volume's contributors, they will be directed to the Huntington's Disease Society of America, in John and Pat Feinberg's names. It is the hope of the contributors to this volume that by our supporting research into Huntington's Chorea, the day will hasten when the riddle of this disease will be solved and prevention or even a cure will be discovered.

As the editors of this volume, and writing for Crossway and the other contributors, it is our sincere desire to express our love for our dear friend, colleague, professor, and mentor, John Feinberg, by honoring him with *Building on the Foundations of Evangelical Theology*. May this work not only express our gratitude to the Lord for the gift of John to the church, but may it also in some small way help the church to remain faithful in our day as we seek to do theology well for God's glory and for the good of the church.

Gregg Allison and Stephen Wellum, Editors

Contributors

Gregg R. Allison, Professor of Christian Theology, The Southern Baptist Theological Seminary

Graham A. Cole, Anglican Professor of Divinity, Beeson Divinity School

Bruce L. Fields, Chair of the Biblical and Systematic Theology Department, Associate Professor of Biblical and Systematic Theology, Trinity Evangelical Divinity School

Gary R. Habermas, Chair of the Department of Philosophy, Distinguished Research Professor, Liberty University

Walter C. Kaiser, Jr., President Emeritus, Colman M. Mockler Distinguished Professor Emeritus of Old Testament and Old Testament Ethics, Gordon-Conwell Theological Seminary

John F. Kilner, Director of Bioethics Programs, Franklin and Dorothy Forman Chair of Christian Ethics and Theology, Professor of Bioethics and Contemporary Culture, Trinity Evangelical Divinity School

Thomas H. McCall, Associate Professor of Biblical and Systematic Theology, Director, Carl F. H. Henry Center for Theological Understanding, Trinity Evangelical Divinity School

John Douglas Morrison, Professor of Philosophy and Theology, Liberty University

Harold A. Netland, Professor of Philosophy of Religion and Intercultural Studies, Trinity Evangelical Divinity School

Thomas A. Provenzola, Professor of Philosophy and Theology, Liberty University

Robert L. Saucy (1930–2015), Distinguished Professor of Systematic Theology, Talbot School of Theology

Willem VanGemeren, Professor Emeritus of Old Testament and Semitic Languages, Trinity Evangelical Divinity School

Kevin J. Vanhoozer, Research Professor of Systematic Theology, Trinity Evangelical Divinity School

Bruce A. Ware, T. Rupert and Lucille Coleman Professor of Christian Theology, The Southern Baptist Theological Seminary

Stephen J. Wellum, Professor of Christian Theology, The Southern Baptist Theological Seminary

Keith E. Yandell, Julius R. Weinberg Professor of Philosophy (retired), University of Wisconsin

I

DESIGNING THE ARCHITECTURE OF EVANGELICAL THEOLOGY

I

Improvising Theology according to the Scriptures: An Evangelical Account of the Development of Doctrine

KEVIN J. VANHOOZER

INTRODUCTION: DEVELOPING DOCTRINE BIBLICALLY

- "Christian Thought, for $1,000."
- *The most baffling and difficult problem of Christian theology.*[1]
- "What is the development of doctrine?"

No real *Jeopardy* contestant, to my knowledge, has ever had to ask this question. Yet the church is in jeopardy of losing its identity, and biblical moorings, if Christians do not ask and answer it: "no task confronting Christian theology today is more vital than the demand that it face this issue squarely."[2] The challenge is to show how Christian doctrine truly is "in accordance with the Scriptures" (1 Cor. 15:3). This is a particularly pressing problem for evangelical theologians, who affirm the supreme

---
[1] From dust jacket of Jan Hendrik Walgrave, *Unfolding Revelation: The Nature of Doctrine Development* (Philadelphia: Westminster, 1972).
[2] Jaroslav Pelikan, "Theology and Change," *Cross Currents* 19 (1969): 384.

16 *Kevin J. Vanhoozer*

authority of Scripture yet identify with diverse denominations, theological traditions, and doctrines.[3]

There are three reasons why giving an evangelical account of the development of doctrine is a particularly apt way to honor John Feinberg. First, John was for more than twenty years head of the Department of Biblical and Systematic Theology at Trinity Evangelical Divinity School, and the Department's name contains the very problem I wish here to address. "Biblical theology" has come to have two potentially contrasting meanings. The strict sense refers to the theology of the biblical books themselves (or to the historical task of determining and describing it), the broader sense to any theology that accords with the Bible. To speak of "development" of doctrine suggests that one is going beyond, but not against, biblical theology in the narrower sense of the term. That raises the question: is there something theologians have to do "after biblical theology"—after reconstructing the theology of the biblical authors—and, if so, what?

Second, John contributed an essay to and edited a highly regarded volume dealing with the problem of continuity and discontinuity, though John was addressing the problem of the relationship between the Old and New Testaments (and the difference between covenantal and dispensational systems for dealing with this), whereas I am addressing the problem of the relationship between Scripture and Christian doctrine.[4] The underlying problem is the same, namely, how to account for both the *sameness* between what the Scriptures and later creeds teach (i.e., continuity) while acknowledging some kind of *change* (i.e., discontinuity).

Third, in his chapter in the aforementioned volume and elsewhere, John has shown himself to be a dual threat, a person who does theology as both exegete and philosopher. For example, in his chapter he helpfully cautions against confusing a biblical *word* (*oikonomia* = "dispensation") with a *concept* (dispensation), much less a conceptual scheme or theo-

---

[3] Alister McGrath refers to this as "the Achilles' heel" of contemporary evangelicalism: "Evangelicalism, having affirmed the supreme authority of Scripture, finds itself without any meta-authority by which the correct interpretation of Scripture could be determined" ("Faith and Tradition," in *The Oxford Handbook to Evangelical Theology*, ed. Gerald R. McDermott [Oxford: Oxford University Press, 2010], 82). Cf. Malcolm B. Yarnell III, who says, "Evangelicalism has not offered a uniformly accepted doctrine of development" (*The Formation of Christian Doctrine* [Nashville: B&H Academic, 2007], 107).
[4] John S. Feinberg, ed., *Continuity and Discontinuity: Perspectives on the Relationship between the Old and New Testaments. Essays in Honor of S. Lewis Johnson, Jr.* (Westchester, IL: Crossway, 1988).

logical system (dispensationalism).[5] It is just such conceptual analysis that proves important in discussions of doctrinal development as well. A case in point: must doctrines be *identical* to retain their *identity* over time? Much depends on what "identical" and "identity" mean, and how one views change over time. These are philosophical questions. In light of John's work at the interstice of Bible, theology, and philosophy, then, I want to ask whether the continuity and discontinuity intrinsic to the development of doctrine is best understood by recourse to either analytic or Continental philosophical resources. Which best accounts for doctrinal development: analytic or hermeneutic theology?

The present essay responds to this either-or question, not by choosing one option but by incorporating aspects of both into a larger, properly *dogmatic* account of doctrinal development. Whereas church historians helpfully *describe* and *interpret* doctrinal change over time, systematic theologians need, and seek to provide, a *normative* account that assists the church in discerning which changes reflect genuine understanding and which do not. We need properly theological categories if we are to distinguish the development of orthodox doctrine from the kinds of changes that characterize things in general. To give a dogmatic account is to distinguish the *special development* of doctrine from theories of *general development*. What, then, is "special" about doctrinal development? My contention will be that (right) development of doctrine is an entailment of the gospel of the triune God: the Spirit "enlarges" the word in the process of its regional expansion in an economy of creative understanding that both preserves the good deposit and collects interest on truth's account.

DOCTRINAL DEVELOPMENT: THREE CASE STUDIES

Doctrine is what, on the basis of the Bible, the church believes, teaches, and confesses—both explicitly in its creeds and statements of faith and implicitly in its most characteristic practices.[6] Evangelicals are willing to speak of progressive revelation *in* the Bible, but most do not believe that revelation progresses *beyond* the Bible.[7] Jesus Christ is God's final word,

---
[5] Feinberg, "Systems of Discontinuity," in *Continuity and Discontinuity*, 69.
[6] See Jaroslav Pelikan, *The Christian Tradition: A History of the Development of Doctrine, Vol. 1: The Emergence of the Catholic Tradition* (Chicago: University of Chicago Press, 1971), 1.
[7] Some scholars contend, however, that there is doctrinal development within the thought of the human authors of Scripture. See, for example, E. P. Sanders, "Did Paul's Theology Develop?" in *The Word Leaps*

and he is "the same yesterday and today and forever" (Heb. 13:8). Hence revealed truth, the objective content of the faith, is fixed. By way of contrast, the church's appropriation of that truth is still in flux: the search for doctrinal understanding goes on.

Here, in two nutshells, is the problem: (1) evangelicals confess the sufficiency of Scripture but disagree as to what it teaches; (2) evangelicals proclaim *sola scriptura,* yet some doctrines are not explicitly taught in the Bible. It is impossible to study church history for long without being struck by both the continuities and the discontinuities in what the church believes, teaches, and confesses on the basis of the Word of God. As Jaroslav Pelikan notes, "The fact of the development of doctrine . . . is beyond question; what is at issue is the legitimacy and limits of development."[8]

What does it mean for a doctrine to develop? What actually happens? We can begin by distinguishing minimal from maximal development. Development is minimal (i.e., there is least change) when the church does not add anything to what Scripture says but simply comes to understand it. Development is maximal (i.e., there is most change) when the church introduces a teaching that cannot be derived from Scripture, such as the Roman Catholic doctrine of the Assumption of Mary, about which we can say, "There was a time when it was not!" Many doctrinal changes lie somewhere between these two extremes. Consider, for example, the following three case studies.

THE DEITY OF THE HOLY SPIRIT

The Bible does not explicitly teach the doctrine of the Trinity as expounded at the Council of Nicaea in 325. That Council affirmed the Son was of "the same substance" (*homoousios*) as the Father, but it fell to Basil of Caesarea to complete the case for—to develop the doctrine of—the deity of the Holy Spirit, and he did so in the face of considerable opposition. Some in the fourth century thought the Spirit was a creature; others refused to commit themselves. The so-called *Pneumatomachians* (lit., "enemies of the Spirit") accepted the divinity of the Son but not of the Spirit, and appealed to differences in the language

---
the Gap: Essays on Scripture and Theology in Honor of Richard B. Hays, ed. J. Ross Wagner, C. Kavin Rowe, and A. Katherine Grieb (Grand Rapids, MI: Eerdmans, 2008), 325–350.
[8] Pelikan, "An Essay on the Development of Christian Doctrine," *Church History* 35 (1966): 4.

Scripture uses to speak of each. They were particularly fond of reading theology off of prepositions, insisting that "from whom" applies to the Father, "through whom" to the Son, and "in whom" to the Spirit (cf. 1 Cor. 8:6; Rom. 8:9).[9]

Basil opens his treatise *On the Holy Spirit* by acknowledging, "not one of the words that are applied to God in every use of speech should be left uninvestigated."[10] Basil is vigilant in his use of language: he refrains from calling the Spirit "God" because the Bible does not; he is reluctant to say the Spirit is *homoousios* because the Nicene Creed fails to do so. However, he prays "to the Father, through the Son, in the Holy Spirit," and he vehemently protests the heretics' claim that, in doing so, he is denying the deity of the Spirit.

In a tour de force of prepositional theology, Basil painstakingly examines the biblical use of "through," "from," "with," and "in." He shows that Scripture uses the prepositions flexibly (e.g., "from whom" is often posited of the Spirit as well as the Father). More importantly, he argues that Scripture consistently ranks the Spirit with the Father and the Son, as when Jesus commands disciples to baptize "in the name of the Father and of the Son and of the Holy Spirit" (Matt. 28:19). Basil pointedly asks his opponents how to understand this passage if this common name and rank "is not indicative of some [ontological] communion or union."[11]

Basil's arguments carried the day at the Council of Constantinople in 381, which reaffirmed Nicaea, rejected the doctrine of the Pneumatomachians and, most importantly, confessed the deity of the Spirit, "who with the Father and the Son together is worshiped and glorified."[12] Call it a "level-1" doctrinal development—one that identifies *who* the God who works salvation is, and thus a doctrine on which the integrity of the gospel itself likewise depends.[13] The doctrines of the Trinity and the incarnation, formulated by the Nicene-Constantinopolitan (381) and Chalcedon (451) Creeds respectively, would be other examples. If neither the Son nor the Spirit were fully God, then at some point, the good news that believers

---

[9] Gregory of Nazianzus also engages this argument in the fifth of his "Five Theological Orations" (see his *On God and Christ* [Crestwood, NY: St. Vladimir's Seminary Press, 2002], 132).
[10] Basil, *On the Holy Spirit* 1.1 (Yonkers, NY: St. Vladimir's Seminary Press, 2011), 27.
[11] Ibid., 10.24 (55).
[12] This is one of the lines added by the Nicene-Constantinopolitan Creed (381) to the Nicene Creed (325).
[13] Cf. Al Mohler's classification of first, second, and third order doctrines in his "Confessional Evangelicalism," in *Four Views on the Spectrum of Evangelicalism*, ed. Andrew Naselli and Collin Hansen (Grand Rapids, MI: Zondervan, 2011), 77–80.

who are "in Christ" enjoy communion with God is fatally compromised. To deny a level-1 doctrinal development—a development that issues in a *dogma*—is to fall into heresy.[14]

"He Descended into Hell"

Our second case study presents a quite different problem, focusing not on the divine agents but on the divine action. Not only does it concern what happened to Jesus Christ at a key moment in salvation history, but it also figures in the Apostles' Creed and claims some, albeit slim, biblical support (1 Pet. 3:18–20). The number of interpretations of "he descended into hell" is staggering, and we cannot here do justice to them all. My main purpose for including this second case study is twofold: it is a prime exhibit of doctrinal development because it encapsulates the problem of the relationship between Scripture and tradition; it pertains to the gospel, at least in indirect fashion, because it addresses the issue of what happened to Jesus after he died, and thus touches on matters pertaining to his person and saving work (i.e., soteriology).

"He descended into hell" is part of the second article of the Apostles' Creed, which begins, "I believe in Jesus Christ."[15] Why was it included, and what does it mean? J. N. D. Kelly suggests that the historical occasion of the *descensus* was Docetism, the heresy that denies the reality of Jesus's embodied existence. "He descended into hell" underscores the reality of his physical death.[16] As to what "descended into hell" means, there are a variety of suggestions, including: (1) Jesus preached the gospel to those who died before his incarnation, to give them an opportunity to believe (early church; Pannenberg);[17] (2) Jesus proclaimed victory to and liberated the Old Testament patriarchs in Hades (Aquinas); (3) Jesus triumphed over sin, death, and Satan (Luther);[18] (4) Jesus finished the work of redemption by suffering more (John Aepinus); (5) Jesus suffered

---

[14] If doctrine is what the church believes and professes on the basis of the word of God, then we may define dogma as "a formal, official, public, and binding statement of what is believed and confessed by the church" (Jaroslav Pelikan, *Credo: Historical and Theological Guide to Creeds and Confessions of Faith in the Christian Tradition* [New Haven and London: Yale University Press, 2003], 88).
[15] In fact, the phrase had a checkered history. It first appeared in Rufinius's version of the Apostles' Creed around 400, where it took the place of "and was buried." By 700, both phrases were included.
[16] J. N. D. Kelly, *Early Christian Creeds*, 3rd ed. (New York: Longman, 1972), 383.
[17] Interestingly, Philastrius of Brescia includes this belief in a catalogue of heresies, citing Psalm 6:5 and Romans 2:12 in rebuttal. See Martin F. Connell, *Descensus Christ Ad Inferos*: Christ's Descent to the Dead," *Theological Studies* 62 (2001): 265.
[18] See esp. Luther's 1533 sermon, reproduced in full in Richard Klann, "Christ's Descent into Hell," *Concordia Journal* 2 (1976): 43–47.

not only dying, the moment of death, but also *being dead* and *the second death/damnation* (Balthasar).[19]

Wayne Grudem will have none of it, insisting in a hard-hitting essay that evangelicals dissent from the "descent" on the grounds that the clause is unbiblical: "It has no clear warrant from Scripture."[20] Moreover, it flies in the face of biblical texts that clearly oppose it.[21] For example, Jesus's words to the criminal crucified next to him, "Today you will be with me in Paradise" (Luke 23:43), leave no time for a descent; and Jesus's next words, "Father, into your hands I commit my spirit!" (Luke 23:46), suggest that he fully expected to ascend, not descend.[22]

Somewhat surprisingly, John Calvin devotes more attention to this phrase than to any other in the Apostles' Creed. He knows it was a later addition; nevertheless, he thinks it makes an important contribution: "But we ought not to omit his descent into hell, a matter of no small moment in bringing about redemption. . . . if it is left out, much of the benefit of Christ's death will be lost."[23] Calvin and the Reformed tradition affirm the descent in two ways: (1) The descent of Jesus's body. Question 50 of the Westminster Larger Catechism is, "Wherein consisted Christ's humiliation after his death?" and answers, "Christ's humiliation after his death consisted in his being buried, *and continuing in the state of the dead, and under the power of death till the third day*."[24] The biblical support is Jesus's own statement: "For just as Jonah was three days and three nights in the belly of the great fish, so will the Son of Man be three days and three nights in the heart of the earth" (Matt. 12:40). (2) The descent of Jesus's soul. Here Calvin is careful to stress the symbolic meaning of "descent." Jesus endured the kind of death we all endure, the separation of soul from body, but he also suffered a hellish agony of the soul specific to his messianic office: separation from God. Calvin is not bothered about the chronology of the events. Jesus suffered death in his soul (i.e., descended into hell) while on the cross (after his death his soul went to

---

[19] See Alyssa Lyra Pitstick, *Light in Darkness: Hans Urs von Balthasar and the Catholic Doctrine of Christ's Descent into Hell* (Grand Rapids, MI: Eerdmans, 2007); and David Lauber, *Barth on the Descent into Hell: God, Atonement, and the Christian Life* (Burlington, VT: Ashgate, 2004), esp. chapters 2–3.
[20] Wayne Grudem, "He Did Not Descend into Hell: A Plea for Following Scripture instead of the Apostles' Creed," *Journal of the Evangelical Theological Society* 34/1 (1991): 113.
[21] Grudem is also aware of the spotty evidence for the antiquity of the phrase, noting its absence from the earliest versions of the Apostles' Creed.
[22] We could also mention Jesus's words "It is finished" (John 19:30), which indicate that his suffering was over, effectively rebutting Balthasar's thesis that Jesus's suffering would continue a bit longer in hell.
[23] Calvin, *Institutes* 2.16.8.
[24] Emphasis mine.

heaven even as his body was in the tomb): "The Creed sets forth what Christ suffered in the sight of men, and then . . . speaks of that invisible and incomprehensible judgment which he underwent in the sight of God in order that we might know . . . that he paid a greater and more excellent price in suffering in his soul."[25] Jesus conquered not only death but also the dread of death: "And surely, unless his soul shared in the punishment, he would have been the Redeemer of bodies alone."[26]

That Jesus died for our sins is part and parcel of the gospel (Rom. 5:8; 1 Cor. 15:3). The event of atonement—the reconciliation of God and humanity made possible by the cross—is a *sine qua non* of salvation. That is why *crucicentrism* is one of David Bebbington's four distinguishing marks of evangelicalism.[27] However, when it comes to explaining the mechanism of the atonement, we are dealing with a level-2 doctrine. Level-2 doctrines deal with some aspect of the history of redemption—not with the divine persons per se, but with what they have done (and with what humans have or have not done in response). However, though Christians affirm *that* Jesus died "for us," they disagree about *what* happened (i.e., the meaning of the events in question). Calvinists and Arminians agree that Jesus's death has atoning significance, but they disagree about the nature and extent of the atonement. "He descended into hell" is not like the deity of the Holy Spirit. It is a level-2 doctrine that seeks to understand the significance of Jesus's death.[28] Denominations may divide over their understandings of the cross, yet they continue to acknowledge one another as fellow Christians: "Bible-believing Christians can allow themselves to differ on the nature of Jesus's descent into hell. Some will be able to recite this part of the Apostles' Creed with conviction, while others may choose to remain silent."[29]

The Salvation of Unbaptized Infants

Our third case study involves not the meaning of Jesus's saving work but one of its entailments: the fate of unbaptized infants. If all human beings

---

[25] Calvin, *Institutes* 2.16.10.
[26] Ibid., 2.16.12. For a fuller presentation of the Reformed view, see Daniel R. Hyde, *In Defense of the Descent: A Response to Contemporary Critics* (Grand Rapids, MI: Reformation Heritage, 2010).
[27] David W. Bebbington, *Evangelicalism in Modern Britain: A History from the 1730s to the 1980s* (London: Routledge, 1993), 3.
[28] Ideally, a doctrine of the atonement should do justice to the full range of biblical metaphors for explaining the saving significance of the cross: (penal) substitution, satisfaction, ransom, victory, etc.
[29] Millard Erickson, "Did Jesus Really Descend to Hell?" *Christianity Today* 44/2 (February 7, 2000): 74.

share in Adam's sin from the moment of conception (Ps. 51:5; Rom. 3:23), then it seems to follow that infants are lost unless the Spirit unites them to Christ too. What can we say to bereaved parents after the loss of an unbaptized child? This is an important issue for systematic and pastoral theology alike.

B. B. Warfield wrote a booklet in which he demonstrates that, while the church has always had a doctrine on this topic, there has been "a progressive correction of crudities in its conception."[30] The Fathers agreed that, with the exception of martyrs, "no infant dying unbaptized could enter the kingdom of heaven."[31] Augustine held the more moderate view that, though unbaptized children are condemned to hell, they suffer "the mildest punishment."[32] The medieval consensus was that only those who committed actual sins would suffer the torments of hell, with infants paying only the penalty for original sin—the deprivation of the vision of God—in "limbo," on the fringes of hell.[33] By the time of Vatican II, however, many Roman Catholic theologians felt that this exclusion of unbaptized infants was incompatible with God's universal salvific will. Jean Galot appealed to the idea of a "hierarchy of truth" to argue that the necessity of baptism "is secondary to the salvific will."[34] The *Catechism of the Catholic Church* (1997) explicitly addresses the question of children who have died without baptism: "the Church can only entrust them to the mercy of God . . . who desires that all men should be saved."[35]

Reformed theologians approached the question differently by (1) emphasizing membership in the invisible rather than the visible church, (2) insisting that such membership proceeds from divine election and, on account of the grace of God, (3) viewing death in infancy as either a possible or likely sign of election.[36] Warfield notes that Reformed

---

[30] Benjamin Breckenridge Warfield, *The Development of the Doctrine of Infant Salvation* (New York: Christian Literature, 1891), 5.
[31] Ibid., 7.
[32] Augustine, *Enchiridion* chapter 93.
[33] Pope Innocent III confirmed this in 1201.
[34] Cited in Francis A. Sullivan, "The Development of Doctrine about Infants Who Die Unbaptized," *Theological Studies* 72 (2011): 8.
[35] *Catechism of the Catholic Church*, 2nd ed. (New York and London: Doubleday, 1997), para. 1261, 353. See also the 2007 International Theological Commission statement, "The Hope of Salvation for Infants Who Die Without Being Baptized, http://www.vatican.va/roman_curia/congregations/cfaith/cti_documents/rc_con_cfaith_doc_20070419_un-baptised-infants_en.html (accessed February 27, 2014).
[36] Warfield is putting a happy face on the Reformed tradition. The actual situation on the ground was considerably more complicated, and less optimistic vis-à-vis the fate of nonelect children. Lutheran theologians viewed the Reformed position differently (see C. P. Krauth, *Infant Baptism and Infant Salvation in the Calvinistic System: A Review of Dr. Hodge's Systematic Theology* [Philadelphia: Lutheran Book Store, 1874]).

Confessions "with characteristic caution refrain from all definition of the negative side of the salvation of infants."[37] There is no presumption here. Indeed, Warfield is aware that the greatest obstacle to the development of this doctrine is "the unchristian conception of man's natural innocence."[38] In this regard, he argues that neither Roman Catholicism nor Wesleyan Arminianism can comfortably accommodate infant salvation into their respective systems. In Rome's ecclesiastical conception, there is no salvation outside the church, hence the necessity of baptism, the means of saving grace. In Arminianism's synergistic conception, free will must improve upon the grace given to all, but infants have no opportunity to do this. According to Warfield, only the Reformed tradition can coherently explain how unbaptized infants may be saved, namely, by being graciously elected, and thus united to Christ and the people of God. How do we know which infants who die unbaptized are elect? *All those who die in infancy* is "as legitimate [a scriptural] and as logical an answer as any, on Reformed postulates."[39] Indeed, if all infants are saved, it is not because they have been baptized into the visible church or have improved upon a universal grace, but only because the Spirit regenerates those whom God elects.

As Warfield admits, there are a variety of opinions even within the Reformed tradition, largely because we cannot presume upon God's gracious election. The doctrine of infant salvation is therefore a level-3 doctrine: one that does not threaten the integrity of the triune God (i.e., the identity of the divine persons) or the gospel (what the divine persons have done, are doing, and will do for us and our salvation), and over which there is disagreement even within one's theological tradition. Whereas disagreements over level-2 doctrines lead to different denominations, there can be debate about level-3 doctrines without compromising fellowship at either the denominational or congregational level.

THE IDEA OF DOCTRINAL DEVELOPMENT: A BRIEF TYPOLOGY

Doctrine—what the church believes, teaches, and professes on the basis of the Scripture—develops. This much is incontestable, as our three case

---
[37] Warfield, *Development of the Doctrine of Infant Salvation*, 44.
[38] Ibid., 50.
[39] Ibid., 60.

studies have shown.[40] Such developments, even if they prove to be mistaken, are not altogether irrational. If we wish to understand the development of doctrine, however, we need to examine the relationship of reason and history more closely. What is the logic or force or principle behind such development?

Theology as Biblical Reasoning

Christian theology is the human attempt to understand and respond to God's self-communication in the redemptive-history that culminates in the event of Jesus Christ and its apostolic witness. John Webster describes theology as a kind of biblical reasoning, "the redeemed intellect's reflective apprehension of God's gospel address through the embassy of Scripture."[41] The aim is to learn what God is making known about God, and doing in Christ, by following the words of the text: "Dogmatics is the schematic and analytic presentation of the matter of the gospel."[42] Webster is not asking theologians for a formalized set of deductions; rather, theology is systematic "in the low-level sense of gathering together what is dispersed through the temporal economy to which the prophets and apostles direct reason's gaze."[43]

Types of Biblical Reasoning

The challenge in formulating doctrine is to attend to the truth of revelation preserved in Scripture, *unfolding* without betraying it either by changing it into something else or by corrupting it by adding foreign particles. Of course, one theologian's healthy development may be another's pathology. Everything depends on (a) the nature of the objective revelation, (b) the ways in which reason processes it, and (c) the criteria for evaluating this process. There are three basic types of theories when it comes to evaluating reason's role in doctrinal development: conservative, liberal, and moderate.[44]

---

[40] "If Christian theology is to be taken seriously as an enterprise of 'faith seeking understanding,' it must come to terms with the fact that its doctrines have developed in history" (Jaroslav Pelikan and John P. Whalen, "General Editors' Foreword" to Walgrave, *Unfolding Revelation*, xi).
[41] John Webster, *The Domain of the Word: Scripture and Theological Reason* (London and New York: T. & T. Clark, 2012), 128.
[42] Ibid., 131.
[43] Ibid.
[44] For a similar typology that distinguishes between static, (r)evolutionary, and dynamic types, see Rolf J. Pöhler, *Continuity and Change in Christian Doctrine: A Study in the Problem of Doctrinal Development* (Frankfurt am Main: Peter Lang, 1999), esp. chapter 3.

*The Conservative Approach: Logical Development (*Idem *Identity)*
"Guard the good deposit entrusted to you" (2 Tim. 1:14).

Evangelicals who affirm *sola scriptura* and the sufficiency of Scripture will perhaps sympathize with Patristic theologians like Vincent of Lérins, who worried that doctrinal development risked opening up the deposit of faith to corruption. Vincent appealed to church consensus as a stabilizing factor because, as he well knew, not everyone understands Scripture in the same way. In Vincent's words, "we can find almost as many interpretations as there are men."[45] Accordingly, the so-called Vincentian canon states, "care must be taken so we hold that which has been believed everywhere, always, and by everyone [*semper, ubique, et ab omnibus*]."[46]

The Patristic watchword was not *semper reformanda* ("always reforming") but *semper eadem* ("always the same"). Vincent believed that ecumenical councils preserved the propositional deposit of the faith: "The classical theory of doctrinal development is that there is no real development in doctrine."[47] Yes, there is conceptual polishing, but this is simply a matter of refining the propositional content already revealed in Scripture. The words (e.g., *homoousios*) may have changed, but not the meanings or thoughts they convey. Development here resembles logical entailment: to conclude "John is a bachelor" from premises (1) "bachelors are unmarried men" and (2) "John is unmarried" is simply to restate the same thought in other terms. On this view, then, doctrines preserve the conceptual content of Scripture and so partake of *idem* identity (i.e., conceptual sameness or permanence over time).

Permanence over time—immutability—is a form of *hard* continuity. Discontinuity appears here as a kind of damaging mutation. This was precisely Adolf von Harnack's objection to orthodoxy.[48] Harnack adopted a critical stance toward the development of Christian dogma, concluding that creedal orthodoxy corrupted the "essence" of Christianity—the pure faith of the gospel—by seeking to understand it in terms of Hellenistic philosophy. For Harnack, to develop doctrine is to intellectualize what ought to be a matter of interior faith, effectively exchanging the fatherhood of God for a formula of deity (viz., the Trinity).[49]

---

[45] Vincent of Lérins, *Commonitorium* 2.2.
[46] Ibid., 2:5.
[47] Yarnell, *Formation of Christian Doctrine*, 107.
[48] See Adolf von Harnack, *The History of Dogma*, 3rd ed. (1885; repr., Eugene, OR: Wipf & Stock, 1997).
[49] Several recent works have rebutted Harnack's hypothesis: instead of speaking of the Hellenization of the gospel we do better to speak of the evangelization of Hellenistic culture and thought. See, for example,

As our case studies have shown, doctrines at all three levels have developed. Even something as fundamental as the deity of the Holy Spirit does more than restate the explicit teaching of Scripture. To confess the deity of the Spirit on the basis of God's Word involves considerably more than deducing that John is a bachelor. Vincent himself knew this, which is why he formulates a second rule for assessing acceptable progress: "Yet it must be an advance [*profectus*] . . . and not an alteration [*permutatio*] in faith. For progress means that each thing is enlarged within itself, while alteration implies that one thing is transformed into something else."[50] As an example of the kind of development he has in mind, Vincent offers an analogy with the growth of bodies: from childhood to adulthood I may grow larger, but I remain the same person. The emphasis is still on conservation. Even where there is growth, then, it must not upset the earlier consensus about the deposit of faith: "speak newly, but never say new things [*dicase nove, non dicas nova*]."[51]

The Liberal Approach: "Free Radical" Development (Non-Identity)

If the watchword of conservative theology is "continuity for the sake of fidelity," that of many liberal-leaning theologians might well be "discontinuity for the sake of intelligibility—and liberation." Maurice Wiles, a liberal Anglican, argues that the most important criterion for formulating doctrine is not whether it preserves old formulations but whether it continues the aims of the church "in a way which is effective and creative in the contemporary world."[52] Wiles thinks that many of the earlier doctrinal formulations have become either irrelevant or meaningless and are in dire need of revision. He is therefore willing to "remake" certain doctrines, and infamously tried to do so when, with John Hick, he dismissed Chalcedonian two-nature Christology (i.e., the deity of Jesus) and instead promoted the "truth" behind the myth of God incarnate—that Jesus, though not himself God, nevertheless lived a life that displayed obedience to God and communicated God's very character.[53]

Paul Gavrilyuk, *The Suffering of the Impassible God: The Dialectics of Patristic Thought* (Oxford: Oxford University Press, 2004), esp. chapter 1, "The Case Against the Theory of Theology's Fall into Hellenistic Philosophy."
[50] Vincent, *Commonitorium* chapter 23. See also Thomas G. Guarino, *Vincent of Lérins and the Development of Christian Doctrine* (Grand Rapids, MI: Baker, 2013).
[51] Vincent, *Commonitorium* 22.7.
[52] Maurice F. Wiles, *The Making of Christian Doctrine: A Study in the Principles of Early Doctrinal Development* (Cambridge: Cambridge University Press, 1967), 177.
[53] See Maurice F. Wiles, "Christianity without Incarnation," in John Hick, ed., *The Myth of God Incarnate* (Philadelphia: Westminster, 1979), 1–11. See also Maurice F. Wiles, *The Remaking of Christian Doctrine*

Wiles thinks that theologians must always "remake" Christian doctrine to keep in step with today's world.[54] Indeed, theologians are free to make even radical revisions to doctrinal formulations: "True continuity ... is to be sought not so much in the repetition of [the Fathers'] doctrinal conclusions or even in the building upon them, but rather in the continuation of their doctrinal aims."[55] By "doctrinal aims" Wiles has in mind the church's concern to keep in mind Scripture, the practice of worship, and the (contemporary) experience of salvation. The interpretive paradigm that wins the day in a doctrinal revolution is not the one that simply tidies up old formulas of the past but rather the one that opens up new possibilities for the future.[56]

The Balanced Dynamic Approach: Organic Development (Ipse *Identity*)
John Henry Newman's *Essay on Development* is probably the most famous treatise on the topic and represents a third approach, one that attempts to strike a happy medium by giving equal time as it were to both continuity and discontinuity by acknowledging *real growth*.[57] The Christian tradition is not an immutable deposit (contra Vincent) or a series of relativistic revolutions (contra Wiles) but rather something living and growing, which is why Newman employs an organic model to explain doctrinal development. What we have in Scripture is a seed—a seminal idea, to be precise—which eventually blossoms into a mature plant (i.e., a doctrinal system).

Organic growth involves both continuity and change. What stays the same is not an already developed set of propositional truths but rather a prereflective intuition: the idea of Christianity. Newman preached a sermon at Oxford University in 1843 on doctrinal development, taking Luke 2:19 as his text: "But Mary treasured up all these things, pondering them in her heart."[58] Theologians should go and do likewise, inasmuch as they too have not only to profess the faith but also to work out its

---
(London: SCM, 1974).
[54] Whereas continuous (evolutionary) development was the watchword of the nineteenth century (see below on Newman's idea of development), the twentieth century saw cataclysmic changes in both history and science. As Pöhler rightly observes, our present-day cultural context is thus more disposed toward thinking in terms of heterogeneous discontinuity rather than homogeneous continuity (see his *Continuity and Change in Christian Doctrine*, 81).
[55] Wiles, *Making of Christian Doctrine*, 173.
[56] Ibid., 171.
[57] John Henry Newman, *An Essay on the Development of Christian Doctrine*, 6th ed. (1878; repr., Notre Dame, IN: University of Notre Dame Press, 1989).
[58] John Henry Newman, "Sermon 15: The Theory of Developments in Religious Doctrine," *Fifteen Sermons Preached before the University of Oxford between A.D. 1826 and 1843* (Notre Dame, IN: University of Notre Dame Press, 1997), 312–351.

implications. The basic idea that Mary and the church ponder—the incarnation—remains the same, but over time the seedling idea grows into a mature dogmatic system. Organic growth, from acorn to oak, partakes of *ipse* identity, the kind of identity that a self has as it grows from infant to adolescent to adult. In one sense, I am the same person I was when I was five years old, with the same name, same narrative, and same DNA. In another sense, however, I am different; my fifty-something self knows more and is wiser than my five-year-old forebear.

For Newman, the idea of Christianity grows because it is part of a living tradition. The church, as the body of Christ, has its being-in-time. Time is the operative concept: it takes time for ideas to develop. Whereas the young Anglican Newman saw later doctrinal developments as corruptions, the mature Roman Catholic Newman believed later developments, such as purgatory or the merits of the saints, to be part of the original idea of incarnation; they simply needed time to mature. Newman eventually had to appeal to ecclesial authority (i.e., the *magisterium*) as a criterion for discerning proper development (maturation) from improper (mutation).[59] In addition to this formal question concerning doctrinal authority (Whose say-so counts in determining legitimate from illegitimate development, continuations rather than reversals of the essential idea?), Newman's account also raises a material question concerning doctrinal content: how do we know whether a given doctrinal development reflects a growth in understanding rather than a positive increase in the deposit of faith—a new revelation—in which case it would constitute a development *beyond* the "idea" embodied in Jesus Christ?[60] The distinction between Roman Catholic and Protestant approaches may indeed boil down to the latter's claim that we ought to discern the difference between development that unfolds what is implicit in Scripture and development that adds something new to the content of the faith.

Analytics versus Hermeneutics: A Methodological House Divided?

Into which of the above three types do evangelicals best fit? We can probably dispense with what I have called the liberal approach, because it

---

[59] Newman proposed seven criteria for judging doctrinal developments, but admitted that they would not work by themselves apart from the *magisterium*. See the discussion in Jaroslav Pelikan, *Development of Christian Doctrine: Some Historical Prolegomena* (New Haven and London: Yale University Press, 1969), 12–24.
[60] Yarnell objects to Newman's misapplication of the biblical metaphor of growth, which concerns the kingdom of God, not the development of doctrine (*Formation of Christian Doctrine*, 59n53).

cedes too much to discontinuity when it comes to the identity of revealed truth over time. That leaves the first and third approaches, marked by two kinds of identity (*idem* and *ipse*) and two kinds of development (logical and organic). I submit that these two approaches to doctrinal development are closely related to two types of theology—the analytic and the hermeneutic—and their philosophical counterparts, Anglo-American and Continental philosophy respectively.[61] These connections may not be obvious, but I think they are worth pondering in our hearts, particularly because each approach has something to contribute when it comes to doing theology "according to the Scriptures." The way forward for evangelical theology lies not in choosing to inhabit one house or the other, but in integrating aspects of each into a unified theory of development.

Analytic theology draws on the strengths of analytic philosophy.[62] These include putting a premium on definitional clarity, conceptual precision, and logical coherence.[63] With regard to doctrinal development, then, this approach excels in making distinctions and drawing out consequences—in a word, *explication* (i.e., *logical* development). Explication is a ministerial use of reason in which what is implied (*implicatus*: "folded in") by the text is *unfolded* (i.e., made explicit). Calvin defended something similar: "But what prevents us from explaining in clearer words those matters in Scripture which perplex and hinder our understanding?"[64] Doctrine develops largely through analysis: clarifying concepts (e.g., God), scrutinizing, and then systematizing the logical relationships between propositions. Analytic theology has particular affinities with the way in which Basil analyzed biblical prepositions as part of his case for the deity of the Holy Spirit.

Hermeneutic theology takes its cue from Continental philosophy (i.e., European philosophy in the nineteenth and twentieth centuries). In this extended family of approaches, the emphasis is not on explanation but on understanding. Though both analytic and Continental philosophers are concerned with interpreting language and texts, when the latter speak of hermeneutics they are not thinking about a scientific "method" for ex-

---

[61] See C. G. Prado, ed., *A House Divided: Comparing Analytic and Continental Philosophy* (Amherst, NY: Humanity, 2003); James Chase and Jack Reynolds, *Analytic versus Continental: Arguments on the Methods and Values of Philosophy* (Montreal: McGill–Queen's University Press, 2010).
[62] See Oliver D. Crisp and Michael C. Rea, eds., *Analytic Theology: New Essays in the Philosophy of Theology* (Oxford: Oxford University Press, 2009), esp. the introduction and chapters 1, 2.
[63] To my knowledge, no analytic theologian has yet proposed a theory of doctrinal development.
[64] Calvin, *Institutes* 1.13.3.

plicating texts or analyzing propositions; rather, they are thinking about the problem of what it is for human beings, rooted in a particular place and time, to understand people, and texts, from other times and places. For hermeneutic philosophers, human finitude and historicity (life) problematize attempts to gain objective knowledge via interpretive methods (logic).[65] For Continental thinkers, it is as important to describe the conditions of historical existence out of which statements emerge and, in particular, to which they are directed (i.e., readers today), as it is to examine the statements themselves.[66]

If *analytic* theology stresses cognitive continuity, a *hermeneutic* theology of doctrinal development puts the accent on historical discontinuity, on understanding *at a distance*. The apostles' context is not ours, hence we hear them through the filter of historical tradition, a history and a tradition that no one can entirely escape. That is why Hans-Georg Gadamer says that interpretation is both reproductive and productive: on the one hand, it tries to recover how the original readers understood the text; on the other hand, it tries to answer what the text means for us today.[67] Understanding is the result of a "fusion of horizons," where what the reader understands is in part a result of where (and who) the reader is: "In other words, our interpretations are always relative to the location—linguistic, historical, cultural—from which they are made."[68] If analytic theology resembles the conservative (logical) approach to doctrinal development, hermeneutic theology finds its analogue in the idea of dynamic (organic) development: growth over time, which is another way of referring to tradition.

In sum: calling attention to the analytic/Continental philosophical divide brings to the fore the fundamental problem underlying the various approaches to doctrinal development. The problem, again, is how to do justice to both continuity and discontinuity, sameness and otherness. Whereas analytic theology sees the development of doctrine as a kind of translation (i.e., saying the same thing in clearer terms), hermeneutic theology sees development as a kind of dialogue at a (temporal) distance, which is another way of describing human being-in-tradition. The process

---

[65] See further Andrew Cutrofello, *Continental Philosophy: A Contemporary Introduction* (New York and London: Routledge, 2005).
[66] Simon Oliver's review of Crisp and Rea's *Analytic Theology* repeatedly makes this point ("Analytic Theology," *International Journal of Systematic Theology* 12/4 [2010]: 464–475).
[67] Hans-Georg Gadamer, *Truth and Method*, 2nd rev. ed. (New York: Continuum, 2002), 369–379.
[68] Merold Westphal, "Hermeneutics and Holiness," in *Analytic Theology*, 275.

of development on this view is more like application or contextualization than translation: the attempt "to hear Scripture's meaning speak in new contexts."[69] With this basic analytic/hermeneutic distinction in hand, then, we turn now to examine some evangelical accounts of doctrinal development.

RECENT EVANGELICAL ACCOUNTS: "GENERAL" OR "SPECIAL" DOCTRINAL DEVELOPMENT?

Nineteenth-century Protestant responders to Newman's theory of doctrinal development, while willing to accept the fact of historical development, were unwilling to accept the premise that the apostles taught things that were neither contained in nor deducible from the Bible. Such a premise would directly contradict the confession of the sufficiency of Scripture. So, while Protestants acknowledged "subjective" development (i.e., greater understanding), they rejected the idea of "objective" development, if this means the actual growth of the deposit of revelation. What God says in Scripture is invariant; by way of contrast, what Christians from different times and places understand God to have said may vary in quantity and quality.[70] From another angle, James Orr rebutted Harnack's charge that the development of orthodoxy was a corruption of the gospel, arguing instead that the history of dogma is an evolutionary history that progresses further and further toward (but never reaches) completion.[71] By and large, evangelical Protestants tended to treat doctrinal development as a problem for biblical hermeneutics.

Peter Toon

Peter Toon's *The Development of Doctrine in the Church* made the first post–World War II evangelical case for a treatment of the topic that would be distinct from hermeneutics.[72] In particular, he called evangelicals to (1) accept the historical and cultural conditions of doctrinal statements, including creeds, (2) declare as historically inadequate all "static" theo-

---

[69] Jeannine Brown, *Scripture as Communication: Introducing Biblical Hermeneutics* (Grand Rapids, MI: Baker, 2007), 25.
[70] See William Cunningham, *Discussions on Church Principles: Popish, Erastian, and Presbyterian* (Edinburgh: T. & T. Clark, 1863), esp. chapter 2; Robert Rainy, *The Delivery and Development of Christian Doctrine* (Edinburgh: T. & T. Clark, 1874).
[71] James Orr, *The Progress of Dogma* (London: Hodder & Stoughton, 1901).
[72] Peter Toon, *The Development of Doctrine in the Church* (Grand Rapids, MI: Eerdmans, 1979).

ries that effectively deny development, and (3) acknowledge that a high view of Scripture does not by itself ensure doctrinal agreement.

Toon compares the actual process of development to what Thomas Kuhn calls "normal science," namely, the pursuit of a particular research paradigm. Toon gives six criteria for discerning whether a doctrinal formulation indeed represents progress—understood as a deeper insight into God's word written—including the requirement that new developments *"must positively cohere with (that is, be entailed by, not merely consistent with) what is already believed at other points."*[73] Toon's account has clear affinities with analytic theology. Yet he is also aware of cultural conditioning, and for this reason appeals to the Spirit's guidance of the early church in its formulation of the doctrines of the Trinity and Christology: "This is not to deny that these doctrines are integrally related to their historical situation in reference to concepts and language; but, properly understood, they are accurate statements addressed to our intellects and, therefore, though they can possibly be improved, they can never be denied."[74]

ALISTER MCGRATH

Charles Hodge thinks doctrine—our grasp of the "facts" of Scripture—progresses in the same way as science's knowledge of the Book of Nature, through cumulative inductive study.[75] Alister McGrath agrees up to a point: the development of doctrine is formally parallel to scientific theorizing, but science does not work the way Hodge thought it did. Like Toon, McGrath appeals to Kuhn, though not to highlight "normal science." On the contrary, McGrath points out that science does not always progress in smooth linear fashion, but sometimes as a result of radical paradigm shifts (e.g., from Newtonian to Einsteinian physics). Science is the work of an interpretive community that shares the same paradigmatic assumptions and that, under various kinds of pressure, may as a community adopt new paradigmatic assumptions: "There are clear parallels between the development of doctrine and the emergence of new paradigms within the scientific community."[76] Indeed, one might describe the Reformation, and the doctrine of justification by faith, as a consequence

---

[73] Ibid., 117 (emphasis his).
[74] Ibid., 120.
[75] See ibid., 51–53.
[76] Alister E. McGrath, *A Scientific Theology, Vol. 3: Theory* (Grand Rapids, MI: Eerdmans, 2003), 233.

34 Kevin J. Vanhoozer

of the community's changing the paradigm for thinking about the way we get God's grace.

McGrath's account of doctrinal development is "Continental" to the extent that it calls evangelicals to acknowledge how everyone "is condemned to live and speak in history and historical forms."[77] The focus is therefore on particular interpretive communities—in a word, theological traditions—in which all Christians, including theologians, live and move and have their being. Indeed, the very term "doctrine" implies "reference to a tradition and a community," because doctrine "is essentially the prevailing expression of the faith of the Christian community with reference to the content of the Christian revelation."[78] The development of doctrine is a response to the "generative event" of the history of Jesus that is mediated to the community through the gospel narrative: "Doctrine is an *activity*, a process of transmission of the collective wisdom of a community."[79] McGrath here recalls Gadamer's idea of tradition as an ongoing conversation between a community and its founding text.[80]

Tradition is the process of handing on the narrative of Jesus and its understanding. McGrath agrees with Gadamer: one cannot know the history of Jesus apart from the history of its reception in the church.[81] The continuity that counts is, for McGrath, as *communal* as it is *conceptual*; for tradition is not simply a collection of static beliefs, but a set of dispositions and practices that preserve the memory of Jesus and embody the mind of Christ. In sum: apart from the church's ongoing historical existence, we would have neither doctrinal development nor doctrine itself. Put differently: both doctrine and the church are effects of the history of Jesus.[82]

---

[77] Alister E. McGrath, *The Genesis of Doctrine: A Study in the Foundation of Doctrinal Criticism* (Oxford: Basil Blackwell, 1990), 81.
[78] Ibid., 10–11.
[79] Ibid., 11.
[80] For the significance of Gadamer in McGrath's account, see Steven L. Oldham, "Alister E. McGrath and Evangelical Theories of Doctrinal Development" (PhD diss., Baylor University, 2000), 115–126.
[81] I would have liked to include a discussion of Anthony Thiselton's hermeneutical variation on a Gadamerian theme, if space had permitted. Like McGrath (and Continental thinkers in general), Thiselton is reluctant to treat doctrine apart from the historical life of the church. Unlike McGrath, Thiselton deploys the full resources of hermeneutical theory to understand the process of doctrinal development. Tradition for Thiselton is an ongoing corporate conversation—a question-and-answer dialogue—about the meaning of the Christ event. Following Gadamer, Thiselton views meaning as poised between the two horizons of text and contemporary community, such that understanding is always application/contextualization. See his *The Hermeneutics of Doctrine* (Grand Rapids, MI: Eerdmans, 2007); and Rhyne Putman, "Postcanonical Doctrinal Development as Hermeneutical Phenomenon" (PhD diss., New Orleans Baptist Theological Seminary, 2012).
[82] "Doctrine cannot be regarded as an isolable aspect of the Christian faith, as if it could be detached from the community of faith and treated as a purely ideational phenomenon" (McGrath, *Genesis of Doctrine*, 193). Thiselton would say "Amen": doctrines are not simply true propositions but self-involving claims

Malcolm Yarnell

Malcolm Yarnell, a Southern Baptist, has written an account of doctrinal development from a believers' church perspective. Though he is aware of the other two evangelical models we have discussed, he is unimpressed. Toon is too *analytic* for assuming "rational tests may discern true developments from corruptions," while McGrath is too *hermeneutic* for assuming "tradition necessarily supplements Scripture."[83] Furthermore, "both are weak with regard to pneumatology and ecclesiology."[84] Yarnell believes their theories come to grief largely due to a faulty conception of the church. We might say that Yarnell faults Toon and McGrath for falling short of a *special* (i.e., properly theological) account of doctrinal development, one that makes full use of what the Bible teaches about itself, the Holy Spirit, and discipleship.

At the heart of Yarnell's theological method is the idea that the church is a community of disciples who follow Christ by listening to the Spirit as they read Scripture together: "The free churches begin their theology of discipleship with a personal relationship with Jesus Christ, seek to understand His ordinances through His word illumined by the Spirit, and institute those ordinances within the church, according to the biblical order."[85] Neither *analytic* nor *hermeneutic* does justice to the kind of *pneumatic* development Yarnell has in mind. Yarnell believes that the Spirit continues to lead the church, by which he means *local* churches, "into all the truth" (John 16:13), and he contrasts this leading with the "rationalism" of evangelical exegetes who rely on analytic and hermeneutic methods for a deeper understanding of Scripture.[86] There is "more truth and light yet to break forth out of [God's] holy word," but this is due to the Spirit's illumination of that word, not to further revelation or the "supplement" of tradition.

Yarnell's believers' church theory of doctrinal development derives from his free church theology of history. The history of the church is neither a prolongation of the incarnation (contra the Roman Catholic conception of visible catholicity) nor the story of the visible church being

---

that serve "*to nail the speaker's colors to the mast* as an act of first-person testimony and commitment" (*Hermeneutics of Doctrine*, 13 [emphasis his]).
[83] Yarnell, *Formation of Christian Doctrine*, 126.
[84] Ibid., 127. Yarnell thinks Reformed theology, represented by Herman Bavinck, is guilty of both rationalism and traditionalism, faults that he traces to the doctrines of common grace and the invisible church respectively (see 49–59).
[85] Ibid., 70.
[86] Ibid., 137.

reformed in light of its spiritual ideal (contra the Reformed conception of invisible catholicity). Yarnell rather insists that the New Testament speaks of the church in local terms only. He views what happened at the Jerusalem Council (Acts 15) as the template for all subsequent doctrinal development: "Christ, by His Spirit, moves among the churches sovereignly and mysteriously. No church has any priority over any other. . . . Every church is under the direct headship of Christ and responsible to Him for the way it reads the Bible and follows the Spirit."[87]

Why, then, should free churches be Trinitarian, if the doctrine of the Trinity is a product not of a local church but of ecumenical councils (Nicaea and Constantinople)? Yarnell cites Athanasius, who saw that the pattern the early churches used for interpreting Scripture came from Scripture itself. Yarnell also appeals to Basil of Caesarea, who notes that proper interpretation of Scripture is due to "the government of the Holy Spirit."[88] Yarnell concludes, "A true free church may err, but heretical it cannot be, for free churches are willing to be corrected but only by the Word of God illumined by the Holy Spirit of God."[89]

Yarnell's account of doctrinal development is "special" because his appeal to the Spirit's leading local congregations of disciples draws on distinctly theological resources (e.g., it is *pneumatic*) and so transcends the *analytic/hermeneutic* divide. I believe his account to be flawed, however, due to an inadequate ecclesiology—inadequate not because of what it affirms but because of what it denies: *catholicity*. Yarnell thinks each local congregation should profess what is right in its own eyes, assuming its willingness to be corrected by Word and Spirit. However, he does not seem to realize that the Spirit often uses the universal (i.e., catholic) church to correct the local church.[90] It was, after all, the catholic church that developed the doctrine of the Trinity and continues to maintain it.

Ironically, Yarnell turns a deaf ear to what other theologians (and local churches!) have to say about the nature of the church. He criticizes Herman Bavinck—and Reformed theology in general—for holding "an extrabiblical view of the universal church as invisible."[91] According to Bavinck, catholicity qualifies the church "as a unified whole in contrast

---

[87] Ibid., 178.
[88] *De Spiritu Sancto* 77, cited in Yarnell, *Formation of Christian Doctrine*, 189.
[89] Yarnell, *Formation of Christian Doctrine*, 203.
[90] He does, however, affirm the congregation's role in correcting individuals.
[91] Yarnell, *Formation of Christian Doctrine*, 54.

to the dispersed local congregations that make up the whole."[92] Yarnell complains that Bavinck gives only one biblical passage in support of the idea of catholicity, and a disputed one at that: Acts 9:31, which refers to "the church [singular] throughout all Judea and Galilee and Samaria." On Yarnell's free church understanding, the text should read "the churches" (plural), and this is what we find in the *textus receptus*—but, significantly, *only* in the *textus receptus*. Yarnell fails to appreciate the irony of a biblicist appealing to tradition, which is what *textus receptus* means (and what it is). Bavinck's reading is on much stronger text-critical ground, and most translations now reflect this by using "church" in the singular. It thus appears that the notion of a translocal church is biblical after all.[93]

Yarnell worries that the notion of an invisible catholic church confuses what in his view can only be an eschatological reality with something present, and results in a tyranny of (Reformed) theologians who appeal to the notion to impose their systems on others. I understand his concern. Nevertheless, my own concern is that Yarnell, in refusing to recognize any authority whatsoever to the deliverances of regional (i.e., ecumenical) church councils, is in danger of failing "to discern the body" (see 1 Cor. 11:29).[94] For what is the invisible church if not the "body" that is composed of many members (Eph. 4:4–5), the sum total of saints who are "in Christ"?[95]

The local church is a particular instantiation of the church universal. Yarnell "confines the body of Christ to the local presence of Christ" as opposed to seeing the body of Christ as having "a trans-local reality."[96] He insists that the local church stands under the authority of Christ alone and is thus free from coercion from any outside human authorities. But Christ rules in ten thousand places. It is therefore inconsistent to say that Christ rules one's own local church and not others. However, if Christ and Christ's Spirit illumine other local churches, then should not

---

[92] Herman Bavinck, "The Catholicity of Christianity and the Church," *Calvin Theological Journal* 27 (1992): 221 (trans. John Bolt, from an address originally delivered in 1888).
[93] This is significant not least for understanding evangelicalism as a transdenominational and translocal movement. "Translocality" has become an important concept in recent social geography and anthropology. See Clemens Greiner and Patrick Sakdapolrak, "Translocality: Concepts, Applications, and Perspectives," *Geography Compass* 7/5 (2013): 373–384.
[94] Of course, the authority I have in mind is only ministerial, one that derives from the magisterial authority of the triune God speaking in the Scriptures.
[95] Cf. Yarnell's critique of Timothy George, a fellow Baptist, for focusing on the invisible church, and hence ecumenical dialogue, at the expense of the local church (*Formation of Christian Doctrine*, 71).
[96] Paul S. Fiddes, "Christian Doctrine and Free Church Ecclesiology: Recent Developments among Baptists in the Southern United States," *Ecclesiology* 7 (2011): 205.

every local church interpret the Bible in conversation with other local churches as well as with members of its own congregation? This too is a way of discerning the body. It follows that local congregations, while free, are also interdependent: members of a larger *koinonia*.[97] Clearly, these different conceptions of the nature of the church have important consequences for how we understand the normative element in the process of doctrinal development. To reject the invisible catholic church is to reject the normed norm of postapostolic ecclesial tradition.[98]

A NEW EVANGELICAL ACCOUNT: DOCTRINAL DEVELOPMENT AS MISSIOLOGICAL IMPROVISATION

Alister McGrath perfectly captures the challenge of balancing continuity and discontinuity as the church attempts to say what it believes on the basis of the word of God: "The genesis of doctrine lies in the exodus from uncritical repetition of the narrative heritage of the past."[99] We need a "deuteronomy" of doctrine: a "second normative statement" of the faith once confessed.[100] Because doctrine is a *second* statement, we can rule out *replication* (i.e., repetition of Scripture); because it is a *normative* statement, we can rule out *innovation* (i.e., departure from Scripture). How, then, do we arrive at this second statement of biblical doctrine?

The word "develop" has a range of meanings, including to unfold, expand by degrees, make explicit what is implicit, actualize the potential of, evolve, etc. What exactly are we doing to Scripture when we develop doctrine from it? The suffix *-ation* pertains to "the action or process of doing something." We have already eliminated *replication* and *innovation* as possibilities for genuine development. The former takes continuity to a pathological extreme (too much sameness); the latter does something similar with discontinuity (too much difference). Models of development

---

[97] Fiddes points out that seventeenth- and eighteenth-century Baptists affirmed three forms of the church—a visible local church, an invisible catholic church, and a visible universal church—all of which cohere: "the local is *wholly* the church and yet is not the *whole* of the church" ("Christian Doctrine and Free Church Ecclesiology," 206).

[98] Fiddes contends that Yarnell is on the verge of admitting the ministerial role of tradition but holds back out of fear of admitting the invisible catholic church through the back door: "Belief in the rule of Christ in the church in all its dimensions, local, regional, and universal, might well provide the context for a non-oppressive concept of the catholic church" ("Christian Doctrine and Free Church Ecclesiology," 219).

[99] McGrath, *Genesis of Doctrine*, 7.

[100] It should be noted that the normativity of dogmatic statements is ministerial. What authority they have is secondary to and derivative from the magisterial authority of Scripture. Cf. Carl R. Trueman: "if Scripture is the *norming* norm, then creeds and confessions, when adopted by churches as statements of their own faith, are the *normed* norms" (*The Creedal Imperative* [Wheaton, IL: Crossway, 2012], 80 [emphasis mine]).

that favor the analytic approach have translation (i.e., re-textualization) as their goal and tend to see the process of growth in terms of *explication* and *elucidation*. What change there is exists only for the sake of clarification; nothing new is added, for the emphasis is on conceptual sameness. By way of contrast, models of development that favor the Continental/hermeneutic approach have application (i.e., contextualization) as their goal and tend to see the process of growth in terms of *maturation* and *amalgamation* (e.g., the fusion of two horizons). Such models excel not in preserving sameness but in acknowledging difference.

I believe there is a more excellent way, one able to preserve the sufficiency of Scripture and the sameness of the gospel (continuity) on the one hand, while acknowledging genuine growth and otherness (discontinuity) on the other. Further, I agree with Yarnell that we must draw on the resources of Christian theology itself in order to do justice to what is "special" about the process of doctrinal development.[101]

Evangelization: Mission as Gospel Transmission

A properly theological account of doctrinal development begins with the realization that it is part and parcel of the triune God's missionary movement in our world, a means by which the Spirit leads the church further into the light of God's Word. To take the most conspicuous example: the doctrine of the Trinity exemplifies not the Hellenization of the gospel but the *evangelization* of Hellenism. Doctrine develops as missionaries restate the gospel in new languages, cultures, and conceptualities.

Andrew Walls, a missiologist, roots Christian missionary activity in God's own mission to the world: "Christian faith rests on a divine act of translation: 'the Word became flesh, and dwelt among us' (John 1:14)."[102] What ultimately gets translated in subsequent Christian mission is the mind and way of Christ. The church evangelizes by taking every thought and practice captive to Christ, demonstrating in the process what discipleship, and thus the lordship of Christ, means in specific situations. The history of the church's transmission of the faith exposes the inadequacy

---
[101] For further discussion of various kinds of *-ation* and doctrinal development, see my "May We Go beyond What Is Written after All? The Pattern of Theological Authority and the Problem of Doctrinal Development," in *"But My Words Will Never Pass Away:" The Enduring Authority of the Christian Scriptures*, ed. D. A. Carson, 2 vols. (Grand Rapids, MI: Eerdmans, forthcoming).

[102] Andrew Walls, "The Translation Principle in Christian History," in *The Missionary Movement in Christian History: Studies in the Transmission of the Faith* (Maryknoll, NY, and Edinburgh: Orbis and T. & T. Clark, 1996), 26.

of *idem* sameness: there is no one Christian language or culture because Christian faith is *infinitely* translatable.[103] To be sure, there is constancy and continuity: what gets transmitted is faith in the one Jesus Christ. However, what Walls finds marvelous about the process of transmitting the gospel is the way in which it leads to further growth in faith's understanding: "As Paul and his fellow missionaries explain and translate the significance of the Christ in a world that is Gentile and Hellenistic, that significance is seen to be greater than anyone had realized before. *It is as though Christ himself actually grows through the work of mission.*"[104]

The book of Acts says something similar about the word of God. On three occasions Luke states that "the word of God increased [*ēuxsanen*]" (see Acts 6:7; 12:24; 19:20). Calvin understands Luke to be referring to the word's geographic and demographic spread: as more and more people come to faith in response to the apostolic preaching, the domain of the word enlarges. Yet according to Calvin, the word of God grows in two ways: first, when new disciples come to faith; second, when those who are already disciples "go forward therein."[105] Walls's point is that transmitting the faith cross-culturally results in both kinds of enlargement: a greater number of believers, yes, but also greater understanding: "Translation did not negate the tradition, but enhanced it. The use of new materials of language and thought . . . led to new discoveries about Christ that could not have been made using only the Jewish categories of messiahship."[106]

Dialogization: Time and Talk as Conditions for Creative Understanding

If Walls is right, then the passing of time (i.e., history) does not necessarily erode the truth but may, on the contrary, serve as the condi-

---

[103] Ibid., 22. Cf. Lamin Sanneh, who describes the history of Christianity as a "vernacular translation movement" (*Translating the Message: The Missionary Impact on Culture* (Maryknoll, NY: Orbis, 1989), 7.
[104] Ibid., xvii (emphasis mine). Cf. James Risser: "The fact that understanding is not an action of subjectivity but an entering into—a participation in—an event of transmission is perhaps the central insight of Gadamer's philosophical hermeneutics" (*Hermeneutics and the Voice of the Other: Re-reading Gadamer's Philosophical Hermeneutics* [Albany, NY: SUNY Press, 1997], 74). The merit of Walls's account is that it frames understanding missiologically, highlighting the progress of the biblical word in the economy of redemption.
[105] Calvin, *Commentary upon the Acts of the Apostles*, vol. 1 (Edinburgh: Calvin Translation Society, 1844), 239. See further Jerome Kodell, "The Word of God Grew: The Ecclesial Tendency of the Logos in Acts 6:7; 12:24; 19:20," *Biblica* 55/4 (1974): 505–519.
[106] Andrew F. Walls, *The Cross-Cultural Process in Christian History* (Maryknoll, NY, and Edinburgh: Orbis and T. & T. Clark, 2002), 80.

tion for truth's full blossoming. Time is God's gift to the church that enables evangelization and discipleship.[107] Consider, for example, the time it took the disciples on the road to Emmaus to talk with one another about the things that had happened to Jesus in Jerusalem (Luke 24:14–15). Similarly, it took time for the apostles to understand that the gospel was meant for Gentiles as well as Jews, and this was arguably the most radical doctrinal development of all in the earliest church (Eph. 2:11–21). Most of all, it takes time to communicate the gospel to outsiders. Walls's term for two people from different cultures coming together to learn Christ is "the Ephesian moment." Here is how Walls describes the process: "We need each other's vision to correct, enlarge, and focus our own; only together are we complete in Christ."[108] It takes time and space for the church to attain "the measure of the stature of the fullness of Christ" (Eph. 4:13).

We do well to pair Walls's account of the way in which transmission of Christian faith across cultures results in a growth of understanding to Mikhail Bakhtin's account of creative textual understanding. There is space here merely to highlight two remarkable parallels. First, Bakhtin resists Gadamer's notion of the fusion of horizons on the grounds that "outsideness"—historical or cultural distance—is not an obstacle to, but rather the very condition of, a deeper understanding of an other (i.e., author). If we simply recovered the author's understanding we would have replication, which is no advance at all. Gadamer's fusion of horizons is monologic; in a genuine dialogue, neither conversation partner is absorbed into the other. In contrast, Walls's idea that Christ grows as a result of cross-cultural transmission finds its counterpart in Bakhtin's notion of creative understanding: "Creative understanding does not renounce itself, its own place in time, its own culture; and it forgets nothing. . . . It is only in the eyes of *another* culture that foreign culture reveals itself fully and profoundly."[109]

Bakhtin's central idea is that only dialogue can fathom the full meaning potential of a text: it takes at least two cultural perspectives to enlarge one's own understanding of "all these things that had hap-

---
[107] For time as "space" for communicative action, and divine patience as the time God gives sinners to repent, see my *Remythologizing Theology: Divine Action, Passion, and Authorship* (Cambridge: Cambridge University Press, 2010), 321–323 and 449–451.
[108] Walls, *Cross-Cultural Process in Christian History*, 79.
[109] Mikhail Bakhtin, "Response to a Question from the *Novy Mir* Staff," in *Speech Genres and Other Late Essays* (Austin: University of Texas Press, 1986), 7.

pened" to Jesus in Jerusalem (Luke 24:14). "Meaning potential" is the operative concept: the dialogue that is doctrinal development does not *add* something to the biblical text, but we need outsideness—different languages, concepts, and cultural locations—to mine the treasure buried in Scripture (i.e., its implicit, latent meaning). Interpreters do not invent but discover truth in and through the process of dialogue: "Semantic phenomena can exist in concealed form, potentially, and be revealed only in semantic cultural contexts of subsequent epochs that are favorable for such disclosure."[110] Bakhtin is not referring to doctrinal development in this quote, but he may as well be, so close is the connection. Christian mission to other cultures is a paramount instance of evangelization through dialogization, and thus becomes "an occasion for exploring the potentials of the work in a way not available to its original authors and readers."[111]

It takes time to dialogue, particularly when the topic is the depths of the wisdom of God (Rom. 11:33). To confine a text to its own time only is to enclose it in its own epoch, thus reducing its significance to what Bakhtin calls "small time." By way of contrast, the word of God "increases" (in a sense that combines Acts 12:24, Walls, and Bakhtin) over time. We see this both in the time span between the Old and New Testaments and between the closing of the Canon and subsequent church history. Scripture is sufficient, and is the supreme norm of theology, but it need not follow that theological *understanding* is confined to the past. Both Walls and Bakhtin insist that it is a mistake to think that one gains a "purer" understanding if one forgets one's own place, time, and culture (as if that were even possible!) and simply duplicates past understanding (i.e., what the original readers would have understood). Rather, the goal is to achieve a "creative" understanding that does not merely replicate the past but mines its resources for the sake of the present. It took time for the early church to achieve a creative understanding of what Paul said about the Son's "equality" with God (Phil. 2:6). The result of that century-long dialogue between East and West was the Nicene concept *homoousios*. And, as we saw in our first case study, it took even more time for the church to understand that the Spirit was

---
[110] Ibid., 5.
[111] Gary Saul Morson and Caryl Emerson, *Mikhail Bakhtin: Creation of a Prosaics* (Stanford, CA: Stanford University Press, 1990), 429.

homoousios too. It takes what Bakhtin calls "great time" to achieve creative understanding.[112]

Improvisation: Continuing the Same Gospel in New Cultural-Linguistic Terms

God has graciously given the church time, great time, to take the gospel to every tribe and nation. This great time also affords the church a precious opportunity to achieve a deeper understanding of her faith, for we do not really understand something until we are able to explain it in our own words to others. Christ—which is to say our *understanding* of Christ—grows as the church interprets and acts out the truth of the gospel in ten thousand places.

The company of faith *transmits* the faith not only by translating Scripture but also by *transposing* it: performing the gospel; living out what is in Christ; speaking and displaying creative understanding. In a word: the church *improvises*, in new terms for new contexts, the faith once delivered to the saints. Improvisation is ultimately another way of speaking about creative understanding. Note well: it is important not to confuse improvising with innovating. A jazz musician improvises freely within certain melodic and rhythmic constraints.[113] Theatrical improvisers, similarly, act spontaneously in ways disciplined by the initial premise of the scene. In each case, there is something historical, in the sense of a prior action, which anchors and orients improvisation. Peter's sermon in Acts 2:14–36 clearly sets out the central themes of redemptive history. *Improvising is the process of discovering the full meaning potential of Scripture by continuing the disciples' story, speaking new lines and acting out new scenes in new cultural contexts in ways that preserve the evangelical truth and action at the heart of the drama of redemption.* Developing doctrine in the church is one more in a series of improvisations: the disciples' story is an improvisation on the history of Israel. Jesus Christ is himself an improvisation on a covenant theme: God's steadfast

---

[112] Mikhail Bakhtin, "Toward a Methodology for the Human Sciences," in *Speech Genres and Other Late Essays*, 170. For a fuller discussion of "great time," creative understanding, and doctrinal development, see my *The Drama of Doctrine: A Canonical-Linguistic Approach to Christian Theology* (Louisville: Westminster/John Knox, 2005), 346–354.

[113] See Bruce Ellis Benson, "The Improvisation of Hermeneutics: Jazz Lessons for Interpreters," in *Hermeneutics at the Crossroads*, ed. Kevin J. Vanhoozer, James K. L. Smith, and Bruce Ellis Benson (Bloomington and Indianapolis: Indiana University Press, 2006), 193–210.

love and righteousness.[114] In each case, there is both creativity (newness) and fidelity to what preceded (sameness).[115]

Improvisation accents the importance of both speaking and acting out faith's understanding. As we saw in our three case studies, the development of doctrine belongs not to speculative but to *pastoral* theology. In each case, doctrine helps the church to know what to say, think, and do in the face of new challenges. Is it proper to speak of the Holy Spirit as God? Should we affirm Jesus's "descent into hell," and if so, what should we mean by it? What kind of comfort can we offer to the bereaved parents of unbaptized children? These questions are similar to the ones faced by the church fathers at Nicaea: does Scripture depict the Son as the greatest of God's creations or as the same as God? Walls rightly reminds us, "The purpose of theology is to make or clarify Christian decisions. Theology is about choices; it is the attempt to think in a Christian way. And the need for choice and decision arises from specific settings in life. In this sense, the theological agenda is culturally induced; and the cross-cultural diffusion of Christian faith invariably makes creative theological activity a necessity."[116] The development of doctrine is a matter of *thinking biblically* in new situations. *Scripture shapes our vision of the whole, instills mental habits, forms the desire of our hearts, and trains us in the way of discipleship.* Doctrine is essential for training in discipleship, and that includes missiological improvisation—knowing how to go on in the same gospel way in different situations.

Here is the end of the evangelical matter: the triune God has acted in our world and summons the church to play a part in the triune drama of redemption, spreading and embodying the good news that the Father is renewing all things in the Son through the Spirit. Doctrine helps the church understand God, the gospel, and her own nature and mission. The challenge of theology is to direct the church rightly to participate in the *same* drama of redemption in *different* conceptual contexts and cultural-linguistic forms.[117] It is not that doctrine is infinitely revisable,

---

[114] Improvisation is how the execution of God's plan of salvation appears to us, human beings in time, but not to God, who is eternal.
[115] God improvises by making good on his promise in new ways. However, the Word of God becoming flesh is more than an improvisation; it is a new revelatory act, as is the New Testament itself (Heb. 1:1–2).
[116] Walls, *Cross-Cultural Process in Christian History*, 79.
[117] The sameness in question here is, of course, *ipse* (same drama of redemption; same divine wisdom) rather than *idem* (same lines; same formulas) identity.

but rather that doctrine is infinitely realizable, for biblical judgments may be formulated in a variety of languages and cultural settings. Doctrinal development is ultimately a matter of the church's faith improvisation in accordance with the Scriptures and with earlier faithful improvisations (e.g., creedal formulations).

CONCLUSION

"Truth in God . . . is unchangeable; but truth in man, or the apprehension of it, grows and develops with man and with history. Change . . . is not necessarily a mark of heresy, but may be a sign of life and growth, as the want of change, on the other hand, is by no means always an indication of orthodoxy."[118]

The development of doctrine is part and parcel of the mission of the church. Doctrine helps disciples individually and corporately to make right decisions about what to say and do in order to participate rightly in and continue the same drama of redemption in which Israel, Jesus Christ, and the apostles played leading parts. The purpose of theology is to make disciples, players in God's drama of redemption who are able to play their parts with faithful and creative understanding.

Thus far I have described the process of doctrinal development in terms of dramatic improvisation. I conclude by anticipating an obvious yet important objection: How do we know whether a particular doctrinal development represents a genuine growth in understanding, and hence a faithful improvisation, rather than a misunderstanding or false innovation?

IMPROVISATORY CORRESPONDENCE (CANONICITY)

An evangelical account of the development of doctrine will give pride of place to evangelization, the translation of the gospel in new cultural-linguistic settings. The content of the gospel—the good news of what is "in Christ"—is the *material* principle of doctrinal development. This principle generates the all-important criterion of canonicity, because there is no other gospel than the one attested by the prophets and apostles (Gal. 1:6–7). In addition to corresponding to "the faith that was once for all delivered to the saints" (Jude 3), contemporary improvisations should

---

[118] Philip Schaff, *The Creeds of Christendom*, 6th ed. (New York, 1931), 87.

also embody the same evangelical wisdom—conformity to the new order inaugurated by the risen Christ—that has been paradigmatically instantiated in the occasional writings that comprise the New Testament. Just as what happened to Israel served as an example to the early church, "written down for our instruction" (1 Cor. 10:11), so what happened to the apostolic church serves as an example to us.[119] The church is a company charged with improvising gospel wisdom in continuity with its authoritative transcript (holy Scripture). However, it is not the exact words, concepts, and actions of the New Testament authors that we must preserve (this way lies the replication of *idem* identity), but rather the evangelical judgments embodied in their words, concepts, and actions (the *ipse* identity that continues the same drama albeit in new scenes).[120]

IMPROVISATORY CONDUCTIVITY (CONTEXTUALITY)

The material principle—what is in Christ—generates a second criterion for discerning genuine from spurious doctrinal developments whose focus is not text but context, in particular, the edifying effect of our improvisations in the church. Do our doctrinal improvisations enable others to participate rightly and thus continue the drama of redemption in their own contexts? This second criterion highlights evangelical conductivity, the property of transmitting not heat, electricity, or sound, but rather the light and energy of Jesus Christ. The purpose of the development of doctrine is ultimately to enlarge our understanding, yes, but also to expand the sphere of Christ's lordly influence, that is, the kingdom of God. Doctrinal development serves the church when it deepens our understanding of what discipleship looks like in new situations and expands the kingdom of God.

IMPROVISATORY COHERENCE (CATHOLICITY)

The previous two criteria are helpful as far as they go, but some readers may feel they do nothing to help regulate the evangelical quickstep, namely, the fancy exegetical footwork by which one attempts to move

---

[119] See Nicholas Lash on Newman: we have to ask "whether the 'development' in question expresses or embodies a style of life, an ethical response, which is in conformity with the style of life commanded or recommended by the gospel" (Lash, *Newman on Development: The Search for an Explanation in History* (London: Sheed & Ward, 1975), 142.

[120] For more on the difference between "concepts" and "judgments," see David Yeago, "The New Testament and the Nicene Dogma: A Contribution to the Recovery of Theological Exegesis," in *The Theological Interpretation of Scripture: Classic and Contemporary Readings*, ed. Stephen Fowl (Oxford: Blackwell, 1997), 87–100.

directly from biblical text to application without passing hermeneutical "go." Even heretics argue from Scripture, and many traditions claim to be biblical, so how do we know which improvisations are most faithful to the biblical text or most fruitful in their context? It is not enough to have bare criteria; we must also determine *whose use* of these criteria is authoritative. We therefore need a *formal* principle, and a third criterion, to complete our evangelical account of the development of doctrine.

Whereas the material principle pertains to the substance of the gospel, the formal principle concerns the scope of its authorized reception—authorized, that is, by the Holy Spirit, who guides the church in discerning the truth of the gospel. The *formal* principle of doctrinal development is therefore *catholicity*. By "catholic" (i.e., whole, universal) church I mean the company of the faithful, the sum total of saints who have believed and creatively understood (i.e., improvised) the gospel across space and time. After all, the church is not simply a theme of the gospel but its lived exhibit. The church is not simply local but *translocal*: the people of the gospel hail from every tribe and nation. In invoking catholicity, then, I am claiming that *the scope of the body of Christ is relevant to the task of discerning genuine doctrinal developments.* Hence our third criterion: Is what we are proposing to say and do at least congruent with the catholic tradition—the ways in which Christians from other times and places have participated in the drama of redemption in their own words and in their own contexts? It is important to respect these catholic precedents as the church improvises what it means to be biblical in new situations.

In *Why Study the Past? The Quest for the Historical Church*, Rowan Williams puts the question of doctrinal continuity and discontinuity into perspective by contemplating the body of Christ. The saints from earlier times and other places "are helpful to us not because they are just like us but in fancy dress, but because they are who they are in their own context."[121] To put it in Bakhtinian terms: they are helpful because they are *outside* us. We can say something similar about the ancient creeds: they display what it means to be biblical in their own contexts. While no single way of embodying the gospel or identifying Jesus Christ is exhaustive, occasional performances—and all attempts to articulate theological understanding are "occasional"—may produce permanent gains. Nicaea and Chalcedon provide concrete examples of the kind of things Christians

---

[121] Rowan Williams, *Why Study the Past?* (Grand Rapids, MI: Eerdmans, 2005), 26.

ought to say about God and Jesus Christ on the basis of the word of God. What the rest of us ought to imitate is not their fancy dress (i.e., Greek philosophical concepts) but their good theological judgment and biblical wisdom: they knew what they had to say to carry on the same drama of redemption in their own particular contexts.

Reading with the Spirit-led church—the community of the Canon extended in space and time—serves as a helpful subsidiary criterion. Church tradition provides a rich resource of case studies in how other members of the company of Jesus have made judgments concerning canonical correspondence as they sought to continue the apostolic tradition. By studying past improvisations, Christians today can learn how best to extend in new situations the same pattern of thinking, feeling, and acting instantiated by Christ and the apostles. Improvisatory coherence means that the beliefs and practices of local churches today must continue the same understanding action exemplified by the fathers and councils of the early church.

While the Canon alone is the norming norm, the consensus of the early ecumenical councils is a normed norm insofar as it displays biblical judgment in the context of Hellenistic culture and philosophy. Vincent was right: local churches ought to affirm what everyone has believed everywhere, at all times. Yes, there is development: the council of Nicaea did not replicate but improvised the concept of *homoousios*. Yet, because *homoousios* is now part of the catholic tradition, churches today must improvise in ways that go on in the same *homoousios* way, even if they do not explicitly invoke the same Greek concept.[122] However churches speak of Jesus Christ in new contexts, there must be continuity as concerns the underlying judgment instantiated by Nicaea: the Son who took on humanity has the same being—nature, properties, characteristics, etc.—as God the Father.

To invoke catholic sensibility as our third criterion for discerning right doctrinal development is to acknowledge the importance of doing theology in communion with the saints. By studying earlier creedal formulations, the church today gains a precious insight into the God of the gospel: who God is, who Jesus Christ is, and what is in Christ.[123] These

---

[122] Minimally, this would mean not going against (i.e., explicitly denying) it.
[123] The doctrine of the Trinity is not simply a complicated aspect of the doctrine of God, but rather a summary or *précis* of the gospel itself. There can be communion with God only if Father, Son, and Spirit alike are each God. It is the Spirit who unites us to Christ and thus relates us to God. For a fuller treatment of this idea, see Fred Sanders, *The Deep Things of God: How the Trinity Changes Everything* (Wheaton,

formulations yield true insights, and for that reason must be valued and affirmed, even if there is more to be said.

Catholicity also affords us a practical gauge for distinguishing between levels of doctrine. Catholic sensibility alone allows the church to maintain a healthy tension between coherence (on essentials) and contingency (on nonessentials). Briefly: a first-level doctrine—a doctrine that identifies the persons of the triune God on whom the integrity of the gospel depends—is one in which the communion of the saints has already formed a consensus.[124] Surprising though it may at first appear, we must conclude that an evangelical account of the development of doctrine will at some point have recourse to ecclesiology: *catholicity is implicit in the idea of doctrinal rank*. It is difficult to distinguish between essential and nonessential doctrines without the criterion of catholic consensus. Level-1 doctrines represent the agreed universal judgments of the church: what Christians at all times and places must confess in order to preserve the intelligibility of the gospel (material principle) and partake of the fellowship of the saints (formal principle). Level-2 doctrines treat events (e.g., atonement, resurrection) and aspects of salvation history (e.g., image of God; sin; justification) that must be affirmed, though there is some scope for different interpretations. Disagreements about level-2 doctrines do not disqualify one from the fellowship of the saints, though they often represent points where there are "regional" differences (i.e., points at which confessions, theological traditions, denominations, and congregations diverge). Level-3 doctrines, though important, are usually not regarded as church-splitting differences, but teachings on which there can be a legitimate diversity of opinion, even in the local church.[125]

The church is relevant to the development of doctrine in one other important respect: it is the place where Christians learn theology, the sum total of beliefs and practices that, when embodied in a local church, represent the church universal. The disciple-improviser learns the way of Jesus Christ through imitation and instruction when local churches go on in the same way as (i.e., continue) the catholic tradition. The develop-

---

IL: Crossway, 2010), and my "At Play in the Theodrama of the Lord: The Triune God of the Gospel," in *Theatrical Theology*, ed. Trevor Hart and Wesley Vander Lugt (Eugene, OR: Cascade, forthcoming).

[124] Of particular note is the focus of the first six ecumenical councils on the identity of the triune God and, in particular, the person and natures of Jesus Christ.

[125] It is no coincidence that these three levels of doctrine more or less correspond to the universal, translocal, and local manifestations of the church. This is what we would expect given what I have called the "formal principle" of doctrinal development: catholicity (i.e., the length and breadth of the Spirit-indwelt body of Christ).

ment of doctrine is part and parcel of the church's task to fulfill the Great Commission to make disciples who know how to go on in the same way in different situations. Scripture is the norming norm, but it takes great time, and a Spirit-led company, to plumb its depths. Great Commission (evangelization); great time (tradition); great church (catholicity): a threefold great is not quickly broken (Eccles. 4:12).

In sum: doctrine serves the cause of discipleship, the project of following and embodying Christ in ten thousand places. Doctrine develops in order to advance the cause of discipleship, and the gospel, forming disciples who know how to embody the mind of Christ at all times and in all places, disciples who exhibit *great understanding* of "the measure of the stature of the fullness of Christ" (Eph. 4:13).[126]

---

[126] I here acknowledge my gratitude to the members of the Deerfield dinner-discussion group for their helpful interaction with an earlier draft.

2

Hermeneutics and Evangelical Theology[1]

WALTER C. KAISER, JR.

Hermeneutics derives its name from the Greek god Hermes, who was the deity in charge of interpretation and communication. Even though the name for this discipline sounds so formal, hermeneutics is an essential part of communication and important in the whole process of understanding what we read, everything from digesting the local or international news in all of its print forms to reflecting on our comprehension of the textbooks we used in grade school or college. In fact, as we learned to talk and enter into conversation with others, we instinctively began simultaneously to practice the discipline of hermeneutics, for it all required interpretation. Most disciplines do not pause long enough to provide a course for the hermeneutics for each subject we study (e.g., "the Hermeneutics of Shakespeare"), yet the study of hermeneutics has become particularly important for those who study the Bible in more detail.

EARLY STUDY OF HERMENEUTICS

The study of hermeneutics became a more formal subject in the time of William Ames (1576–1633), when he wrote *The Marrow of Theology*,

---

[1] It is a delight to honor my friend and former colleague John Feinberg with this essay. It is impossible to say how enriched my own life has been by the consistency of his scholarship, the faithfulness of his Christian life, and the joy I had in serving with him for so many years at Trinity Evangelical Divinity School.

which became the standard text for hermeneutics at Harvard College. The focus of this study was at first the Scriptures. In that work, Ames contended that,

> [T]here is one meaning for every place in Scripture. Otherwise the meaning of Scripture would not only be unclear and uncertain, but there would be no meaning at all—for anything which does not mean one thing surely means nothing.[2]

This emphasis on the single meaning of a text—unless the text gave clear signals to the contrary—held sway all the way up to the twentieth century. For example, the same emphasis could be seen in the writings of the conservative bishop of Liverpool J. C. Ryle (1816–1900). He expressed his opinion on hermeneutics in this way:

> I hold it to be a most dangerous mode of interpreting Scripture, to regard everything which its words may be tortured into meaning, as a lawful interpretation of the words. I hold undoubtedly that there is a mighty depth in all Scripture, and that in this respect it stands alone. But I also hold that the words of Scripture were intended to have one definite sense, and that our first object should be to discover that sense, and adhere rigidly to it. I believe that, as a general rule, the words of Scripture are intended to have, like all other language, one plain definite meaning, and that to say words *do* mean a thing, merely because they *can* be tortured into meaning it, is a most dishonourable and dangerous way of handling Scripture.[3]

The views of Ames and Ryle are not shared by many biblical interpreters today. The idea that Scripture basically has only one meaning or sense, which meaning can be found in an author's own assertions, is thought to be a limited reading of the text for a number of reasons. For the conservative reader, who wants to account for the fact that Scripture has two authors—God and the human writer—Scripture will have at least two meanings: the divine meaning and the human writer's thoughts. For the secular interpreter, the Bible will need to be interpreted according to the reader's response to the writing rather than being limited to what the author meant.

---
[2] William Ames, *The Marrow of Theology* (1629; repr., Boston: Pilgrim, 1968), 188.
[3] J. C. Ryle, *Expository Thoughts on the Gospels: St. Luke, Vol. 1* (London: William Hunt, 1858), 383.

THE LITERARY SHOT HEARD ROUND THE WORLD

Despite the long tradition in general hermeneutics, going back at least to Ames, that each text would have a single meaning, a megashift took place in the middle of the twentieth century—sometime around 1946. The literary "shot" that was heard round the world came from two literary critics, William K. Wimsatt and Monroe Beardsley. Although Wimsatt and Beardsley set up three types of internal evidence for discovering the meaning of a passage, their distinctions were generally swallowed up, in the popular version of their work, as the idea of the "intentional fallacy"[4] gained ascendancy among the new generation of literary scholars. This emphasis, which was later to be part of the "New Criticism," found the main problem in understanding a literary piece to be the fallacy of depending on what the author meant to say by his or her own words as the sole basis for interpreting that text. Furthermore, adherents of the New Criticism concluded that trying to understand what the author meant was impossible anyway, since no one could get into the mind of another person. The author could have his say, mind you, but his readers should be free to substitute their own senses or meanings for what they were reading.

A whole new standard, therefore, was introduced in the interpretation not only of the Scriptures but of all literature as well. It even affected areas such as jurisprudence. A reader's response to the text became more important than the assertions of the author. The classics and literature of all sorts took on previously unheard-of meanings as readers declared what a given text personally meant to them instead of what the author had intended the text to say. In the area of jurisprudence, legal experts began to give new meanings to the law—meanings not found in such things as constitutions or legal precedents—as it seemed best in their eyes, rather than trying to ferret out what the original framers of laws had in mind. The world and culture were undergoing a megashift, and not in a good direction.

EVANGELICALS AND THE PRINCIPLE OF SINGLE MEANING OF THE TEXT

Evangelicals had used the textbook of Milton S. Terry, *Biblical Hermeneutics*,[5] for well over the first half of the twentieth century, for

---

[4] William K. Wimsatt and Monroe Beardsley, "The Intentional Fallacy," *Sewanee Review* 54 (1946): 3–18.
[5] Milton S. Terry, *Biblical Hermeneutics: A Treatise on the Interpretation of the Old and New Testaments* (1885; repr., Grand Rapids, MI: Zondervan, 1947), 205.

he too held to the principle of the single meaning of the text of Scripture. He taught that,

> The fundamental principle in grammatico-historical exposition is that the words and sentences can have but one significance in one and the same connection. The moment we neglect this principle we drift out upon a sea of uncertainty and conjecture.[6]

Likewise, as late as 1970, Bernard Ramm endorsed the same principle in his hermeneutical textbook:

> But here we must remember the old adage: "Interpretation is one; application is many." This means there is only one meaning to a passage of Scripture which is determined by careful study.[7]

This line of thought could be extended even further into the twentieth century, for on November 10–13, 1982, the "International Council on Biblical Inerrancy," composed of evangelical leaders in the church worldwide and gathered in Chicago, issued in its "Articles of Affirmation and Denial," in Article VII, the following declaration:

> We affirm that the meaning expressed in each biblical text is single, definite and fixed. We deny that the recognition of this single meaning eliminates the variety of its application.

However, even with all of these impressive statements on the authorial meaning of the text, a gentle disaffection began to set in among the new evangelical leaders, so that by the last quarter of the twentieth century it was beginning to be difficult to find a younger scholar who still held to the older affirmation of a single meaning to the text.

For example, James DeYoung and Sarah Hurty[8] deliberately sought a meaning *beyond* the grammatico-historical meaning of the text. They called the meaning of grammatico-historical interpretation the "existential meaning," but the deeper meaning they entitled the "essential meaning." They allowed a single passage to have a number of essential meanings that

---
[6] Ibid.
[7] Bernard Ramm, *Protestant Biblical Interpretation: A Textbook on Hermeneutics*, 3rd rev. ed. (Grand Rapids, MI: Baker, 1970), 113.
[8] James DeYoung and Sarah Hurty, *Beyond the Obvious: Discover the Deeper Meaning of Scripture* (Gresham, OR., Vision House, 1995), 67–80.

might differ with what the sentence in Scripture actually said according to its existential meaning, or within the story in which it was embedded. Even though they tried to limit the possible essential meanings to what they called a "kingdom center," it was not obvious that this center, or any other criteria, had any impact on their freedom to discover whatever deeper meaning they wished to announce.

This same tendency to go beyond the fixed and definite meaning of the author could be observed in a book by Dan McCartney and Charles Clayton. In fact, they tended to go even further, calling the principle of finding only a single meaning in a text "ridiculous from a general hermeneutical point of view"; moreover, they pronounced such a search "perverse from a theological [point of view]." They easily indulged in eisegesis (a "reading into" a text) by reading New Testament meanings back into the Old Testament, with the result that these ended up being either *additional* meanings to what the author was asserting or *reinterpretations* of what the author had wanted to say.[9]

Another recent textbook, coauthored by William Klein, Craig Blomberg, and Robert Hubbard,[10] offered some of the same advice as they discussed meaning. Here they included the legitimate form of inaugurated eschatology with its "now and not yet" aspects in the prophetic literature of the Bible along with words having what they deemed to be double entendre—in John 3:3, for example, the Greek word *anōthen*, meaning "again" and "from above." The issue of inaugurated eschatology should not, however, be used as a point against the single meaning of the author, just as the Antiochene exegesis of the fifth-century church argued for a unified single meaning of text where, according to their view of Theoria, the prophet "saw" as one meaning both the "already/now" and the distant "not yet."

One could mention many other evangelical leaders who seemed to go along with the new development in hermeneutics, but the trend was clearly one that deviated from several centuries of scholarship. However, in 1967, a wake-up call came from a nonevangelical professor of literature at the University of Virginia, E. D. Hirsch, Jr. Though he later modified his views on interpretation, he was the one to sound the alarm that

---

[9] Dan McCartney and Charles Clayton, *Let the Reader Understand: A Guide to Interpreting and Applying the Bible* (Wheaton, IL: Victor, 1994), 157, 161, 164.
[10] William W. Klein, Craig Blomberg, and Robert L. Hubbard, Jr., *Introduction to Biblical Interpretation* (Dallas: Word, 1993), 122.

the best and only way to validate the meaning of a text was to return to what the author had meant to say.

VALIDITY IN INTERPRETATION; AUTHORIAL INTENTIONALITY

Hirsch's *Validity in Interpretation* (Yale University Press, 1967) was a solid endorsement of the need to return to the author's meaning and intentionality. Hirsch admitted that he had been influenced in part by the work of Emilio Betti, an Italian historian of law.[11] Among Hirsch's key concepts:

1. Verbal meaning is whatever someone (the author or speaker) has willed to convey by a particular sequence of words.
2. The author's truth-intention provides the only genuinely discriminating norm for ascertaining the valid or true interpretation from invalid and false ones.
3. The primary objective in the interpretive process is to make clear the text's meaning.
4. Meaning is represented by the linguistic signs in the text that represent what the author meant to say.
5. Significance names a relationship that a text's meaning, once it is established by grammatico-historical interpretation, has with another person, situation, or other possible associations.
6. Meaning is fixed and cannot change once it is written, but the significance of a text may, and often does, change depending on the times, culture, or historical circumstances in which it is read.
7. If the author changes his mind, he must either retract what he said or oppose it with another explanation.

At first evangelicals regarded Hirsch's views as being in accord with many of their own views, for they saw them as a continuation of those methods used by the older Reformed and Puritan writers. But modernity very quickly caught up with and began to overwhelm the evangelical movement. Many of the younger evangelical scholars, having graduated from secular doctoral studies, attempted to use some of the methods they

---
[11] Emilio Betti, "Hermeneutics as a General Methodology of the *Geisteswissenschaften*," trans. Josef Bleicher, in Josef Bleicher, *Contemporary Hermeneutics: Hermeneutics as Method, Philosophy and Critique* (Boston: Routledge & Kegan Paul, 1980), 51–94.

had been taught, often including "New Criticism" or "New Hermeneutic" in their work of biblical interpretation.

Added to this confusion were the leftover effects of Marcion, who saw a real division between the God of the Old Testament, whom he labeled as a demiurge, and the God of love found in the New Testament. Interpretation of the Old Testament began to emphasize that teaching from the Old Testament was not complete, or even Christian, until it was somehow connected to the story of Jesus. What had been a Christocentric view of the Bible began to be a "Christo-exclusive" view of the Old Testament. Precedent for this approach was seen in the so-called loose view of the New Testament writers in quoting the Old Testament (which they did some three hundred times).

NEW TESTAMENT USE OF THE OLD TESTAMENT

Of course, evangelicals rightly felt that the Bible had depths to it that many scholars did not see or appreciate.

For example, evangelicals who taught the Old Testament in a stultifying and dreary academic way, merely recounting the principal facts of the narratives or the genre, needed to find some new way to get at a deeper meaning of the text of Scripture—for, after all, it was God's communication to us. Scripture could not be all that boring and deadening. If interpreters were to avoid allegorizing, psychologizing, and spiritualizing in order to falsely make the text come alive, then another avenue had to be sought besides the grammatico-historical method of exegesis. The complaint, of course, had some truth in it, for all too many had stopped short of showing how the Bible had any contemporary relevance, claiming that such was the work of the Holy Spirit in each person's own life. But did the New Testament use of the Old Testament point the way to show us how to reinterpret the Old Testament? Was it true that there were at least two meanings to such biblical texts: a divine and a human meaning? All of this was a new direction for biblical hermeneutics. It was a real matter of dispute that the New Testament either exercised an alternative meaning or that it gave us as interpreters permission to derive "deeper meanings" from the text. The search continued for another way to find what was hoped would be the "deeper meaning" of the text.

In more recent times, some traction has been gained by the view that the New Testament writers used Second Temple Jewish exegetical methods (often referred to as the "Midrashic" or "Pesher" methods) in interpreting the Old Testament. This Second Temple period of scholarship was at its height during the days of Jesus's life and ministry. Instead of beginning with a straightforward, natural, or plain meaning of a text, Second Temple scholars looked for a deeper meaning.

In the Midrashic method, the interpreter would begin with the Scripture but would seek to locate a hidden or embedded meaning that was supported by the general spirit of the text. In order to accomplish this, he had to follow interpretive rules known as *middoth*. At first there were only seven rules, attributed to Rabbi Hillel, who lived in the generation immediately preceding the Christian era. But these seven rules were expanded to thirty-two rules by Rabbis Ishmael ben Elisha and Eliezer ben Jose. The rules involved techniques such as *gematria*, the computation of the numerical value of letters to get a deeper meaning, and *notrikon*, which involved the breaking up of one word into two or more words, or even constructing an entirely new word by using the initials of many words. Obviously, this method was rather subjective.

Another factor in Second Temple interpretation came to light after the discovery of the Dead Sea Scrolls, which reflected the last days of the Second Temple period in Israel. While the word "pesher" meant "solution" or "interpretation," it too was not a straightforward explanation of the Scriptures. Instead, it relied on the "Teacher of Righteousness," who was thought to be able to see veiled references to eschatological meanings in the ancient words of Scripture. He would therefore intone the following: "This [eschatological event that will come in the last days] is [what] that [biblical text] is saying!" For example, a commentary on the book of Habakkuk was found among these scrolls, but whereas the ancient prophet spoke of the "Chaldeans/Babylonians" who posed a threat to Judah, the Teacher of Righteousness in his Pesher interpretation said the "Chaldeans" were the "Romans" and their Essene community was the one being threatened. Even though the Teacher of Righteousness was the only source for such modernization of the text, his word was considered as authoritative as the original Scripture.

These Second Temple methods fired the imagination of many evangelical interpreters who were searching for "thicker" meanings to the text. But such a search would often take them away from the authoritative senses or meanings of the original authors of Scripture.

THE WORLD OF *SENSUS PLENIOR* INTERPRETATION

Scripture, of course, is the product of both a human and a divine author, and perhaps that was the clue from which this longing for a deeper, thicker, more insightful access into the Bible might find resolution. In fact, already in 1927 Father Andre Fernandez[12] had introduced the idea of *"sensus plenior,"* or a "deeper sense" to Scripture, but this concept did not take hold among evangelicals until some time after Raymond E. Brown published his 1955 doctoral dissertation on *sensus plenior*. Brown described *sensus plenior* this way:

> The *sensus plenior* is that additional, deeper meaning, intended by God, but not clearly intended by the human author, which is seen to exist in the words of a biblical text (or group of texts, or even a whole book) when they are studied in light of further revelation or development in the understanding of revelation.[13]

Brown said that this deeper meaning had "not clearly [been] intended by the human author," but later he would deny that this sense was even intended by that author. As Brown explains,

> Let us apply the term *sensus plenior* ["fuller sense"] to that meaning of his [the author's] text, which by the normal rules of exegesis would not have been within his clear awareness of intention, but which by other criteria we can determine as having been intended by God.[14]

Brown's purpose (and the purposes of those who followed him) was to get at the "deeper" or "fuller" sense that God had intended in the text. The problem came in trying to identify what the criteria were for discerning this additional meaning. Brown and those who followed his method denied that this deeper or fuller meaning was to be found in the words, syntax, or grammar of the passage, for in that case it would have been part of the author's intentionality. This denial created another problem. If the prophets claim that what they spoke came from God, how could there be a division between what God had intended and what the human author wrote?

---

[12] Andre F. Fernandez, "Hermeneutica," in *Institutiones Biblicae Scholis Accommodatae*, 2nd ed. (Rome: Pontifical Biblical Institute, 1927), 306.
[13] Raymond E. Brown, *The Sensus Plenior of Sacred Scripture* (Baltimore: St. Mary's University, 1955), 92.
[14] Ibid., 268–269.

Moreover, if this deeper sense was *not* to be found in the words of Scripture, where was it to be located? The only place left was in between the lines of the text of Scripture, or somewhere in the larger message and bigger picture of the whole book, or of the whole Bible. But if it were in between the lines, then it was not the inspired Word of God, for 2 Timothy 3:16–17 taught that "all writing" (Greek *graphe*) was inspired—and this deeper meaning was not put into writing. By this theory, it fell in between the lines. If it came from the whole book or whole Bible, then how could we be sure it was on the same topic, and correctly linked to this passage, and divinely authorized?

The motivation of these readers of Scripture to find this "fuller" or "deeper" meaning was in the right direction, but where was the authority for what was being affirmed? Here at last was a deeper meaning, but it was one that needed to be anchored in the authority of the One who gave Scripture. And who better to give such a meaning than those writers God had called to be the messengers of his revelation? If they had not gotten the message in the first place, then we would be left trying to identify the so-called hidden codes in Scripture. But that concept would be opposed by the teaching of the perspicuity of Scripture. So we are left with the words of the writers of Scripture, who claimed that they had stood in the council of God and received their teaching.

THE TOOL OF BIBLICAL THEOLOGY

In recent years, help in solving at least part of this problem has come from the study of biblical theology. However, even that has presented a special difficulty in that the very definition of the discipline of biblical theology is a matter of great dispute. Even though there is uniform agreement on what generally constitutes biblical theology, the briefest definition of this discipline has been offered by Robert W. Yarbrough:

> *Biblical Theology.* Study of the Bible that seeks to discover what the biblical writers, under divine guidance, believed, described, and taught in the context of their own times.[15]

But what this definition, along with many others, fails to capture is that this discipline has an important historical and diachronic feature to

---
[15] Robert W. Yarbrough, "Biblical Theology," in *Baker Theological Dictionary of the Bible*, ed. Walter A. Elwell (Grand Rapids, MI: Baker, 1996), 61.

it, so that it can be used first of all by exegetical theology, rather than what most see it as serving primarily—systematic theology. All this is to say that the interpreter needs to know what concepts, doctrines, or issues had appeared earlier in the text of Scripture, so that the interpreter could see the way in which a particular new revelation supplements what preceded it. Only after the meaning of the target text of Scripture has been explained would it be proper to go on to see how the whole canon of Scripture develops that same thought.

The views of the entire Bible in all its wholeness must, of course, be a part of the interpreter's final summary of any given passage. But to introduce it prematurely in the interpretive process itself would be a form of "reading into" the text what was not clearly present as represented by its words, grammar, and syntax. There is no question that there is a unity to Scripture, for each part of the text has a contribution to make to the theological wholeness of the story of the Bible. But one must beware of presenting a "flat Bible," as if what it says anywhere is equal to what it finally says as it comes to its closing books and chapters. Of course, no Christian interpreter is going to pretend that God did not give the rest of his revelation in the Bible. That is not in question. Instead, it is a matter of using an accurate methodology.

But by now it should be clear that biblical theology is a technical term that signifies more than the fact that it is a collation of theology that comes from the entire Bible. Many of the biblical theologies seem to be more like systematic theologies, which simply collect texts around predictable topics such as God, man, sin, Christ, salvation, the church, and last things. Many of these so-called biblical theologies use what is called the "analogy of faith" method as their main operating procedure. Verses that seem to include the same topic or subject are gathered together to form a collection of teachings on a particular subject, but without any reference to the time period from which they came or the context from which they were taken. It is almost as if the mere citation of the chapter and verse were enough to establish that all these texts are speaking of the same subject. But this only replicates the method used in systematic theology, where verses are collected that bear on the same topic generally without regard to the time period or context from which they came.

Some of the foundational principles for doing biblical theology can now be described. First, of course, is the centrality of the text of Scripture. The text should be the focus of our attention as we begin. If we waver from this principle, we forfeit the great advantage of the divine authority of the text, which can be found in what the author is asserting and intending to say.

After we have examined the text according to its grammatico-historical bases, we must next look for an intertextuality from similar allusions, quotations, concepts, or persons that appeared earlier in the divine revelation. For example, when preparing the text of 1 Kings 19:1–21 for preaching or teaching, one finds that the prophet Elijah fled to Mount Sinai in a state of deep despondency over the fact that the press, the populace, and the palace had not repented despite the divine demonstration of fire that fell from heaven on Mount Carmel when the prophet prayed. So Elijah fled, under the threat of Queen Jezebel. Twice, on Mount Sinai, God had to ask him, "What are you doing here?" (1 Kings 19:9, 13). To Elijah's weak answer, God commanded him to come out and stand on the mountain, there at Sinai, "for the LORD [was] about to pass by" (1 Kings 19:11b, NIV). What this despondent prophet needed most of all was a whole new vision of who God was, just as Moses had needed years before him.

A biblical theology that is organized generally in a diachronic or chronological way will note that a very similar incident had happened to Moses in connection with the golden calf narrative. In Exodus 34:6 the Lord "passed in front of Moses" (NIV) as he proclaimed his name. In fact, in Exodus 33:19, the Lord said,

> I will cause all my goodness to pass in front of you, and I will proclaim my name, the LORD, in your presence. I will have mercy on whom I will have mercy, and I will have compassion on whom I will have compassion. (NIV)

Surely, the words of the Lord to Elijah, that he was about to "pass in front of [him]" on Mount Sinai, must have brought to mind the word God had given previously to Moses. But even if these words did not help Elijah's recall, we as interpreters should use the earlier words in Exodus to help us get to the deeper meaning, if that teaching is now one of the goals of 1 Kings 19. This is a great example of what the tools of biblical theology should help us with. Here then lies a "deeper" meaning, but one that is embedded in the text and that has an antecedent theology to it on which to build God's progressive revelation.

Finally, since the Bible is not a potpourri of disconnected readings, but shows close connections with what came before the text under examination was written, and with what came after that text, then we must go on to show whatever development that concept or theology had in the later revelations from God. The theology of God's abiding presence and the theology of the power and comfort of his name are enhanced as Scripture enlarges upon that theme.

The concept we are arguing for here was opposed by Graeme Goldsworthy. He contended that it was a fundamental error "to think that the historical structure of progressive revelation is best observed by a simple chronological approach."[16] Surprisingly, he argued that such a diachronic approach "ignor[ed] the final word of God in Jesus Christ . . ."[17] Goldsworthy does acknowledge that what the Old Testament writers wrote was all that they had up to that point in time, but to teach only what they had at that point was to ignore the gospel that came later, of which we should be aware as interpreters. But to begin our uncovering the sense of a passage by applying the New Testament gospel structure to any and every passage is to run the risk of eisegeting a text and leveling the Bible into a "flat Bible." Furthermore, not every verse or chapter in the Bible must bear a Christocentric meaning in order to be a Christian message. Such an approach boils all theology down to a soteriological track, but a creation track is broader and encompasses much more theology than a soteriological emphasis.

Therefore, the search for the "thicker" and "deeper" meaning can be found in the words, grammar, and syntax of the Old Testament, when it also uses the tools of a diachronic or an antecedent theological appreciation of biblical theology. Such a method also preserves the ancient call for a single meaning or sense as the basic approach to interpreting the Bible.

THEOLOGICAL INTERPRETATION OF SCRIPTURE

One more attempt to get into a "thicker" sense of the Bible began to emerge for evangelicals sometime in and around the 1990s. Various Bible

---
[16] Graeme Goldsworthy, *Preaching the Whole Bible as Christian Scripture* (Grand Rapids, MI: Eerdmans, 2000), 97.
[17] Ibid.

teachers began to notice that there had been a steady decline in an appreciation of the theological interpretation of Scripture. In fact, some had deliberately replaced systematic theology with the newer texts on biblical theology.

This theological decline had begun under the impact of the rise of the "historical-critical" view of the Bible in the nineteenth and twentieth centuries. But already early in the twentieth century—in 1921—Karl Barth would publish his famous commentary on the book of Romans, which historians have insisted on labeling as the "bombshell [that was] dropped on the playground of theologians." That is what it was indeed!

Barth had complained that, as he mounted the pulpit to preach, it felt as if the word of God was slipping out of his hands. He preached as he had been trained, in the historical-critical methodology, but this left him and his audience feeling bankrupt, with little or no sure words from God week after week. But when he read Luther's introduction to his commentary on Romans, he suddenly changed his direction and the content of his preaching.

Barth's influence would extend all the way from Switzerland to Yale University, where Brevard S. Childs in 1977 developed what he called the "Canonical Approach" to Scripture. Though he still retained his training in the historical-critical method, Childs argued that preachers and teachers should give priority to the "final form" of the text of Scripture. In his view, someone had to explain to God's people the text that was in front of them rather than trying to get behind the text to see how the Bible had emerged. Childs has had an extensive influence on evangelical interpreters, for his work has given them permission to work with the text that is in front of them instead of a text that is behind the text. Thus, under the influence of Barth and Childs, a theological interpretation of the Scripture was being rehabilitated, and this began to supply part of the deeper meaning some longed for.

Even though some might conclude that E. D. Hirsch's author-centered approach to the Bible is no longer as dominant in evangelical circles as one would want it to be, many evangelicals claim they begin their approach to the text from that standpoint and then go on to locate thicker meanings by means of various options such as *sensus plenior*, New Testament alleged reinterpretations of the Old Testament, Second Temple methods, or new theological approaches to the Bible. The question of the hour is this: can these added features show divine authority for what they allege to have found in the text? The final assessment of these initiatives must await another day and another time, for we seem to be in a period of transition in evangelical hermeneutics. The question that remains to be answered is, will evangelicals emerge with an authoritative word from God, or will it feel as if that text is beginning to slip through our hands as well?

3

Does the Apostle Paul Reverse the Prophetic Tradition of the Salvation of Israel and the Nations?

ROBERT L. SAUCY

The Bible is more than a book of timeless truths that explain how to be right with God. It is the story of creation, rebellion, and redemption. The bulk of the story—from the entrance of sin and the promises of its defeat in Genesis 3:15 to the new heavens and new earth in Revelation—is the history of God's victorious program of salvation against the destructive power of sin.

As is evident in Scripture, the little nation of Israel, created and commissioned by God to be a special channel of his revelation and salvation for all the people of the world, has a central role in God's plan of salvation.[1] As Jesus succinctly summed it up to the Samaritan woman, "Salvation is from the Jews" (John 4:22). Israel's role in salvation since their rejection of their Messiah at his first appearance, however, has been much disputed. Our purpose in this essay is to consider one limited but important issue in this discussion, namely, the relationship of the salvation of Israel and the salvation of the Gentiles, especially the temporal relationship. This is a rather global biblical issue that I will be able only to sketch out in this brief essay.

---
[1] See, for example, Genesis 12:2–3; Exodus 19:5–6; Psalm 67:1–2, 7; 102:13–15; Isaiah 41:8–9; 44:23; 60:1–3.

THE ISSUE

Most biblical interpreters, as we will see, agree that the primary plan expressed in the hope of the Old Testament prophets involved a divine restoration of Israel through which the glory of God would be revealed to all nations, with the consequences that they would come to acknowledge the true God of Israel. But as a result of Israel's rejection of their Messiah at his first appearance, many understand this picture of Israel's restoration leading to the salvation of the nations or Gentiles to be changed. This purported change is based particularly on Paul's discussion of Israel in Romans 9–11, especially his statement that "a partial hardening has come upon Israel, until the fullness of the Gentiles has come in. And in this way all Israel will be saved" (11:25–26). With many commentators, I take "in this way" in the last sentence to have a temporal sense in addition to expressing the manner in which Israel comes to be saved, and thus indicating that Israel's salvation is consequential to the coming in of the fullness of the Gentiles and the lifting of the partial hardening presently affecting Israel.[2]

On the basis of the "fullness of the Gentiles" coming in, presumably to salvation prior to the salvation of Israel, most interpreters today understand Paul to be reversing the dominant Old Testament prophecy, which saw the nations coming to salvation following the salvation and restoration of Israel. For example, after noting the Old Testament teaching that "God's glory revealed in a rejuvenated and regathered Israel" would stimulate the Gentiles to join in the worship of the Lord, Moo says of Paul's teaching, "But wholly novel was the idea that the inauguration of the eschatological age would involve setting aside the majority of Jews while Gentiles streamed in to enjoy the blessings of salvation and that only when that stream had been exhausted would Israel as a whole experience these blessings."[3]

---

[2] Cf. C. E. B. Cranfield, *The Epistle to the Romans*, International Critical Commentary, vol. 2 (Edinburgh: T. & T. Clark, 1979), 574–575; James D. G. Dunn, *Romans 9–16*, Word Biblical Commentary, vol. 38B (Dallas: Word, 1988), 681; Scott Hafemann, "The Salvation of Israel in Romans 11:25–26: A Response to Krister Stendahl," *Ex Auditu* 4 (1988): 53; Arland J. Hultgren, *Paul's Letter to the Romans: A Commentary* (Grand Rapids, MI: Eerdmans, 2011), 416–417; Robert Jewett, *Romans: A Commentary* (Minneapolis: Fortress, 2007), 701; Ernst Kasemann, *Commentary on Romans* (Grand Rapids, MI: Eerdmans, 1980), 313.

[3] Douglas Moo, *The Epistle to the Romans*, New International Commentary on the New Testament (Grand Rapids, MI: Eerdmans, 1996), 684n2; 716–717. Similarly, Dunn says, "Paul has inverted the more typically Jewish expectation that the eschatological pilgrimage of the Gentiles would be the final climax and would underscore the triumph of Israel's faith . . . ; here the restoration of Israel is to be a consequence of the incoming Gentiles" (Dunn, *Romans 9–16*, 682). See also Hafemann, "Salvation of Israel," 47; Jewett,

This perspective of a reversal also generally entails the proposition that the future salvation promised for "all Israel" is similar to the present salvation for the church, which is essentially spiritual, thus having no import for Israel as a nation with a land[4] and a role yet to play among the nations in salvation history.

In seeking to understand God's plan of salvation for Israel and the nations, and especially whether the New Testament and in particular the apostle Paul reverses the Old Testament prophecy of eschatological salvation, I will consider: (1) the Old Testament teaching of the salvation of Israel and the nations; (2) Paul's teaching in Romans 9–11; and (3) the salvation of the nations in the book of Revelation. Of necessity my discussion of such a broad issue entailing great portions of Scripture will have to be brief. But hopefully, the overall plan of salvation will be seen.

THE OLD TESTAMENT TEACHING ON THE SALVATION OF ISRAEL AND THE NATIONS

An examination of the Old Testament teaching concerning the salvation of Israel and the nations actually reveals two scenarios: (1) the dominant plan noted above, in which the nations come to God following the final restoration of Israel, and (2) another picture of the salvation of Gentiles when Israel is in disobedience.

THE DOMINANT THEME OF THE SALVATION OF THE NATIONS WHEN ISRAEL IS RESTORED

The scenario of the salvation of the nations as a result of their encounter with God in his restoration of Israel is widely recognized and therefore will be touched upon only summarily. This theme is especially prominent in the prophecies of Isaiah. Immediately, in chapter 2, the prophet says,

> It shall come to pass in the latter days
>   that the mountain of the house of the LORD
> shall be established as the highest of the mountains,
>   and shall be lifted up above the hills;

Romans, 698; Otfried Hofius, "'All Israel Will Be Saved': Divine Salvation and Israel's Deliverance in Romans 9–11," *The Princeton Seminary Bulletin* (1990): 34–35.

[4] In this perspective, the inclusion of land and a national existence for Israel may be acknowledged, but these have no significance above any other nation and its land, as is the case with reference to the present salvation.

> and all the nations shall flow to it,
>   and many peoples shall come, and say:
> "Come, let us go up to the mountain of the Lord,
>   to the house of the God of Jacob,
> that he may teach us his ways
>   and that we may walk in his paths."
> For out of Zion shall go the law,
>   and the word of the Lord from Jerusalem. (Isa. 2:2–3)[5]

Peter Ackroyd's discussion of the restoration of Israel and its saving effect on the nations in the so-called Deutero-Isaiah (i.e., Isaiah 40–55) captures the prophet's teaching. Referring to Israel, Ackroyd says,

> The limit of God's purpose is not reached in the restoration of Israel, but in the extension of his saving power to the ends of the earth (49.6). The nations will see and prostrate themselves because of Yahweh's choice again of Israel; for in this it is clear, they will see the justice of divine action (49.7). The exaltation of the servant of God brings in the nations as the witnesses in amazement at what God has done (52.13–53.12). . . . And the result will be the acknowledgement of Yahweh as the savior.[6]

Similar expressions of this theme, often referred to as the eschatological pilgrimage of nations to the mountain of God, emerge in one way or another in other prophetic writings. For example, Jeremiah writes, "At that time Jerusalem shall be called the throne of the Lord, and all nations shall gather to it" (3:17; cf. 33:9; Ezek. 36:22–26; 37:28; 39:27; Zech. 2:11; 8:13, 20–23). Likewise the psalmist says, "You will arise and have pity on Zion; . . . Nations will fear the name of the Lord, and all the kings of the earth will fear your glory" (Ps. 102:13, 15). And, again, the prayer, "God be gracious to us and bless us, and cause His face to shine upon us [Israel]—that Your way may be known on the earth, Your salvation among all nations. . . . God blesses us, that all the ends of the earth may fear Him" (Ps. 67:1–2, 7, NASB).

---

[5] Cf. 19:21–25; 42:4; 45:22–23; 52:7–10; 55:3–5; 60:1–3. For a good overview of the prophecy of Isaiah concerning Israel and the salvation of the nations, see Christopher T. Begg, "The Peoples and the Worship of Yahweh in the Book of Isaiah," in *Worship and the Hebrew Bible: Essays in Honour of John T. Willis*, ed. M. Patrick Graham, Rick R. Marrs, and Steven L. McKenzie (Sheffield, England: Sheffield Academic Press, 1999), 35–55.
[6] Peter R. Ackroyd, *Exile and Restoration* (Philadelphia: Westminster, 1968), 136.

McNicol aptly sums up the prophetic teaching of the salvation of the nations as the result of God's restoration of Israel: "Concern for the incorporation of the nations into ultimate recognition of Yahweh in a restored Zion was pervasive in the prophetic scriptures. Any faithful Jew of the late Second Temple period interested in forming an eschatological vision of the last days could hardly miss this emphasis."[7]

THE MINOR THEME OF THE SALVATION OF THE GENTILES WHEN ISRAEL IS IN DISOBEDIENCE

Those who see the New Testament, especially Romans 11:25–26, reversing this dominant picture usually base this change on the failure of Israel to receive her Messiah, i.e., her disobedience to God. In line with Old Testament prophecy, Jesus came to Israel first and not to the nations (Matt. 15:24; cf. John 1:31; Luke 1:54). He charged his disciples likewise (Matt. 10:6). Had Israel received its Messiah, it seems reasonable to surmise that salvation would have come first to Israel and then to the Gentiles in accord with the prominent prophecies mentioned above. Thus, there would be no reversal of the prophesied sequence of salvation.

But as logical as a reversal on the basis of Israel's disobedience may seem, it flounders on the reality that the same prophets who proclaimed the dominant eschatological theme of Gentile salvation resulting from the salvation of Israel also foretold of that nation's disobedience and failure to receive its Messiah. The New Testament writers continually assert that their message of Christ and his salvation is according to the Scriptures (e.g., Rom. 1:1–4; 16:25–26) and lace their writings with citations from the Old Testament in support of their teaching. Thus the apostle Paul, as well as others, sees the present failure of Israel, including its ultimate unbelief in rejecting its Messiah, as already foretold by the Old Testament.

---

[7] Allan J. McNicol, *The Conversion of the Nations in Revelation* (London, New York: T. & T. Clark, 2011), 88. McNicol sets forth the broad scenario of the "key texts" of the Old Testament prophets concerning the salvation of the nations as follows: "l. The nations assemble against the holy city and the Lord's anointed; the nations are defeated. 2. The Lord brings a new creation with analogues to elements of the first creation. 3. The covenant with the house of David and his servants is renewed in the form of a people-covenant. 4. Jerusalem and its temple are renewed beyond its former glory. 5. The covenant with the nations is renewed. They come to Zion to acknowledge the sovereignty of Yahweh" (93). Furthermore, the significance of Israel in the salvation of nations according to the prophets is evident in Urbach's statement that "the stronger the stress placed by the prophets on universalism, the greater is their emphasis upon the special position of Israel" (E. E. Urbach, "Self-Isolation or Self-Affirmation in Judaism in the First Three Centuries: Theory and Practice," in *Jewish and Christian Self-Definition, Vol. 2: Aspects of Judaism in the Graeco-Roman Period*, ed. E. P. Sanders, A. I. Baumgarten, and A. Mendelson [Philadelphia: SCM, 1981], 273).

Israel would be hardened, its ears and eyes would be dull through unbelief (Deut. 29:4; Isa. 6:9–10; 29:10; cf. Matt. 13:14 and par.; John 12:40; Acts 28:26; Rom. 11:8). It would be a blind and deaf servant of God (Isa. 42:19–20). Its rebellion as the people of God would lead to the point where God would no longer call it "My People" (Hos. 1:9–10; 2:23; cf. Rom. 9:25–26). It would be reduced to a "remnant" (Isa. 1:9; 10:21–23), language that, while implying hope for the remnant (Rom. 11:1–6), also speaks of failure and judgment of the remainder (e.g., Rom. 9:27–29).[8]

Finally, even Israel's rejection of its Messiah is foretold in the prophets: The stone that God would lay in Zion would be a stumbling block to many (Isa. 8:14; 28:16; cf. Rom. 9:33). The builders would reject the chief cornerstone, ultimately the Messiah (Ps. 118:22; cf. Matt. 21:42; Acts 4:11). They would not believe God's good news announced through Isaiah of the coming Messiah who would come in an unexpected way (Isa. 53:1; cf. John 12:38; Rom. 10:16). They would despise and afflict their Messiah and finally, along with the Gentiles, pronounce judgment upon him as wicked (Isa. 53:2–4, 7–8; cf. Psalms 22; 69).

The Old Testament not only contained revelation of Israel's rebellious unbelief issuing in the rejection of their Messiah. It also hinted that the salvation that would come through the life and death of Christ would go out to the Gentiles when Israel as a nation was in disobedience and under the judgment of partial hardening. I say "hinted," because this theme is minor compared to the dominant theme of Gentile salvation resulting from the restoration of "all Israel," as noted above. But both themes are found in the prophecies and are utilized, especially by Paul, in the understanding of God's present work of salvation.

In the Song of Moses (Deut. 32:1–43), in which Moses gives a summary of Israel's history from inception on to the future end of days, God predicts the final salvation of Israel and the nations rejoicing with Israel (vv. 36–43). But prior to that time we see another scenario in which Israel is unfaithful and God responds by turning to the Gentiles: "They have made me jealous with what is no god; they have provoked me to anger with their idols. So I will make them jealous with those who are no people; I will provoke them to anger with a foolish nation" (v. 21). Many have seen this "foolish nation" as a reference to historical enemies

---

[8] Hafemann, "Salvation of Israel," 49–50.

that God would use to judge Israel,[9] but little support is offered for these proposals. This imprecision as to identification of the "foolish nation," according to Eugene Merrill, suggests that the prophecy looks forward to eschatological times.[10] Moreover, God's use of this "no people" is not so much to punish Israel as to evoke Israel's jealousy.

God was provoked to a righteous anger of jealousy because Israel had violated their exclusive relationship by turning to other gods. So God would use another people—described as "not a people," similar to the language of Hosea 1:10 and 2:23[11]—to stir Israel's jealousy for him. God's turning his affection to another people would evoke a jealousy of "anger" over seeing others receive the blessing of God (e.g., Acts 13:45; 17:5), but would also lead some to salvation through the jealousy of emulation (Rom. 11:11, 14).

The prophet Isaiah's words also look to the salvation of Gentiles while Israel is in disobedience: "I was ready to be sought by those who did not ask for me; I was ready to be found by those who did not seek me. I said, 'Here I am, here I am,' to a nation that was not called by my name" (Isa. 65:1). Most modern commentators understand this verse in its original context as God's gracious invitation to a rebellious Israel. But some, along with the older interpreters including Luther[12] and Calvin,[13] understand it as Paul uses it in Romans 10:20, i.e., as a reference to God extending salvation to Gentiles.[14]

Derek Kidner notes that the construction of the verbs "ready to be

---

[9] Suggestions have included Canaanites, Philistines, Babylonians, and many others, including Moabites or Ammonites, Arameans, Assyrians, and Samaritans (Richard H. Bell, *Provoked to Jealousy: The Origin and Purpose of the Jealousy Motive in Romans 9–11* [Tübingen: J. C. B. (Paul Siebeck) Mohr, 1994], 215).

[10] Eugene Merrill, *Deuteronomy*, The New American Commentary, vol. 4 (Nashville: Broadman & Holman, 1994), 418n25.

[11] Although Mark Seifrid identifies the "foolish nation" in its Deuteronomy setting as an "unnamed enemy of Israel," he aptly explains Paul's use of this text in Romans 11:11–16 as the church made up of the Jewish remnant and Gentiles and not simply Gentile nations, which would be plural (Mark A. Seifrid, "Romans," in *Commentary on the New Testament Use of the Old Testament*, ed. G. K. Beale and D. A. Carson [Grand Rapids, MI: Baker, 2007], 664).

[12] Martin Luther, *Lectures on Isaiah chs 40–66*, in *Luther's Works*, ed. Jaroslav Pelikan, Hilton C. Oswald, and Helmut T. Lehmann, 55 vols. (St. Louis: Concordia, 1972), 17:375–377.

[13] John Calvin, *Commentary on the Book of the Prophet Isaiah*, trans. William Pringle, 4 vols. (Grand Rapids, MI: Eerdmans, 1948), 4:377–380.

[14] See Joseph Addison Alexander, *Commentary on the Prophecies of Isaiah* (1867 ed.; repr., Grand Rapids, MI: Kregel, 1992), 437; Geoffrey W. Grogan, "Isaiah," in *The Expositor's Bible Commentary on the Old Testament*, Frank E. Gaebelein, gen. ed., vol. 6 (Grand Rapids, MI: Zondervan, 1986), 349; Derek Kidner, "Isaiah," in *New Bible Commentary*, 3rd edition, ed. Donald Guthrie and J. A. Motyer (Leicester, England: Inter-Varsity, 1970), 624; Alec Motyer, *Isaiah: An Introduction and Commentary* (Leicester, England: Inter-Varsity, 1999), 393–394; Carl Wilhelm Eduard Nägelsbach, "The Prophet Isaiah," in John Peter Lange, *Commentary on the Holy Scriptures: Critical, Doctrinal, and Homiletical*, ed. Philip Schaff, vol. 11 (New York: Charles Scribner's Sons, 1884), 689; Edward J. Young, *The Book of Isaiah*, vol. 3 (Grand Rapids, MI: Eerdmans, 1972), 502.

sought" and "ready to be found" refers to actual events, that is, they do not simply indicate an attitude of grace on God's part, but also the result of his action in people actually seeking and finding God; this could not be a reference to rebellious Israelites, as the next section indicates (Isa. 65:2–7).[15] Moreover, according to the Hebrew text, the description of those to whom God presented himself is "a nation that was *not called by my name*" (ESV; cf. ASV, HCSB, KJV, NKJV) rather than the reading of the ancient versions followed by most modern versions, "a nation that did *not call on my name*" (NIV and TNIV; cf. RSV, NRSV, NASB, CEB, Douay-Rheims; cf. 63:19). Nowhere else is Israel said to be a nation not known as God's people. As Motyer says, "There was no time when Israel could be described as *a nation that did not call on my name*, for there were always those who did call; even if we understand the words to imply 'but not sincerely', the accusation is still too sweeping; and even if it were not, there is nothing in the Hebrew to warrant importing the required thought of insincerity."[16]

Finally, in Malachi 1:11, in the midst of expressing his displeasure with the hypocritical offerings of Israel's present priests, God says, "For from the rising of the sun to its setting my name will be great among the nations, and in every place incense will be offered to my name, and a pure offering. For my name will be great among the nations, says the LORD of hosts." Since Malachi later predicts the restoration of Israel (3:1–4:6), this reference to God's name becoming great among the nations probably refers to God's salvation going to the Gentiles while Israel, represented by her priests, is in disobedience. As Keil says, it speaks of a future "reception of the heathen into the kingdom of God in the place of Israel, which would be rejected for a time."[17]

Admittedly, there is disagreement over whether the writers were actually referring to Gentile salvation in every text discussed above, although the evidence for rejecting this reference to the Gentiles as such is far from

---

[15] Kidner, "Isaiah," 624. He says that to understand these verbs as simply indicating that God was ready to be sought and found, without his actually being sought and found, "goes beyond the known use of the 'tolerative Niphal': nowhere else does this construction simply imply a non-event."
[16] Motyer, *Isaiah*, 393.
[17] Carl Friedrich Keil, *Biblical Commentary on the Old Testament: The Twelve Minor Prophets* (Grand Rapids, MI: Eerdmans, 1949), 2:437. See also Peter Verhoef, who sees Malachi 1:11 as a reference to "Pentecost and the NT dispensation." Although not mentioning that this occurs during the temporary rejection of Israel, Verhoef does see the restoration of Israel later in Malachi's prophecy as possibly suggesting that the Gentile salvation of 1:11 occurs before Israel is restored (Peter A. Verhoef, *The Books of Haggai and Malachi* [Grand Rapids, MI: Eerdmans, 1987], 231); Robert L. Alden, "Malachi," in *The Expositor's Bible Commentary*, Frank E. Gaebelein, gen. ed., vol. 7 (Grand Rapids, MI: Zondervan, 1985), 713.

overwhelming. It is sufficient to note at this point that the apostle Paul clearly used the first two passages (Deut. 32:21; Isa. 65:1) and several other Old Testament texts in his explanation of his ministry and the present age of God's salvation history. In this regard, Cranfield's comment in relation to Paul's use of Deuteronomy 32:21 in Romans 10:19 is significant: "It is a striking feature of the argument here that, instead of appealing directly to the actual course of the Gentile mission in which he himself had played so important a part, Paul keeps steadfastly to the OT."[18]

In sum, the Old Testament prophecy of salvation history beginning with the coming of Christ involves two themes of Gentile salvation—one while Israel is disobedient, including the rejection of their Messiah; and another when the nations come to recognize God through the promised restoration of Israel. The overall eschatological salvation history thus looks like this: (1) Israel's spiritual rebellion, climaxing in the rejection of the Messiah by the nation, although a remnant receive him; (2) salvation going out to the Gentiles, beginning through the believing remnant of Israel during the present age, while the nation of Israel largely is in disobedience; (3) the salvation and restoration of Israel as a nation in connection with the parousia of Christ; and (4) the salvation of the nations as they see the restoration and glorification of Israel and come to acknowledge and worship Yahweh along with Israel as the true God.

Before turning to the teaching of the apostle Paul in Romans 9–11, it will be helpful to very briefly note the teaching of the Gospels, especially that of Jesus, who clearly taught that the Gentiles are included in God's salvation plan. The nations would be judged and the saved among them ("sheep") would "inherit the kingdom prepared for you from the foundation of the world" (Matt. 25:31–40). As the "Son of Man," Jesus fulfilled the prophecy of Daniel 7:13–14, which foretold of "all peoples, nations, and languages" serving him.

In the so-called triumphal entry into Jerusalem just prior to his crucifixion, Jesus rode on a donkey in a fulfillment of Zechariah 9:9–10—a prophecy that spoke of the one coming as "righteous and having salvation" who, among other actions, would "speak peace to the nations." Prophesying over the child Jesus, Simeon spoke of him as God's salvation

---

[18] Cranfield, *Epistle to the Romans*, 2:539. His statement is worth pondering in this discussion despite the fact that, with many others, he sees Deuteronomy 32:21 as referring to various Gentile nations that God has used throughout history to punish Israel for her infidelity.

who would be "a light for revelation to the Gentiles, and for glory to your people Israel" (Luke 2:32; citing Isa. 42:6; 49:6).

But Jesus also spoke of Israel's disobedience and rejection of him, and saw it as prophesied in the Old Testament. Israel and its leaders would be judicially hardened and unable to receive his teaching (Matt. 13:14–15; 15:7–9, citing Isa. 6:9–10). As predicted in the Old Testament, they would stumble over the messianic stone laid by God (Matt. 21:42, citing Ps. 118:22–23), and would strike the shepherd (Matt. 26:31, citing Zech. 13:7; cf. Matt. 26:56). According to Jesus all the events of his life, death, and resurrection were things about which "the prophets have spoken" (Luke 24:25; see vv. 19–27).

Like the Old Testament, Jesus also spoke of salvation going to the Gentiles while disobedient Israel was judicially set aside for a time. Early in his ministry he mentioned God extending mercy to non-Israelites when that nation was disobedient (Luke 4:25–27). Later he declared that "many will come from east and west and recline at table with Abraham, Isaac, and Jacob in the kingdom of heaven, while the sons of the kingdom will be thrown into the outer darkness" (Matt. 8:11–12). In sum, the salvation history of Jesus and the Gospels not only conforms to what we have seen in the Old Testament above, but is said to be based on it.

THE TEACHING OF PAUL IN ROMANS 9-11

Paul's teaching in Romans 9–11 is the most extensive discussion in the New Testament of the eschatological situation of Israel, and is therefore central to the New Testament perspective on the fulfillment of Old Testament prophecies concerning that nation in the remaining history of salvation. This issue arises in the letter as a result of Paul's explanation of the nature of God's salvation in Christ and the nation of Israel's rejection of it.

Hints of Israel's priority in God's plan of salvation are found in prior chapters. The gospel "is the power of God for salvation to everyone who believes, to the Jew first and also to the Greek" (Rom. 1:16). The Jews were advantaged, having been entrusted by God with the revelation of God with its many promises (3:1–2). But what about Israel now that God's salvation is going out to the nations, seemingly bypassing the nation of Israel that rejects it? What about the prophecies concerning that nation that remain unfulfilled? Are they being fulfilled in the church in another way in a "new Israel," the church?

Israel's Rejection and Hardening Have Not Voided the "Covenants" and "Promises"

The full presentation of the gospel in Romans 1–8, and Israel's failure to receive it, inevitably raised the question of the fulfillment of all of the prophecies found in the Old Testament revelation. Already addressed in 3:3—"What if some were unfaithful? Does their faithlessness nullify the faithfulness of God?"—the question is again raised at the beginning of Paul's discourse on Israel and again answered negatively: "But it is not as though the word of God has failed" (9:6). The issue of the fulfillment of the prophetic word of God concerning Israel not only affected that nation but, as J. C. Beker notes, it was fundamental to the gospel and Christians as well: "What is at stake is nothing less than the faithfulness of God. If it could be argued that God has rejected the people of the election, Israel, and that therefore God's promises to Israel have become null and void, how are the Gentiles to trust the confirmation of these promises to them through God's righteousness in Christ?"[19] In response to the question of the present status of God's promises to Israel, Paul, without qualification or indication of reinterpretation, affirms the validity of God's prophetic word to that nation, even in its present state of unbelief and in light of the existence of the new messianic community composed of believing Jews and Gentiles.

Referring to the unbelieving "Israelites," whom he identifies as "my kinsmen according to the flesh," Paul declares that "to them belong the adoption, the glory, the covenants, the giving of the law, the worship, and the promises" (Rom. 9:3–4).[20] Focusing particularly on "the covenants" and the "promises": the former surely included the various covenants made with Abraham, the nation at Sinai, and David, and the promised new covenant; the "promises" certainly included those given to Abraham, which the apostle refers to elsewhere in his writings (cf. 4:13–22; Gal. 3:16–29). But, as Cranfield notes, Paul probably "also had in mind many other OT promises, particularly the eschatological and messianic promises."[21]

---

[19] J. C. Beker, "The Faithfulness of God and the Priority of Israel in Paul's Letter to the Romans," in *Christians among Jews and Gentiles*, ed. George W. E. Nickelsburg with George W. MacRae (Philadelphia: Fortress, 1986), 14.

[20] For a good discussion of this list, which constitutes a summary of the divinely promised prerogatives of Israel and their Old Testament heritage, see John Piper, *The Justification of God* (Grand Rapids, MI: Baker, 1983), 15–25.

[21] Cranfield, *Epistle to the Romans*, 464. Referring to the many other Old Testament promises, he adds, "Such passages as 2 Sam. 7.12, 16, 28f; Isa. 9.6f; Jer. 23.5; 31.31ff; Ezek. 34.24ff spring to mind. There are many references in Judaism to God's promises."

Again, in Romans 11:28–29, Paul speaks of contemporary Israel, declaring that while the people are presently enemies for the sake of the gospel going to the Gentiles, they are still "beloved for the sake of [because of] their forefathers. For the gifts and the calling of God are irrevocable." This confidence obviously flows from the earlier statement that "God has not rejected his people whom he foreknew" [i.e., "deliberately joined them to himself in faithful love"[22]] (11:2). It is generally agreed that the irrevocable "gifts" refer back to the formal list of Israel's divinely bestowed attributes in 9:4–5.[23]

With regard to Israel's permanent "calling," most interpreters appear to think of it in terms of salvation, or as Dunn explains, "promise and election," that also belongs to Gentile believers.[24] But there is no reason not to see in Israel's "calling" also a function of service in salvation history for which they were originally called and made "God's people" (see Ex. 19:5–6). If the gifts refer to covenants and promises (Rom. 9:4–5) that involved service, it seems reasonable to understand this "calling," with Cranfield, as "God's calling of Israel to be His special people, to stand in a special relation to Himself, and to fulfill a special function in history."[25]

Paul's strong affirmation of the continued validity of God's Old Testament promises to the nation of Israel, even after its rejection of the Messiah and the beginning of the church, raises the question of the content of these continuing covenants and promises. For our purpose I will mention only three important things frequently found in the prophecies concerning Israel. First, Israel was created to be a nation, not just a spiritual people. God promised Abraham that his descendants would be "a great nation" (Gen. 12:2; cf. 17:5; 18:18; Ex. 19:6; 33:13; Deut. 4:34; 26:5). In the Old Testament, three major elements defined a nation: race, government, and territory.[26] Israel in its beginning clearly met these criteria. While

---

[22] Ibid, 545.
[23] Jewett, *Romans*, 708; Cranfield, *Epistle to the Romans*, 581; Dunn, *Romans 9–16*, 694; Moo, *Epistle to the Romans*, 732.
[24] Dunn, *Romans 9–16*, 694. This is probably due to the fact that these commentators understand Paul to see the bringing of Israel into salvation following Gentile salvation as the fulfillment of the promises to that people, rather than as saving them and using them in a further role in salvation history.
[25] Cranfield, *Epistle to the Romans*, 581. Everett Harrison expresses a similar thought, defining Israel's "calling" here as "the summons of Israel to a unique place in the purpose of God" ("Romans," in *The Expositor's Bible Commentary*, Frank E. Gaebelein, gen. ed., vol. 10 [Grand Rapids, MI: Zondervan, 1976], 125).
[26] Ronald E. Clements, "גוי, goy," *Theological Dictionary of the Old Testament*, vol. 2 (Grand Rapids, MI: Eerdmans, 1975), 428–429.

it has not continually endured as nation, due to God's judgment of its unfaithfulness, the Old Testament prophets promised a spiritual renewal (e.g., Ezek. 36:25–29; 37:12–14, 20–27; Isa. 46:13; Jer. 31:31–33) and the restoration of its status as a nation (e.g., Ezek. 37:21–22; 20:42; Jer. 23:5–6; Hos. 1:11; Zech. 10:6–12).

Second, Israel as a nation entailed a territory, i.e., a national land. This is reflected in Ronald Clements's comment concerning the book of Deuteronomy: "A pervasive assumption throughout the book is that Israel is a nation, and it can scarcely be said to countenance the possibility that Israel might continue to live as Yahweh's people in some form other than that of a nation."[27] Although Israel was exiled from her land, as just noted above, the promise of national restoration included the promise of a return to and occupation of the land that God had given it (e.g., Isa. 49:6–8; Jer. 3:18–19; 24:6; Ezek. 20:39–42; 36:8–12). According to the Old Testament, "for Israel to live . . . is to return to the land of Canaan."[28]

Third, Israel was called to a special role in God's plan of salvation: the nation was to be a "kingdom of priests" (Ex. 19:6). In the words of Martin Noth, Israel was "to have the role of a priestly member in the number of earthly states . . . to do 'service' for all the world (cf. Isa. 65:5f.); this is the purpose for which Israel has been chosen."[29] As we have seen above, the Old Testament prophecies see this ministry of Israel for the world as culminating through God's salvation and restoration in the eschatological times of the Messiah.

Aside from all of the other promises related to Israel, if these three fundamental promises related to Israel are included in the "covenants" and "promises" that Paul affirms are valid—restoration as a nation, occupation of the Promised Land, and the divine function of bringing God's blessing to the nations through its restoration and glorification before the nations—then it is difficult to see how these things are not still to be expected. We would expect the apostle to give some explanation if the nature of these promises have been altered from their Old Testament meaning, but nowhere does he give such indication.

---

[27] Ronald E. Clements, *Old Testament Theology* (Atlanta: John Knox, 1976), 89.
[28] Donald E. Gowan, *Eschatology in the Old Testament* (Philadelphia: Fortress, 1986), 25.
[29] Martin Noth, *Exodus* (Philadelphia: Westminster, 1962), 157. Brevard Childs similarly states, "Israel as a people is dedicated to God's service among the nations as priests function with a society" (*The Book of Exodus* [Philadelphia: Westminster, 1974], 367).

The Present Salvation of Gentiles Is Not the Final Fulfillment of the Prophesied Salvation of the Gentiles

Those who see Paul as reversing the Old Testament prophecies, making the salvation of Gentiles now precede that of Israel, nevertheless see him as teaching that this change is the fulfillment of the Old Testament prophecies. The coming in of the full number of Gentiles during this age before the salvation of Israel (Rom. 11:25–26) is with various interpretations viewed as the fulfillment of the Old Testament prophecies described as the eschatological pilgrimage of the Gentiles to Zion (Isa. 2:1–4) or the ingathering of the nations.[30]

However, there are a number of things, which can only be briefly stated, that make it difficult to accept this interpretation:

(1) Rather than the nations acknowledging God and streaming to Zion to worship him, the New Testament clearly sees them during the "times of the Gentile" essentially in rebellion against God: they will tread down Jerusalem until the Messiah returns to restore Israel (Luke 21:23–24). This rebellion is evident especially in the book of Revelation, where the nations are enraged at the establishment of Christ's kingdom (11:18) and are under the sway of Babylon until it is brought down at the end of the age (14:8; 17:15; 18:3). The present world's anti-Semitism is contrary to the prophesied exaltation of Israel among the nations (Isa. 59:21–60:3, 14; 62:10–12).

(2) According to Jesus and the writers of the New Testament, this age is one of persecution for followers of Christ. It is difficult to see how such would be the case if the nations are coming to know and worship the true God. Again, this point is highlighted in Revelation, as the nations come under the Antichrist in the last days.

(3) According to the New Testament, Christ enters into judgment with the nations at his future coming. But if the nations are coming to acknowledge and worship God in this age in fulfillment of the prophecies, as is commonly claimed, why this coming devastating judgment on the nations when Christ returns, as prophesied in Revelation 19:15ff.? To be sure, there is a final judgment of individuals at the great white throne judgment

---

[30] E.g., Dunn, *Romans 9–16*, 680; Hultgren, *Paul's Letter to the Romans*, 418; Joachim Jeremias, *Jesus' Promise to the Nations* (Philadelphia: Fortress, 1982), 56ff., 72n2.; Bruce W. Longenecker, "Different Answers to Different Issues: Israel, the Gentiles, and Salvation History in Romans 9–11," *Journal for the Study of the New Testament* 36 (1989): 111.

following the millennial reign of Christ and the saints (Rev. 20:11ff.). But there is no mention of a judgment of the nations at that point, which fact harmonizes with the prophecies that, under the reign of Christ following his return, they have come to acknowledge the true God of Israel.

(4) The inversion of the order, with the final Gentile salvation coming prior to the salvation of Israel, is finally radically contrary to the basic contour of the Old Testament. Terence Donaldson gets to the heart of this dissonance when he says,

> [T]his approach slides too easily over the problems posed by the putative inversion of the order of salvation of Israel and the Gentiles. Such an inversion would represent not a simple modification in detail, but the abandonment of the foundation of the tradition itself. In the eschatological pilgrimage tradition, the salvation of the Gentiles follows the redemption of Israel as a matter not simply of sequence but of *consequence*: it is *because* they see the redemption of Israel and the glorification of Zion that the Gentiles abandon their idols and turn to worship the God of Israel.[31]

(5) In his discussion of the salvation of Gentiles and Israel in Romans 9–11, Paul does not use the primary Old Testament prophecies focusing on Gentile salvation, and certainly not the texts supporting the pilgrimage of the nations to Zion (e.g., Isa. 2:2ff.; Mic. 4:2; Isa. 56:7; 60:3); rather, he uses texts related to what I have called above the minor prophetic theme of Gentile salvation. He portrays his ministry as an apostle to the Gentiles not as fulfilling the ultimate prophecies of Gentile salvation but as saving Gentiles in order to stimulate Israel to jealousy and bring that nation to salvation (Rom. 11:13–14).

In light of these discrepancies between the apostle's teaching in Romans 9–11 and the central Old Testament prophecies related to the salvation and restoration of Israel and the salvation of Gentiles, it is difficult to see how the interpretation that sees Paul as inverting the dominant eschatological prophecies can make peace with his strong affirmation of the continuing validity of Israel's "covenants" and "promises." What makes it especially difficult is the fact that nowhere does he indicate that he is modifying these covenant promises.

---

[31] Terence L. Donaldson, "'Riches for the Gentiles' (Rom 11:12): Israel's Rejection and Paul's Gentile Mission," *Journal of Biblical Literature* 112/7 (1993), 92.

The Future Blessing to the World through Israel's Restoration

I come now to the crucial issue of how we are to understand Paul's teaching concerning the future blessing of the world that will take place when Israel is restored (Rom. 11:12, 15)—i.e., the salvation of "all Israel" (v. 26)—and his teaching that Israel's salvation will occur after the "fullness of the Gentiles has come in."

The Future Blessing of the World (Rom. 11:12, 15)

Paul's concern that Gentile believers at Rome not be arrogant over their privileged position of participating in the promised messianic salvation, while the bulk of Israel was under the hardening of God, led him to insert two brief statements to the effect that a much greater blessing is in store for the world when Israel recognizes its Messiah and is restored:

> Now if their trespass means riches for the world, and if their failure means riches for the Gentiles, how much more will their full inclusion mean! (v. 12)

> For if their rejection means the reconciliation of the world, what will their acceptance mean but life from the dead? (v. 15)

While there is considerable disagreement as to the precise meaning of the people of Israel's "full inclusion" and their "acceptance," it is generally agreed that the expressions relate to the future conversion of "all Israel" (cf. v. 26). My concern here is the meaning of the phrases that speak of the benefit that will occur for the Gentiles and the world when Israel (and not just a remnant of it) will come to salvation.

The contents of the "much more" for the Gentiles, which is anticipated following the salvation of Israel, are variously described but often without a specific definition.[32] There seems to be good reason, however, to see this "much more" as a reference to greater riches of salvation for Gentiles, including the concept of conversion.

---

[32] For example, Dunn says that Paul "in this rhetorically shaped phrasing . . . is not attempting a specific meaning, but simply seeking a way to contrast the deprived condition of Israel in the final building up to the climax of God's purpose for the world, with the blessing of salvation newly opened up to the Gentiles" (Dunn, *Romans 9–16*, 654–655); Moo, on the other hand, sees the "much more" of verse 12 as the "life from the dead" in verse 15, i.e., "the new life that comes after the resurrection" (*Epistle to the Romans*, 689, 695).

For example, Cranfield understands the meaning of "riches" that will be "much more" when Israel comes to salvation as "substantially the same" as what is expressed by "salvation" in the previous verse (Rom. 11:11).[33] While not explicitly saying that this salvation means conversion, he does say that the "much more" salvation is more "of the benefits" that came to Gentiles as a result of Israel's unbelief,[34] which surely included conversion. John Murray explains the "much more" as "a greater enjoyment of gospel blessing," or "the expansion of the success attending the gospel and of the kingdom of God."[35] This also suggests more Gentiles responding to the gospel to enjoy its salvation. Jewett agrees that the "much more" that will ensue from the fulfillment of Israel is much more of the "riches" that the Gentiles presently enjoy, which he defines as "spiritual and material" prosperity; again, this notion would seem to involve spiritual conversion.[36] Robert Haldane expressed this same opinion, declaring that the restoration of the Jews "will yet prove a far greater blessing to the Gentiles. It will be connected with a calling of the nations to an extent beyond anything yet witnessed, and also with a great enlargement of their knowledge of the Gospel."[37] John Stott sees the "much more" explained in verse 15—"life from the dead," which he clearly sees as involving a greater conversion of the Gentiles (to be discussed below).[38]

The promised "life from the dead" (Rom. 11:15) receives two prominent interpretations. For many it is the "general resurrection that will take place after the return of Christ in glory, or . . . the blessed life that will follow that resurrection." Others, taking it metaphorically, see it either as a "spiritual quickening of the whole world," or less commonly as the spiritual conversion of the Jews.[39] A reference to the spiritual conversion of Israel seems unlikely here, as Paul's statement seems analogous to verse 12, in which the restoration of Israel brings worldwide blessing, not just blessing to Israel.

The resurrection view is possible, as Scripture clearly teaches a resur-

---

[33] Cranfield, *Epistle to the Romans*, 556–557. Unfortunately, Cranfield does not discuss what he means by salvation.
[34] Ibid., 556.
[35] John Murray, *The Epistle to the Romans, Vol. 2: Chapters 9–16* (Grand Rapids, MI: Eerdmans, 1965), 79.
[36] Jewett, *Romans: A Commentary*, 676–677.
[37] Robert Haldane, *Exposition of the Epistle to the Romans* (1874; repr., London: Banner of Truth, 1958), 533.
[38] John Stott, *Romans: God's Good News for the World* (Downers Grove, IL: InterVarsity Press, 1994), 296, 298–299.
[39] Moo, *Epistle to the Romans*, 694. Moo provides a good list of the advocates of these three views in notes 61, 62, and 63 respectively.

rection associated with the coming of Christ (1 Thess. 4:16; Rev. 20:4). But there is no reference in the context to the radical transformation of all things that takes place at the time of the general resurrection and the end of history. The only possible thought of Christ's coming here is to bring salvation to historical Israel (Rom. 11:26), which in turn will bring greater blessing to the world. Moreover, as has been noted, Paul's language used in 11:15, "life from the dead," is different from the terminology used for the resurrection of Christ and people throughout the New Testament and by Paul himself, namely, "resurrection of [or from] the dead" (Rom. 1:4; 6:5; 8:6; 1 Cor. 15:12, 13, 21, 42; Phil. 3:10).[40] It should be noted that nowhere in the Old Testament are the prophecies of the blessing of the world through Israel's restoration related to the final resurrection. Thus, if resurrection is what Paul intends, he would not simply be reversing the Old Testament scheme; he would not be following prophecy at all.

The metaphorical use of life and death for spiritual realities is frequently found in Scripture (e.g., Ezek. 37:1–10), more frequently in the New Testament and especially in Paul's letters (e.g., Rom. 5:18; 6:4, 11, 13; 8:6; 2 Cor. 2:16; Eph. 2:1, 5; 4:18; Phil. 2:16; Col. 2:12). This meaning is also appropriate to the context of Paul's discussion of rich blessing coming to the world through the salvation of Israel. Thus, Murray explains "life from the dead" as "an unprecedented quickening for the world in *the expansion and success of the gospel.*"[41] Stott cites Murray's words approvingly and suggests that Paul might be using Ezekiel's vision of Israel receiving life from the dead (Ezek. 37:1–10) as an analogy of what Paul promises for the Gentiles.[42] The eminent Swiss Catholic theologian Charles Journet also understood both verses 12 and 15 of Romans 11 as referring to a future blessing of the world through Israel's salvation: "For Israel must one day come back to its Messiah, so that nations, enlivened and enriched by its return, may at that moment enter the second stage of their conversion. . . . Israel holds back the supreme outpouring of grace on the world and thus the course of redemptive history."[43]

---

[40] Murray, *Epistle to the Romans*, 83; see also Joseph A. Fitzmyer, *Romans: A New Translation with Introduction and Commentary*, The Anchor Bible (New York: Doubleday, 1993), 613. As we saw above, Moo sees this point as strong enough to suggest that "life from the dead" does not refer to the resurrection but to the life that comes after it.
[41] Murray, *Epistle to the Romans*, 84 (emphasis mine).
[42] Stott, *Romans*, 298–299; see also Harrison, "Romans," 120–121.
[43] Charles Journet, "The Mysterious Destinies of Israel," in *The Bridge: A Yearbook of Judaeo-Christian Studies*, vol. 2 (New York: Pantheon, 1956), 69–70.

No doubt this metaphorical view of these verses would be more common were it not for the fact that many interpreters are convinced that Paul clearly teaches the ultimate end of Gentile salvation when he refers to the coming in of "the fullness of the Gentiles" prior to the salvation of Israel (Rom. 11:25).[44] But is it possible that Journet is correct when he refers to the future salvation of the Gentiles as "the second stage of their conversion" and the present salvation of Gentiles, which according to Paul is designed to provoke Israel to jealousy and lead to their salvation, as only the "first stage of the world's conversion"?[45]

Without attempting a full discussion of what Paul means by the coming in of "the fullness of the Gentiles,"[46] several things argue against the common view that it refers to the ultimate number of Gentiles that will be saved. First, Paul's prior references to a greater blessing of the Gentiles when Israel is restored (Rom. 11:12, 15), if this includes a numerical increase of salvation as noted above, precludes the end of all Gentile salvation prior to Israel's salvation.

Second, according to the New Testament, the salvation of the nations prior to the return of Christ is quite different in scope than the nations coming to God foretold in prophecies for the messianic age, which we have seen above. Several statements of Jesus point to a relatively few coming to salvation during this time (e.g., Matt. 7:14; Luke 18:8; cf. Luke 13:23–24; Matt. 24:11–13). The prediction of persecution of believers for this entire age also argues against the nations turning to worship the God of Israel as seen in the prophecies. The activity of God's salvation among the nations presently is depicted by James as taking from among the Gentiles "a people for his name" (Acts 15:14). Paul's reference to his goal of bringing about the obedience of faith "among all the nations" (Rom. 1:5), which Dunn sees as possibly suggesting his recognition that the Gentile response would be "patchy,"[47] fits this picture of the present salvation of the nations.

Third, the terminology of "the fullness" or "the completeness" of

---

[44] In support of his view that Romans 11:12 and 15 refer to the new life that comes after the resurrection, Moo says, "And vv. 25–26 suggest that the salvation of Israel comes only after God has brought into the kingdom all Gentiles destined to be saved. No room is therefore left for a spiritual quickening of the world: all that remains is the consummation" (Moo, *Epistle to the Romans*, 695; see also Cranfield, *Epistle to the Romans*, 563).
[45] Journet, "Mysterious Destinies of Israel," 69–70.
[46] For a brief reference to the different views and their advocates, see Michael G. VanLaningham, "Romans 11:25–27 and the Future of Israel in Paul's Thought," *The Master's Seminary Journal* 3/2 (Fall 1992): 152–156.
[47] James D. G. Dunn, *Romans 1–8*, Word Biblical Commentary, vol. 38A (Dallas: Word, 1988), 18.

Gentile salvation does not by itself signify whether this fullness of Gentile salvation refers to all of salvation history or to a particular time of that history. Hübner, for example, explains Paul's reference to "the *full number* of Gentiles" as "a theological concept related to Paul's mission within the framework of the discussion of Israel in Romans 9–11." The full number of Gentiles is thus "the 'prerequisite' for the saving of all Israel."[48]

Understanding Hübner's statements as indicating that the "fullness of the Gentiles" refers to those Gentiles saved during this age until God's mercy again brings the salvation of Israel, harmonizes well with other scriptural teaching that sees the present age especially related to Gentile salvation. Clearly, the context of Romans 9–11 portrays the present time as the time of Gentile salvation as compared to the salvation of Israel—the time when Gentiles are receiving God's mercy and Israel is not (11:28–31).

We might also add Jesus's teaching of the wedding feast when, due to the rejection of the invitation by Israel's leaders and thus by the bulk of the nation, the vacancies will be made up by compelling others (including Gentiles) to come in, so that his "house may be filled" (Luke 14:12–24; cf. Matt. 8:11–12; 22:1–14). The statement that "this gospel of the kingdom will be proclaimed throughout the whole world as a testimony to all nations, and then the end will come" (Matt. 24:14) also suggests a particular period of Gentile salvation. Moreover, the "end" at this point cannot be the ultimate end of salvation history, for the end of the "fullness of the Gentile" brings God's mercy and salvation for "all Israel."

The Nature of Israel's Salvation

The nature of Israel's salvation in Romans 11:26 is also entailed in the question of whether Paul's "mystery" includes the reversal of the prophesied order of the salvation of Israel and the Gentiles. For those who see such a reversal, the future salvation received by "all Israel"[49] is that salvation explained in the previous chapters of Romans, i.e., the blessings of forgiveness and justification by God's grace, or essentially "a large scale

---

[48] Hans Hübner, "πλήρωμα," in *Exegetical Dictionary of the New Testament*, ed. Horst Balz and Gerhard Schneider, vol. 3 (Grand Rapids, MI: Eerdmans, 1993), 110–111.
[49] Based on the Old Testament and other Jewish sources, "all Israel" is generally accepted today as "a collective designation for the people of Israel in its entirety," without the connotation of every individual Israelite (Hofius, "'All Israel Will Be Saved,'" 35).

conversion of Jewish people."[50] The idea that it could include the Old Testament hope of national restoration with land and primacy of Israel among the nations is rejected.[51]

To be sure, Paul does not refer to any explicit prophecies concerning the restoration of Israel to the land as a nation. But a number of reasons that can only briefly be stated suggest that this silence does not of itself mean that Paul is thereby excluding these prophesies of Israel's national restoration as concomitant with the "salvation" he predicts for "all Israel."

(1) While the focus of Paul's concern is the salvation of Israel through the mercy of God, i.e., by grace through faith, the citations from the Old Testament, in their context, clearly involve more than spiritual salvation. Isaiah 59:20–21 is immediately followed with promise of the glory of the Lord shining on Israel and drawing the nations to its brightness (60:1–4). Similarly, Isaiah 27:9 is surrounded by references to the blossoming and sprouting of Israel, filling the whole world with its fruit (v. 6), and its regathering to worship Yahweh "on the holy mountain at Jerusalem" (vv. 12–13). The reference to "my covenant with them when I take away their sins" (Rom. 11:27) is also probably an allusion to Jeremiah's prophecy of a new covenant (Jer. 31:31–34). Along with its promise of forgiveness of sins, this covenant also promises the restoration and perpetual existence of Israel as "a nation before me forever" (v. 36, see also vv. 35–40). Paul gives no indication that his reference to the salvation of Israel excludes these prophesied aspects of Israel's salvation, which he and all of the Jewish writers and Jewish hearers of the New Testament message knew very well.

Moreover, as Stamm explains, the Old Testament understanding of forgiveness, or the taking away of sins (Rom. 11:27) (which would seem applicable to the Old Testament citations), is more than the forgiveness of justification. It is "an act of God in response to humanity that, along with liberation from sin and the removal of punishment, also brings a comprehensive restoration or renewal."[52]

(2) Paul's concern in his discussion of Israel in Romans 9–11 is to set Israel into the salvation in Christ that, as he has been explaining

---

[50] Moo, *Epistle to the Romans*, 724.
[51] Ibid., 724n59; Dunn, *Romans 9–16*, 682.
[52] J. J. Stamm, "סלח, *slḥ* to forgive," *Theological Lexicon of the Old Testament*, ed. Ernst Jenni and Claus Westermann (Peabody, MA: Hendrickson, 1997), 803.

through the earlier chapters, is by grace through faith alone. As Hofius expresses it, "The Pauline doctrine of justification . . . forms the background against which the exposition of Romans 9–11 is to be viewed and understood."[53] Thus, as Nils Dahl explains,

> Paul has no interest in giving a detailed description of what is going to happen at the end of time. He does not speak abstractly about the distant future but concretely about a course of events already in progress, of which his own work as apostle to the Gentiles is an important part. . . . Paul applies scriptural quotations about Israel's disobedience, the hardening of the Israelites' hearts and their temporary rejection to their refusal to accept Christ. He identifies the faithful remnant with those Jews who do believe in Christ. That God in the last days will again show mercy and restore his disobedient people to favor means that he has promised that all Israel will share in the salvation Christ alone makes available. Paul does not discuss what else the future holds for Israel, because for him Israel's relation to Christ is the decisive problem.[54]

Paul's focused concern on the merciful nature of God's salvation and therefore the absence of repeating all of the prophecies concerning Israel's restoration cannot be a strong argument that he no longer anticipated the fulfillment of these prophecies.

(3) Finally, viewing the salvation of Israel as essentially only conversion into the new community of Christ, the church, is contrary to the prophecies in several ways. It does not account for the many political, economic, and material aspects related to the restoration and exaltation of Israel as a nation among the nations inhabiting a fruitful land. It does violence to the prophetic picture of a restored Israel as the place from which the light of God's saving glory radiates to the nations for their

---

[53] Hofius, "'All Israel Will Be Saved,'" 23; similarly, Dahl says that "Romans 9–11 illustrates Paul's doctrine of justification by faith" (Nils Alstrup Dahl, "The Future of Israel," in his *Studies in Paul: Theology for the Early Christian Mission* [Minneapolis: Augsburg, 1977], 156).

[54] Dahl, "Future of Israel," 154–155. Barrett sees Paul's discussion as leading to a conclusion in 11:30–32: "For just as you [Gentiles] were once disobedient to God, but now have been shown mercy because of their [Israel's] disobedience, so these [Israel] also now have been disobedient, that because of mercy shown to you they also may now be shown mercy. For God has shut up all [Gentile and Jew] in disobedience so that He may show mercy to all." In other words, the Gentiles were disobedient (Romans 1), and the Jews in their disbelief in Christ have also come and remain in that place, all demonstrating that salvation in Christ can come only through the mercy of God—"only sinners can be the objects of his mercy, and only those who know that they are sinners can know that they are loved" (C. K. Barrett, *The Epistle to the Romans*, rev. ed. [Grand Rapids, MI: Baker, 2011], 208–209).

salvation. In other words, it does not provide a fulfillment of God's purpose for Israel to be God's priestly nation among the nations and her final salvation for the sake of the salvation of the nations.

In this connection it could be argued that the understanding of Israel's salvation as basically spiritual conversion seriously weakens Paul's warning against Gentile arrogance over their enjoyment of God's salvation while Israel is outside (Rom. 11:18, 20, 25). If Israel's salvation is simply conversion to participate in what the Gentiles already have, without any future role in salvation history, then the Gentiles could think of themselves as being the ultimate messenger of salvation in bringing in many Jews. The final stage of salvation history would then be "salvation is from the Gentiles" and not "from the Jews."

THE SALVATION OF THE NATIONS IN THE BOOK OF REVELATION

The book of Revelation, which brings us to eternity and thus includes the end of the biblical history of salvation, has much to say about the nations in these last days of salvation history. Space precludes more than a very brief outline of John's portrait of the history of the nations through these end times.

(1) Although God's people are seen as *drawn from the nations* in the early part of the book (Rev. 5:9; 7:9), the *nations themselves* are pictured as unbelieving—increasingly giving their allegiance to and coming under the control of wicked Babylon and the Antichrist (13:3, 7, 8, 12ff.; 11:2; 14:8; 17:15, 18; 18:3, 9, 23) until their destruction by Christ at his coming.

(2) When Christ returns "to strike down the nations" in battle "with their armies" (19:15, 19), the kings of the nations and their vast armies are destroyed (19:20–21), and possibly also all those among the nations who worshiped the beast and received his mark on their forehead (14:9–11).

(3) In harmony with the previous points, there is no evidence of a mass number of Gentiles coming to salvation, and certainly none for the nations and their kings coming to acknowledge God and streaming to Zion to worship and learn from him during the time prior to the return of Christ and destruction of the armies of the rebellious nations.

(4) In the last portrait in Revelation, we see the grand scene of the

nations and their kings walking in the light of the new Jerusalem and bringing "into it the glory and the honor of the nations" (21:24, 26).

In the words of McNicol, there seems to be in this picture of the nations a "deep tension in . . . [John's] narrative between the destructive defeat of the kings and the nations in Revelation 19.15–21 and the joyous welcome extended to them in 21.24–26." To phrase the problem in another way pertinent to the issue in this essay, if the domination of Satan and his Antichrist over the nations is broken only through their defeat and destruction at the coming of Christ, and the coming of Christ to save all Israel also signals the end of Gentile salvation, how do we account for these eschatological nations who are now worshiping God and bringing their glory into the new Jerusalem?[55]

Different nuanced answers are given to this question, but for the issue of this essay, they resolve down to two. On the one hand, with those who understand the end of Gentile salvation to be prior to the salvation of Israel in a reversal of Old Testament prophecy, one can see eschatological nations and their kings as the result of the present salvation and the coming in of the "fullness of the Gentiles," the end of which is related to the coming of Christ and prior to the salvation of "all Israel." The evidence for such a salvation of nations (and especially kings) during this period in which the nations and their kings are moving toward a final destructive confrontation with Christ is difficult to find, not only in Revelation but in all of the New Testament.

On the other hand, one can understand John as elaborating the Old Testament prophecies that see the nations coming to recognize and worship God as a result of the display of his power in the restoration and glorification of Israel. The many allusions in Revelation to the Old Testament, especially the focus on prophecies from Psalms, Isaiah, Ezekiel, and Daniel, along with others including Zechariah, give support to McNicol's thesis that "the views of the prophet John on the end times were deeply formed by reading key passages of scripture on the pilgrimage of the nations. . . . From this foundation he began to formulate a coherent eschatological vision."[56] If John is indeed following these Old Testament prophecies, his teaching not only cannot be harmonized with the

---

[55] This is the question that McNicol so aptly poses in *Conversion of the Nations in Revelation*, xiv, 2–3, 86.
[56] Ibid., xiv. More specifically McNicol says, "John's account of the pilgrimage of the nations to Jerusalem reflects themes drawn from such key texts as Isaiah 60, 66, and Zechariah 14. There we find featured the pilgrimage of compliant nations coming to the new Jerusalem in recognition of God's sovereign power" (87; see also 88–92).

alleged reversal of these prophecies by Paul; rather, it fully agrees with the apostle's reference to greater blessing for the world following the salvation of Israel.

CONCLUSION

Our brief study suggests that the New Testament and particularly Paul's teaching in Romans 9–11 is best understood as a confirmation of the Old Testament prophecies concerning the sequence of the salvation of Israel and the nations, rather than the reversal of this prophetic tradition as many today espouse. According to a minor prophetic theme, there would be a time of Gentile salvation when Israel is in disobedience, including the rejection of her Messiah. But this period of the evangelization of the nations is destined to end with the nations and their rulers under the sway of the Antichrist and their defeat by Christ at his coming.

Beyond this first period of salvation for the Gentiles, the major theme of the prophets saw a much greater final salvation of the nations: they and their kings would one day come to acknowledge the true God and would stream to Jerusalem to worship him. This worldwide salvation would be the result of the manifestation of God's power and glory in his restoration and sanctification of Israel before the eyes of the world. In this way, Israel will finally complete her original calling to be God's witness to the nations.

4

Epistemic Eucatastrophe:
The Favorable Turn of the Evidence

THOMAS A. PROVENZOLA

INTRODUCTION

In his recent assessment of Alvin Plantinga's Reformed Epistemology, John Feinberg argues that, while much of Plantinga's approach to belief in God as a properly basic belief is rationally defensible, there are certain aspects of his account that can be firmed up only by evidence and argument that Christian theism is in fact true.[1] As Feinberg rightly notes, Plantinga is *not* saying that everyone does or even must come to have rational belief in God apart from argument and evidence, or that persons come to hold such belief *only* in a way that is analogous to the way in which we come to have many of our everyday beliefs.[2] More to the point, as Feinberg further notes, many who come to believe in God in the properly basic way that Plantinga suggests may later come to have doubts for a wide variety of reasons, and they may find it necessary to make an evidential case in order to shore up their initial belief in God.[3] In the final analysis, Feinberg argues that the epistemic deliverances (the arguments for one's beliefs) for both believers and nonbelievers may come closer to representing the

---
[1] John S. Feinberg, *Can You Believe It's True? Christian Apologetics in a Modern and Postmodern Era* (Wheaton, IL: Crossway, 2013), 247.
[2] Ibid., 239.
[3] Ibid., 247.

common experiences of typical persons who likely will at some point want to know that Christian beliefs are not only *warranted* for those who hold them apart from argument or evidence (i.e., being within one's epistemic rights to be considered rational in holding them), but that those beliefs are also *right* in the sense that they are true, or likely true, in the robust sense of the term.

Now if we grant Plantinga's argument that it is possible to have rational belief in God apart from marshaling evidential arguments for that belief, perhaps the question worth exploring is whether the rational deliverances of an evidential approach along the lines of Feinberg's account ultimately reflect a more preferable cognitive experience for the typical person, all things considered. It seems somewhat intuitive, for example, that the typical person is at least at some level aware of the possibility that the evidence could go either way, perhaps arguing quite convincingly against rational belief in God.[4] In recognizing this possibility, Philip Quinn argues that Plantinga's account of properly basic belief in God fails to consider the possibility that individual potential defeaters can combine to compose a cumulative case that may be strong enough to defeat theistic belief that would otherwise remain properly basic with respect to warrant.[5] In appealing to the typical person's awareness of the potential defeaters intrinsic to such issues as the problem of evil and religious diversity, just to name two of the commonly accepted strongest forms of potential defeaters, Quinn thinks it is quite likely that, for many people at least, such potential defeaters would require them to abandon the firmness with which they hold properly basic belief in God. Consequently, Quinn thinks belief in God will have sufficient warrant to count as knowledge for some persons (i.e., that belief in God is both rational and right) only if it is supported by a cumulative case that includes evidential arguments and, *a fortiori*, cannot be considered properly basic on Plantinga's conception.[6]

---

[4] Paul K. Moser, ed., *The Oxford Handbook of Epistemology* (New York: Oxford University Press, 2002), 14–15. On our proposed model of rationality, we are assuming a general affinity with Moser's reliance on instrumental epistemic rationality, an approach that appeals to the various cognitive objectives of different epistemic systems and does not pretend to escape evidential circularity, namely, the stance that there is no noncircular test for effectiveness in acquiring truth. Since we cannot escape the human predicament of using our cognitive faculties to show that they are reliable, we are forced (no different than the skeptic) into a kind of evidential circularity. All things being equal, then, the rational conception in review is a system that encourages us to appeal to the available evidence for a belief whenever we are in a position to do so, when it is deemed beneficial to the other person, and when the threat of potential defeaters calls for it.
[5] Philip L. Quinn, "Epistemology in Philosophy of Religion," in Moser, *Oxford Handbook of Epistemology*, 537.
[6] Ibid.

Perhaps, then, in light of our ponderings on what may be a more preferable rational deliverance for the typical person, we may make the somewhat modest suggestion that one can arrive at a model of rationality in which a cumulative case approach to the evidence can be augmented not only to involve the more *explicit* forms of evidence we normally glean from propositional argument but also to include appeals to the more *implicit* forms of rational deliverance (or evidence) that are often the common experiences of the typical believer. Such experiences may be at least consistent with Plantinga's notion of warrant, and particularly with his conception on the rational deliverances of our affective capacities, suggesting that an appeal to the deliverances of the affective capacities can be viewed as part of a rational approach to the evidence.

Additionally, our modified model recognizes that, in agreement with Plantinga, it is too high a standard to maintain that one is rational in holding a belief only when a person has in fact *verified* (i.e., marshaled the appropriate evidence) that belief as true on propositional evidence. Of course, one may be rational in holding a belief arising out of a reason-based conception of justification in which sufficient evidence can rest on other basic or nonbasic beliefs, but it can also rest on mental or perceptual states that a person believes he has good reasons to think are true, even if a person makes no attempt to verify his beliefs as true, or even if those beliefs, mental states, or perceptual states turn out to be false.

So long as a person holds those beliefs for reasons he *thinks* are likely true (a seemingly intuitive minimal criterion for having a reason), he is rational in holding them. But unlike Plantinga's system, our model of rationality further suggests that the more likely it is that others will challenge the truthfulness of a belief due to insufficient or underdetermined evidence, or in the face of potential defeaters, the more the typical person will likely want to think that there is good evidence for that belief if one is to be rational in holding it, although that evidence need not be indubitable or involve conclusive arguments.[7] It also suggests that, given insufficient or underdetermined data, a person is more likely to be rational in holding such a belief more tentatively. All the same, while our augmented model of rationality allows room for the possibility that some

---

[7] See, for example, Paul K. Moser, Dwayne H. Mulder, and J. D. Trout, *The Theory of Knowledge: A Thematic Introduction* (New York: Oxford University Press, 1998), 185. The authors suggest that such a model of rationality aims at the twofold cognitive goal of achieving truth in the correspondence sense and avoiding error.

of a person's beliefs may be provisional on evidence, it does not expect the tentativeness of a belief to be a governing criterion for the rationality of one's beliefs.[8]

RATIONALITY, JUSTIFICATION, AND TRUTH

It is difficult to deny the cognitively intuitive sense that we regularly hold true beliefs while also holding those beliefs in the absence of adequate reasons for *why* we hold them. If I only feel a hunch that my friend is holding four aces in his hand, my belief, while it may turn out to be true, is not based on good reasons or evidence. In contrast, my friend, because he can see the cards in his hands, has more than likely appealed to the best evidence that his cognitive equipment has to offer for saying that he is holding four aces. We would say that he has *perceptual grounds* for his belief. So while both beliefs are true, only my friend has appealed to reasons that appear consistent with being both rational and right.[9]

On this conception of rationality, justification (i.e., our reason-giving theory or conception for why we think a belief is in fact true) involves the reasons, evidence, or arguments for holding a given belief. Where possible, it may involve *attempts* to verify one's beliefs as true with good arguments and appropriate evidence. But it does not necessarily demand that a person *verify* a belief as true on evidence, or even attempt to verify a belief as true. And this points to a significant distinction in our proposed model of rationality. Our augmented model suggests that there are two different senses in which a person can be rational in holding a belief. In the first place, there is a sense in which rationality is tied to the stronger notions of truth and verification. In this sense, one is rational in holding a belief in virtue of the *fact* that one has verified one's belief as true by appealing to the appropriate kind, quality, and amount of evidence for the belief in question. In other words, one can do no better than to verify one's belief as true on evidence.

But there is another sense in which rationality relates to the way in which the typical person can recognize that, while we are not always in an *epistemic position* to verify a belief as true on evidence, we are often

---

[8] For a similar and extended treatment of the use of modified foundationalism in fallibilist conceptions of rationality, see Steven L. Porter, *Restoring the Foundations of Epistemic Justification: A Direct Realist and Conceptualist Theory of Foundationalism* (Lanham, MD: Rowman & Littlefield, 2006).

[9] Matthias Steup, *An Introduction to Contemporary Epistemology* (Upper Saddle River, NJ: Prentice-Hall, 1996), 6–7.

in an epistemic position to at least *attempt* to offer *reasons* (arguments and evidence) for why we *think* our beliefs are true. In doing so, we are dealing with a sense of rationality in which one is rational for holding a belief that, while it may not *in fact* be verified as true, there is at least an attempt to offer a reason-based conception for why one thinks it is true. The implication here is that there is a sense in which Plantinga is essentially right in arguing that one can be justified in holding a belief that one has in fact *not* verified on evidential grounds, that is, not verified in terms of offering publicly available and unbiased evidential arguments. All the same, at those times in which we are in a position to offer evidential reasons for a belief, it doesn't mean that the reasons offered must be irrefutable if that belief is to be justified. As many epistemologists acknowledge, it is difficult to argue against the simple thesis that a person may be rational in believing x at time t given a background set of beliefs y. So while a person's belief *may* be justified without verifying it as true, or even attempting to verify it, nevertheless, it is not held arbitrarily or without some basis in reason.[10]

Consequently, on our model of rationality, justification is a reason-based conception in which a person could mistakenly hold a false belief but be rational in doing so.[11] As stated above, this approach recognizes that one's reasons may not in fact verify a belief as true, but it does suggest that one at least *has* reasons for one's beliefs, reasons for which a person thinks a given belief is true, even if that belief turns out to be false. Such reasons may be based on other beliefs a person thinks are true, but one's reasons can also be based on a person's nondoxastic states, that is, states of mind other than a person's current set of beliefs of which that person is in some way aware. As John Pollock reminds us, for example, a person may be aware that reasoning according to *modus ponens* is somehow a correct cognitive process, and yet initially not go so far as to form a belief about it.[12] But once again, a person's justification for a belief can be a different matter from a belief's truthfulness. Still, as our model of rationality suggests, the reasons that a person offers in support of a belief can be

---

[10] See Richard Swinburne's five different kinds of rationality in his *Faith and Reason* (New York: Oxford University Press, 1991), 13–26.

[11] See Stephen Robert Jacobson, "What's Wrong with Reliability Theories of Justification?" (PhD diss., University of Michigan, 1989), 122. Cf. Swinburne's first two notions of rationality in his *Faith and Reason*, 45–49.

[12] Cf. John L. Pollock and Joseph Cruz, eds., *Contemporary Theories of Knowledge*, 2nd ed. (Lanham, MD: Rowman & Littlefield, 1999), 25.

considered justified only to the extent that they are reasons that a person *thinks* are true. And such reasons may seem initially intuitive to a person, further suggesting that one's reasons can also include appeals to testimony, or authority, or particularly to prior beliefs that one already accepts as true. And further still, reasons can also be based in perception, or memory, or some other experiential or rational state of which a person is aware. But the point is that a person at least thinks she has some nonarbitrary reasons for thinking that her belief is true, even if it turns out to be false.

Additionally, the criteria for rationality outlined above, while not necessarily restricted to a specific epistemic system, seems to work well within a modified form of foundationalism, reflecting a fallibilist position that does not commit a person to holding to the indefeasibility of foundational beliefs. That is, the typical person can be open to the possibility that further evidence could show one's basic belief to be false, even though it is not expected that such will be the case. Such an epistemic structure argues for a fallibilist system in at least three ways. First, one's foundational beliefs may turn out to be unjustified *or* false, or unjustified *and* false; second, nonbasic (or inferential) beliefs are only inductively, and consequently, fallibly justified by foundational beliefs. One's nonfoundational beliefs can turn out false, even when the foundational beliefs from which they are inferred are true. And third, the possibility of discovering error, even among one's foundational beliefs, is left open.[13] A further implication of this model is that we are not necessarily forced to trace all our nonbasic beliefs back to basic beliefs.[14] Of course, this is not to say that a person *could* not trace one's nonbasic beliefs back to basic beliefs, but instead that there is no need to do so once enough evidence has been supplied.

And finally, a fallibilist position seeks to address the further question of the way in which potential defeaters, as a form of counterevidence, relate to a person's foundational beliefs. If it is granted that there is always the possibility of discovering error among one's basic beliefs, then it seems reasonable to suggest that a person may at some point legitimately reassess those beliefs in light of additional evidence. That is, if at some later point, at least for me, my basic beliefs are challenged by me, I may apply

---

[13] See Robert Audi, *The Structure of Justification* (Cambridge: Cambridge University Press, 1993), 135.
[14] See, for example, Alvin Plantinga, "Is Belief in God Rational?" in *Rationality and Religious Belief*, ed. C. F. Delaney (Notre Dame, IN: University of Notre Dame Press, 1979), 7–27; cf. idem, "Is Belief in God Properly Basic?" in *Contemporary Perspectives on Religious Epistemology*, ed. R. Douglas Geivett and Brendan Sweetman (New York: Oxford University Press, 1992), 135.

evidence against those beliefs in a manner similar to the way in which I apply evidence against my nonbasic beliefs. For example, as my wife and I frantically rush out the door to do our Christmas shopping, I may have the basic perceptual belief that the book I put in my front pocket is in fact the checkbook. This seems to meet the criteria for a belief that is evident to my senses, and as such, it rightfully belongs among my basic beliefs. But suppose my wife challenges my basic belief. She suggests that it's quite possible that the book I have in my pocket is the savings book, and not the checkbook that I perceived it to be. She gently reminds me that both books have blue covers, look exactly the same on the outside, and are kept in the same desk drawer. What choice do I have but to quickly open the book to see if the transactions recorded in the book's register are what we would expect them to be if it is in fact the checkbook? In such a case, it's not all that clear whether my basic belief at that point should continue to remain among my foundational beliefs. But it is perhaps reasonable to suggest that, should I be in a position to marshal enough of the appropriate kind of evidence so as to satisfy my own challenge and become so rationally convinced that it no longer makes sense to reasonably maintain a doubt, then there seems to be no good reason why my belief cannot once again resume its place among the basic beliefs of my noetic structure.[15]

VARIABILITY OF BELIEF AND AFFECTIVE EVIDENCE

Given our awareness of the fallibility of belief, even among one's basic beliefs, perhaps we are now in a more congenial epistemic position to suggest some possible ways in which the reciprocity between our cognitive and affective capacities can offer up rational deliverances for a given belief that may strike the typical person as being both rational and right, particularly when considering the more implicit side of the evidence. In an insightful analysis of Plantinga's argument for warrant and properly basic belief in God, James Beilby indicates that part of the workability of the model hinges on the crucial distinctions Plantinga makes between the typical believer and the paradigmatic believer, or between typical cases in which believers come to have *true beliefs about God* and paradigmatic cases in which believers come to have *warranted belief in God*.[16] To put

---
[15] Robert Audi, *Epistemology: A Contemporary Introduction to the Theory of Knowledge* (New York & London: Routledge, 1998), 205.
[16] The central features of this discussion are found in James Beilby, *Epistemology as Theology* (Burlington, VT: Ashgate, 2005), 179–215.

this succinctly, paradigmatic cases are epistemic situations in which believers enjoy the maximal conditions for rational and true belief in God (e.g., properly functioning faculties, suitable belief-forming environments aimed at truth, no defeaters, appreciable depth of ingression [i.e., how crucial an issue is] for one's theistic belief, etc.), a kind of *maxi-environment* in which the cognitive process cannot fail to function properly and deliver *knowledge* that God exists.[17] As such, the *paradigmatic* believer experiences no defeaters for warranted belief in God and thereby has the warrant necessary for knowledge. By contrast, the *typical* believer experiences only a *mini-environment*, one suitable for forming true beliefs about God yet falling short of the maximal conditions for knowledge enjoyed by the paradigmatic believer.

Additionally, in reflecting on Plantinga's distinction between what he calls the A/C and the extended A/C models (models that are somewhat loosely constructed on the combined theological insights of Thomas Aquinas and John Calvin), Beilby rightly shows that Plantinga thinks there is within a person's original cognitive faculties a *sensus divinitatus*, that is, an innate tendency, triggered by various person-relative circumstances, for human persons to see the hand of God in nature.[18] On this account, the deliverances of the *sensus divinitatus* are not inferential beliefs but beliefs that arise immediately and noninferentially as a result of the relevant experience that gives rise to such beliefs. Like beliefs of perception and memory, beliefs produced in a person via the *sensus divinitatus* are properly basic, that is, they are epistemically direct, spontaneously arising in the individual in psychologically convincing ways.[19] More specifically for our purposes, since the A/C model and the extended A/C model are meant only as possible states of affairs, there is no requirement on Plantinga's part to actually *show* that either model is in fact true.[20] As such, the A/C model is offered up as an explanation for how it is *possible* for human persons in a *prelapsarian* (i.e., prefall) world to have warranted beliefs about God. All the same, while the A/C model may work as a satisfying account in a prelapsarian context, Plantinga claims it is insufficient for warrant in a *postlapsarian* (i.e., postfall) epistemic situation.

A postlapsarian epistemic situation, in contrast to its prelapsarian

---

[17] Alvin Plantinga, *Warranted Christian Belief* (New York: Oxford University Press, 2000), 246n10; cf. Beilby, *Epistemology as Theology*, 184.
[18] Plantinga, *Warranted Christian Belief*, 170–174.
[19] Ibid., 175.
[20] Ibid., 169–170.

counterpart, must account for the *noetic effects of sin* and its devastating consequences on our moral, volitional, affective, and cognitive capacities. Sin damages and suppresses the ability of the *sensus divinitatus* to deliver the natural knowledge of God we would normally have in a prelapsarian epistemic situation. And, crucial to our current conception of rationality, sin introduces a ruinous affective condition, so that there is both an affective resistance and hostility to the deliverances of the *sensus divinitatus*. We simply lack the desire to see, cognitively or affectively, what we ought to see by way of the *sensus divinitatus*.[21] As a consequence, the extended A/C model is a needed corrective to the damaged *sensus divinitatus*, since it includes God's plan of salvation and thereby overcomes objective metaphysical barriers, resulting in spiritual regeneration and rebirth.[22] Further still, in light of what he calls the internal instigation of the Holy Spirit—a feature of the extended A/C model intentionally designed for a postlapsarian context—Plantinga thinks a person in this cognitive process meets, by faith, the conditions that are jointly sufficient and severally necessary for knowledge that God exists (i.e., warrant).[23]

On the other hand, one might readily see that typical cases, unlike paradigmatic cases, are a bit more epistemically tenuous. The epistemic circumstances for typical believers, persons who come to have *true* beliefs about God, is such that beliefs produced in this context—what Plantinga calls the *mini-environment*—initially may have sufficient immediate warrant and yet fall short of the warrant necessary for *knowledge*. Plantinga thinks this is the case, since such beliefs are not accompanied by a sufficient degree of intrinsic strength from one's cognitive content, and often appear tenuous and open to defeaters.[24] More particularly, it is in the case of the typical believer that we find the problem of the *variability of belief* on the extended A/C model. This stands to reason, since the degree of intrinsic strength of a belief in light of a typical believer's cognitive content is open to defeaters.

What is particularly striking at this point is that not only is it *not* uncommon for the typical believer to have her initial warrant augmented through other inferential beliefs, but it also may be at times precisely because of this kind of epistemic situation that one can come to a more

---
[21] Ibid., 205; cf. Beilby, *Epistemology as Theology*, 181.
[22] Plantinga, *Warranted Christian Belief*, 205.
[23] Ibid., 258.
[24] Beilby, *Epistemology as Theology*, 186, 194.

appreciably enhanced cognitive and affective state of mind. More specifically, one wonders whether such a process could be an *intentional* feature within a design plan (i.e., a divinely intended strategy) aimed at truth. Through his intentional use of the agency of those in community and the testimony of others, together with the deliverances of the affective capacities (e.g., the implicit awareness of what is virtuous in our grasp of moral intuition, beauty, nature, and the ubiquitous sense of virtue in good stories), could it not be possible that God may be encouraging us away from a *purely* spectatorial account of the evidence, by which some of the most convincing and intimate forms of rational deliverance would otherwise not be had? And this seems especially critical if it represents the typical experiences of most persons grappling with belief in God. And further, as our common experiences seem to suggest, this does not seem to strike the typical person as a fixed process. Instead, and more directly, the question at issue is whether paradigmatic cases of theistic belief, even though thought to be warranted (i.e., even though they are in fact knowledge), are to be preferred over typical cases. The question may at first seem somewhat counterintuitive, but is it not possible, after all, that contingent and significantly free human persons could ultimately experience more favorable cognitive and affective deliverances by going through rational processes that seem to line up with the tensions of our putative experiences, particularly since, as Beilby insightfully notes, the typical person tends to cycle back and forth on whether one's belief in God is a basic or nonbasic belief?[25]

Additionally, as Beilby further indicates, the variability of belief problem seems difficult to reconcile solely on Plantinga's extended A/C model.[26] The tension is that the deliverances of the internal instigation of the Holy Spirit are thought to be certain and firm for the paradigmatic believer, and yet our typical experiences seem to indicate that the paradigmatic believer can still experience doubt, notwithstanding the internal instigation of the Holy Spirit and a repaired *sensus divinitatus*. But on Plantinga's account, doubt should apply only in the case of the typical believer, suggesting that this may be accounted for on the basis of some residual dysfunction of the *sensus divinitatus* from which the paradigmatic believer is somehow im-

---

[25] Ibid., 195–197; for a further discussion of "depth of ingression," see Alvin Plantinga, "Reason and Belief in God," in *Faith and Rationality*, ed. Alvin Plantinga and Nicholas Wolterstorff (Notre Dame, IN: University of Notre Dame Press, 1983), 50.
[26] Plantinga, *Warranted Christian Belief*, 264n43; cf. Beilby, *Epistemology as Theology*, 204.

mune.[27] But why should it be so difficult for us to think of the persistence of the variability of belief as being an intentional part of God's design plan aimed at truth? If part of the design plan of God involves his intention to encourage agent participation in the discovery of truths otherwise not made available to the person, perhaps the extended A/C model can be slightly augmented to include this feature without any real threat to Plantinga's central claims concerning the internal instigation of the Holy Spirit and his work in repairing the cognitive and affective deliverances of the *sensus divinitatus*.[28] More specifically, if the variability of belief is best explained on the basis of the noetic effects of sin on the believer, as Plantinga wants to suggest, then it seems we are making an appeal to the evidential deliverances of one's native cognitive capacities, and not to what God is apparently willing and able to do in circumventing the limitations of those capacities by *causing* the relevant belief in a person.[29] Consequently, what seems likely to many is that the effects of sin on the mind, even the mind of the believer, are not wholly cured by the regenerating effects of the internal instigation of the Holy Spirit, suggesting the variability of belief on evidence.[30] And perhaps more to the point, as Beilby further indicates, it is difficult to imagine how a person's new rational awareness in light of the deliverances of the internal instigation of the Holy Spirit can be completely divorced from a person's previous evidential reflection on the matter.[31] This seems to be a critical point. It is difficult to imagine that our awareness of the synergism between our cognitive and affective capacities, along with our awareness of potential defeaters, does not make it problematic to think that belief in God is not sustained for a person apart from reciprocity among the full range of one's native capacities.

Since, on Plantinga's account, it is difficult to reconcile his conviction of the firm and certain knowledge arising out of the deliverances of the cognitive aspects of faith with his claim that the noetic effects of sin can sometimes continue to undermine that same unwavering knowledge in the case of the paradigmatic believer, perhaps this tension can be viewed as divinely intentional on a more participatory account of warrant. The problem is that the presence of the variability of belief among those who have received the internal instigation of the Holy Spirit seems to work

---

[27] Plantinga, *Warranted Christian Belief*, 260n35; 343; cf. Beilby, *Epistemology as Theology*, 205.
[28] Beilby, *Epistemology as Theology*, 205.
[29] Ibid., 206.
[30] Ibid., 196.
[31] Ibid.

against the environmental condition of Plantinga's account of warrant. On this conception, whatever causes a belief to fall short of one or more of the conditions for warrant (e.g., properly functioning faculties, suitable environments aimed at truth, no-defeater conditions) is considered a warrant defeater.[32] If, as Beilby indicates, the presence of the variability of belief is explained by the continued influence of the noetic effects of sin on the cognitive aspects of a believer's faith, then there is a problem with the epistemic environment, and the condition for warrant is not met. This means that the presence of the variability of belief may be an indication of a warrant-defeater for beliefs about God. For we have no way of being certain that beliefs formed by the extended A/C model, even if they are true and even if they are held with a high degree of confidence, are warranted, since the very presence of the variability of belief is an indication that Plantinga's environmental condition has not been met.[33]

Again, it is important to keep in mind the distinction between the typical believer and the paradigmatic believer of Plantinga's account. As Beilby indicates, even if Plantinga is right in claiming that a design plan aimed at truth is congenial to the production of warranted beliefs about God in the cognitive *maxi-environment*, we have no way of being certain that the same congeniality holds for the cognitive *mini-environments* in which typical believers find themselves.[34] Since the only qualification Plantinga gives for a favorable cognitive mini-environment is that it can be relied upon to produce true beliefs, the qualification fails to cover the *firm and unwavering conditions* necessary for warrant. This implies that the presence of the variability of belief will result in a hostile environment with respect to warrant. Additionally, as Beilby recognizes, this problem conjures up the possible limitations placed on an omnipotent being, for it may be that God cannot guarantee that firm and unwavering beliefs will be produced in significantly free persons experiencing a postlapsarian epistemic environment.[35]

EVIDENCE AND THE AFFECTIVE CAPACITIES

What may be critical to our augmented model is that, on a more participatory account of the evidence, beliefs formed out of the typical person's cognitive and affective equipment need not be firm and certain, may well

---
[32] Ibid., 207; cf. Plantinga, *Warranted Christian Belief*, 251.
[33] Beilby, *Epistemology as Theology*, 208; cf. Plantinga, *Warranted Christian Belief*, 159.
[34] Beilby, *Epistemology as Theology*, 208.
[35] Ibid.

be consistent with the variability of belief, and yet may also be sufficient for rational and right belief in God. Instead, it may be the case that the variability of belief is worked into the very fabric of a design plan that need not look so disparagingly on potential defeaters. Variability of belief may be accounted for on the basis of an intentional design plan that encourages greater degrees of involvement on the part of the individual. If, on a more generous model, a person may come to have warranted belief in God partially from immediate, noninferential beliefs and partially from inferential beliefs, then it is possible that the internal instigation of the Holy Spirit may be working to encourage a person to use the full range of his or her cognitive and affective equipment in seeking more tenacious and reflective reasons for rational belief in God. Such an account may be a way of recognizing a person's divine right and affective desire, via the *imago Dei*, to participate in the discovery of truth on both explicit and implicit levels.[36] Perhaps another way of saying this is that it may be precisely because the evidence is hidden or separated from us by some kind of cognitive or affective boundary, that we find it interesting. We reflect on it. We introspect. And we gain not only the intuitive sense of its universal applicability but also a richer appreciation for the conflicting states of mind among those who find their beliefs open to defeaters in light of the often tenuous cognitive and affective deliverances of faculties, environments, and experiences less robust in aiming at truth.

In light of these qualifications, then, it seems reasonable to suggest that typical cases may be more preferred than paradigmatic cases, given that typical cases strike us as being the more likely common experiences of the two, all things taken into consideration. Still, in thinking along these lines, as Beilby claims, it seems unavoidable that something gets lost in transfer. In giving up the paradigmatic cases, we lose the *maxi-environment* in which the cognitive process cannot fail to function properly. But it seems we also acquire something humanly indispensable in the exchange, for a seemingly critical feature of such an approach is that it allows for the varying degrees of doubt and the variability of belief that are the common experiences of the typical believer.[37] And furthermore,

---

[36] As we shall see later, J. R. R. Tolkien refers to this ability as the sub-creative capacity in the human condition. For a detailed discussion of his conception of the features of sub-creation, see J. R. R. Tolkien, "On Fairy-Stories," in *The Monsters and the Critics*, ed. Christopher Tolkien (London: HarperCollins, 1990), 109–161.

[37] Beilby suggests that such an approach will typically trade clarity for applicability; cf. *Epistemology as Theology*, 211.

it is this approach to the evidence, one that seems to naturally arise out of a person's free choice, which seeks a more cooperative relationship between the internal instigation of the Holy Spirit and a person's native cognitive faculties. It may be, for example, that there is a natural (and divinely purposive) tension intended for the typical believer, namely, that she will want to know that the beliefs formed in her by the Holy Spirit's influence are at the same time beliefs that flow from her native cognitive faculties, and not produced apart from them. And perhaps the typical believer would find this type of belief-forming process to be more consistent with the kind of inward transformation we would expect from a personal agent like the Holy Spirit.

So, again, whether this type of rational activity is viewed as divine testimony, or as a cognitive process designed to encourage us to consider either the noninferential or inferential grounds of our beliefs, the argument here is whether it is crucial for the typical person to see that it is native cognitive faculties that ultimately produce the relevant beliefs in question.[38] This may suggest that a more robust version of warrant (a model which includes a design plan aimed at truth) is one that seems consistent with my role as an intentionally reflective agent, in this case, an agent who can at least recognize on some level that the reasons for my beliefs are found in my own native faculties to which I have some degree of reflective access. On such an account of warrant, I am more than a person who is cognitively acted upon by something external to me, say, for example, the internal instigation of the Holy Spirit. There is instead an intellectual assenting that is genuinely acknowledged by my own reflective awareness of the partial role that my cognitive and affective capacities play in the deliverances of knowledge.

If such a conception of rational belief has some resonance for the typical person, then, could not a maximally good God have a design plan that intentionally makes certain kinds of evidence elusive, like the doubt inherent in a story's uncertain ending, in order to encourage our participatory and sub-creative activity in the discovery of theistic belief by way of our repaired volitional and affective capacities? In this sense, God could be purposive, knowing in his divine wisdom that we experience a deeper and more profound appreciation for truth that we discover through participation. And what is deep and profound in its broadly

---
[38] Beilby, *Epistemology as Theology*, 201, 212.

evidential deliverances may not necessarily translate into what is firm and unwavering in the extended A/C model.

If this is the case, and if the typical person is likely to have multiple sources of warrant,[39] then a person's defense against defeaters need not be restricted to one's strong sense of inner conviction that belief in God is properly basic (i.e., the intrinsic defeater-defeater in the paradigmatic cases of Plantinga's extended A/C model). Again, while such cases seem possible, there seem to be compelling reasons for thinking that such a model may not be preferable. For it is always possible that a more preferable model for significantly free and contingent beings is one that relies at least in part on the full range of the evidential deliverances of a person's native cognitive and affective capacities. Such rational deliverances could direct a person to consider the wide variety of defeater-defeaters found in evidences that are based partly on immediate, noninferential grounds and partly on inferential grounds.

Additionally, if our augmented model strikes us as more likely the case, could not the experiences associated with the internal instigation of the Holy Spirit be broadened to include those truths discovered implicitly by participating in God's purposive evidence, evidence intentionally hidden in order to encourage our participation and to steer us away from purely spectatorial accounts of belief in God? There seem to be compelling reasons to think that such a cognitive process may be purposively designed by God to produce such beliefs and affections within the boundaries of one's native cognitive equipment. Plantinga, for example, seems to suggest the possibility of such a feature in his reference to indexing a person's *depth of ingression* that can be associated with belief in God.[40] According to Plantinga, a person can experience this phenomenon when one's belief on the cognitive side of faith, including the belief both that the Christian God exists and that one should have a positive orientation of religious affections toward God, is held with such psychological conviction that the abandonment of such a belief would require appreciably significant changes in one's noetic structure.[41] It could be argued, for example, that it is precisely this kind of phenomenon of belief that seems to be consistent with what many sense when, like the good ending we so

---
[39] Ibid., 212.
[40] Alvin Plantinga, "Reason and Belief in God," in *Faith and Rationality*, 50.
[41] Beilby, *Epistemology as Theology*, 197.

earnestly desire in an enchanting and virtuous story, we refuse to abandon belief in God in the face of potentially recalcitrant evidence.

Since Plantinga holds that the first-person perspective is crucial in determining whether a person has a defeater (since defeaters are relative to a person's noetic structures) if one's depth of ingression is deep enough, then even if the evidence against one's belief is extremely strong, one does not necessarily have a defeater for that belief. Given this possibility, it may be that, as Beilby suggests, a fuller account of warranted belief in God is one that takes into account the full range of our cognitive equipment, one that, along with Plantinga's notion of the internal instigation of the Holy Spirit, also relies partially on arguments and propositional evidence. Perhaps it is possible that the warrant for one's original belief, that is, one's belief in God, is stronger than the warrant for the potential defeater precisely because of a person's *awareness* that the full range of her cognitive equipment, including its *implicit* and *explicit* features, far exceeds the strength of the potential defeater. As Beilby further notes, even if beliefs about God are originally held in the basic way, that is, apart from evidential considerations, the presence of defeaters for Christian belief often causes typical Christians to turn to evidential support as defeater-defeaters for their religious beliefs.[42]

On this account, it may be that a more robust epistemic situation, in the attempt to circumvent a purely spectatorial view of the evidence, could benefit from a design plan of divine hiddenness that recognizes that a fuller epistemic recovery process requires forms of evidence made available only on a participatory basis.[43] While this approach creates various epistemic tensions, such tensions could be the result of God's intention to encourage the human desire to participate in the discovery of certain kinds of evidence that otherwise may not be made available. Such a design plan, far from suggesting a cognitively subpar approach to the evidence, stacks the deck in a favor of a positive response to the evidence.[44] Additionally, this approach may serve to augment the effusive

---

[42] Ibid., 196–197. In making this case, Beilby suggests an important difference between *generative* and *sustaining* grounds for a belief (196).
[43] This approach is somewhat reminiscent of David E. Cooper's *Existentialism*, 2nd ed. (Malden, MA: Blackwell, 1999), 49. Cooper refers to this as the "spectatorial premise," that is, the existentialist discernment, and rejection of, traditional philosophy's refusal to divest itself of the epistemological premise that only Enlightenment evidentialism can weigh the rational merits of most of our beliefs, leaving us as detached and passive *spectators* of *de facto* matters rather than active and participating *agents* in nondualistic engagements with the world (e.g., subject versus object, mind versus body, reason versus passion, and fact versus value).
[44] While this position has certain affinities with Paul Moser's argument concerning our willingness to apprehend God's purposively available authoritative evidence in his *The Elusive God: Reorienting Religious*

cognitive and affective deliverances of warrant by following a design plan of epistemic benevolence, one that encourages a person to acquire and tender good reasons for one's beliefs, including belief in God, when in a position to do so.

As we have been indicating, on our model there is some suggestion that Plantinga's notion of the deliverances of the internal instigation of the Holy Spirit may have greater cognitive and affective appeal if those deliverances are viewed as coming alongside a person's native cognitive faculties and working cooperatively with them to produce belief in God. That is, the deliverances of the Holy Spirit's influence could be seen as part of a rich and robust *relational causality* designed to engage a person's native cognitive faculties in the deep wonder and profound splendor of Christian belief. We mean by relational causality a particular state of affairs, including certain states of mind, that arise only in the context of the interaction between two or more personal agents. While it produces commonly instantiated properties in persons (e.g., love, faith, hope, fidelity, desire, affection), each instance produced by relational causality is unique, or at least has unique existential components, for the agents experiencing the properties in question. On this conception, some states of affairs, including the deliverances of certain kinds of evidences, can come about only as a result of engagement between persons, and while many of these will be analogous to each other, they will likely not be identical. Personhood, it would seem, demands that these properties are unique instances of analogous experiences. This is at least consistent with Plantinga's reliance on the internal instigation of the Holy Spirit, but it is not exclusive to his model.

Such deliverances, then, would be indicative of a design plan that has as one of its aims the intention of participating with, and flowing out from, a person's native cognitive faculties. On such an account, the internal instigation of the Holy Spirit may be the immediate cause of the belief in question, but the means of sustaining that belief may be found in reasons stemming from the broader range of one's cognitive and affective faculties, at least some of which a person is consciously aware of.[45] To put it another way, it may be precisely because of a person's awareness that beliefs about

---

Epistemology (Cambridge: Cambridge University Press, 2008), 12–13, the current suggestion of participation is intended as a fairly generous model that includes non-obstructive engagements in relational causality between God and human persons, resulting in evidences otherwise hidden, apart from such a causality.
[45] Beilby, *Epistemology as Theology*, 201.

God originally held on grounds of proper basicality can be challenged by the presence of defeaters that one instinctively responds by seeking to support the generative grounds for one's Christian beliefs by developing defeater-defeaters. And while this clearly involves appeals to propositional evidence or inferential reasons, it is also much broader than such deliverances. It may also include the more affective aspects of a person's cognitive equipment, that is, epistemic features that, while more implicit in nature, nevertheless tend to involve a significant degree of a person's reflective and introspective capacities. To be sure, while it may be difficult to specify the criteria for implicit forms of evidence, the suggestion is that some beliefs formed on the basis of immediate and noninferential experiences can strike us with a kind of intuitive awareness of a proposition's truth-indicative features.[46] Perhaps, then, there is good reason to think that this can play some role in a suitable environment aimed at truth and, consequently, can be a part of the conditions for warrant.

THE EUCATASTROPHE OF THE IMPLICIT

Now if such an account of the phenomenology of belief seems to line up with what our intuitions are telling us, then it may be that there is a kind of symmetry and beauty in the way that a person is causally related to a belief-forming process, one that emerges out of the synergy of both inferential and noninferential beliefs. At some point in the belief-forming process, one becomes intuitively aware that one is *not* rationally required to accept Christian belief solely on the basis of propositional evidence. Rather, a person may be in some type of cognitive position that allows her to recognize that she is volitionally free to accept or reject such belief in light of the perceived axiological properties that emerge from all the relevant features of specific belief-forming processes aimed at giving rise to a true belief. During such a cognitive process, she either recognizes, or fails to recognize, the axiological properties (aesthetic, ethical, or virtuous) that supervene on the external conditions and other states of mind that could potentially give rise to theistic belief for that person.[47] So there

---

[46] Porter, *Restoring the Foundations of Epistemic Justification*, 26.
[47] Humphrey Carpenter, ed., *The Letters of J. R. R. Tolkien* (Boston: Houghton Mifflin, 1981), 100–101. Tolkien speaks of the eucatastrophe in fairy-story as giving us a sudden glimpse of the truth, one that transforms us in ways powerfully reminiscent of Plantinga's properly basic belief in God. Tolkien recounts an experience he had one day while bicycling through Oxford. On becoming aware of a sudden burst of clarity, a clarity that sometimes comes in dreams, Tolkien writes, "I remember saying aloud with absolute conviction: 'But of course! Of course that's how things really do work'. But I could not produce any argu-

is a kind of metaphor here. The propositional evidence, when falling short of convincing a person of the deliverances of a true belief, and, consequently, knowledge for a person, is met by a *eucatastrophe*—a joyous turn to favor the evidence for a given belief, and particularly belief in God, in light of the depth of ingression that a person has for that belief.

In other words, is it possible that something cognitively supervenes on the inferential and noninferential processes that give rise to certain kinds of beliefs for a person, namely, a higher-ordered state of mind, a kind of meta-introspection that results in a favorable turn to the collective evidence emerging out of the belief-forming process, one that results in positive epistemic status for that person, and, consequently, knowledge? Perhaps another way of putting this is to suggest that the category of the beautiful supervenes on our being made in the image of God and actively bearing that image. This category is essential because, though God is the greatest conceivable being (which means that he is also the greatest conceivable being with the highest conceivable ability to draw us to himself), if our nearness to him is not of our own making, it may be that, while we are likely to accept him, we are not likely to accept him freely. The free exercise of our affective capacities would become eclipsed by a disposition that is no longer sub-creative in the making. For as Pascal tells us, it is for our own goodness and well-being that God is partially concealed, and partially revealed.[48] And the effects on us are deleterious if this dialectical balance is not struck just right.

On this conception the beautiful serves as a kind of pre-causal accelerator, as it were, but one that requires our participation, the favorable leaning of our affective capacities in order for the causal effect to take place, that is, in order for the richness of meaning and beauty and truth and goodness to blossom forth. And it is precisely this deeply personal type of causality that is sometimes missed in our epistemic systems, but often powerfully captured in story. Perhaps *Mythopoeic* writers like J. R. R. Tolkien and C. S. Lewis saw that God, in his omnisapience and

---

ment that had led to this, though the sensation was the same as having been convinced by *reason* (if without reasoning). And I have since thought that one of the reasons why one can't recapture the wonderful argument or secret when one wakes up is simply because there was not one: but there was (often maybe) a direct appreciation by the mind (sc. reason) but without the chain of argument we know in our time-serial life" (101). It is perhaps worth mentioning that Tolkien's description of "sudden clarity" is also remarkably similar to a direct realist account of perceptual beliefs being formed out of noninferential states of awareness.
[48] Blaise Pascal, *Pensées*, trans. Alban Krailsheimer (New York: Penguin, 1995), thoughts 232 and 446. Cf. Thomas V. Morris, *Making Sense of It All* (Grand Rapids, MI: Eerdmans, 1992), 85–108.

supererogatory goodness,[49] anticipates this sort of problem—if he draws near too fast, our sense of freedom can quickly evaporate to the point that there is just an irresistible compulsion to surrender (or, perhaps an equally forceful compulsion in the opposite direction, to reject his goodness in a way that strikes one as lacking the free expression of one's affective qualities). Similar to the way we enter into story and myth, not as detached spectators or passive observers, but as engaged participants longing for a favorably enhanced experience of our ordinary world, we enter into participatory evidence in hopes of the divine eucatastrophe, the sudden and joyous turn of the evidence in favor of belief in God.[50] In order to activate our hearts and wills as we are, though, as humans in this environment, God draws near through the written Word, through story, through history, through shared experience, through art and music and literature and, yes, even through the evidence and arguments of philosophy, that is, all the representations of "The Good" that he is in himself, but that can implicitly be a sort of signifier of his presence—the practical, the beautiful, the fitting, the true, the useful, the pleasant, the uplifting, the thrilling, the jubilant, the victorious, the celebratory, the dedicatory, the remembering, and the remembrance (of things past, but with a present and future significance).[51]

The virtue of beauty is that it strikes us as a property that can transcend any model of epistemic justification, much in the same way that most apologetic systems, artistic expressions, stories, and nature appear to put some people, at least some of the time, within their epistemic rights in responding favorably to the belief or state of mind seemingly expressed by those features of a relational causality. And perhaps experiences like beauty and goodness, and even doubt, are intentional in the design plan for the typical person that most of us find ourselves to be. Apart from such qualities, our beliefs are not as robust and psychologically convincing, and often fall short of basicality and knowledge. Like story, affective evidence is participatory; and in a way similar to the storyteller's technique, affective evidence and desire (or intentionally designed evidence) have human interests at heart and are often easier to express. The features of such expressions and experiences are inherent and intrinsic. And it

---

[49] See, for example, J. R. R. Tolkien's poem "Mythopoeia," in *Tree and Leaf* (London: HarperCollins, 2001), 85–90.
[50] Tolkien, "On Fairy-Stories," 109–161. Verlyn Flieger, *Splintered Light: Logos and Language in Tolkien's World*, rev. ed. (Kent, OH: Kent State University Press, 2002), 21.
[51] I am indebted to Edward N. Martin for much of this crescendo of expression.

is also about being epistemically right in a way that is attractive to the other person, that is, when my intention is to engage the other person in ways that bring truth, beauty, and goodness together in a kind of cohesive whole, one that is sensed and appreciated by the other person. For it may be there is something about this approach that appears fundamentally relational and teleological, and it is this very quality that makes it well-suited for an epistemology that takes seriously the true agency and personhood of the other person.

And further still, it is quite possible that what we are suggesting here is an implicit recognition of the very causative nature of personal relationships, a relational causality that reflects the unique way we have been designed to retrieve information about the world and form beliefs as rational agents in possession of the image of God. What can be expressed as a kind of relational causality, for example, may be viewed as a kind of epistemic recovery process that argues that what was lost in the fall—what brought about the tensions in nature, virtue, beauty, truth, language, and meaning—cannot be recovered entirely through an explicit and analytic investigation, suggesting that the implicit and the imaginative in the dynamics of our relationships also contribute real virtue and value in knowledge, theologically and culturally. Relational causality seeks to resolve the tensions arising out of the fractured relationship between reason and imagination, the explicit and the implicit in knowledge, truth, and virtue. On such a conception, it is suggested that relational causality supplements, rather than dismisses, putative forms of evidentialism. It complements the explicit and allows us to see with greater clarity the beauty of what is implicit in a kind of *epistemic charity*. By epistemic charity we mean a quality of epistemic justification that is a natural result of relational causality, a form of rational deliverance that essentially involves the reasons, evidence, and arguments one offers in support of a belief, when in the position to do so, and for the sake of the other person. It implies some sense of awareness of the reasons that are internal to the person.[52] And finally, epistemic charity is primarily

---

[52] This notion is somewhat reminiscent of William L. Power's insights on the way we come to have positive affirmation, on both metaphorical and literal conceptions, in interpreting the image of God, in his "*Imago Dei-Imitatio Dei*," *International Journal for Philosophy of Religion* 42 (1997): 131–141. Power argues that a cataphatic sense of *metaphorical* use and interpretation is parasitic on the cataphatic way of *literal* use and interpretation (134). The implication is that we must have some literal affirmation or positive understanding of God if we are to have any basis for thinking we are coming close to imitating the character of God in demonstrating the affective qualities of epistemic charity and relational causality.

motivated by the example of supererogatory goodness demonstrated to human persons in divine intentionality, and not solely for deontological reasons.

CONCLUSION

While clearly departing somewhat from Plantinga's notion of properly basic belief, the approach we have presented may come closer to representing what most of us experience not only in terms of Christian belief but also in terms of other axiological and aesthetic beliefs that seem to require our affective capacities in order to strike us as being a closer and fuller accounting of rational belief in general. And this suggests that, while our modified approach may have specific application to rational theistic belief, it does not seem that it should be limited only to belief in God. Its features may tell us something about how we come to form and hold many of our other seemingly ordinary beliefs. Aesthetic properties and qualities may be designed by God for the specific purpose of producing a favorable turn of the evidence, a turn that may at first reflect a favorable turn toward the agent, either the divine agent (in the case of the Holy Spirit), or in the case of the human (or angelic) agent conveying aesthetic qualities for our good (e.g., the powerfully aesthetic language in the angelic announcements of the birth of Christ to Mary, and later to the shepherds).

A favorable turn in the direction of the evidence for a belief, and particularly theistic belief, may be contingent upon the inherent connection between what one is rationally convinced of and what is aesthetically pleasing in light of a relational causality that respects and encourages a person's intuitive desire to exercise one's affective capacities in forming true beliefs.[53] If the current suggestion is found to have some merit, it could be that when epistemic justification is so coercive that it eclipses a person's affective qualities, such an approach may fail to reflect the transcendental virtues of truth, goodness, and beauty that are so endemic to supererogatory actions, and particularly the kind of intrinsic goodness

---

[53] It seems likely that Feinberg hints at such a relational causality in suggesting the possibility that God could choose not to be consciously aware of everything he knows. Feinberg argues, for example, that perhaps a more robust notion of fellowship among the members of the Trinity, or our ability to draw God's attention to our specific concerns, or our ability to take seriously God's willingness to forget our sins, begins to emerge if God is not always thinking of everything he knows. Cf. John S. Feinberg, *No One Like Him: The Doctrine of God*, Foundations of Evangelical Theology, John S. Feinberg, gen. ed. (Wheaton, IL: Crossway, 2001), 317–320.

that seeks to enhance personal human agency.[54] The absence of such affective qualities in the knowing process may result in a potential dehumanizing of the person, especially if one senses that one is rationally coerced to respond exclusively on the basis of an explicit presentation of the evidence.

On this conception, when intentionally exercised, various aesthetic qualities endemic to our cognitive and affective capacities can serve to create reciprocity between the beauty of belief and the endemic human desire to be both rational and right about one's beliefs. Affective evidence on our approach may serve merely to broaden the cumulative case argument for rational belief in God. And while beauty is not a surrogate for true belief,[55] a God of supererogatory goodness, for example, can see to it that certain beliefs, while not satisfying the more stringent requirements for evidence in more traditional forms of evidentialism, may strike us, all things considered, as being cognitively attractive in engaging and encouraging the typical person to consider certain aesthetic elements within the free exercise of one's native faculties in arriving at an indispensably rich and robust acceptance of rational belief in God's existence.

---

[54] One can imagine here Hans Urs von Balthasar's powerful insight on the place of beauty in the formation of beliefs. See, for example, his *The Glory of God: A Theological Aesthetic*, 2nd ed., trans. Erasmo Leiva-Merikakis, ed. Joseph Fessio, SJ, and John Riches (San Francisco: Ignatius, 2009), 18. Von Balthasar writes, "Our situation today shows that beauty demands for itself at least as much courage and decision as do truth and goodness, and she will not allow herself to be separated and banned from her two sisters without taking them along with herself in an act of mysterious vengeance."
[55] Roger Scruton, *Beauty* (New York: Oxford University Press, 2009), 2–5.

5

Christian Miracle Claims and Supernatural Causation: Representative Cases from the Synoptic Gospels and Contemporary Accounts[1]

GARY R. HABERMAS

Defining the term "miracle" is a challenging and thorny issue in itself.[2] But rather than filling the majority of this essay by surveying potential candidates for a definition, we will simply begin by stating that perhaps the predominant contemporary view is that, in addition to the historical event itself, a miracle requires the intervention or causation of God or another supernatural source. Philosopher David Basinger asserts, "a religious miracle is usually defined as an unusual, observable event caused by a god."[3] Another philosopher, Richard Swinburne, is slightly more detailed: "we may say very generally that a miracle is an event of an extraordinary kind, brought about by a god, and of religious significance."[4]

The initial issue of whether or not particular events actually occurred

---

[1] An earlier version of this essay, though unpublished and less than two-thirds of the present length, was invited and read to the Synoptic Gospels Study Group at the annual meeting of the Evangelical Theological Society in Baltimore, November 19, 2013.
[2] For my own approach and definition, see Gary R. Habermas, *Philosophy of History, Miracles, and the Resurrection of Jesus*, 3rd ed. (Sagamore Beach, MA: Academx, 2012), esp. 8.
[3] David Basinger, "Christian Theism and the Concept of Miracle: Some Epistemological Perplexities," *The Southern Journal of Philosophy* 18 (Summer 1980): 137.
[4] Richard Swinburne, *The Concept of Miracle* (London: Macmillan, 1970), 1.

in space and time is largely historical in nature and will not be the primary emphasis in this essay, though a few hints will be provided. Rather, we will be chiefly occupied with the latter portion of the definition of miracles, concerning the intervention or causation of God or supernatural forces for reasons of religious significance or purpose. These concluding characterizations introduce many potential factors chiefly of a philosophical or theological nature.

Our chief purpose, then, is to pursue the subject of the supernatural causation of potential candidates for miraculous events. Along the way, though we will make some observations regarding the facticity of the occurrences themselves, we are primarily interested in potential paths for justifying, indicating, or even requiring some sort of intervention by nonnatural forces. In focusing on these wider philosophical and theological causal concerns, then, we are not constructing the central apologetic argument per se. Given the potential existence of some miraculous candidates from the Synoptic Gospels as well as from a few very recent medical cases, are there any probable parameters that may point to or identify the presence of any supernatural actions and purposes in these events? If so, what might serve as such recognizable conduits from events back to causes, in the sense of divine actions?

THE PHILOSOPHICAL REQUIREMENTS

According to two of the very best-known atheistic philosophers of the late twentieth century, Antony Flew[5] and J. L. Mackie, two conditions must obtain in order to indicate that a miracle has actually happened: the event must have occurred, and it must be opposed to a known law of nature.[6] I have argued at great length that the two prerequisites for a miraculous event have been satisfied in the case of the resurrection of Jesus, which actually occurred, and which certainly would have contravened or overridden natural law.[7]

---

[5] Here I am discussing Flew's position *prior* to his becoming a theist or deist. Regarding what Flew referred to as his "conversion," see "My Pilgrimage from Atheism to Theism: A Discussion between Antony Flew and Gary Habermas," *Philosophia Christi* 6 (2004): 197–211; Antony Flew with Roy Abraham Varghese, *There Is a God: How the World's Most Notorious Atheist Changed His Mind* (New York: HarperCollins, 2008).

[6] Antony Flew, "Introduction" to David Hume, *Of Miracles* (La Salle, IL: Open Court, 1985), 7–8; J. L. Mackie, *The Miracle of Theism* (Oxford: Clarendon, 1982), 26.

[7] Flew and I have debated both the historicity of the resurrection and its relation to nature's laws on at least three separate occasions, all of which have been published. Our volumes include *Did Jesus Rise from the Dead? The Resurrection Debate*, ed. Terry L. Miethe (San Francisco: Harper & Row, 1987); *Resurrected? An Atheist and Theist Dialogue*, ed. John F. Ankerberg (Lanham, MD: Rowman & Littlefield, 2005); *Did*

Elsewhere Flew mentioned an additional requirement: the event itself cannot be a sufficient condition for concluding that a miracle occurred. It is also necessary to have an interpretive system in which to understand these events.[8] Are there further worldview criteria, then, which, if they were present, would constitute a philosophical context and framework that, along with the extraordinary events, would allow us to conclude that those events are most likely acts of God? We wish to address this paramount focus here.

Basinger's analysis is quite instructive at this point, especially since he also rejects a strongly epistemic grounding for identifying such events as acts of God. Still, outlining examples or aspects of what might qualify, he helpfully terms this the establishing of a potential "divine action pattern." Basinger identifies the following as possible candidates for such a path: (1) "divine healing in response to human petition," (2) if the Scripture is trustworthy, then there is "little reason to deny" the knowledge that such designed paths can be detected there, or (3) special events today "which seem clearly to be identified as direct acts of God" in Scripture.[9]

Basinger concludes that, while there can be "no epistemological certainty" in such cases, this "is not to say that the theist cannot justifiably consider it more probable than not that an occurrence is a direct act of God if it stands as the consequent in an instantiated divine action pattern." Yet, he still unfortunately concludes that "the identification of a miracle becomes a very subjective matter," since theists can only conclude this matter for themselves.[10]

Swinburne addresses similar issues, including what it means to transgress a law of nature. He concludes that we may designate certain events, if they occurred, as violations of nature's laws: levitation,[11] the resurrection of a man who meets the current criteria for death, turning water into wine by command alone, and, more relevantly for our study here, "a man getting better from polio in a minute." As Swinburne states, "We know quite enough about how things behave to be reasonably certain that . . . these events are physically impossible."[12]

---

the Resurrection Happen? A Conversation with Gary Habermas and Antony Flew, ed. David Baggett (Downers Grove, IL: InterVarsity Press, 2009).
[8] Antony Flew, "Miracle," in The Encyclopedia of Philosophy, ed. Paul Edwards (New York: Macmillan/Free Press, 1967), 348, 353.
[9] Basinger, "Christian Theism and the Concept of Miracle," 142–144.
[10] Ibid., 144, 148–149.
[11] Personally, I doubt that levitation qualifies as a miracle. I think that it belongs in Swinburne's other category of repeatable events, which are less likely to be miraculous (see Swinburne, Concept of Miracle, 9–10).
[12] Swinburne, Concept of Miracle, 29–32; see also 58–60.

Rather incredibly, even as an atheist philosopher, Mackie makes seemingly similar concessions. He points out that a resurrection from actual death would indeed constitute a miracle.[13] He also makes a further, rather striking clarification. Regarding the criteria for divine intervention, he allows that "anyone who is fortunate enough to have carefully observed and carefully recorded, for himself, an apparently miraculous occurrence is no doubt rationally justified in taking it very seriously. . . ."[14] So personal participation in or observation of an apparent miracle could be another criterion that might contribute to a sufficient case being made.

In our first debate on the resurrection, still in his atheist days, Flew conceded from the outset that if it is shown that Jesus was raised from the dead, then this event "is the best, if not the only, reason for accepting that Jesus is the God of Abraham, Isaac, and Israel."[15] Later, I inquired that, if the resurrection occurred, would a naturalist at least have to be open to Jesus's claims to be deity and that he was God's spokesman? Flew responded, "Yes, that seems to be clear . . . yes, you've put it rather nicely . . . clearly there would have to be some ears opened to some radical new thinking."[16] So for Flew, as well, there is a potential path to fulfilling the required interpretive or worldview system that would give the needed meaning to the miraculous events.

So if we accept the particular delineations of Basinger and Swinburne, and even those of Mackie and Flew, certain criteria could at least theoretically both fit and fulfill the schema that, when combined with the particular evidenced events, may identify these combinations of occurrence plus religious significance as at least potential qualifying cases for the miraculous. Moreover, at least Swinburne, Mackie, and Flew all specify that the resurrection of Jesus would be such a candidate. Further, especially for our purposes in this essay, Basinger, Swinburne, and Mackie each stipulate additionally that contemporary extraordinary events, especially when witnessed personally, are likewise quite relevant to the discussion. And having had many private discussions with Flew on similar topics, I am quite certain that he would agree heartily.

Beyond these more theoretical and largely isolated philosophical

---
[13] Mackie, *Miracle of Theism*, 24.
[14] Ibid., 28.
[15] Flew, in *Did Jesus Rise from the Dead?*, 3.
[16] Ibid., 49–50.

considerations, then, what if we introduce two very specific contexts? Could such conditions and qualifications regarding the combination of evidenced event plus religious message and context also be applied appropriately to the miracles plus the teachings associated with Jesus, as recorded by the Synoptic Gospel authors? Further, what about the application of such similar qualities to contemporary miracle claims of an extraordinary sort, if there are such events that are also paired with religious significance, as referred to by at least Basinger, Swinburne, and Mackie? We will now focus on these last two subjects.

DIVINE ACTION PATTERNS IN THE SYNOPTIC GOSPEL MIRACLES

What is the contemporary scholarly attitude toward the miracle claims of Jesus as they are depicted in the Synoptic Gospels? And, are these occurrences also grounded in a divine landscape, perspective, and worldview? The answer to the initial question is that the scholarly attitude has changed significantly in the past few decades.[17] Even a more skeptical researcher, prominent Jesus Seminar member Marcus Borg, attests that, "Despite the difficulty which miracles pose for the modern mind, on historical grounds it is virtually indisputable that Jesus was a healer and exorcist."[18]

Few scholars have provided more meticulous analyses here than either John Meier or Graham Twelftree. Meier concluded his four hundred–plus page study by judging that more than 40 percent of the miracle claims presented in the Gospels actually correspond to specific historical occurrences in the life of Jesus. He quite amazingly concludes, "In sum, the statement that Jesus acted as and was viewed as an exorcist and healer during his public ministry has as much historical corroboration as almost any other statement we can make about the Jesus of history. Indeed . . . it has much better attestation than many other assertions made about Jesus, assertions that people often take for granted."[19] Coming from a major

---

[17] This can and should be ascertained from the recent scholarly sources themselves, which are quite clear on this conclusion. But as a personal example from my own graduate student experiences in the 1970s, if one believed back in that decade that Jesus was indeed a miracle worker and an exorcist, others could probably surmise that that individual was most likely an evangelical!

[18] Marcus J. Borg, *Jesus, A New Vision: Spirit, Culture, and the Life of Discipleship* (San Francisco: Harper-Collins, 1987), 61, for the quotation; cf. also the greater context in 59–61, 65–71.

[19] John P. Meier, *A Marginal Jew: Mentor, Miracles, and Message*, 4 vols. (New York: Doubleday, 1994), 2:970 for the quotation; Meier's historical conclusions are found on 2:968–970.

scholar such as Meier, who is about as influential as anyone in recent historical Jesus research, this is indeed a significant conclusion.

In an even longer critical study, Twelftree thinks that a much higher percentage (approximately 76 percent) of the Gospel miracle accounts accurately portray historical events in Jesus's life. His bottom line is also quite similar to Meier's: *"there is hardly any aspect of the life of the historical Jesus which is so well and widely attested as that he conducted unparalleled wonders."* In fact, his miracles *"were the most important aspect of Jesus's whole pre-Easter ministry."*[20] Further, it is crucial to state that neither Meier nor Twelftree discount the remaining Gospel miracle accounts where we possess insufficient historical evidence to establish them as individual events. A lack of evidence is decidedly not the same thing as the nonoccurrence of the events in question.

Craig Keener is another scholar who treats the topic of miracles in great detail, though his treatment of Jesus's miracles is not as detailed, since his emphasis is on contemporary miracle claims. Rather than examining the intricacies of the Gospel texts, as do Maier and Twelftree, Keener chiefly and helpfully treats the overall state of the current scholarly discussion. He argues that all ancient sources agreed that Jesus performed miracles, including ancient non-Christian texts from the Jewish rabbis and from the critic Celsus. Surprisingly, none of these ancient texts attempted to deny or refute the Christian claims. Moreover, Keener lists approximately a dozen different ancient texts that assert Jesus's miracles, including the five commonly identified Gospel sources (Q, Mark, M, L, and John).[21] He also finds that there is very little of the modern notion of development over the time between the Gospels, and concludes that, "The essential substance of the miracles themselves remains unchanged."[22]

Keener likewise addresses briefly the state of recent scholarly views on the subject of Jesus's miracles, especially from within the ranks of the Third Quest for the Historical Jesus. Several exceptionally positive affirmations are reproduced from these critical scholars, including even the radical critic Morton Smith, whom Keener terms the "most skeptical

---

[20] Graham H. Twelftree, *Jesus the Miracle Worker: A Historical and Theological Study* (Downers Grove, IL: InterVarsity Press, 1999), 345 for the quotation (emphasis his); Twelftree's historical conclusions are found on 328–330.
[21] See Craig S. Keener, *Miracles: The Credibility of the New Testament Accounts*, 2 vols. (Grand Rapids, MI: Baker Academic, 2011), 1:22–25, 29–33.
[22] Ibid., 1:31–32.

toward the Gospel tradition." Yet, while Smith dismisses Jesus's miracles, he still "argues that miracle working is the most authentic part of the Jesus tradition." Keener ends this chapter by posing two methodological sorts of questions for later discussions: the potential contrast of Christian with non-Christian miracle claims, and the huge issue of contemporary a priori assumptions against miraculous events.[23]

According to Borg, it might even be stated, in fact, that the major concern in Jesus's time was not the miracles themselves, which were recognized as actual events. Rather, the chief concern was the teachings brought by the wonder worker. What did individual miracle workers teach as following from their miracles? In the view of the Gospel authors as well as of Jesus, his mighty acts were done by the power and authority of God.[24]

So the scholarly attitude has changed rather significantly during the past few decades with regard to whether or not Jesus actually performed supernatural events such as those recorded in the Synoptic Gospels. It is almost unanimous, even among quite skeptical scholars, that Jesus was in some sense a miracle worker and an exorcist, however these events are ultimately explained or interpreted. The Synoptic authors also maintain that these events were linked to the hand of God, and were performed by God's power. As such, Jesus's miracles were seen as an integral part of the overall divine plan. This is especially the case when understood within the ancient Jewish context, as we shall see.

So how do the Synoptic Gospels make this vital connection between Jesus's miracles and his being from God? How are these amazing events connected to God, indicating that they are woven into the divine plan? Can the supernatural occurrences reported straightforwardly as historical events by the Synoptic authors plausibly be traced to a divine hand and power, as these writings clearly argue? As indicated throughout, such linking of event with supernatural activity is necessary if it is to be argued that these occurrences were actually miracles. We want to pursue this connection, while noting carefully that, in our search for these signals of divine action as revealed through the Synoptic Gospels' miraculous events (and later in modern miracle claims), we will basically only be able to

---

[23] Ibid., 1:26; for the other topics, see 1:24–34. In chapter 2, Keener addresses the first of these questions by quite intriguingly contrasting early Christian miracle claims with ancient non-Christian miracle claims.
[24] Borg, *Jesus, A New Vision*, where these two points are made, respectively, on 180–185 and 66–67.

list many of these potentially divine indications. Space limitations do not allow detailed elaboration or interaction with each of these indications.[25]

First, even by their very nature, miracles tend to point beyond themselves to a religious message. This is why some of the most-used synonyms include terms such as "signs/pointers," or "wonders." This is the case whether in a Christian, Jewish, or non-Christian context. Once having decided that an event is (or even possibly could be) a miracle, the next question, either then or now, seems to pertain to its purpose, or to what it signified, or to who the miracle worker is, or to what the event is teaching. What does the event "sign(ify)" or where does it point? Swinburne asserts that this is a distinctive and central feature: "To be a miracle an event must contribute significantly towards a holy divine purpose for the world." Conversely, extraordinary happenings that clearly lack religious significance are "more appropriately characterised as magical or psychic phenomena rather than as miracles."[26]

Second and more directly, according to the Synoptic Gospel reports, Jesus claimed that his miracles were signs that God had certified the truth of his teachings. For instance, after being accused of committing blasphemy for claiming to do something that only God could do, Jesus responded to his critics in the earliest Gospel by declaring boldly that his healing of a lame man would show clearly that they could "know that the Son of man has authority on earth to forgive sins" (Mark 2:10, RSV). In a very early text, when John the Baptist experienced doubts regarding whether or not Jesus was God's promised Messiah, Jesus again pointed to his miracles (Luke 7:18–28) as the answer. In two other circumstances, when asked by his critics for a sign of his authority, Jesus indicated that his resurrection would be his primary evidence (Matt. 12:38–42/Luke 11:29–32; Matt. 16:1–4). These miracles served as signs that were designed to point beyond Jesus's words, as attestation for the authority of his message.

A third sign of a divine action pattern being indicated by Jesus's miracles is that, beyond the events themselves, recent research has indicated at least a half-dozen strong historical reasons to hold that Jesus also predicted his death, resurrection, and/or his exaltation,[27] as pointers to

---
[25] For such elaboration and interaction, see Gary R. Habermas, *The Risen Jesus and Future Hope* (Lanham, MD: Rowman & Littlefield, 2003), esp. chapters 1–3, as well as other works.
[26] Swinburne, *Concept of Miracle*, 7–10.
[27] For examples, see Mark 8:31; 9:31; 10:33–34; 14:27–28. For the best summaries of the data, see Michael Licona, "Did Jesus Predict His Death and Vindication/Resurrection?" *Journal for the Study of the Historical*

his supreme vindication. This is very significant with regard to ascertaining the presence and involvement of a divine action pattern. Besides any force from the resurrection event itself, Jesus's knowing about it ahead of time would signify that this occurrence was not some freak event of nature. Rather, Jesus's foreknowledge indicated that it was *part of an overall, intelligently designed, divine plan*, certainly extending beyond the historical happening itself by pointing to God's provision of salvation and the eternal life of the kingdom. It is difficult to imagine a much better indication of divine interaction.

Fourth, the early Christian believers agreed that Jesus's miracles confirmed the truth of his message. For example, we read the claims that many people believed after they saw Jesus's miracles.[28] In the initial post-resurrection sermon, Peter reportedly declared that Jesus's miracles, and the resurrection in particular, were the chief indications that God placed his stamp of approval on Jesus's teachings (Acts 2:23–32). Later, we are told that Paul also used the resurrection event as assurance that God had confirmed Jesus's teachings, hence Paul's challenging the Greek philosophers to repent (Acts 17:30–31). In citing an early tradition that utilizes at least two lofty Christological titles ("Son of God" and "Lord"), Paul proclaimed that the resurrection was God's confirmation of Jesus Christ's deity (Rom. 1:3–4). So the New Testament authors repeatedly made use of Jesus's miracles, above all his resurrection, in order to indicate that Jesus's teachings were both true and authoritative.

So the Synoptic Gospels as well as other New Testament texts indicate that Jesus's followers freely cited Jesus's miracles as indicating that his teachings were true. In this, they both shared the view taught by Jesus himself and tapped into the very common notion—both then and now, as well as across world religious lines of demarcation—that miracles serve as pointers to or indicators of truth. When we add that Jesus most likely predicted his resurrection and/or his vindication before it happened, these four considerations, when lined up side by side, certainly seem to point to a pattern of interconnection between these miracle claims and the message they were meant to convey. Together, we catch a glimpse of some crucial portions of the "divine action pattern" that surrounded these events and connected them to the hand of God.

Jesus 8 (2010): 47–66. See also Licona's excellent volume, *The Resurrection of Jesus: A New Historiographical Approach* (Downers Grove, IL: InterVarsity Press, 2010), 284–302.
[28] Mark 2:12; Matthew 8:27; 14:32–33.

More specifically in terms of the various messages themselves, we see miraculous occurrences utilized in the texts as the vindication for Jesus being able to forgive sins; to argue repeatedly that he was the Messiah and that he both had claimed and had been given other divine titles; to show that Jesus was God's chosen messenger, especially regarding the message of God's kingdom; and to show that his teachings were true. In him, God was confronting people with a choice. In short, what they did with Jesus determined whether or not they could enter God's kingdom. Intriguingly, even Jesus's exorcisms were employed as pointers to messages such as his triumph over Satan (Mark 3:22–27) and the presence of God's kingdom (Luke 11:20). All of this and more was said to follow from the occurrence of Jesus's miracles and exorcisms.

Perhaps even a majority of recent critical scholars hold that Jesus thought that his miracles confirmed both his person and his message.[29] In fact, Twelftree remarks that the evidence indicates that *"because of his miracles*, Jesus appears to have been conscious that he was God's key figure. . . ."[30] I. Howard Marshall affirms that Jesus's resurrection served as "the decisive stimulus" in causing the early Christians to recognize that Jesus was deity.[31] Such critical recognition is not surprising, since the Gospel comments indicating that Jesus thought in terms of the miraculous confirmation of his message are reflected by very strong multiple attestation, being found in at least four sources (Mark, Q, M, and John).

In other words, against this general backdrop, Jesus apparently predicted his resurrection, performed miracles and exorcisms, and then

---

[29] This is quite incredibly the case even among many theologians and Scripture scholars who reject the literal resurrection event as well as the doctrines Jesus taught! A few examples, across a wide critical spectrum and spread over more than a half century, of those who think that at least Jesus believed this about his teachings, would include Rudolf Bultmann, *Theology of the New Testament*, trans. Kendrick Grobel, 2 vols. (New York: Charles Scribner's Sons, 1951), 1:7; Reginald H. Fuller, *The Foundations of New Testament Christology* (New York: Charles Scribner's Sons, 1965), 107; Wolfhart Pannenberg, *Jesus: God and Man*, trans. Lewis L. Wilkins and Duane A. Priebe (Philadelphia: Westminster, 1968), 63–64; Willi Marxsen, *The Resurrection of Jesus of Nazareth*, trans. Margaret Kohl (Philadelphia: Fortress, 1970), 125, 147, 169, 183; Ulrich Wilckens, *Resurrection: Biblical Testimony to the Resurrection: An Historical Examination and Explanation*, trans. A. M. Stewart (Edinburgh: Saint Andrew, 1977), 124–132; Murray J. Harris, *Raised Immortal: Resurrection and Immortality in the New Testament* (Grand Rapids, MI: Eerdmans, 1983), chapter 5, for instance; Borg, *Jesus, A New Vision*, esp. 59–61, 65–71; Raymond E. Brown, *An Introduction to New Testament Christology* (Mahwah, NJ: Paulist, 1994), 61–67; Howard Clark Kee, *What Can We Know about Jesus?* (Cambridge: Cambridge University, 1990), 112; Meier, *Marginal Jew*, 2:967–970; Twelftree, *Jesus the Miracle Worker*, 328–330, 343–348; E. P. Sanders, *The Historical Figure of Jesus* (London: Penguin, 1993), chapter 10, esp. 167. Cf. Geza Vermes, *Jesus in His Jewish Context* (Minneapolis: Fortress, 2003), 97; cf. Bart Ehrman, *Did Jesus Exist? The Historical Argument for Jesus of Nazareth* (New York: HarperCollins, 2012), 316–317.
[30] Twelftree, *Jesus the Miracle Worker*, 346–347 (emphasis his).
[31] I. Howard Marshall, *The Origins of New Testament Christology*, updated ed. (Downers Grove, IL: InterVarsity Press, 1990), 128–129.

taught that all these actions were the accrediting signs that verified his claims. Then many scholars have argued repeatedly that Jesus was also raised from the dead, just as he had predicted. What would this overall scenario look like from the Jewish perspective? As Borg explains, Jesus's opponents did not deny his miracles. Rather, they admitted them while attributing them to evil powers. But this move actually only succeeded in pointing both to Jesus's holiness and to his healing authority.[32]

What, then, follows next, if Jesus was actually raised from the dead? Negatively, it would be difficult to name many more crucial areas as candidates for heresy than those major doctrines affirmed by Jesus of himself, particularly in terms of his deity and his being God's path of salvation. How highly unlikely would it be that God would have raised such a colossal blasphemer from the dead?[33] Positively, it must have been disarming for his opponents to realize that Jesus's miracles and, above all, his resurrection from the dead, just might indicate the supreme acts whereby God placed the ultimate stamp of approval on Jesus's teachings—as taught by Jesus himself as well as by the early church.

From yet another angle, what if some unknown individual, or even a nonreligious person, had performed these sorts of miraculous events? Especially if there was a lack of interpretive pattern accompanying this person's actions, some might call these occasions just freak events of nature. But since they accompanied Jesus, the very individual who was surrounded by these rather bombastic claims and his one-of-a-kind life, this certainly favors the conjunction of a very positive "divine action pattern." As world religions specialist Stephen Neill asserted rather boldly, "Jesus is not the least like anyone else who has ever lived. The things he says about God are not the same as the sayings of any other religious teacher. The claims that he makes for himself are not the same as those that have been made by any other religious teacher."[34] Stated briefly, it could be argued that history's most unique messenger was the focus of history's most unique events.[35]

---

[32] Borg, *Jesus, A New Vision*, 61.
[33] For an overall assessment of some of the major philosophical issues involved, see Richard Swinburne, "Does God Permit Massive Deception?" *Philosophia Christi*, n.s., 15 (2013): 265–270.
[34] Stephen Neill, *Christian Faith and Other Faiths: The Christian Dialogue with Other Religions*, 2nd ed. (London: Oxford University Press, 1970), 233. Neill repeated a very similar comment in an updated edition of this volume published by InterVarsity Press (Downers Grove, IL) in 1984 (286).
[35] There is additional potential to construct a more philosophical context for Jesus's life and ministry as well, featuring items such as the connection between the existence and attributes of the God of biblical theism, and the necessary requirements of healing events like those narrated in the Synoptic Gospels, as well as Jesus's resurrection. This could be explored from the perspectives of both the Father and the Son. For

DIVINE ACTION PATTERNS IN CONTEMPORARY MIRACLE CLAIMS

Repeated public polls have indicated that most Americans today are at least open to the occurrence of miracles, and do not rule out the possibility of supernatural events. So in spite of the many skeptical or naturalistic views toward supernatural events that are often heard today, it seems that a clear majority of respondents in several recent polls think that miracles are at least possible, if not likely. In one poll, a little more than one-third of the respondents even declared that they had experienced or witnessed miracles for themselves.[36]

But perhaps those who are skeptical or nonreligious might be more interested and open than is sometimes thought, to being convinced of miracles by good historical evidence. In another of the American polls that Keener cites, even a majority of those who apparently were largely nonreligious still believed that miracles probably do occur.[37]

Can contemporary miraculous events also be traced to divine causes? Earlier we observed Basinger's suggestions of potential indications of "divine action patterns" that also might be present in certain recent miracle claims. Those suggestions include healing in the presence of prayer and petition to God, and the seeming occurrence of circumstances that appear to be similar to those patterns found in the New Testament. We also noted Swinburne's reference to the importance of a disease being healed immediately (in order to be considered miraculous), or even Mackie's recognizing that individuals who personally witness particular events that appear to be miraculous are rationally justified in taking such experiences seriously.

Although a number of other significant research efforts have also examined the question of recent miracle claims,[38] our focus here will be on

---

details, see Habermas, *The Risen Jesus and Future Hope*, chapters 1–3. Swinburne also favors approaching the miracles issue from the angle of God's existence (*Concept of Miracle*, chapter 6). In fact, Swinburne asserted that if the traditional God exists, we would need "only slender historical evidence" for a miracle, because such events would follow from God's character (*Concept of Miracle*, 68–69; also 69–71). Most intriguingly, Antony Flew, even during his atheist days, similarly admitted that, "Certainly given some beliefs about God, the occurrence of the resurrection does become enormously more likely" (see Habermas and Flew, *Did Jesus Rise from the Dead?*, 39). For other approaches that still come at these subjects from distinctly different perspectives, see the recent issue of *Philosophia Christi* devoted to the theme of "Ramified Natural Theology" (n.s., 15 [2013]).

[36] Craig Keener produces an array of reputable polls which generally show that a rather high majority of recent respondents believe that miracles occur. See Keener, *Miracles*, 1:204–205, for several examples.

[37] Ibid., 1:204.

[38] Other research efforts include books written by medical doctors, such as Rex Gardner's *Healing Miracles: A Doctor Investigates* (London: Darton, Longman, & Todd, 1986) and H. Richard Casdorph's *The Miracles: A Medical Doctor Says Yes to Miracles* (Plainfield, NJ: Logos, 1976). These texts have also investigated

Craig Keener's massive exploration. In keeping with our primary theme of potential connections between miracle reports and divine involvement, Keener makes numerous, largely philosophical comments about worldviews, paradigm changes, and especially his conviction that many of these testimonies of miracles actually involve supernatural activity.[39] In spite of his caveats here and there,[40] it would be helpful to detail some of the more philosophical portions of the miracles discussion, where this emphasis on what would qualify epistemically as supernatural or miraculous activity has a long research history. But unless at least some of his cases are caused by supernatural actions, his project loses perhaps even most of its force. Without such, critics could charge that these testimonies relate hearsay testimony, or at best, something like odd, freak events of nature.

Therefore, it seems that supplementing or accenting what is already present in Keener's incredible research with these chiefly philosophical emphases will hopefully bolster his excellent efforts. My intent, then, is to provide ammunition and augmentation in these more theoretical but necessary areas. After all, if the testimonies recorded by Keener and others are to provide evidence for supernaturalism in general or for Christian theism in particular, then the accounts must be more than merely hearsay or anomalous occurrences. But when a common response by Christians seems to be that such testimonies are so evidential, strange, or incredible that God *must* have performed them, they have just played into the hands of the naturalists and, frankly, have botched the potential causal case.[41] No matter how strong Keener's miracle reports may be, we *must* have more than even the outstanding medical or other evidence alone in order to make the necessary case for miracles, contemporary or otherwise.

What might be observed if we looked for some potential divine involvement configurations in the recent miracle claims recorded in the pages of Keener's detailed volumes? Might some of his accounts provide possible or even likely candidates for the presence of bridges from the occurrences themselves to divine activity behind them?

---

contemporary healing cases, including providing some impressive medical confirmation. See also philosopher Robert A. Larmer, *The Legitimacy of Miracle* (Lanham, MD: Rowman & Littlefield [Lexington Press], 2014), especially the four healing cases included in the appendix. A brief popular treatment of a few more examples can be found in Gary R. Habermas, *Why Is God Ignoring Me? What to Do When It Feels like He's Giving You the Silent Treatment* (Carol Stream, IL: Tyndale, 2010), chapter 1.

[39] Keener, *Miracles*, 1:2, 4–9, 16, 103, 201, 241, 249, 254–255, 261; 2:752–759, for some examples.
[40] Ibid., 1:241.
[41] It should be noted that Keener does not make these moves, though they seem to be common enough among believers.

The most common action pattern reported by Keener is the occurrence of healing in the presence of prayer, especially when the prayers appear to be correlated directly in time, specific focus, content, and so on.[42] Often, these cases are quite dramatic in themselves, as well as being confirmed by pre- and post-medical testing such as MRIs, CT scans, or X-rays. Sometimes, specialized medical testimony was immediately available. However, I will be able only to cite briefly a small number of these reports. Many more are found in these volumes.

Several cases concern the immediate and unexpected vanishing of cancerous tumors after God was petitioned, such as "the sudden disappearance of a brain tumor after prayer, before any medical treatment could begin." The tumor covered almost one-fourth of a girl's brain, with MRI confirmation of the cancer from before the incident, while, just two days after the prayer, another MRI was administered and the tumor had already disappeared.[43] *Time* magazine reported that a baby with a type of malignant brain tumor that always proved fatal was also healed specifically after both prayer and anointing by a minister. The absence of the cancer was confirmed, though the tissue had earlier been biopsied as cancerous. The girl was almost thirteen years old when the article was written.[44]

In still another case, this one involving metastasized breast cancer, the doctor noted that the patient was cured immediately after prayer. Testing the very next morning established the result.[45] In another account, a woman's cancer had spread to several organs and she was very close to death. Though the physicians could do no more for her, she was cured instantly, with her damaged organs even healing.[46]

Keener cites many other such examples. After much prayer, including a service at his church for this purpose, a boy with two holes in his heart, affecting his lungs, was taken to the hospital for surgery. How-

---

[42] This category could potentially be buttressed further by some double-blind prayer experiments, published in medical journals, where the intercessory prayer factor is even more clearly linked to healing. This is a difficult research question not without its own issues, though a further discussion cannot of course be pursued in this context. Yet, it would seem that there is still some possible significance for at least some of these medical prayer studies. For examples, see Randolph B. Byrd, "Positive Therapeutic Effects of Intercessory Prayer in a Coronary Care Unit Population," *Southern Medical Journal* 81 (July 1988): 826–829; and W. S. Harris et al., "A Randomized, Controlled Trial of the Effects of Remote, Intercessory Prayer on Outcomes in Patients Admitted to the Coronary Care Unit," *Archives of Internal Medicine* 159 (October 1999): 2273–2278.
[43] Keener, *Miracles*, 1:428.
[44] Ibid.
[45] Ibid., 1:435.
[46] Ibid., 2:682n206.

ever, as both the attending pediatric cardiac surgeon and a pulmonologist observed films of the boy's heart just prior to operating, the pictures indicated that the holes, which had been clearly visible on films from the previous day, were no longer present—in fact, they were now covered by some sort of wall inside the heart. Both the heart and the lungs were now normal as well. As a result, they never did the scheduled surgery and, rather incredibly, the eight-year-old was allowed to play baseball just three days later![47]

While away from home attending a Christian retreat, a man broke his ankle rather severely and went to a hospital, where an orthopedist set the ankle in a cast. He was even required to spend that night in the hospital. Upon later arriving back home, in another state, he was sent to a local hospital for some follow-up X-rays. After studying them, the physician informed the man that his ankle was never broken, as indicated by the lack of a break or even tissue damage where the break had been. But the earlier X-rays were ordered from the first hospital and clearly confirmed the break. Keener even received a set of the radiology reports.[48]

Dr. Cecil Titus, from St. Luke's Hospital in Cleveland, Ohio, testified that he personally observed as a ten-year-old girl's club foot just "straightened before my very eyes." This occurred precisely during a minister's prayer.[49]

Another of Basinger's "divine action patterns" consists of miracle claims that fit configurations that were similar to biblical accounts. Keener's two volumes of miracle reports were actually written during his work on an extensive four-volume commentary on Acts, whose first two volumes, which have already appeared, total more than two thousand pages.[50] He recounts that his interest in present-day miracles was born of his interest in the New Testament healing narratives. After his study, he realized that "the miracle reports in the Gospels and Acts are generally plausible historically. . . . Similar claims, often from convinced eyewitnesses, circulate widely today, and there are no a priori reasons to doubt that ancient eyewitnesses made analogous claims."[51] Keener's subtitle, "The Credibility of the New Testament Accounts," reflects his convic-

---

[47] Ibid., 1:431–432.
[48] Ibid., 1:440.
[49] Ibid., 1:463.
[50] These two volumes are Craig S. Keener, *Acts: An Exegetical Commentary* (Grand Rapids, MI: Baker Academic, 2012, 2013).
[51] Keener, *Miracles*, 1:7; cf. esp. 1–9.

tion that the modern cases similarly confirm the biblical reports, as with Basinger's proposal.

We have no desire to extend this last point too far, as if we need some sort of 1:1 ratio between the New Testament miracle accounts and modern ones, for this is decidedly not the case at all. But many of the healing descriptions in Keener (minus the modern accoutrements such as MRIs, CT scans, X-rays, and casts) at least appear to be in the vicinity of what might be expected from Jesus's ministry and that of the early church, even if superficially. For instance, the last account above, of the ten-year-old girl being healed of her club foot while the minister prayed, reminded me of Jesus telling the man with the withered hand to stretch it out, after which he was healed (Matt. 12:9–10a, 13). Just as we said that prayer is the most common connection to a divine healing pattern, texts like Acts 9:40–42 might come to mind, where prayer is also a precursor to healing.

Lest we forget the cognate point of Jesus's exorcisms also being central in this discussion, Keener likewise presents a large number of such modern cases.[52] Perhaps the most extraordinary accounts are the so-called power encounters, where Christian ministers often contend face-to-face with various sorcerers, witch doctors, and voodoo practitioners in cases of evangelism, healing, and exorcisms. In many of these accounts, not only are the Christians the ones who secure the desired result, including amazing examples of physical protection, but sometimes the occultist is actually converted![53]

While originally reading Keener's exorcism material, I thought that some of the stories were reminiscent of Paul confronting the girl who was described as having a spirit of divination, and then casting out the demon, after which she lost her powers (Acts 16:16–18). Jesus's comment, while speaking of Satan, might also be recalled—that a strong man's treasure cannot be taken unless the strong man is first secured (Mark 3:27).

Basinger denies that one can assert with epistemic certainty that God performed particular supernatural feats, but he does not reject the argument that a theist may be able to conclude that it is "more probable than not that an occurrence is a direct act of God."[54] This is especially the case when it is supported by indications of a "divine action pattern." We have argued here that such a pattern can be established, made up

---
[52] Ibid., vol. 2, appendices A and B in particular.
[53] Ibid., 2:843–852.
[54] Basinger, "Christian Theism and the Concept of Miracle," 144.

of individual strands of historical data plus an appropriate connection indicating the likelihood of supernatural involvement in the events. Such can be constructed both from cases in the Synoptic Gospels and from some of the best-evidenced accounts today. Perhaps this contributes to the widespread agreement noted above, even among critical scholars, that Jesus did indeed perform supernatural events such as those recorded in the Synoptic texts.

CONCLUSION

Three conclusions seem to follow from what we have considered. The first of these admittedly can be made only from research that extends far beyond this present essay, although it was referenced here several times. I have argued elsewhere at great length that the resurrection of Jesus Christ is a historical event, and have presented the clear philosophical and theological indications of an accompanying worldview perspective that identifies this event as an act of God.[55] In short, if this argument were to obtain, I think the divine action pattern is stronger than it is for any ancient occurrence.

Second, contemporary critical scholarship is almost completely agreed that, besides being a great teacher, Jesus Christ was also a miracle worker and an exorcist, at the very least in the minimal sense that he performed actions like those frequently described in the Synoptic Gospels. As many (James D. G. Dunn[56] and Marcus Borg, for example) have added, it is "virtually indisputable" that this conclusion can be established on historical grounds.[57] Further, there are several strong indications that these events were also clearly due to the manifestation of supernatural power.

Third, at least the best of the contemporary miracle claim cases are indeed exceptionally impressive, particularly when they are accompanied by pre- and post-X-rays, MRIs, or CT scans, and/or when they are further supplemented by specialized medical testimony. There is simply an astounding, almost overpowering number of such empirically evidenced examples, seemingly with detailed cases to fit almost everyone's interests.[58]

---

[55] See especially Habermas, *Risen Jesus and Future Hope*, esp. chapters 1–3.
[56] James D. G. Dunn, *Jesus Remembered*, vol. 1 of *Christianity in the Making* (Grand Rapids, MI: Eerdmans, 2003), 670–694, esp. 670–673.
[57] This quotation is from Borg, in *Jesus, A New Vision*, particularly 61.
[58] Soon after Keener's volumes appeared, I recommended them highly to two philosophically minded, agnostic friends with whom I'd been having conversations. They immediately purchased and studied Keener's books. The next time we talked, they began by telling me that they were completely convinced that at least

Especially when the reports themselves are also occasioned by the presence of these divine action patterns involving prayer, anointing, faith, and features that are sometimes strikingly similar to the stories in the Gospels and Acts, they are not only quite extraordinary but may be said to indicate the likely presence of God's hand.

So altogether, the case for Jesus Christ being caught up with the supernatural realm at any of many points appears to be exceptionally strong. This applies to both the historical side and to philosophical, worldview considerations involving divine action. Along with Stephen Neill, it indeed may be affirmed that no one like this has ever lived and taught before or since. Contemporary miracle claims increase the relevance and evidential force of these conclusions.[59]

---

several of the best-documented cases had actually occurred and were miraculous. They are not Christians, but they find the evidence for present-day miracles very convincing.
[59] Neill, *Christian Faith and Other Faiths*, 233.

II

SETTING THE FOUNDATIONS OF EVANGELICAL THEOLOGY

6

The Glory of God in the Doctrine of God

BRUCE A. WARE

It is my hope and prayer that the pages that follow will not only inform but also stimulate you to love, worship, and serve our great God even more! I trust as well that they will help us all recapture a sense of the wonder and grandeur of God. Most of all, I pray that what I have written will be pleasing to God himself and will bring him glory. He is most deserving of all our worship and praise, for there is no one like him![1]

Though God has many purposes [for his decree and for all creation], the ultimate reason for all of it is to bring him glory.[2]

If I may, I would like to begin with a few personal reflections. I recall distinctly the student assembly at Western Seminary, spring quarter of 1976, when an announcement was made that Mr. John S. Feinberg (he was, at that time, ABD in his PhD program in philosophy at the University of Chicago) would be joining the theology faculty. These were uncharted waters at Western—a professor with a degree in philosophy from a major university? How would this go over? Answer: we soon found out!

---
[1] John S. Feinberg, *No One Like Him: The Doctrine of God*, Foundations of Evangelical Theology, John S. Feinberg, gen. ed. (Wheaton, IL: Crossway, 2001), xxvii.
[2] Ibid., 515.

My first course with Dr. Feinberg would be in the winter quarter, 1977, but I recall well the cries that went around campus his inaugural fall quarter of 1976, when a significant number of students in his apologetics course failed their midterm exams. We realized right away that we were witnessing a brilliant mind, demanding standards, and an incredibly knowledgeable and capable lecturer in the person of John Feinberg. From that point on, I took nearly all of my required theology courses with Dr. Feinberg, and because I learned and benefited so very much, I took several theology electives with him as well. In God's kind providence, I stayed on for a ThM degree following the completion of my MDiv, and I had the privilege of working as Dr. Feinberg's teaching assistant. I got to know him well, and he befriended me in deeply loving and personal ways. And through all this, my respect for him and his incredibly penetrating mind only deepened.

His influence in my life continued. When I was contemplating where I should go for graduate studies, Dr. Feinberg knew I would benefit from additional work in philosophy, and he found for me (recall, these are days long before Internet searches!) a wonderful one-year MA program in philosophy at the University of Washington. I'm deeply grateful for that rich year of study, which happened only at his suggestion and urging. Then, near the completion of my own doctoral program, I received a phone call out of the blue from Millard Erickson, saying that Bethel Seminary had an opening (his opening, actually, as Dr. Erickson had been appointed dean of the seminary) in theology, and that my name had been given to him by John Feinberg. In God's kindness I got that position, and so began my now thirty-year career of teaching theology because John Feinberg believed in me and recommended me. What grace! Then also, at another point in my life, a theology teaching position opened at Trinity Evangelical Divinity School, and John once again supported me and, in God's mercy, I had the privilege of teaching with him—colleagues in the same department—for seven years at TEDS. I cannot even begin to calculate the benefit I had, and have, from studying theology under him and also through growing in a deep and enduring friendship with him. Few men have had a more profound influence in my life, and I wish to state publicly the depth of my gratitude and love for this capable theologian, teacher, mentor, and friend.

It is a distinct privilege, then, to contribute a chapter in this book written and published in honor of John S. Feinberg. And for this Festschrift, I took as my chapter title and theme "the glory of God in the doctrine of God" for two reasons: First, John's own life's work and publications, as well as my own, have focused in significant part on the doctrine of God, and so I know this is a topic near and dear to his heart as well as to my own. Second, while this book is produced in honor of John, it, along with all else, has legitimacy only as it serves the ultimate glory of God. How appropriate, then, to reflect a bit on what it is about God that undergirds and accounts for the ultimate glory that belongs to him alone. Indeed, God is *exclusively* God—there is no one besides him—and God is *incomparably* God—there is no one like him—such that he alone deserves ultimate and highest glory.

What is it about God, then, that elicits the rightful and exclusive glory of God above all else? Although a full answer to this question is large and expansive, this chapter will focus on one main aspect of the doctrine of God to show that ultimate glory is rightly directed only to him, in light of who he is and what he has done. Both the nature of God and his work direct us to the same conclusion—that ultimate glory is rightly given only to him. While there are a number of pathways one could walk in unfolding the glory of God in the doctrine of God, my focus here will be through considering the fundamental biblical teaching on God's transcendence as the prelude to and grounding for rightly understanding his immanence. Indeed, God is both "apart from us" in the fullness of his eternal existence, and gloriously "with us" as he has come to us in his revelation, particularly in his revelation in Christ. Each of these central aspects of the doctrine of God—his transcendence and his immanence—points in the same direction: that ultimate glory, in its fullness and for all time and eternity, belongs exclusively to God alone.

THE PRIORITY AND CENTRALITY OF THE DIVINE TRANSCENDENCE IN THE DOCTRINE OF GOD

Contemporary Christian culture is marked by a "rush" to the divine immanence. That is, when thinking and talking about God, we tend to default almost always to talking about God's love, grace, mercy, kindness, compassion, goodness, presence, attentiveness, and watch care, but we do so by bypassing almost altogether God's glorious and eternal transcendence. By rushing to immanence and missing transcendence, two problems result: First, we do not truly know the fullness of the God who is loving, gracious, merciful, and so forth because we don't know the awesomeness, greatness, grandeur, glory, transcendent independence, otherness, and holiness of this God who has chosen, amazingly, to do what he need not do, to do what we do not deserve, that is, to show the likes of us love and kindness. Second, we don't rightly know even the true nature of the love of God that we have rushed to embrace, because of lofty views of self and diminished views of God. We may sing "Amazing Grace," but we don't really consider this grace all that amazing. Rather, because, in our own estimate, we're so important, and God is, after all, perfectly loving, his grace to us seems altogether "entitled" and "expected" and the amazement is all but lost. In our rush to immanence, we know aright neither the infinite greatness of God nor the nature of the very love of God that we claim to cherish.

A. W. Tozer was exactly right when he declared, "What comes into our minds when we think about God is the most important thing about us."[3] What's behind this declaration of the importance of knowing God rightly? Here's part of the burden Tozer had: "The Church," he bemoans, "has surrendered her once lofty concept of God and has substituted for it one so low, so ignoble, as to be utterly unworthy of thinking, worshiping men."[4] Again, Tozer comments, "the Christian conception of God current . . . is so decadent as to be utterly beneath the dignity of the Most High God."[5] David F. Wells has also discussed the enormity of this problem. He writes, "It is one of the defining marks of Our Time that God is now weightless. I do not mean by this that he is ethereal but rather that he has become unimportant. He rests upon the world so inconsequentially as not to be noticeable."[6] And John Feinberg detected the same problem, for in the preface of his magisterial *No One Like Him* he expressed his desire that readers would "recapture a sense of the wonder and grandeur of God."[7]

The glory of God in the doctrine of God starts here. We must understand God as infinitely and eternally rich in the fullness of his glorious being who, as such, has condescended to come and show weak, finite,

---
[3] A. W. Tozer, *The Knowledge of the Holy* (New York: Harper & Brothers, 1961), 9.
[4] Ibid., 6.
[5] Ibid., 10.
[6] David F. Wells, *God in the Wasteland: The Reality of Truth in a World of Fading Dreams* (Grand Rapids, MI: Eerdmans, 1994), 88.
[7] Feinberg, *No One Like Him*, xxvii.

and sinful creatures his love and devotion. The transcendence of God must be understood first as the platform for understanding rightly and appreciating the astonishing truth of God's immanent presence and kindness. Our rush to immanence has cost us dearly—we have lost sight of the transcendent greatness, grandeur, and independent excellence of God in the fullness of his being, and as a result, we have also diminished the significance of the immanent love and kindness that is expressed from none other than this infinitely and eternally glorious God.

THE CENTRAL EXPRESSION OF THE DIVINE TRANSCENDENCE IN THE SELF-SUFFICIENCY OF GOD

The transcendence of God finds full expression in biblical teaching concerning God's absolute self-sufficiency. God exists eternally by his own will and nature, and his existence is of such a quality as to contain intrinsically and eternally every quality[8] in infinite measure. The eternal existence of God, then, is the eternal existence of all perfection, infinitely and intrinsically possessed, within the eternal triune nature of God. Just as it is unthinkable from a biblical point of view that God could ever not be, so too it is unimaginable that God could ever receive some quality, some value, some knowledge, some power, some ability, some perfection that he previously lacked. The apostle Paul echoes the Old Testament prophets' understanding of God when he writes,

> "For who has known the mind of the Lord
>   or who has been his counselor?"
> "Or who has given a gift to him
>   that he might be repaid?"
>
> For from him and through him and to him are all things. To him be glory forever. Amen. (Rom. 11:34–36; cf. Isa. 40:12–28)

If God were ever in need of food, says the psalmist, he would not inform his creatures, for the world and all it contains are his (Ps. 50:7–12). His greatness so surpasses the created realm that the earth itself is the mere footstool for his feet (Isa. 66:1). The God of the Bible, the true and living God, is in need of nothing from any created being; quite the opposite,

---
[8] By "quality" I have in mind everything that is qualitatively good or, more simply, every perfection.

whereas he is not dependent on anything whatsoever, all else is dependent entirely on him. As Tozer comments,

> To admit the existence of a need in God is to admit incompleteness in the divine Being. Need is a creature-word and cannot be spoken of the Creator. God has a voluntary relation to everything He has made, but He has no necessary relation to anything outside of Himself. His interest in His creatures arises from His sovereign good pleasure, not from any need those creatures can supply nor from any completeness they can bring to Him who is complete in Himself.[9]

And C. S. Lewis contributes this insight:

> God has no needs. Human love, as Plato teaches us, is the child of Poverty—of a want or lack; it is caused by a real or supposed good in its beloved which the lover needs and desires. But God's love, far from being caused by goodness in the object, causes all the goodness which the object has, loving it first into existence and then into real, though derivative, lovability. God is Goodness. He can give good, but cannot need or get it. In that sense all His love is, as it were, bottomlessly selfless by very definition; it has everything to give and nothing to receive.[10]

Concerning God's unqualified self-sufficiency, the apostle Paul declares,

> The God who made the world and everything in it, being Lord of heaven and earth, does not live in temples made by man, nor is he served by human hands, as though he needed anything, since he himself gives to all mankind life and breath and everything. (Acts 17:24–25)

As the supreme Creator of the world and everything in it, and as the sole "Giver" of "everything" that is given to "all mankind," God, then, possesses within himself intrinsically[11] all perfections that there are, and

---
[9] Tozer, *Knowledge of the Holy*, 39.
[10] C. S. Lewis, *The Problem of Pain* (New York: Macmillan, 1962), 50.
[11] It is important to affirm not only that God possesses every quality or perfection within himself, but that he possesses these qualities within himself *intrinsically*. The reason is simple: it is possible to possess qualities within oneself that are not intrinsic to the person possessing them. For example, when we breathe, the air we breathe is within us, but that air is not intrinsic to us. Rather, that air is extrinsic, and we need to live in an environment where we take within us what we lack and what we need for our existence. The point, then, in affirming that God possesses every quality that there is within himself *intrinsically* is to say that God doesn't receive any of these qualities from some outside source, as if God were dependent upon

absolutely nothing can exist independent of him that could contribute in some way to enrich his very being or enlarge his possessions. God is supremely independent of the world, and hence he simply does not need the world he has made. His transcendence is manifest most clearly by his independent and infinite self-sufficiency. He possesses within himself, intrinsically and eternally, every quality in infinite measure. As Karl Barth rightly comments, "God is not dependent on anything that is not Himself; on anything outside Himself. He is not limited by anything outside Himself, and is not subject to any necessity distinct from Himself. On the contrary, everything that exists is dependent on His will."[12]

God utterly transcends all lesser reality, then, in that he alone exists eternally and of necessity, and his existence encompasses the fullness of all value and perfection entirely within itself. Any and all other existence, goodness, perfection, power, holiness, beauty, or whatever value one might mention, is strictly derivative in nature, coming from the eternal God who alone has all such perfection infinitely and intrinsically. The question of Paul to the Corinthians, "What do you have that you did not receive?" (1 Cor. 4:7), is appropriate in regard to all finite beings. The thought that somehow we frail creatures of his making may somehow contribute value to or fill some void within the divine nature is utterly abhorrent to biblical thought. God stands supreme and above all as the one who exists in his infinite fullness, independent of all. And our finite existence bears testimony, not to any human capacity to be anything in itself, much less to some supposed ability to add anything to God, but only to God's gracious will in creating out of nothing all that is and granting to all his creation each and every quality it possesses (cf. James 1:17).

The doctrine of process theologians and others, whereby God is understood as the eminent recipient of value apprehended from the world, is here utterly rejected. Surely one may wish to imagine that God so benefits intrinsically from human existence and activity, but the self-revelation of God, as given in Holy Scripture, simply will not bear this out. The fundamental (but misguided) religious intuition that underlies this unbiblical doctrine of the divine dependence is that, if God is viewed as self-sufficient and thus in no need whatever of humankind or other contingent

---

anything external to himself. No, God possesses every quality that there is, and he does so by his nature as God. There are no qualities or perfections that are not God's qualities or perfections, and every one of them, to their infinite fullness, is the eternal, intrinsic, and exclusive possession of God.

[12] Karl Barth, *Church Dogmatics*, ed. G. W. Bromiley and T. F. Torrance (Edinburgh: T. & T. Clark, 1956–1975), II/1. 560.

reality, then surely it must make no difference to God whether we exist at all or whether we are happy in our existence.

For example, Charles Hartshorne writes, "If God be in all aspects absolute, then literally it is 'all the same' to him, a matter of utter indifference, whether we do this or do that, whether we live or die, whether we joy or suffer. This is precisely not to be personal in any sense relevant to religion or ethics."[13] In another place, Hartshorne speaks of the essence of "true religion" as found "most essentially" in humans "contributing value to God which he would otherwise lack."[14] In other words, codependence marks the process view of the god-world relation: god depends on the world just as much as the world depends on god. Such is the perversion of God's true and eternal independent self-existence and self-sufficiency. Process theology's endeavor to secure our importance to God by making him dependent upon us for what he otherwise would lack comes at the cost of falsely ascribing to us capacities and abilities we simply do not have while denying of God the fullness of his own independent and eternal excellency. Making much of us (wrongly) results inevitably in belittling the glory of God.

IMPLICATIONS FROM THE DIVINE TRANSCENDENT SELF-SUFFICIENCY OF GOD FOR THE GLORY OF GOD

The implications of this discussion for God's glory should be apparent from our consideration of God's eternal and transcendent self-sufficiency. If, as Scripture supports over and again, God possesses within himself, intrinsically and eternally, every quality in infinite measure, one startling consequence should be clear: God alone possesses all that is qualitatively good (i.e., all perfections), and hence, all that is worthy of commendation, admiration, praise, honor, and worship. If it is true that we should honor only that which rightly is worthy of honor, and praise what truly is praiseworthy, and exalt what is highest and greatest so as to warrant the expression of such exaltation; and furthermore, if it is true that God

---

[13] Charles Hartshorne, *The Divine Relativity: A Social Conception of God* (New Haven, CT: Yale University Press, 1948), 143.
[14] Charles Hartshorne, "The Dipolar Conception of Deity," *Review of Metaphysics* 21 (1967): 274. The full statement surrounding this claim is worth noting. Hartshorne writes, "I take 'true religion' to mean serving God, by which I do not mean simply admiring or 'obeying' him, or enabling him to give benefits to me and other non-divine creatures, but also, and most essentially, contributing value to God which he would otherwise lack. Even in this religious case, to 'serve' is to confer a benefit, in precisely the sense that the served will to some extent depend upon the server for that benefit. This is genuine dependence."

alone possesses within himself, intrinsically, eternally, and infinitely every quality that is worthy of honor, and is praiseworthy, and is highest and greatest without qualification; then it follows that God alone is deserving of being the recipient of ultimate and highest glory and honor. Here, then, is ontological grounding for the ultimate glory of God above all else. Because of who God is, and who he is alone, he is exclusively worthy of the highest and greatest and the only ultimate praise that can rightly be expressed. Because he possesses the fullness of every quality, he alone deserves the fullness of rightful praise and honor. A right doctrine of God, then, undergirds and accounts rightly for the only ultimate glory, which belongs to God alone.

And we must be quick to add another corresponding yet sobering implication. Just as this doctrine is the ontological grounding for God's ultimate and maximal glory, it also serves as the ontological grounding for our dependence and humility before him. Discussions of humility often move directly and automatically to a focus on our sinfulness, depravity, and unworthiness as background for understanding better the grace of God shown to us in Christ—as if this were the only basis for Christian humility. While this focus on our sin and on God's gracious redemption in Christ is altogether appropriate, it needs to be seen that the first and more fundamental basis for our dependence on God rests not in his gracious redeeming work in Christ but in our being made creatures of the infinitely glorious and self-sufficient Creator. That is, before the ethical grounding of our humility in God's gracious redemption of us as sinners, the more fundamental grounding for our humility is ontological—it is grounded in God's unconstrained and freely chosen act (Rev. 4:11) to bring into existence those who are by nature and by necessity wholly dependent creatures.

As a human race, before we are sinners, we are creatures. And of course, after we are sinners, we are creatures. And as creatures, we depend upon God for all that we are, all that we have, and all that we will become. Just as there are no qualities that are not God's, possessed by him intrinsically, eternally, and infinitely, so there are no qualities we possess that are not his. His possession of the qualities that are his (which is every quality that there is, in infinite measure) is intrinsic; our possession of the few and limited qualities that are ours is derivative. Every true thought, every ounce of strength, every ability, every capacity, every moment of life—all is ours only as we have received these from him. As Paul put it, "he himself gives to all mankind life and breath and everything" (Acts 17:25). So, yes of course, our sinful state as background for God's gracious and merciful redemption in Christ is rightly a basis for our humility before God. But also, and in significant ways more fundamental, our humility is found in our identity as wholly dependent creatures before this glorious, eternal, and infinite, self-sufficient God. Andrew Murray provides a beautiful and illuminating expression of this truth in the opening chapter of his powerful treatment of humility:

> When God created the universe, it was with the one object of making the creature partaker of His perfection and blessedness, and so showing forth in it the glory of His love and wisdom and power. God wished to reveal Himself in and through created beings by communicating to them as much of His own goodness and glory as they were capable of receiving. But this communication was not a giving to the creature something which it could possess in itself, a certain life or goodness, of which it had the charge and disposal. By no means. But as God is the ever-living, ever-present, ever-acting One, who upholdeth all things by the word of His power, and in whom all things exist, the relation of the creature to God could only be one of unceasing, absolute, universal dependence. As truly as God by His power once created, so truly by that same power must God every moment maintain. The creature has not only to look back to the origin and first beginning of existence, and acknowledge that it there owes everything to God; its chief care, its highest virtue, its only happiness, now and through all eternity, is to present itself an empty vessel, in which God can dwell and manifest His power and goodness.
>
> The life God bestows is imparted not once for all but each moment continuously, by the unceasing operation of His mighty power. Humility, the place of entire dependence on God, is, from the very nature of things, the first duty and the highest virtue of the creature, and the root of every virtue.[15]

These twin truths—God is eternally and without qualification *independent* from all else as the exclusive possessor, within himself, infinitely

---
[15] Andrew Murray, *Humility* (Lexington, KY: Fig, 2012), 1–2.

and intrinsically, of all that is qualitatively good; whereas we are for the whole of our existence and without qualification entirely *dependent* upon God for our very existence along with any and every quality of that existence that marks our lives for now and for eternity—are central in understanding correctly the glory of God. The first truth, as we have seen, is foundational for comprehending why God alone is deserving of ultimate glory. Because everything worthy of praise and honor is his exclusive, eternal, and infinite possession, it follows that only he is deserving of ultimate glory. To put it simply, he ought to be glorified in the greatest and only ultimate sense precisely because he is intrinsically and infinitely glorious. That is, the self-sufficient being of God comprises his intrinsic and inexhaustible glory.

But second, it also follows that we owe to God alone the ascribing of glory to him above all else both because he alone deserves being so glorified, and because we owe to him everything that we are and have: no exception, and no qualification. We have, that is, a moral obligation to honor what is honorable and so to honor God, who alone is infinitely honorable, above all else; and we have a moral obligation to offer praise, thanksgiving, and glory to the one who has provided for us all that we are and possess. No doubt this is what Paul has in mind as he levels against sinful humanity this charge: "For although they knew God, they did not honor him as God or give thanks to him, but they became futile in their thinking, and their foolish hearts were darkened" (Rom. 1:21). Implied in this are these twin truths: God is deserving of all ultimate honor and glory, and we his creatures are morally obligated so to honor and glorify him. To fail to do so is at the heart of our sinful disregard, rebellion, and treason. God alone is deserving of all ultimate glory because he alone possesses all that is worthy of such glory. And God alone is deserving of all ultimate glory because we are indebted to him, and to him alone, for absolutely everything good that we are and have. Our rightful glorification of God above all is grounded in God's own intrinsic and transcendent being that is infinitely, eternally, and inexhaustibly glorious.

SELECT QUESTIONS AND ISSUES ARISING FROM GOD'S TRANSCENDENT SELF-SUFFICIENCY

Questions often arise at this point. First, some wonder, isn't God benefited and perhaps made more glorious by the glory we ascribe to him as his creatures? Isn't it the case that the glory of God couldn't be what it is without the creation, and particularly without creatures who give glory to him? To get at an answer to this, perhaps it will help to distinguish between the "glory of God" and the "glorification of God." The former, the glory of God, is absolute and infinite, and as such can admit no increase or decrease. The glory of God is his own intrinsic weightiness, worth, and value that is grounded in God being who he is, the self-sufficient possessor of all that is of eternal worth. In this sense, the glory of God is the God-ness of God. All that makes God who he eternally is provides the basis for God being infinitely glorious. Hence, this glory that is God's is absolute, and no creatures, or universes, or expressions of praise can either increase or diminish the infinite fullness of this glory.

The *glorification* of God, however, is a different matter. This involves two aspects: first, the revelation of God in physical, visible form such that something of his intrinsic character is shown forth and put on display; and second, the recognition of his revealed character and work that results in his creatures ascribing to him something of the worth and glory that is his. Both senses of glorification are contingent, it should be clear, on God's free choice to create a world, and to populate it with moral creatures whose capacities include an awareness of his divine character and work through creation.

Must God create? Absolutely not. This is one place where the distinction between the glory of God and the glorification of God becomes crucial. God is intrinsically glorious whether or not he creates, and whether or not he creates has no bearing on any supposed increase or decrease of the intrinsic glory that is his eternally. But for glorification to take place, it requires, as it were, that God go public; that is, he must manifest something of himself in some manner extrinsic to his own being, such that a revelation of God—his character and his work—is now brought into existence. Furthermore, for this glorification to find its fullest expression, he must create moral beings who have the God-given capacity to see and understand something of his character and work through the revelation of himself in the created order. So, while the glory of God is absolute and admits no degrees, the glorification of God admits degrees of expression in revelation and in recognition by God's moral creatures. It is only in this second sense, then, that we can rightly talk about giving to God the glory that he deserves or failing to glorify God as we ought.

Both the revelation of the glory of God and the recognition of the glory of God can vary, but the intrinsic glory that is God's is constant, eternal, infinite, and untouchable.

By way of illustration, consider a large windowless room that has within it one very large and bright light. This light is at the center of the room, and it is the only source of light that the room has. Now imagine next someone entering the room, holding a large mirror. With that mirror, the person holding it can reflect the light and shine its light to various places around the room, but one thing that the mirror cannot do is increase or decrease the actual light that is in the room. Now imagine a thousand such mirrors in this large room, all reflecting the brightness of this light, showing a great display of the light's brightness and beauty. Surely it is the case that the light would not be reflected in the ways that it is were it not for the presence of the mirrors. It is equally true that none of those mirrors, nor the totality of them taken together, can add one fragment of light to the room; nor can the mirrors diminish any amount of light that comes from the only source of light, in the center of the room, were they to be covered or removed from the room. On this last point, one might recall a memorable statement by C. S. Lewis: "A man can no more diminish God's glory by refusing to worship Him than a lunatic can put out the sun by scribbling the word 'darkness' on the walls of his cell."[16] Indeed, the glory that is God's is infinitely great and unalterable, whereas the glorification of God admits degrees of increase or decrease. Although creation affects the latter, it can in no way affect the former. God *is* glorious whether he create or not, whether he reveal himself or not, and whether his creatures ascribe to him the glory due him or not.

Second, how can God truly be personal and loving if he does not need the created order that he has made? If God doesn't need us or depend on us at all, doesn't this call into question whether he really cares about and loves us? There can be no doubt that God cares deeply and intimately for humankind. The full range of God's self-disclosure bears witness to this truth, and in particular the Father's gift of his Son to bear the sin of the world testifies in the greatest way possible to God's love for his creatures, even his sinful creatures. But does God's love for the world imply or entail some kind of divine dependence upon this world that he loves? Is it the case that *because* the true and living God is personal and intimately in-

---
[16] Lewis, *Problem of Pain*, 53.

volved in the world, this means that he must need us? The logic of this line of thinking is dangerously misleading. Simply put, the inference indicated here is a non sequitur. Surely, if a being were in fact utterly self-sufficient (as has been described above), then one might naturally wonder of what concern the world would be to him. After all, the world and all it contains can in no way benefit his inherent excellence, for indeed that excellence is infinite and hence eternally and intrinsically incorporating of all value and perfection. Admittedly, then, one might naturally be led to conclude that God is indifferent concerning the world, when it is first shown that he is absolutely self-sufficient. But while the conclusion of God's indifference may follow naturally from his self-sufficiency, it does not follow necessarily, nor does it follow rightly. In fact, the glorious reality is that God is both infinitely self-sufficient and lavishly loving.

So, how can this self-sufficient God love a world he doesn't need? And why, if we do not fulfill some deep need in God, did he choose and act to bring us into existence? The answer here is as glorious as it is humbling: although God doesn't need us, he loves us, and his purpose in creating and redeeming us is not that we might fill up some lack in him (for indeed, he has none!), but that he might fill us up with himself. He made us, his dependent and fallen people, empty to be filled with his fullness, thirsty to drink of the water of life, weak to receive his strength, foolish to be instructed and corrected by his wisdom. In his love, he longs to give, to share the bounty. He wants us to experience in finite measure the fullness of joy and blessing that he knows infinitely—all to redound to the praise and glory of his name, the Giver and Provider of all the good we enjoy. Recall again the statement quoted above from C. S. Lewis, that God's love is not like ours, helping another while needing also to be helped. No, God's love, says Lewis, is "bottomlessly selfless, by very definition; it has everything to give and nothing to receive."[17]

We reach a point in contemplating these truths where it is almost impossible for us finite and needy humans to comprehend the reality we know is there. God's love for us truly is unconditional, in the greatest sense possible. Precisely because God is self-sufficient, it is impossible for him to receive something that he lacks. He lacks nothing! We cannot contribute to God something that he needs. He needs nothing! So, should we conclude that God must not love us, then? Absolutely not! Instead, we

---
[17] Ibid., 50.

realize that God's love has nothing at all to do with what he gains, but rather with what he has to give. Our reason for being, in short, is to be a recipient of all that God has for us, and what he has for us is principally himself. God has created and redeemed us in order that we might know him (Isa. 11:9; Jer. 9:23–24)—to receive from his infinite fullness the holiness, wisdom, and goodness that are his. Created to be loved by one who needs none of what we supposedly can give him—this is at the heart of a correct understanding of both God and us, and it shows why God alone is deserving of ultimate glory.

Third, if God is self-sufficient and doesn't need us or anything that we have to offer, why does he demand our obedience to him? Although much more could be said, here is the core of the answer: Because he loves us and wants our best, and because he knows that our only true joy is found when we follow in his ways, he demands (yes, demands!) that we obey him. His commandments lead us to life. That is, his demands are given as from a Lover. C. S. Lewis comments concerning the commandments of God, "Those divine demands, which sound to our natural ears most like those of a despot and least like those of a lover, in fact marshal us where we should want to go if we knew what we wanted."[18] Ah, yes! If we truly knew and believed that his commands are demands of life and joy and fulfillment, we would follow them. Our sinful tendency, though, is to think that only if *we* decide how we should live can we truly enter into a life of satisfaction and joy. But God knows better. His ways are always best, and his commandments always lead to life. So, in his love for us he calls us, commands us, to follow his ways and enter into the only true and lasting joy there is.

Fourth and finally, why does God enlist our service when, as self-sufficient, he is not "served by human hands, as though he needed anything" (Acts 17:25)? Yet Psalm 100:2 commands us to serve the Lord with gladness! So, how can we reconcile these two passages? Or, how can we serve the God who cannot be served? God doesn't need our service (Acts 17:25), so his call for us to serve (Ps. 100:2) is a call to *participate in the privilege and joy of the ministry of grace* that flows *from* him, *into* us, and then *through* us into the lives of others. We can take no credit. All we have is a gift from him, and he gives us what we have to be used in service to others. God is so sharing! He is so generous! Rather than just

---
[18] Ibid., 52.

doing the work unilaterally, he devises a plan by which he intends that some of his work be done in and through others, by calling and equipping and using them. We have absolutely no basis for boasting, before God or others. Human pride is utterly shattered; it is devastated when we understand in the depths of our souls the infinite and intrinsic fullness that is God's alone for all eternity. It not only is not about us; it is not of us, or from us, or because of us! All that we are—every quality that we possess; all that we have—every good and worthwhile characteristic; and all that we can do—every ability, both in its kind and in its degree—all are gifts to us from God. We simply cannot rightfully take credit for anything we ever are or ever do. All glory, in short, belongs exclusively with God!

CONCLUSION

Why should God alone receive ultimate, final, and exclusive glory? In light of what we've seen, consider these three summary answers: (1) It is our *highest duty* to glorify God, for *in him alone* is the fullness of infinite perfection (see Isa. 42:8; 1 Cor. 10:31). (2) It is our *greatest delight* to glorify God, for *from him alone* do we receive the fullness of everlasting joy and satisfaction (see Isa. 55:1–3; John 15:11). (3) It is our *ultimate destiny* to glorify God, for *to him alone* are we drawn to know the intimacy of his glorious presence (see Isa. 11:9; John 17:24).

The glory of God in the doctrine of God is grounded, then, in the transcendent excellency and self-sufficiency of God. Only when we understand more of the fullness of his glorious independence from this world that he has made can we begin to comprehend rightly how amazing it is that he loves and cares for what he has created. He is in himself the God of glory, and because of this we owe to him the glory due his name. May God be pleased to enable his people more fully to understand his greatness as the basis for marveling afresh at his grace; his majesty to see more profoundly his mercy; his fullness to marvel more humbly at his forgiveness. He is the God of glory. May our lives be lived to see his glory made known more broadly and magnified more deeply.

7

The Doctrine of the Trinity: Consistent and Coherent

KEITH E. YANDELL

PREFACE

John Feinberg's massive (887 small-print but readable pages), impressive *No One Like Him*[1] challenges the traditional doctrines that the Father eternally begets the Son, and that the Holy Spirit eternally proceeds from the Father (Eastern church), or from the Father and the Son (Western church). In addition, he holds that the biblical God is temporal—not timelessly eternal (i.e., having no temporal properties, and so existing *at* no time) but everlasting (i.e., existing at every time). Both are significant departures from the majority tradition. Thus we read,

> ... *in regard to relations within the ontological or immanent Trinity, the church historically has affirmed that the Son is eternally generated and the Spirit eternally proceeds. Despite their firm entrenchment in both Western and Eastern traditions, the doctrines of eternal generation and eternal procession are unclear and are not required by Scripture. In saying this I part company with a host of theologians throughout church history.* . . . Despite the firm hold of

[1] John S. Feinberg, *No One Like Him: The Doctrine of God*, Foundations of Evangelical Theology, John S. Feinberg, gen. ed. (Wheaton, IL: Crossway, 2001).

these doctrines within the Christian tradition, we must see what they mean and whether Scripture warrants them.[2]

INTRODUCTION

There are two parts to this essay. Part One concerns the question as to what role, if any, the terms *begotten by* and *proceeding from* properly play in understanding the *metaphysics* of the Trinity. Feinberg presents strong linguistic-exegetical reasons for not accepting the traditional metaphysics-of-the-immanent-Trinity uses of these terms. He adds philosophical considerations as well, but does so very briefly. I will briefly present his linguistic-exegetical case, and explore his philosophical and theological criticisms of begetting and proceeding, taken as intra-Trinitarian essential relations. Part Two discusses one way of making intra-Trinitarian distinctions in a manner that is not self-contradictory[3] without appeal to begetting and proceeding.

PART ONE: BEGETTING AND PROCEEDING
Exegetical-Linguistic

Feinberg reviews the salient passages that are proposed as sources of the begetting doctrine. The passages discussed include Proverbs 8:22–25, where Wisdom is personified and we are told that God created Wisdom:

> The LORD brought me forth as the first of his works, before his deeds of old; . . . at the very beginning, when the world came to be. (vv. 22–23, NIV)

I take it that the alternatives are that the author is not speaking of Jesus (a genuine possibility), that the passage is saying that Jesus was created (older than the hills, but finitely so), that what is personified is God's property of having wisdom, or (compatibly with the most recent possibility) that the passage should be translated "The LORD possessed me at the beginning of His work"—an NIV alternative reading. On the first reading, that passage is irrelevant to our discussion. The second alternative

---
[2] Ibid., 488–489 (emphasis his).
[3] I take the notion of relative identity to be mistaken; I contend that there necessarily is no such thing as relative metaphysical identity. Thus I have not appealed to it as a way of arguing for the logical consistency of Trinitarian doctrine. If it turned out that the notion of relative identity is consistent, and can be used in defending the doctrine of the Trinity, that obviously would not be anything against my claim that the doctrine of the Trinity is not contradictory.

requires the begetting of the Son (if "Wisdom" refers to the Son) as an early, perhaps the first, created being. At that point, begetting is a lot like human begetting, and the "begotten, not made" distinction is rejected. Neither the third nor the fourth alternatives provides any support for the begetting doctrine.

Another verse seems more promising—Psalm 2:7: "Thou art my Son; this day have I begotten Thee" (KJV). The New Testament quotes this passage in Acts 13:32–33 with reference to the resurrection, connecting it to the claim that "God raised him [Jesus] from the dead so that he will never be subject to decay" (v. 34, NIV), adding that this fulfills a promise made by God to David. Hebrews 1:1–5 also quotes Psalm 2:7; it says that God made the universe through his Son, who is greater than the angels, and that the Son is the exact representation of the Father's being. It says of the Son (Heb. 1:3) that having made "purification for sins, he sat down at the right hand of the Majesty on high," thus relating Psalm 2:7 to the incarnation and glorification. Hebrews 5:4–6 quotes Psalm 2:7 in the context of referring to his days on earth (Heb. 5:7) and relating the passage to Jesus becoming a High Priest. These passages link Psalm 2:7 with incarnation, resurrection, and glorification—not eternal begetting. As to John 3:16's "only begotten Son," Feinberg remarks that recent linguistic work has indicated that the words translated "only begotten" are better translated as "unique" or "one of a kind."[4]

Hebrews 11:17 can be rendered "only begotten" regarding the relationship between Abraham and Isaac, but then it is mistaken, since Ishmael was also Abraham's son; Isaac was the unique son through whom God's promise was kept. In Colossians 1:15, Jesus is referred to as "the firstborn of all creation," but the passage can also be translated "preeminent," and the same verb as found in Colossians 1:15 is used in Luke 2:7 in reference to the incarnation. In Revelation 1:5 we have Jesus as "the firstborn of the dead" in a passage that refers to resurrection, and Romans 8:29 refers to the resurrection of Jesus as the "firstborn among many brothers" in a context referring to his soteriological role. So while "begotten" appears in the translation of a variety of passages, none provide any secure grounding for eternal begetting.

As to the procession of the Holy Spirit, Feinberg suggests that the

---
[4] Feinberg, *No One Like Him*, 490.

salient passage is John 15:26, in which Jesus is reported as promising to send the Holy Spirit, who will proceed from the Father. The obvious connection is with Pentecost, not with the eternal procession of the Spirit.

Theological-Philosophical

Feinberg's theological-philosophical critique of the begetting and proceeding doctrines seems to rely on his view that God is everlasting and hence temporal. This is a highly controversial view, as of course is its denial.

Meaning of the Doctrines

Feinberg asks what the begetting and proceeding doctrines mean. This is fully understandable. The "begotten, not [created or] made" distinction does not burn with bright clarity. Human begetting is making, and its result is made. What, then, can "begetting" mean when creating and making are removed? Nor is it obvious what "proceeding" means in this context. In contrast, if applied to Bethlehem and Pentecost, these terms have clear senses. Regarding "begetting" Feinberg writes,

> Eternal generation of the Son is said to mean that the Father communicates the divine essence to the Son. To communicate the essence is to share it in common. . . . Moreover, since Christ is eternal and *has always existed*, we must say that this generating *has been happening as long as God has existed*, which is forever, and it never began to happen. But think of what is being proposed, and one can see that this makes little sense. If Christ does not begin to receive the divine essence because as divine *he always exists as God*, i.e., *he has always had* the divine essence, how does it make sense to speak of the Father making in common with him something *he has always had anyway?* . . . Christ cannot get something he already has, nor does it make sense to say this receiving *has been happening* for all eternity. If we are told that this is a mystery, the proper response seems to be that this is not mystery, but nonsense and confusion.
>
> The same line of explanation is given for the Holy Spirit's eternal procession, and it is just as problematic as eternal generation of the Son for the same sort of reasons.[5]

---
[5] Ibid., 489 (emphasis mine).

I am in complete sympathy with Feinberg's unwillingness to sweep contradictions under a cognitive carpet. But I am not convinced that the criticism offered here is decisive. It seems to rest on the view that God is everlasting (i.e., exists at all times) rather than timelessly eternal (i.e., existing, but at no time). His language concerning the Son "always" having the divine essence and his saying that it makes no sense for the Father to be "making common with him [the Son] what he [the Son] has already" makes this clear. I do not disagree with this view, though as he knows, it is controversial, and he argues in detail for it. My concern lies with something else.

The core of the objection seems to be this: In the present dispute, both those who accept and those who reject eternal generation of the Son agree that the Son is not a creature, and therefore was not created. (Being created, after all, is what makes something a creature.) There was no time at which the Son was not, or was not divine. On the eternal generation view, the Son always (better, timelessly) is included in the Trinity. But then the Son "already has" full deity and has no need to be given it by the Father. Again, "how does it make sense to speak of the Father making in common with him [the Son] something he [the Son] has always had anyway?" If the Son is always (better, timelessly) divine, then not even the Father can make the Son be what the Son "always" is.

Alternatively, the objection can be put in these terms: There is no condition of the Son in which the Son is not fully divine; therefore there is no opportunity for the Father to share the Father's divinity with the Son. That would involve the Father sharing with the Son what the Son has entirely independent of any Fatherly sharing. The view under critique is,

1. The Father shares his divinity with the Son (very roughly, passes divinity on to the Son without relinquishing his own divinity), and does so eternally.

For those who hold that God is everlasting, existing at all times rather than none, the analogous view would be,

2. The Father shares his divinity with the Son (very roughly, passes divinity on to the Son without relinquishing his own divinity), and does so everlastingly.

The problem with the criticism offered above is that the truth of neither (1) nor (2) requires that there be a condition in which the Son lacks divinity and a condition in which, through Fatherly sharing of it, the Son has divinity.

In regard to the eternal procession of the Holy Spirit, Feinberg argues, "The same line of explanation is given for the Holy Spirit's eternal procession, and it is just as problematic as eternal generation of the Son for the same sort of reasons. The Holy Spirit cannot be given what he already possesses, nor does it help to say he has been receiving it for all eternity."[6] I take it that the idea again is that, if there is no condition in which the Holy Spirit is not divine, then he cannot be made divine—i.e., he cannot be given a nature that He "already has." The problem with this criticism is that it is exactly parallel to the criticism of eternal begetting.

The problem is that another way of understanding both "begetting" and "proceeding" is available, namely "emanating," understood as follows:

> Y emanates from X if and only if X has a property, or is in a state, or engages in an activity, such that X having that property, being in that state, or engaging in that activity (or some combination thereof) is a sufficient condition of the existence of Y, and X having that property, being in that state, or engaging in that activity (or some combination thereof) is an essential feature of X.

My suggestion is that we can replace (1) by,

> (1*) The Father emanates divinity to the Son, thereby grounding the Son's divinity without relinquishing his own divinity, and does so eternally.

This gives us an account of eternal begetting, where begetting = emanating. We can also replace (2) by,

> (2*) The Father emanates divinity to the Son, thereby grounding the Son's divinity without relinquishing his own divinity, and does so everlastingly.

This gives us an account of everlasting begetting, where begetting = emanating.

---

[6] Ibid.

Similarly, we can have,

(1**) The Father emanates divinity to the Holy Spirit, thereby grounding the Holy Spirit's divinity without relinquishing his own divinity, and does so eternally.

And we can have,

(2**) The Father emanates divinity to the Holy Spirit, thereby grounding the Holy Spirit's divinity without relinquishing His own divinity, and does so everlastingly.

Thus we have an account of eternal procession and everlasting procession, where proceeding = emanating. (I leave distinguishing the case of emanation of the Son and the case of emanation of the Holy Spirit to others. I can imagine the Western view claiming an advantage here over the Eastern.)

Given this much, it follows that the eternal procession view can be understood as the claim that *the Holy Spirit having the property of being divine*, just as *the Son having the property of being divine*, is due to something asymmetrically true—true of the Father but not true of them. There is some sort of "sharing," namely emanating, in virtue of which this is so. None of this is to say that I think that either the eternal begetting or the eternal procession doctrine, even as emanation, is in order. Feinberg's discussion of the passages that supposedly teach these doctrines, so far as I can see, stands concerning an emanation account as well. There is further philosophical-theological criticism of the doctrines, read as including emanating, as follows.

I have suggested that the notion of *being begotten by* can be understood as expressing an eternal, or an everlasting, intra-Trinitarian emanation relation between the Father and the Son. It is a claim concerning the immanent Trinity. Similarly, the notion of *proceeding from*, taken as a metaphysical concept, can be understood as another version of the notion of emanation, this time (on one reading) a relation between the Father and the Son on the one hand, and the Holy Spirit on the other; or (on another reading) as an emanation relation between the Father and the Holy Spirit. Emanation of the Son occurs because the Father has an essential feature that entails the Son's existence—has an essential quality, or necessarily is in a state, or necessarily engages in an activity, such that his having that quality, being in that state, or engaging in that activity (or some combination thereof) is necessary and sufficient for the existence of the Son. The Father and the Son each have, or just the Father has, as an essential feature having a quality, or being in a state, or engaging in an activity, such that their, or his, having that quality, or being in that state, or engaging in that activity (or some combination of both) is necessary and sufficient for the existence of the Holy Spirit.

Since the existence of the Father entails the existence of the Son (or, if you prefer the more clearly metaphysical terms, emanates the existence of the Son), were the Son not to exist, neither would the Father exist.[7] So while emanation is asymmetrical, existential dependence is symmetrical. Since (1) the existence of the Father and the existence of the Son, or (2) the existence of the Father, entails the existence of the Holy Spirit—or, if you prefer the more clearly metaphysical terms, since the Spirit emanates from both or one—were the Holy Spirit not to exist, neither would the Father exist (on either the Western or the Eastern account), nor (on the Western account) would the Son exist. So again there is emanational asymmetry, but also a symmetry of existential dependence.

To repeat, in the case of both being begotten and proceeding from, there is an asymmetry that entails a symmetry. The begetter begets the begotten, and not conversely. The one who proceeds does so in consequence of the one who produces the proceeding, and not conversely. But since begetting the Son is an essential feature of the Father, and losing an essential feature is tantamount to not existing, were the Son not to exist, neither would the Father. Since producing the proceeding of the Holy Spirit is an essential feature of the Father, were the Holy Spirit not to exist, for the same reason as in the above case, the Son would not exist. Similarly, if the Son also has producing the proceeding of the Holy Spirit as an essential feature, were the Holy Spirit not to exist, neither would the Son exist. There is, so to speak, one direction of emanation but two (mutual) directions of ontological dependence. Note that these doctrines entail that the Father has an essential property that the Son lacks (begetting the Son), and an essential property that the Holy Spirit lacks (producing the procession of the Holy Spirit). The Son has an essential property that the Father and the Holy Spirit lack (being begotten). The Holy Spirit has an essential property that neither the Father nor the Son has (being

---
[7] If P entails Q, then not-Q entails not-P.

produced by procession). This at least binds the Trinitarian members tightly together, but not every way of developing that result is proper.

How this affects the view that each person of the Godhead shares the same nature is something for reflection. One way to handle it is to define the divine nature in terms of properties like omnipotence, omniscience, and omnipresence and treat them as properties had by each Trinitarian person. Then the properties not shared—the ones noted in the last paragraph—are properties essential only to each disparate Trinitarian member who has them. But having different conditions of existence, in terms of the existence of what you must emanate and the difference of by whom you must be emanated, looks very much like a distinctness that yields a difference in essence. It is in the Father's essence to emanate the Son and the Spirit. It is in the Son's essence to be emanated from the Father, and in the Spirit's essence to be emanated from the Father (or the Father and the Son). So the Trinitarian persons have different essences.

In order to avoid this, one might explore the notion of a property that something necessarily has but which is not part of its essence. There are properties such that to exist at all requires their possession—properties such as *being self-identical* or *having properties*. There are also properties such as *being different from the number thirteen*, which is essential to everything but the number thirteen (call these *properties necessarily had by all things but one*). Essential properties typically are taken to be kind-defining properties, and the latter sort of properties are not kind-defining. One could distinguish between a thing's *broad essence* (which contains its kind-defining properties, its existence-entailed properties, and its necessarily-had-by-all-things-but-one properties) and its *narrow essence* (which contains only its kind-defining properties). But none of this gerrymandering prevents the members of the Trinity from having different essences on the begetting and proceeding (as emanations) stories. Asymmetrical emanation relations are not trumped by symmetrical dependence relations in term of canceling out sufficient grounds for essential differences.

It is sometimes held, in contemporary philosophy, that the conditions of origin of an item are essential to that item: if X came to be in a certain manner, *it*—that very thing—could not have come to be in any other manner. This seems obviously false: if a machine is made of a set of parts, it can be true that the same machine would exist were it put together by a worker or a machine, the parts put together in one order rather than another (assuming more than one order would work), and so on. "In any other *manner*" is imprecise. (To be fair, this doctrine is probably most appealed to regarding organisms, and is perhaps most plausible on a materialist view.) I do not appeal to that doctrine here. I mention it to distinguish it from another view. On the emanation account, the Father has no origin at all, and the Son and the Holy Spirit do have origins. "Origin" here does not mean "conditions of first existence" since there is no first or beginning of existence in question. It means "source of existence." If I may so put the point, the Father is by nature an Emanator and the Son and the Holy Spirit are Emanatees. That, I suggest, is an essential difference.

PART TWO: ONE AND THREE

Oneness

If we come to the doctrine of the Trinity from Greek metaphysics, the obvious basic concept or category under which God falls is that of substance. God is not a quality, quantity, relation, place, time, position, state (condition), action, or passivity. The problem we then face is this: is God a simple or a complex substance? A complex substance is composed of simple substances, in this case three of them if God is composite. But a substance can exist on its own, without ontological company. So if God is a composite substance, then God in principle is decomposable into three simple substances. If God is a simple substance, what is God three of? Not substances, but then what? Not qualities, quantities, relations, places, times, positions, states, actions, or passivities. So it seems that either you have a non-Trinitarian monotheism or a triadic polytheism, neither Christianly satisfactory. Of course a Christian theologian can get creative here and propose that God is made up of relations, but the idea of relations without relata is wonderfully unpromising, and God cannot be composed simply of relations. The other available categories are equally unsuitable, so non-Trinitarian monotheism seems the proper route for the Christian theologian to take—at least then she is a monotheist and escapes polytheism. For Judaism and Islam, this is fine. But for Christianity it is not. One reason is that the Christian economy of salvation is at least inherently binitarian. However exactly it is conceived in detail, it is transactional between a human Jesus and a divine Father. But the human Jesus must not be merely human; he must also be divine, and Jesus is not numerically identical to the Father. This leads directly to a problem which can be stated very simply:

1. There is exactly one God.
2. The Father is God.
3. Jesus (the Son of God incarnate) is God.
4. The Father is not numerically identical to Jesus.

The problem is that the set of propositions 1–4 is flatly contradictory. There is no mystery to appeal to here. The conjunction of 1–4 is formally contradictory, as is this set:

(1*) There is exactly one frog.
(2*) Timmy is a frog.
(3*) Jimmy is a frog.
(4*) Timmy is not numerically identical to Jimmy.

We can change things as follows:

(1a*) There is exactly one frogness.
(2a*) Timmy exhibits frogness.
(3a*) Jimmy exhibits frogness.
(4a*) Timmy is not numerically identical to Jimmy.

"Frogness" is the set of properties possession of which is necessary and sufficient to make you a frog. Any number of things can have frogness, so there being two frogs is fine.

Thus this strategy suggests itself:

(1a) There is exactly one divineness.
(2a) The Father exhibits divineness.
(3a) Jesus (the Son of God incarnate) exhibits divineness.
(4a) The Father is not numerically identical to the Son.

"Divineness" is the set of properties possession of which is necessary and sufficient to make one divine. But can any number of things have divineness and thus there be no problem with there being two divinities? The standard classical way of viewing things is that God does not belong to a kind, so *exhibiting divineness* cannot define a kind. But as far as I can see, it is better to say that God belongs to a kind that is necessarily one-membered, thereby giving up the claim that, *Necessarily, if K is a kind, then K can have more than one member*. But whether or not God belongs to a necessarily no-more-than-one-membered kind, having as many as two beings exhibiting divineness is problematic. The problem is not solved.

We need a different approach. Social Trinitarian theories endeavor to secure Trinitarian unity in their view by taking the idea of mutual indwelling—perichoresis—into account. This idea is not the most lucid in the history of human thought, and it tends to be understood in psychological terms—full mutual awareness of the mental states of one Trinitarian person by another, deep mutual love and understanding, unity of purpose and practice, and the like. The problem is that no psychological linkage is sufficient to yield sufficiently strong unity—to provide adequate "oneness." The obvious next move is to ask what relationship brings the most impermeable unity, short of numerical identity, which will leave no room for multiplicity of persons. We need distinctness without separability.

The proper move seems fairly simple, and can be explained as follows. Consider the series 1, 2, 3 and be a realist about numbers—a view embraced by various mathematicians and philosophers—on which view numbers are abstract objects enjoying mind-independent existence. Numerals are, but numbers are not, creatures of our own making. Numbers (or things into which they can be analyzed) are denizens of the real world, abstract objects as real as rocks and rivers, though less obvious to us. On this realist view of numbers (substitute sets, propositions, states of affairs, or the like, if you wish), each exists necessarily (in every possible way the world might be). No world could exist without 1, 2, and 3 belonging in it. But 1 is not numerically identical to 2, or 2 to 3, or 3 to 1. The existence of each entails the existence of all.

This can be put formally. Propositions are the items that are true or false, are believed or disbelieved, bear logical relations to one another, and are asserted by the typical use of declarative sentences. One proposition P entails another proposition Q if and only if to assert P and deny Q produces a logical contradiction. For example, that there are four chairs in the room entails that there are at least three chairs in the room.

If the existence of some item X entails the existence of some item Y, it is not possible that X exists and Y does not exist.[8] If the existence of

---
[8] For purists, that item X exists entails that item Y exists if and only if the proposition *X exists* entails the proposition *Y exists*.

some item X entails, and is entailed by, the existence of some item Y, then it is not possible that either exists without the other. We can express this latter relationship between X and Y by saying that they form *a logically inseparable pair*. Of course there can be items X, Y, and Z so related that the existence of any one of them entails the existence of the other two. We can call this *a logically inseparable triad*. Our first step in building a model for the metaphysical structure of the Trinity is to claim that the members of the Trinity form a logically inseparable triad. The members of a logically inseparable triad are numerically distinct from one another but none can exist without both of the others existing. Numerical distinctness gives us Trinitarian diversity, and logical inseparability gives us Trinitarian unity. So we have a promising beginning.

A further question concerns what it is in virtue of which the members of the logically inseparable triad differ, one from another. This raises the philosophical issue of individuation between individuals. In particular, it raises the question of individuation of primitive or basic individuals. If there are X's that are made up of Y's, then one X differs from another if one X is made up of different Y's than those that compose the other X. Then you have the question as to what individuates one Y from another.

Threeness

The next step involves considering how the members of the logically inseparable triad can be distinct. It is metaphysical individuation that is relevant here, not epistemological. A principle of epistemological individuation proposes a criterion that one can apply in order to distinguish between two things. A principle of metaphysical individuation proposes a way in which two things are distinct, whether or not we can distinguish them by reference to it. The two sorts of principles are quite different, though it is surprising how often they are confused. For example, suppose it is true that we can distinguish between the members of the Trinity in this fashion: the second person of the Trinity is the one who became incarnate, and the third person of the Trinity is the one who came at Pentecost, and the first person of the Trinity is the one who sent the second and the third. This would provide an epistemological criterion for distinguishing among the members of the Trinity. It does not follow that it provides a metaphysical identity criterion.

Two principles of metaphysical individuation are easily identified:

P1. Items x and y are distinct if it is possible that one exist and the other not exist.

P2. Items x and y are distinct if it is possible that one has a property that the other lacks.

The first criterion obviously will not be helpful in providing individuation between the members of a logically inseparable triad; it is that very inapplicability in virtue of which Trinitarian unity satisfies the "only one God" requirement. The second criterion seems more promising.

If one wishes to ground Trinitarian individuation in an application of P2, one needs an account of what is meant by "property." One sensible suggestion is that a property is either a quality or a relation. Accepting that suggestion, and assuming relations are grounded in nonrelational properties, we are left with qualities. Qualities are features of a thing expressible in one-place predicates, to use a standard philosophical phrase; more simply, a quality is a nonrelational property. But focus on qualities does not take us to our goal. That one Trinitarian member becomes incarnate presupposes a distinction it does not explain; similarly for coming at Pentecost.

One familiar doctrine concerning properties is that they are abstract objects—items that are eternal or everlasting, nonspatial, noncausal, without life, mind-independent, and the entities instantiation of which, or exemplification of which, or participation in which, makes concrete things possessors of qualities. So round things instantiate (abstract) roundness and hot things exemplify (abstract) hotness. Various arguments, some from philosophy of language, some from metaphysics, are offered in support of this view. It is not my purpose here to defend or attack it, but merely to note that this is one view of the nature of properties. Leibniz famously offered the Principle of the Identity of Indiscernibles, which we can state as,

> For any items X and Y, and property P, if X has P if and only if Y has P, then X is numerically identical to Y.

But suppose God creates two unnamed angels at the same time. They (let us suppose) are not embodied (and hence have no spatial properties). Once created, they will always be conserved in existence. So there is no question of their being distinct in virtue of a difference in temporal or spatial qualities. Further, every thought that one has, the other also has; they are equally intelligent, have the same knowledge content, the same causal powers, and neither ever brings about any events in the immaterial or material world. They (by fiat) instantiate the same (abstract) properties and satisfy the same descriptions. But they are distinct conscious and self-aware beings. Why not?

One account of how this may be possible appeals to haecceities. A haecceity is an individual nature, say *Barack-Obamaness* or *Socratiety*—necessarily one-owned-if-owned-at-all. A haecceity can be large—Leibniz thought every property a thing has is essential to it and makes it a distinct individual if the Identity of Indiscernibles is true. The "two angels" scenario challenges its truth. Alternatively, a haecceity can be small—*being Socrates*, or *being the only person who is aware of being Socrates*. This is not challenged by the "two angels" scenario. Fans of haecceities can ascribe to each Trinitarian member its own individual essence, and then propose this as grounding three-ness. Whether there are such essences is controversial—that is, it is a philosophical thesis that there are (or are not). If this is sufficient, well and good. But perhaps it is not.

Here is another view of properties. Consider a pencil. It is yellow, as are lots of other things. But its yellow is a distinct property from any other yellow. There is (we shall assume) no (abstract) yellow it instantiates or exemplifies, or in which it participates. If its yellow is removed and replaced by red, it now has its own redness. If its redness is removed and replaced by yellow, its old yellow does not return; it has passed away and will not be made new. I will be philosophically extravagant and assume that the pencil endures throughout this simple process. It can exist without any of the particular color properties it has. Those particular properties cannot exist without it. I think this is what is meant by a substance being "prior to" its properties. It cannot exist without its having properties, but its properties cannot exist without being *its* properties, whereas it could exist having other properties. The pencil could become purple, and then its yellow would cease to be and its purple would depend for its existence on its being had by that pencil and no other. (Other purple pencils are its color twins, not co-owners of its color.) Each property of X exists only if X has it—the property is uniquely embedded in that which bears it. Properties are concrete and uniquely embedded. The fundamental bottom line of metaphysical individuation of properties is *that to which it belongs.* It is ownership that ultimately matters. (This does not require the doctrine of bare particulars.) Individuation must end somewhere, and my proposal is (roughly) that it ends with substances-with-uniquely-embedded-properties.

This view does not deny that things have essences. Descartes, for example, held that being conscious is essential to your being a mind. He did not add that you must always be conscious in the same way. You could be thinking of your own existence, listening to George Jones singing "He Stopped Loving Her Today," fretting over the Celtics' mediocrity, and so on—just so you were conscious in some manner or other, so long as the candle of your awareness glowed just a little. It does not follow that there is a consciousness of which each conscious state is an instance. All there is here (on the view at hand) is that these conscious states resemble one another in a manner perhaps analyzable and perhaps not. So we are now back to instantiation.

Add, then, that the ultimate entities are substances-with-uniquely-embedded-properties. This is (almost) where ultimate metaphysical individuation lies. To remove the "almost": the fundamental entities are *substance-with-its-embedded-properties* and *logically-inseparable-triad*. (If there are good reasons to think that these are logically inseparable units of two, four, or more, they are welcome too.) The units in a logically inseparable triad are property bearers—bearers of embedded properties—that are numerically distinct. The existence of any one entails that of the others. Not every property bearer is a substance. The category of irreducible entities contains both simple substances and logically inseparable triads of property bearers. Complex substances are composed of simple substances and can be decomposed into these substances. Simple substances do not encompass numerically distinct property bearers. So the Trinity cannot be a simple or a complex substance. Like substances, property bearers that are not substances cannot be decomposed into their properties—they are not merely collections of properties. Property bearers that are so related as to form a logically inseparable triad, then, are neither simple nor composite substances, nor are the inseparables made up of the properties that they have. (The "is" of predication cannot be reduced to the "is" of identity or the "is" of composition.)

So—says the current proposal—the Trinity is a logically inseparable triad that is triadic in virtue of there being three numerically distinct property bearers, all of whose properties are embedded properties. The notion of a property bearer is not fully analyzable into the notions of simple or complex substances. It covers both but is broader than the traditional concept of a substance. The notion of a logically inseparable triad has more promise than the traditional notion of a substance for the purpose of expressing Trinitarian doctrine. Obviously lots more remains to be said on this topic. The properties that are embedded must be the right ones for God to have. Completing the account of the metaphysics of the Trinity within this framework cannot be provided here. So I can only suggest here that I think that filling out this bare-bones metaphysical structure is worthwhile and promising. One of its advantages is that, on it, there is no eternal begetting or proceeding.

8

By What Authority Do We Say These Things? Enlightenment Dualism and the Modern Rejection of Biblical Authority

JOHN DOUGLAS MORRISON

"Hath God said . . . ?" Did God actually say these things to you? Cloaked in the forms of inquiry, this deceptive attack by the Tempter, early in the Genesis narrative of human creation and the fall, has real and destructive power. Matthew and Luke parallel the Genesis passage by describing how the Second Adam, Jesus, faced the Tempter, not in the garden but in the arid, desolate wilderness, and there the question was essentially the same: "Hath God said . . . ?" The Christian faith has always faced, and continues to face, many and highly varied forms of attack, but in most cases, one way or another, the force and edge of such has been the antagonistic and often vehement denial of any notion of the absolute lordship of the triune God, and so of any assertion of the authoritative self-revelation of the covenant God of Abraham, Isaac, and Jacob—of Yahweh, supremely revealed in Jesus Christ, and, thereby, by the Holy Spirit, in Holy Scripture.

THE CENTRALITY OF THE DIVINE AUTHORITY OF HOLY SCRIPTURE

The authority, the divine authority of Holy Scripture, is *a*, if not *the* "first order" issue in any proper doctrine of Scripture—yes, even before inerrancy. This no doubt surprises some and concerns others—is this a denial or a playing down of the importance of the truthfulness of Scripture? Not at all. I am simply putting inerrancy in its proper place and order within God's redemptive-kingdom purposes, and so within the *larger* "faith . . . once for all delivered to the saints" (Jude 3). As the late and much missed Carl F. H. Henry—among others—pointed out repeatedly and correctly, biblical authority is *the* central issue here, for it is *that* which *distinguishes* Scripture, and the gospel message therein, as the Word of God, the Word of God written, which will not return to God void. In, under, of, and from Christ, the Word made flesh, the written Word of God derivatively results from God's self-revelation and "inspiration," and so, by the dynamic, powerful, personal, and effective impulse, guidance, and superintendence of the Holy Spirit.[1] While there are surely many works—e.g., textbooks in arithmetic, mathematics, etc.—which are literally "inerrant," these do *not* as such set before us the *authoritative* Word of God. And often brothers or sisters in Christ who do in fact hold a high view of biblical authority, but who, for one reason or another, hold back from affirming full biblical truthfulness, can be best won to a proper inerrancy position regarding Scripture, not by our "beating" them with the inerrancy issue, but by means of the biblical authority which they already espouse at a significant level, but whose apparent implications they have not, perhaps, thought through thoroughly.

But taking this further, much of my argument herein reflects my deep concern that Christians understand, first, the clear fact that Western culture's zealous pursuit and worship of self—subjectivism—is a devastating consequence grounded in and from the destructive effects of prominent but false dualisms that were reinjected into modern Western thinking. This has often resulted in a strong, even violent, *rejection* of the authority of God as self-disclosed in Jesus Christ, and so also of the *divine authority* of Holy Scripture as the written Word of God. I must quickly prepare the reader for the fact that much of my discussion and analysis will be critical, i.e., clearing the ground by showing where, some three centuries ago,

---

[1] Carl F. H. Henry, *God, Revelation, and Authority: God Who Speaks and Shows*, vol. 4 (1979; repr., Wheaton, IL: Crossway, 1999), thesis 11.

Western culture in certain crucial domains went wrong, thinking contrary to the nature of things, etc. These modern shifts in Western thinking, before and especially from the seventeenth century on, have created, again, a supreme *crisis* for the classical or historical orthodox Christian understanding of divine authority—divine authority that is not only sovereign and faithful but also *historical*, and even *textual*. The reason for these shifts and the resulting crises are obviously manifold, but the late Scottish theologian Thomas Torrance was surely correct when he emphasized especially the widespread and deeply negative effects of the modern reintroduction, and the so-called postmodern extension, of cosmological and epistemological dualisms into Western culture as a whole, notably in the physical sciences, philosophy, and, thereby, into Christian theology.[2] In what immediately follows I will attempt, succinctly, to point toward the profoundly influential and destructive dualisms of René Descartes and his pantheistic disciple, Baruch Spinoza, but I will focus especially on the potent cosmological dualism of Isaac Newton, which conceptually "cut God off" from the world, and so from all direct spatiotemporal action and objective self-disclosure or revelation, *and* the epistemological dualism of Immanuel Kant ("Newton's philosopher") whereby real knowledge of reality in itself, and especially of God, became impossible for "pure reason."[3]

The effects of these two thinkers—a mathematician and a philosopher (who was very concerned with the sciences)—have variously and pervasively permeated and distorted modern and postmodern Christian theology and its understanding of the God-human and God-world relationships. Ever since "the Enlightenment," the destructive effects of this dualism, this disjunctive thinking, this "thinking apart" what ought to be thought *unitarily* together, has negatively affected every Christian doctrine, but most notably the classic Judeo-Christian or historic orthodox Christian doctrine of God's gracious self-disclosure, God's revelation *to*, *in*, and *for* the world. This rampant dualism has led and still leads to

---

[2] See, for example, the following titles wherein T. F. Torrance developed his critical and constructive engagement with modern and early postmodern dualisms, cosmological and epistemological: *Space, Time, and Incarnation* and *Space, Time, and Resurrection* (Edinburgh: T. & T. Clark, 2005); idem, *The Ground and Grammar of Theology* (Edinburgh: T. & T. Clark, 2005); idem, *God and Rationality* (Edinburgh: T. & T. Clark, 1987); idem, *Christian Theology and Scientific Culture* (Eugene, OR: Wipf & Stock, 1998); idem, *Reality and Scientific Theology* (Eugene, OR: Wipf & Stock, 2001); idem, *Divine and Contingent Order* (Edinburgh: T. & T. Clark, 2005).
[3] John Douglas Morrison, *Has God Said? Scripture, the Word of God, and the Crisis of Theological Authority* (Eugene, OR: Pickwick, 2006), 37ff.

what Jewish philosopher Martin Buber has called "the conceptual letting go of God."[4]

SPINOZA'S CARTESIAN SEPARATION OF THE WORD OF GOD FROM SCRIPTURE

With acknowledged brevity, I must yet point out that René Descartes's overdeveloped need for *certainty* led, via his methodological doubt, to his well-known "*Cogito, ergo sum*" ("I think, therefore I am").[5] Thereby his portrayal of the solitary sovereign subject ruled early modern thinking about the human being. It led to several very problematic, dualistic emphases—*subject* over against *object*, *mind* over against *body*, and *thought* over against *language*—all of which pulled apart what ought to have remained unitarily together, and which eventually invited "deconstruction" via Jacques Derrida et al.

One of Descartes's multitudinous "disciples," the Jewish philosopher Baruch Spinoza, took this dualism in ways that his mentor would not have approved, but which, in a sense, were unpacked naturally from Cartesian bases. For his own sociopolitical purposes, and so to extricate himself and European culture from the significant impact of any and all religious authority, both Christian and Jewish, that limited human freedom—especially his own philosophical freedom—Spinoza very deceptively sought to undercut the scriptural-revelational bases of both Judaism and Christianity, and thereby their *authority* in European culture.[6] In his *Theologico-Political Treatise*, Spinoza took the literary "disguise" of a pious believer in the Judeo-Christian tradition, but one who "humbly" wanted to "improve" or "correct" and make right and righteous that tradition—to re-form it to faithful propriety, notably in relation to philosophy. According to Spinoza, true religion and true philosophy never overlap. Religion deals *only* with morality and piety; philosophy deals with the *truth*. And both are conducive to an ordered, peaceful state. But, in fact, Spinoza was thereby waging an aggressive attack on Christian and Jewish orthodoxy, which he equated with "superstition,"

---
[4] Martin Buber, *The Eclipse of God: Studies in the Relation between Religion and Philosophy* (New York: Harper Brothers, 1952), 82.
[5] See René Descartes, *Discourse on Method: Meditations and Principles* (Oxford: Oxford University Press, 2008).
[6] Baruch Spinoza, *A Theologico-Political Treatise*, trans. R. H. M. Elwes (New York: Dover, 1951), 157–190.

while thereby actually pursuing radical freedom for his own philosophical goals. "Religion" must change its foundations, nature, and aims. Religion must be devalued, shown to be inferior and only for the ignorant and simple folk—all the while claiming for himself the role of champion for "true piety" and "religion."

Spinoza's primary targets are the authoritative bases claimed by Jewish and Christian orthodoxy. Hence, the nature of miracles, revelation, and especially Holy Scripture, and the relation of each of these to the "Word" or "Truth of God," as viewed by orthodoxy, are of particular negative concern for Spinoza. While carefully mocking the "multitudes" for their "superstitious" homage to Scripture ("the shreds of antiquity") *"rather than* to the Word of God," Spinoza thereby strips Scripture of all divine authority. He reduces Holy Scripture to merely and *only human* writings given to the imagination, evocative and pictorial, and so meant to stir the piety of the ignorant masses. The apostolic writings, he says, are ad hoc teachings with no claim to authority. It is rather philosophy, he says, that deals in Truth. And the "Word of God" cannot be tainted by history, nor can it be *verbal*, and certainly never *textual* or *written*. The "Word," as thus "transcendentalized," stands only outside history, dualistically separated from all things historical and human.

THE RISE OF MODERNITY'S DESTRUCTIVE DUALISMS

But now we enter the real core of the modern and postmodern problem of dualism. Spinoza gave form and example to others who would further separate Scripture from an utterly transcendent "Word of God," but the most potent bases lay in the physics of Isaac Newton and the philosophy/epistemology of Immanuel Kant.

Clearly one's view of God, the God-world relation, and so God's providence, is highly formative as to how one will then regard and/or limit what can be called "revelation," and especially as to whether God can truly and literally give discourse, speak, declare himself *content*-fully, including in *written* form. The real basis of the post-Enlightenment disputes regarding the church's historic "Scripture Principle," and so its "Identity Thesis," i.e., that Scripture *is* literally (and here, *is* means *is*) the written and *divinely authoritative* Word of God, is essentially a *theological* one. What is at stake in the movement of thought, especially from Newton through and beyond Kant, right to the present debates about revelation and Scripture, is ultimately our doctrine of God, and thereby God's relation or nonrelation to us here within the four-dimensional space-time continuum. What is the manner of God's involvement and activity here, and so in and with the wording/text of Scripture? Clearly, one's view of the nature and authority of Scripture is dynamically related to one's view of God. Holy Scripture as the written Word of God is affirmed as a result of affirmation of God's lordly, interactive, and personal relationship to and in the world as Creator, active and caring Sustainer, and Redeemer of the world. As we will observe, the modern reintroduction of cosmological and epistemological dualisms into Western thinking since the seventeenth century, especially via Newton and Kant, effected a false "construal" of God and the God-world relation, which led toward *deism* for some and toward *panentheism* for others. And for all these it meant the rejection of the historic Christian affirmation of both the incarnation and, too, that Scripture *is* the written and divinely authoritative Word of God.

To a large extent, the "modern" (pre-Einsteinian) approach to knowledge of the world arose in the West through Newton and, via Descartes, through Immanuel Kant. Consequently, alien disjunctions were clamped down on modern thought, resulting in the loss of true objectivity. While crucial details of Newton's system must be left out here, note that Newton's rigid, mechanical, deterministic system of cause and effect (the universe as a "big machine") separated absolute space and time (which he equated with the mind of God) from the relative space and time that we ordinarily experience.[7] In this way, Newton made God (for his cosmological system) what he called the *divinum sensorium*, the infinite "containing mind," which statically impresses rationality on the mechanistic universe, but only and always from the *outside*. God must remain deistically separate from the universe and from what occurs therein. But of special concern for us, Newton's dualistic separation of absolute space and time from our empirical space and time conceptually cut God off from the world. This meant that God has no direct relation to anything or anyone therein, and so the negation of all theological objectivity, and so all self-revelatory relations from God to, in, and for the world. Newton's projection of an unbridgeable "chasm" that separates the wholly other Deity from all ordinary empirical

---

[7] See Albert Einstein's criticism of Newton's problematic, mechanistic, and dualistic views of the universe and its effects on Western thinking, and his description of and call for more objective, "unitary," interrelational ways of seeing and portraying the universe in his *Ideas and Opinions* (London: Souvenir, 1973), 290–323. Note also, again, the previously mentioned works by Torrance.

realities, in order to meet his need for mechanistic uniformity, meant the a priori impossibility of miracles, of the incarnation, and of all content-ful divine revelation. Newton's "universe" meant no "Thus says the Lord!" Reflecting the early church heresy, Newton was an "Arian" Christian, the direct result of his absolute-relative, God-world dualism.

In the aftermath of the notable advances of, e.g., J. Clerk Maxwell and then Einstein, it is recognized that apart from narrow, limited usefulness, Newton's physics had harmful effects on the sciences, on scientific methodology, on Western epistemology and, for our purposes, on modern theology's understanding of the God-world relation, and so on the redemptive knowledge of God in the world. In Newton's universe there can be no divine revelation in the classical Christian sense, ergo no *written*, divinely authoritative Word of God.

Subsequently, Kant was central to the destructive reentrenchment of modern dualisms in the West. Kant took Newton's separation of absolute and relative space and time, and so of God from the world, and applied that separation directly to the human mind and its knowing processes. "Waked" from his "dogmatic slumbers" by reading David Hume's apparently skeptical empiricism, Kant reworked his previous rationalism, and, by his consequent and monumental *Critique of Pure Reason*, ushered in his "Copernican revolution" (or "reversal") in epistemology and, thereby, also in theology.[8] Empiricism had assigned a *passive* role to the human mental processes, i.e., no innate ideas, no constructive role for the mind, just an empty vessel receiving "impressions" from the external world. Kant concluded that such claims to mental passivity alone were faulty. Human knowledge needed firmer ground. Hence, Kant postulated that the human mind is *passive* at one level and *active* at another in order to more adequately deal with the varied elements of the human knowing processes, and to overcome the errors of both rationalism and empiricism. While affirming the need for sense data from outside, Kant "reversed" the knowing relation by conceiving that the object to be known must rather conform to and be molded by the *active* mental capacities. But this means that we cannot know objects or the world as they really are. Thus Kant separated the sense data of our experience (*phenomena*) from objects in the world as they truly are, essences, *and* from all nonphysical realities

---
[8] Immanuel Kant, *The Critique of Pure Reason*, trans. Norman Kemp Smith (New York: Macmillan, 1929, 2003), 27–29, 74, 87, 149, etc.

beyond any direct knowledge by human experience, including God, the "self," and the immortal soul (*noumena*).

By this dualistic separation of *phenomena* from *noumena* (which includes God), unknowable by "pure reason," *including God*, Kant thereby applied Newton's dualistic cosmology, his deistic separation of God from the world, to the human mind. For more than two hundred years the effects of that split have been vast in every sphere of the human pursuit of knowledge, notably in Christian theology. All claims to knowledge of the truth of God or of the reality of God by, e.g., direct divine revelation, and so by Scripture, were thereby ruled out of court a priori. If Kant's view is affirmed, can Christian theology exist? Can content-ful revelation from God be affirmed? Can Holy Scripture *be* the written Word of God, the "inscribed Word"? No! Not in the historic orthodox sense of the term. Recalling Martin Buber's aforementioned work, God has been "eclipsed" for Western culture.

MODERN THEOLOGY'S APPLICATION OF NEWTON AND KANT: SEPARATING GOD'S WORD FROM HISTORY AND TEXT

Again, if Kant's dualistic conclusions are affirmed, one cannot *do* theology in any way akin to historical orthodoxy, which assumes the historical reality and scriptural availability of the Word of God. If one accepts Kant's dualistic severance of God from human knowing, one must take another methodological road. And that is precisely what F. D. E. Schleiermacher did. Schleiermacher, "the father of modern theological liberalism," grudgingly accepted Kant's conclusions but sought to make an "end run" around Kant to "God" by a different path. Under the influence of his Pietist upbringing, Romanticism, and Kant, Schleiermacher aimed for a new way of doing theology that escaped Kant's epistemology and dry moralism via "God-consciousness," or the "feeling of dependence on God." If God cannot be known directly and as he is, if content-ful divine revelation and Scripture as the written Word of God have been "ruled out of court," Schleiermacher took the Enlightenment route of subjectivism, making the human religious subject central (rather than the properly objective Word of God). Specifically, he made the religious feelings that result when we choose to depend wholly upon the unknowable God, or "the All," central to the theological task. All is grounded in and from subjective human piety.[9] Thereby, Kant's "Copernican revolution (reversal)" in epistemology led to Schleiermacher's reversal in theology. Rather than focusing on the graciously given, objective self-disclosure of God as found notably in Scripture for *doing* theology, Schleiermacher reversed that by making our human "religious feelings" or "piety" the data for doing theology. Assuming that God is the *indirect* "Source" of these "feelings," the Kantian theologian or religious community must look within the self to analyze what these feelings indirectly *tell us about* their "God" source. Hence the methodological bases for liberal, neoliberal, existentialist, et al. theology ever since. Therein Scripture is clearly *not* regarded as the "Word of God"—a role claimed variously only for subjective pious feelings. But does Scripture have any role in this schema? Obviously, after Kant, revelatory *noumena* cannot partake of or be identified with written *phenomena*. For Schleiermacher, Scripture is merely a human record of religious feeling or experience, a record that can potentially enhance one's own experience. No divine authority.

The pervasive negative effects of these dualisms have continued to permeate culture and theology, and about a hundred years later a second prominent and influential example (among others) of the Newtonian-Kantian paradigm arose via Rudolf Bultmann. Bultmann was known as both an influential New Testament scholar and a prominent theologian. While Bultmann was ironically critical of late nineteenth-century and early twentieth-century liberal (or "Ritschlian") theology for its divine immanentism, its "culture Christianity," he retained much of the liberal theological foundations, methods, and Schleiermacher-like religious subjectivism in "existentialist" form. He was widely known for his "demythologizing" of the New Testament, for his radical form-criticism and historical skepticism in relation to Scripture, all of it the result of these destructive dualisms on his thinking—as on so many in Western culture. If God is "deistically" shut out from any direct relation to the world, and if the "noumenal" God is conceptually cut off from human knowledge, i.e., unknowable as he really is, how can we affirm any kind of God-human connection at all?

Bultmann strongly emphasized God's transcendence, to the extent

---

[9] Friedrich D. E. Schleiermacher, The Christian Faith, trans. H. R. MacKintosh and James S. Stewart (Edinburgh: T. & T. Clark, 1928, 1960), 10–12, 69–76, 87–88. See also the important criticisms by Klaus Bockmühl, *The Unreal God of Modern Theology: Bultmann, Barth, and the Theology of Atheism: A Call to Recovering the Truth of God's Reality*, trans. Geoffrey Bromiley (Colorado Springs: Helmers & Howard, 1988).

that he was a "deist."[10] According to Bultmann, the universe is a closed system of cause and effect. Hence, no miracles, no incarnation, no content-ful Word of God, no "Thus says the Lord." He also emphasized that people are hopeless and helpless in their sin, which he describes for twentieth-century culture in terms of Martin Heidegger's notion of "inauthenticity"—as utterly estranged from God, the world, and our true selfhood ("authenticity"). Though desperately needing redemption unto authenticity, we can do nothing. But *paradoxically* the "wholly other" God, though shut out from *direct* relation to us, somehow indirectly meets or "encounters" us through the kerygma, the telling of Jesus's existential courage on the cross. Through that human declaration of "good news," God is said to encounter us existentially and to empower us to freely choose for authenticity. We are thereby transformed to true selfhood, etc. Clearly, the focus is not God, not Jesus, but the subjective, existing human "I." It's all about "me"!

Where, then, is Scripture and scriptural authority in this highly influential theological approach? Does Bultmann have any authoritative role for Scripture in relation to "the Word of God's personal address to me?" Here, "the message" of the New Testament biblical documents can be the *human* textual *occasion* for God's paradoxical, existential, but empty, content-less "Word," which encounters the individual, calling him/her to choose for authenticity/faith. This transcendent, transformative, but empty "Word" somehow addresses one *through* the New Testament kerygma. But as one true to Newton and Kant, Bultmann must then regard Scripture as necessarily lacking any divine authority. His dualistic commitments mean that God can be "known," i.e., "experienced," only subjectively as he existentially "acts in me."

Also standing prominently in the Newtonian-Kantian dualistic tradition, specifically as a philosophical theologian, is Paul Tillich. Tillich said that he ever worked "on the boundary," e.g., between theology and philosophy, between Christianity and humanism. His numerous works, notably his three-volume *Systematic Theology*, have had monumental influence throughout late-modern and strains of postmodern theology, notably in neoliberal and existentialist schools of thought. His work reflects the influence not only of Newton and Kant, but also of Neoplatonism (mysti-

---

[10] See Rudolf Bultmann, *Jesus Christ and Mythology* (New York: Scribners, 1958), esp. chapters 2 and 3; and his article "How Does God Speak through the Bible?" in *Existence and Faith*, ed. Schubert Ogden (New York: Meridian, 1960).

cism), German Idealism (Hegel, Schelling), Nietzsche, and (like Bultmann) Heidegger. In contrast to Bultmann's "deism," Tillich's theological work was meant to reflect what he regarded as the panentheistic relation of the "Ground of Being," "Ultimate," "Depth Dimension," or in terms of theological symbol, "God," in and through all human culture (and religions). But especially, given his existentialist analysis of estranged and anxious human beings, alienated from "God" because of "fallenness," he says, "my whole theological work has been directed to the interpretation of (revelatory) religious *symbols* in a way that the secular man—and we are all secular—can understand and be (transformed) by them."[11]

How does this relate to the problem of dualism and so to the question of the authority of Scripture? While Schleiermacher claimed that "the feeling of dependence" (for Bultmann, God's nonhistorical, "existential encounter" through the kerygma) *bridged* the dualistic *chasm* between the otherwise totally unknowable God and finite persons in the here and now, for Tillich this is accomplished especially by Christian religious symbols. While true "symbols" are found in *all* human domains, e.g., the American flag or the British Union Jack, *religious* symbols (which can potentially be any finite thing, e.g., the word "God," the Cross, Jesus as the Christ) uniquely "*answer*" the most basic human existential questions by bringing the healing/saving power of "Essence"/the "Ground of Being" (God) across the Kantian "divide" to our anxious, estranged existence apart from God, with the goal being redemptive re-essentialization/salvation. Despite our existential fallenness, finite things can "miraculously" take on the second capacity of becoming to us the channel for the healing presence of "God." Through this process of "revelation," according to Tillich, the "Power of Being" or, symbolically, "God," breaks in "to us." But, if such a "revelation" supposedly crosses the Kantian chasm, what then of Scripture for Tillich and so for the many who follow his influential lead?

As a modern dualist, Tillich *rejects* the classical Judeo-Christian claim that God reveals himself personally, lovingly, truthfully, content-fully,

---

[11] Paul Tillich's "systematic" presentation of his views on the human existential condition, his view of "God" as the "Ground of Being," et al., as "answering" that anxious condition and the role of religious symbols mediating the divine to the historical and human realm, especially observable in his symbol "Jesus as the Christ," are best portrayed in his *Systematic Theology*, 3 vols. (Chicago: University of Chicago Press, 1951–1957), 1:12–14, 23, 64–66, 80, 94, 108–126, 157–159; 2:29–44, 97–99, 113, 117–124, 130–136, 145–146. For a somewhat more accessible introduction, see Paul Tillich, *Dynamics of Faith* (New York: Harper, 1957).

and so verbally and even textually. Tillich regards any such connection between "Word of God" and Scripture, then, to be a serious error. Rather, he says Scripture is a human text that "God" can potentially *use* "symbolically." In that way, Scripture, like a man-made conduit/pipe, can mediate the transforming power of "Being Itself" to us.[12]

EVANGELICAL THEOLOGY AND MODERN DUALISM: FACING THE TEMPTATION

It will have been noticed that, because of the effects of these modern dualisms on theology, and especially on views of revelation and Scripture, the result has been the modern (and postmodern) *rejection* of the classical "identity thesis," the Christian claim that in and under Christ the Word, by the power of the Holy Spirit, Scripture *is* the divinely authoritative, written Word of God. Any claim that God can only "use" the human text of Scripture is herein a case of what we can call "bibliological adoptianism" (from the early church heresy). But still, these are prominent theological liberals and existentialist neoliberals. Surely such dualism, such disjunctive separation, is not found among theologians claiming the stamp "evangelical," and has no connection to historical Christian orthodoxy. Unfortunately, in recent years, this is too often not the case. The historic orthodox and evangelical affirmation that, under Christ the Word and by the working of the Spirit, Holy Scripture is a *crucial* element/aspect in and of the larger economy of God's gracious self-revelation in order to be known objectively and adequately as he is in himself by space-time human beings, has often been giving way among confessed "evangelicals." It has been a subtle and nuanced move away from *identification* of the Word of God and the text of Scripture at any level except, perhaps, in terms, again, of a formal "adoptianist" or, perhaps, an "Arian" sense. I will mention three who have been among the most influential in this way: Donald Bloesch, Gabriel Fackre, and the late Clark Pinnock.

For many years, Donald Bloesch has been a prominent evangelical theologian teaching within mainline Protestant theological circles. In his much used *Holy Scripture: Revelation, Inspiration, and Interpretation*, he seeks a dialectical middle way between historical orthodoxy and clas-

---

[12] See Tillich's notable extension of this formulation in *Systematic Theology*, vol. 2, regarding the "New Testament Portrait of Jesus as the Christ."

sical evangelicalism on the one hand, at which he hurls numerous names (e.g., static, rationalistic neofundamentalism) in *ad hominem* fashion, and modern liberalism on the other hand, so that whatever is in his own middle ground is necessarily the "high ground" of *real* "evangelicalism."[13] Bloesch is subtle, careful, and given often to speaking of Scripture in glowing terms, even "Word of God" for a time. But against the claims to what he calls the "frozen truth" and "Docetism" of historical orthodoxy, Bloesch takes a so-called Barthian path, to the left of even Barth, by dualistically separating the "transcendent content" of divine revelation and its one single historical form in Jesus Christ, from Scripture as the actual historical written Word of God. Rather, he says, Scripture is only a special *human witness* to the one Word, which is only Christ. Yet Bloesch piously says that this human text can "*become* the Word" when, by the Spirit, it is made to communicate the truth and power of Christ to us. But it is *not* the written Word of God as such. It is notable that, except for minimal citations in the notes, Bloesch all but passes by any biblical discussion of inspiration, e.g., 2 Timothy 3; 2 Peter 1—a *very* telling reflection on Bloesch's agenda. For Bloesch, inspiration is not a past action and illumination of Scripture by the Spirit a present act; rather, for him, "inspiration" occurs in the existential "moment" when the Spirit makes the human text of Scripture to function *now*, "adoptianistically," as God's Word *to me*.[14] But the true "Word" transcends all language and all human witness, which is reflective of Bloesch's Neoplatonic fear that, should God's "Word" ever become truly historical, even textual, i.e., Scripture, it would be thereby sullied, stained, tarnished. What, then, of the incarnation?

Gabriel Fackre has also long labored theologically in mainline Reformed circles, teaching at Andover-Newton Theological School in Massachusetts. There he has purposed to do "properly evangelical" theology in the midst of other much more diverse theological currents—a commendable and difficult goal. In his work *The Doctrine of Revelation: A Narrative Interpretation*, Fackre seeks to reformulate an "evangelical" approach to revelation and Scripture, with much formative influence from Catholic scholar Avery Dulles's *Models of Revelation* and, too, his own interpretation and use of Karl Barth. Hence, Fackre wants to *revise* what Dulles interprets as the "Revelation as Doctrine" model, i.e., the

---

[13] Donald G. Bloesch, *Holy Scripture: Revelation, Inspiration, and Interpretation* (Downers Grove, IL: InterVarsity Press, 1994), 65–67, 94–101.
[14] Ibid., 56–60, 69–70, 117f., 126ff.

view of historical Christian orthodoxy, by means of Fackre's "Barthian" emphasis on revelation as emphatically "Christocentric." Indeed, Jesus Christ is surely the *center* and *ultimate* basis of all revelation, but he is *not* the *only* revelation.[15]

Despite Fackre's initial criticism of Tillich's noncognitive "revelation" via symbols and much of so-called Barthian existentialist Christocentrism that seems to make Jesus, "the Word made flesh," the *one and only* Word of God, he finally falls in step with that very same conclusion. For Fackre, too, Jesus Christ is the *one and only* true Word of God, while Scripture is (again) merely the human "witness to that Word." Thus Scripture, for Fackre, while mightily used by the Spirit, at last stands *outside* of what can be rightly regarded as divine revelation, the Word of God.

Again, we find expressed herein a *fear* that any claim to historical and textual identity, continuity, or real God-effected relation between the incarnate Word and Scripture imperils the proper centrality of Christ. Of course, that is not true, but that is the motivating fear. Yet it must be acknowledged that Fackre seems to sense that the problem of dualism must be faced and dealt with, that he wants to close the Kantian "chasm" between God and a "transcendentalized" divine Word *and* historical human existence and our great need for a coherent, content-ful "Thus says the Lord." For that reason, he tries to approach the issue of "inspiration" as Bloesch does not. Unfortunately he does so by trying to dialectically *contrast* his own view from that of historical Christian orthodoxy (as recently reflected in Carl Henry and J. I. Packer et al.), thereby finally placing "the Word," again, *outside* this history, beyond Scripture and (via Jürgen Moltmann) only at the *end* of history in the *eschaton*. The real "Word," then, is nonhistorical, nonlinguistic, and nontextual. Fackre, too, finally submits to a distorting dualism, and so wrongly denies that Scripture *is* the written Word of God.[16]

My third prominent example of theological and bibliological dualism within evangelicalism is the late Clark Pinnock. Clark was a friend with whom, from time to time, I agreed to disagree agreeably. Clark completed his long teaching career at McMaster Divinity School, within McMaster University in Hamilton, Ontario. Years after his notable work *Biblical Revelation*, Pinnock reflected his changed views on the nature of Scripture

---
[15] Gabriel Fackre, *The Doctrine of Revelation: A Narrative Interpretation* (Grand Rapids, MI: Eerdmans, 1977), 31–32, 85, 137f., 147.
[16] Ibid., 167–170, 172–175.

in his controversial work, *The Scripture Principle*.[17] Of the three evangelical works we have examined, this is the best in significant ways. Pinnock is usually more candid, honest, openly grappling with issues that Bloesch and Fackre handle with more calculated ambiguity. Pinnock takes the classic Protestant affirmation "the Scripture Principle" and defines it in two parts: first, he says there is a *place* where the Word of God is *accessible* in human form—the text of Scripture as God's written Word—and so a place that reveals God's mind authoritatively for us to heed; second, there is a need for a *defense* of biblical authority and trustworthiness against the present crisis regarding "the Scripture Principle."

All of this sounds excellent and most commendable. How, then, does he unpack this definition? Like the Christian theological tradition, and like the distinctive directions of Bloesch and Fackre, Pinnock rightly emphasizes that all of God's self-revelation is ultimately *Christocentric* in pattern and *salvational* in purpose. But does Pinnock use the centrality of Christ to *affirm* Scripture's divine authority or, like Bloesch and Fackre, to finally *deny* that authority? Given his own initial use and definition of "the Scripture Principle" as the affirmation that in Scripture the Word of God has taken human *and* textual form, that therefore Scripture is not only a human text (by Isaiah, Paul et al.) but is at the same time also God's own written Word, and given his explanation of "inspiration" as the divinely effected process whereby this occurred, it would *seem* that Pinnock is espousing that "Holy Scripture is the inspired, written Word of God," divinely authoritative in the classic Christian sense.[18] Alas, no. Throughout Pinnock's argument he repeatedly makes use of what turn out to be telling descriptive terms, e.g., Scripture was a mere "medium," "vehicle" or "conveyor" of God's revelation, revelation then being something *other*, different, beyond the text of Scripture, having then only a formal or functional relation to Scripture. Yes, Scripture is obviously given in human language. Yes, orthodoxy has always recognized divine "accommodation"—that God condescended to speak "down" on our level. But does this require disjunction, dualistic separation of Scripture from the revelation of God? Hardly! Quite the opposite. Yet for Pinnock, finally, this dualism becomes dominant.

---

[17] Clark H. Pinnock, *The Scripture Principle* (San Francisco: Harper & Row, 1984), see esp. 32–40, 43–54, 57–62 95–101, 188–191. See also Pinnock's book-length dialogue with process and neoliberal theologian Delwin Brown in Clark H. Pinnock and Delwin Brown, *Theological Crossfire: An Evangelical Liberal Dialogue* (Grand Rapids, MI: Zondervan, 1991), esp. section 1, part 2.
[18] Pinnock, *Scripture Principle*, 15, 32, 39–41, 45–54, 55–57, 62.

Two vivid and picturesque images or metaphors become formative for Pinnock: first, Scripture as a freight train *carrying* the freight, the transcendent Word of God, which is then not the train; and second, Scripture as a product not *of* revelation but *for* revelation, i.e., Scripture as the "switch track" *by* which the transcendent Word *beyond* Scripture is mediated (as through a pipe) into the human situation.[19] This same agenda has been carried forward by some "post-conservative" evangelicals like Roger Olson and others.[20] Again, problematic dualistic conceptualities have falsely gripped such evangelical thinking to its loss, "thinking apart" what ought to be thought together, i.e., Scripture *is* the written, and so divinely authoritative, Word of God.

CRUCIAL RESOURCES TOWARD RENEWED AFFIRMATION OF SCRIPTURE'S DIVINE AUTHORITY

So how are we to respond to this modern dualistic impact, these destructive effects, upon how we regard God's relation to us, upon what we perceive that God can or cannot enact in our midst, and hence upon our understanding of the nature and authority of Holy Scripture? Is such a disjunctive cutting off of Scripture from the Word of God in fact a long-needed corrective to the historical orthodox position of the church and its "Identity Thesis"? Ought we at last to recognize that the real, *ideal* Word of God is utterly other, beyond our space-time continuum and so beyond any humiliating written and textual form, beyond any debasing relation to inadequate human languages? No. In the name of the incarnate Word, the risen Savior, who ever affirmed the divine authority of Scripture, no!

Before restating, reaffirming, and reconfessing Scripture's *divine* authority, I will with much brevity point to three crucial, interrelated clarifications or reminders that properly direct us toward conclusions contrary to these debilitating, dualistic conclusions: human language is adequate; God is a human language user; and Scripture is God's illocutionary "speech act."

First, can human linguistic forms, human language, even *written* human language, ever be properly reckoned as the written Word of God? Again, historically the church has answered yes. The writers of Scripture themselves clearly and often asserted variously that Yahweh, the covenant God of Sinai, the triune God, is the *speaking* God who declares

---
[19] Ibid., 56, 95–97, 100–101, 188, 191.
[20] Roger Olson, *Reformed and Always Reforming* (Grand Rapids, MI: Baker, 2007), 17, 46, 88, 190–192.

himself and his ways to, in, and through his prophets and apostles. But, for reasons we have observed, Western culture has given in to the spurious modern and especially postmodern assumption that all language is an inadequate means of personal communication, thus effecting human isolation; and if so, how much more is this true of God?

In fact, the *opposite* is true. And alongside a resurgence of dualistic and Neoplatonic mysticism there have, in recent decades, been added "Eastern" religious notions, and both of there trends stress the "ineffability" and "inexpressibility" of the utterly remote, amorphous, or undifferentiated "divine." This has resulted in our contemporary doubt that human language can communicate the reality of God at all—even if God were endeavoring thus to act and speak to us. Rather, as John Frame well states the biblical corrective,

> God's transcendence (so understood) implies that God cannot be clearly revealed or represented to us in human words. . . . (But) Scripture never deduces from God's transcendence the inadequacy and fallibility (let alone the impossibility) of all verbal revelation. Quite the contrary . . . verbal revelation is to be obeyed (as authoritative) *because* of the divine transcendence.[21]

Like the Reformers, we ought to emphasize God's gracious condescension, the "humility" of God whereby he powerfully and lovingly identifies with that which is beneath him. Indeed, in the text of Scripture, God willingly and actively became "undignified" for our redemption.

Let me take this a further step with the help of evangelical Christian philosopher Nicholas Wolterstorff. In his influential Wilde Lectures at Oxford University, published as *Divine Discourse: Philosophical Reflections on the Claim That God Speaks*, Wolterstorff examines the "strange but riveting" declaration, introduced to humanity by Judaism, that "God speaks to us on our way, and that our calling as human beings is to listen to that speech from beyond and hear."[22] As we have acknowledged and evidenced previously in our argument, the idea of God speaking—

---

[21] John M. Frame, "God and Biblical Language," in *God's Inerrant Word*, ed. John W. Montgomery (Minneapolis: Bethany, 1977). See also J. I. Packer, "The Adequacy of Human Language," in *Inerrancy*, ed. Norman Geisler (Grand Rapids, MI: Zondervan, 1980). One ought also to examine carefully John Frame's subsequent and excellent book-length development of this and related issues in his *The Doctrine of the Knowledge of God* (Phillipsburg, NJ: Presbyterian & Reformed, 1987); and idem, *The Doctrine of the Word of God* (Phillipsburg, NJ: P&R, 2010).
[22] Nicholas Wolterstorff, *Divine Discourse: Philosophical Reflections on the Claim That God Speaks* (Cambridge: Cambridge University Press, 1996), see esp. ix, 27–28, 70–73, 186, 281–283, 298–299.

historical divine disclosure or discourse—has faced much hostility in modernity. Wolterstorff calls this antagonism "ill-advised" and "self-defeating." Since the Enlightenment especially, any religious reference to "God speaking" is in mainline religious contexts regarded only as nonliteral, metaphorical, symbolic of something else, usually a vacuous subjective experience (recall Schleiermacher and the others after Kant). Yet, as we also saw, even Bloesch et al., finally balk at the radical historicity required for God to be a *literal* human language user, whether at Mount Sinai or in the text of Holy Scripture, and so the proper identity, under Christ, between Scripture and the Word of God.

What of Wolterstorff? Wolterstorff does not balk. Rather, beginning with his detailed opening analysis of the incident in Augustine's *Confessions* of the child's voice saying, "*Tolle lege, tolle lege*," "Take up and read, take up and read," which Augustine took to be *God's* command *there* and *then* to take and read the text from Romans, which changed his life in an instant and altered the course of much of Western culture through him, Wolterstorff asserts that *somehow*, against all such modern opposition, God is capable of using human language to speak to us historically, and he has in fact *done so*. It is the answering of that "somehow," seeking coherent if partial explanation of *how* God discourses with us, that generates the development of Wolterstorff's argument. Notably for us here, Wolterstorff helpfully develops at length the notion of "deputized discourse," e.g., God speaking through a divinely "deputized" prophet or apostle whereby the prophet's/apostle's speaking becomes also God's speaking, and, to be more particular, the prophet's (or apostle's) specifically prophetic/apostolic *writing* is also included therein as *God's own* authorized, hence *authoritative*, "deputized" discourse. He concludes that there is good reason to regard Christian Scripture, the Canon, as the God-given medium of divine discourse, the written Word of God, and, as described, God can rightly be regarded thereby the "author of the Bible."

Finally, it is the conclusion of numerous contemporary evangelical theologians, myself included, that the analogical, carefully principled application of "speech-act theory" to what Scripture itself says about the way God reveals himself to us, has significantly clarified a proper "trinitarian theology of Holy Scripture."[23] Two of those at the forefront of the development

---

[23] Kevin J. Vanhoozer, *Is There a Meaning in This Text? The Bible, the Reader, and the Morality of Literary Knowledge* (Grand Rapids, MI: Zondervan, 1998); idem, *First Theology: God, Scripture, and Hermeneutics*

of these insights are Wolterstorff and especially Kevin Vanhoozer. Vanhoozer, too, reflects constructively on prominent recent developments in the philosophy of language from the later Wittgenstein and especially through J. L. Austin and John Searle. Crucial for our purposes is Austin's breakthrough recognition, and Searle's clarification, of the fact that every human "speech act," e.g., assertion, command, promise, etc., renders the speaker or author a "communicative agent," a *doer* of a speech-action.

All proper saying or writing is a verbal "doing" and has within itself three more distinctive linguistic acts that effect the larger speech act. These are: (1) the locutionary act, i.e., the actual uttering or saying or expression of something; (2) the illocutionary act, i.e., *what* it is we *do* in saying something (e.g., commanding); (3) the perlocutionary act, i.e., what we *effect* in others by our saying something (e.g., persuading). But it is especially the recognition of the *illocutionary* act that enables distinction between the content of what is said (sense and reference) and its force (what a sentence *does*). Illocutions are all-important to the speaker's/author's role as *intentional* communicative agent. This can be applied almost directly over to God's act of speaking or revelation, the recognition of God as a "Trinitarian" communicative agent. Reflecting the biblical data, God the Father is the "utterer"; his action is "locution"; he is the begetter and upholder of *words* (Heb. 1:1–2), who spoke *to* the prophets. The Logos-Son corresponds to the speaking Father's *act* of *illocution*, what the Father *does* by thus speaking. The Son-Word as divine illocution is the content, reference, and intention of the Father's uttering, making him "count as" what the Father intended for us. The Holy Spirit corresponds to the third active element of a divine speech-act, the *perlocution* or the *effect* of an illocutionary act on the actions or beliefs of the hearer or reader. Hence, the triune God, in and by his communicative act, is the Lordly paradigm of all inherently covenantal and missional communication. And therein, according to this Trinitarian theology of Scripture, i.e., God's speaking from the Father, in and through the Son, and in the power of the Holy Spirit, Vanhoozer explains how *Scripture is itself* "God's illocutionary speech action," the written Word of God, and that as a *result* of God's mighty speech acts.

Contrary to the functionalism of the bibliological "adoptianists," Vanhoozer affirms that Scripture has ontological authority. God not only

---

(Downers Grove, IL: InterVarsity Press, 2002). In *Is There a Meaning*, see esp. 19–28, 43–48; in *First Theology*, see esp. 20, 34–35, 148–157.

uses the words of Scripture to speak to us. The Canon is itself an act of God speaking to the world. The Holy Spirit not only is active occasionally in illumination, but *was* active, too, in the formation of the words of the Canon.[24] And his Word will not return to him void (Isa. 55:11).

UNDER CHRIST THE WORD: SCRIPTURE AS GOD'S WRITTEN WORD TO US

Given the limitations required here, we can give only a "taste," or "the hem of the garment" of these recent developments. Nor can we now elaborate at length on the subsequent overthrow of much of Newtonian determinism, mechanism, and dualism that has occurred in the last century via Christian physicist J. Clerk Maxwell, Einstein, and others who have helped to move portions of Western science back toward a proper objectivity, not only in the physical sciences but also in epistemology, and so our ability, not to know everything (potentially) and yet not nothing, but by the gift and grace of God to know *adequately*. We will now tie together a few interrelated elements toward a fresh statement and affirmation that Holy Scripture *is* the divinely authoritative, written Word of God.

First, the so-called Barthian understanding (often different from Barth's own later, mature position) of the Word of God as finally other than and dualistically separated from or beyond Holy Scripture—a view too often influential upon sectors of broader evangelicalism, including Bloesch, Fackre, and Pinnock—is both wrong and right at different levels. Barth's own *Christocentricity*, his point that *the* ultimate Word of God is Jesus Christ, is surely right and biblical.[25] The openings of John, Colossians, and Hebrews tell us, e.g., that the Word (*logos*) who is God became flesh and dwelt among us. Jesus of Nazareth *is* the Word of God in an eternally preeminent way. He is, we may say, the ontological Word of God. But does this fact negate the biblical necessity of affirming that Holy Scripture, too, is the *written* Word of God? Certainly not. While it is indeed also biblical to refer to Scripture as a primary "witness" to Christ,

---

[24] Kevin J. Vanhoozer, "Scripture and Hermeneutics," in *The Oxford Handbook of Evangelical Theology*, ed. Gerald McDermott (New York: Oxford University Press, 2010), 35–52.

[25] Though Barth was clearly working toward theological objectivity in *Church Dogmatics* I:1, yet it is with I:2 and subsequent volumes that one can observe Barth's progress toward a more orthodox view of Scripture. See Bruce L. McCormack, "The Being of Holy Scripture Is in Becoming: Karl Barth in Conversation with American Evangelical Criticism," in *Evangelicals and Scripture: Tradition, Authority, and Hermeneutics*, ed. Vincent E. Bacote, Laura C. Miguélez, and Dennis L. Okholm (Downers Grove, IL: InterVarsity Press, 2004), 55–75; and Geoffrey Bromiley, "The Authority of Scripture in Karl Barth," in *Hermeneutics, Authority, and Canon*, ed. D. A. Carson and John D. Woodbridge (Grand Rapids, MI: Zondervan, 1986).

as Jesus himself teaches in John 5:39, this distinction of Christ the Word from Scripture's Spirit-inspired testimony to him does not thereby negate Scripture's continuity with and nuanced connection/relation in, with, and under Christ the Word as the written, and so divinely authoritative, Word of God. Indeed, the Father and the Holy Spirit also "bear witness" to Christ, and that hardly negates their divine authority. How, then, should these interrelated elements be brought together in a way faithful to Scripture's teaching, and so to "the faith once for all delivered to the saints"?

If Jesus is the *unique* incarnate Word, and if the Old Testament and New Testament Scriptures repeatedly speak of their own status as divine revelation and/or the written Word of God, a status to which Jesus himself constantly testified, and yet Scripture also "testifies" to Christ as distinct (but not dualistically separate) from itself, then we must *avoid* a flat and undifferentiated *identity* between Jesus Christ (the divine-human *person*) and Scripture (the divine-human *product*). At the same time, *contra* Bloesch et al., we must strenuously reject all dualistic, disjunctive thinking that separates Christ the ultimate Word from the "inscripturated" or "in-scribed" Word, as though Scripture were a mere human word after all, which is somehow occasionally, "adoptianistically" and temporarily "made" the Word if and when *used* by the Holy Spirit. Faith-ful, unitary biblical thinking here will "think after" the "identity-in-distinction" inherent in this relationship, relations also similarly observable in the crucial *homoousion* term of the Nicene Creed, and so the "oneness-in-distinction" of the Trinity. Therefore, in, under, of, and from the Word made flesh, Jesus Christ, and by the effective, powerful working of the Holy Spirit via the Spirit's operations of revelation and inspiration (*theopneustos*; 2 Tim. 3:16; 2 Pet. 1:20–21, etc.), Holy Scripture *is*, again *is* thereby, the divinely authoritative, written, and truthful Word of God, its authority and truthfulness grounded not only in itself, but ultimately, by the Spirit, in Christ the Son, and in God the Father, and so finally in and of the perichoretic or coinherent relations within the eternal, triune Godhead.[26] Praise God for his wonderful gift, the written Word of God and the Gospel therein. To God alone be the glory. Amen.

---

[26] In relation to all these crucial issues in Revelation and Holy Scripture and, therein, especially the relation of Scripture as Word of God and Jesus Christ the Word made flesh, and all in relation to the triune Godhead, I must point the reader to my book on these matters, John Douglas Morrison, *Has God Said? Scripture, the Word of God, and the Crisis of Theological Authority* (Eugene, OR: Pickwick, 2006), especially my own new "model" of Revelation and Holy Scripture in chapter 8 (221–244), "Einstein, Torrance, and Calvin: A Christocentric, Multileveled, Interactive Model of Scripture as the Written Word of God."

9

The Many "Yes, buts . . ." of Theodicy: Revisiting John Feinberg's Account of Moral Evil

THOMAS H. MCCALL

INTRODUCTION

The logical problem of evil is well-known. Less well-known is John S. Feinberg's work on it. This is unfortunate, for his proposal regarding the problem of moral evil is well-informed, interesting, and bold. He is well aware of the serious challenges facing not only theists in general but theological determinists in particular. He treats other views with fairness and charity, and he is clear-eyed in his recognition that the Free Will Defense and related defenses and theodicies may be successful but simply are not accessible to the theological determinist. He understands that theological determinism runs the risk of "making God the author of evil." As a convinced theological determinist, he offers his own proposal for a defense that is indeed consistent with theological determinism.

Several decades after the first statement of it, Feinberg's distinctive and important contribution to the discussion of the problem of evil still awaits the full attention that it deserves.[1] As a result, it has not had as

---

[1] His proposal receives no engagement in the impressive *Blackwell Companion to the Problem of Evil*, ed. Justin P. McBrayer and Daniel Howard-Snyder (Oxford: Blackwell, 2013).

much impact as we might have expected from such a serious and substantive contribution. But neither has it been pressed for the fine-tuned clarifications and adjustments that sometimes help seminal contributions. In this essay, I directly engage several fascinating and important features of his proposal. I push for clarification on several points (clarification that might serve to strengthen his defense), and I raise some friendly criticisms of the proposal as it stands. I do not mean to suggest that such criticisms are fatal to his proposal, for I do not doubt that he has much more to say about these matters. I do, however, hope that the friendly criticisms will be helpful as he continues to develop the proposal and the supporting arguments.

JOHN FEINBERG'S "INTEGRITY OF HUMANITY" DEFENSE

Feinberg realizes that the Free Will Defense is not accessible to him (on theological grounds), but he does utilize Plantinga's distinction between a theodicy and a defense. Where a theodicy tries to provide a full explanation for the evil in the world, a defense offers only a *possible* explanation.[2] Much as the Free Will Defender argues that there is no problem with respect to divine omnipotence to say that God can create free creatures but cannot control or determine their actions (as free creatures), so Feinberg suggests that it does not contradict belief in either divine omnipotence or divine goodness to say that God cannot "remove evil without 1) contradicting other valuable things he has decided to do, 2) casting doubts on or directly contradicting the claims that he has all the attributes predicated of him in Scripture, and/or 3) performing actions which *we* would neither desire nor require him to do, because they would produce a greater evil than we already have in our world."[3]

Feinberg first argues that God intended to create non-glorified human beings who are neither identical to one another nor stereotypically similar with respect to distinct capacities. God obviously intended to create beings who are finite both metaphysically and morally. Our finitude does not "necessitate doing evil," but does entail that we do not have the moral perfection of an infinite God. In sum, "God intended to create

---
[2] This is, of course, all that is needed to meet the objection to theism from the logical problem of evil.
[3] John S. Feinberg, *The Many Faces of Evil: Theological Systems and the Problems of Evil*, rev. and expanded ed. (Wheaton, IL: Crossway, 2004), 167.

human beings, not supernatural beings or even gods."[4] Although sin has deeply impacted humanity (and all creation), it has not abolished the basic capacities given to humanity at creation: "The fundamental features of humanity and of our world are still as God created them."[5] We can know this much, according to Feinberg, from looking at the world as it is.

He next argues that non-glorified humans fall into sin because they follow their desires. "In accord with James 1:13-15," Feinberg makes a case that "morally evil actions ultimately stem from human desires."[6] This does not mean that the "desires in and of themselves are evil or that the desires do the evil."[7] He helpfully summarizes "how an evil action comes to be":

> An individual has certain basic desires or needs which aren't evil in themselves. He initially doesn't purpose to sate those desires in a way that disobeys ethical norms. However, a desirable object comes before him, and he is attracted to it. He forms the intention to have it, even though acquiring it is prohibited by moral precept. Then, when the allurement becomes strong enough, he wills to acquire or do the thing he desires. At that point sin is committed.[8]

As to the willing of the action itself, Feinberg holds that "it is done with compatibilistic free will, for there are causally sufficient non-subsequent conditions that decisively incline the will without constraining it to choose." And even though "Some of the conditions surrounding the decision may involve God's bringing about the state of affairs in which the decision is made," nonetheless he insists that "temptation to evil and the actual willing of evil stem not from God but from man."[9] Indeed, the "problem stems ultimately from us."[10]

Because God wanted to create non-glorified human creatures who have desires that may lead to moral evil, then what, Feinberg asks, would God have had to do to get rid of moral evil? He looks at several possibilities: maybe God could have arranged affairs "so that his compatibilistically free creatures are causally determined to have desires only for good and to choose only good without being constrained at all."[11] While

---
[4] Ibid., 168.
[5] Ibid.
[6] Ibid., 169.
[7] Ibid.
[8] Ibid., 170–171.
[9] Ibid., 171.
[10] Ibid., 172.
[11] Ibid.

this might seem plausible and might take little tweaking and fiddling by God "if people are naturally inclined to do what God wants," humanity has now "inherited from Adam a sin nature which positively disposes us toward evil."[12] With this "sin nature," Feinberg argues, our resistance to God makes it unlikely that God could so arrange affairs so that we always did only what is right—at least not without so creating bigger problems. Other ways that God could eliminate evil in nonmiraculous ways look no better to Feinberg.[13] For God to eliminate evil by miraculous means, on the other hand, would "greatly change life as we know it" and indeed would so upset the world that God has created that it would contradict his desire to have *this* kind of world (a good world with non-glorified humans).[14] Feinberg concludes that "God cannot both produce a utopia and create human beings as we know them," and this means that "God must not, cannot, and should not eliminate moral evil . . ." and thus that "the moral evil in our world is justified."[15]

Feinberg's approach is well-informed and thorough. It makes use of important advances in work on the problem of evil over the past several decades, and it offers a unique (or at least very unusual) "Calvinist" defense. It seems to me that it is vastly superior to theodicies that are much more common in "neo-Reformed" circles; indeed, Feinberg offers direct and sharp criticism of theodicies which insist that moral evil in our world is justified because "God uses it to bring himself glory."[16] Despite these strengths (and what I take to be clear advantages over popular "Reformed" defenses and theodicies), however, several questions remain before us.

QUESTIONS FOR CLARIFICATION

First, why not conclude that God did intend for there to be moral evil? Feinberg says that we can know what sort of being God intended to create by looking at what God actually did. He recognizes that "this same line of thinking could be used to say that God also intended for there to be moral evil, because we have it."[17] But Feinberg denies that we should

---

[12] Ibid., 173.
[13] Ibid., 174–177.
[14] Ibid., 177.
[15] Ibid., 180, 190.
[16] Ibid., 187. Cf. Thomas H. McCall, "I Believe in Divine Sovereignty," *Trinity Journal* (2008): 205–226; John Piper, "I Believe in God's Self-Sufficiency," *Trinity Journal* (2008): 227–234; Thomas H. McCall, "We Believe in God's Sovereign Goodness," *Trinity Journal* (2008): 235–246.
[17] Feinberg, *Many Faces of Evil*, 168.

draw this conclusion. He explains that God did not create evil "when he created other things," and he explains further that because evil "isn't a substance at all," it is not even in the scope of things that God created.[18] Feinberg is exactly right that evil is not a substance, and he is right to deny that God either created evil or performs evil actions. But none of this gets exactly to the main—and original—question: Does God *intend* moral evil? There is more than one question here: Did God create evil? Did God perform evil actions in place of created agents? Did God intend for them to perform such actions? Feinberg answers the first two, and he answers them negatively. But this does not address the last question. Surely God did not create the evil or perform the evil actions in place of the created agents, but did God *intend* these evil actions? For the theological determinist such as Feinberg, it seems that the answer must be positive. Of course there is a lot more that could be said about all this, and indeed Feinberg says more about the divine will elsewhere.[19] But it would help for more to be said *here*, in the context of the problem of evil.

Second, why think that God doing something unexpected or undesired—even miraculously—is problematic? God's action in the incarnation and resurrection of Christ surely was both unexpected and miraculous, and much that God does is undesired by sinful human persons. So why should we balk at the thought of God doing what we do not expect or want? It is important to realize that Feinberg is talking about God doing things that would cause us to question divine wisdom; he is talking about extreme cases, and while one might reasonably point out that nothing seems more extreme than the incarnation, Feinberg seems to mean extreme cases that would be done with some regularity. But here it seems that a move that has become fairly standard in the "skeptical theism" response to the "evidential problem of evil" is relevant: just because we cannot *see* good reasons to think that such extraordinary action would befit divine wisdom does not mean that there *are not* any good reasons.[20] So such radical intervention by God "would greatly change life as we know it?"[21] Is not this radical intervention what Christians long for, what Paul says

---
[18] Ibid., 168–169.
[19] John S. Feinberg, *No One Like Him: The Doctrine of God*, Foundations of Evangelical Theology, John S. Feinberg, gen. ed. (Wheaton, IL: Crossway, 2003), 693–698.
[20] For a fine overview of these issues, see Michael Bergmann, "Skeptical Theism and the Problem of Evil," in *The Oxford Handbook of Philosophical Theology*, ed. Thomas P. Flint and Michael C. Rea (Oxford: Oxford University Press, 2009), 374–399.
[21] Feinberg, *Many Faces of Evil*, 177.

the whole creation "groans" for? Would not this be a good thing? Again, there is much more that might be said about such matters, and I have no doubt that Feinberg has more to say. My point here is simply that it would be good to offer further explanation, for it is not at all obvious just what our desires and expectations have to do with divine wisdom. Indeed, if we think about the problem of evil from a Christological center, we might think that we have reason to be suspicious of our desires and expectations.

Let us turn from epistemological issues to those that are more metaphysical and theological. Feinberg rejects the notion that God wanted to create "superhuman" creatures; clearly God wanted regular humans rather than superhumans. But while the basic idea is discernible, it is not completely clear just what he means by "superhuman" (as opposed to "human"). Is the idea that to be superhuman is to be nonhuman? Or is superhumanity genuine humanity that is humanity-plus-something? Feinberg contrasts "superhuman" with "non-glorified human," but it is not obvious that he equates superhuman with glorified-human either.[22] At one point Feinberg seems to rely upon a contrast between superhumans and humans; he objects to a view because, he says, if it were true, then "God would have to make us in a way that would contradict his intention to make human beings and not superhuman beings."[23] Later, he protests (against an objection raised by Carl F. H. Henry) that there is "nothing fatalistic about this arrangement, for God could have created a completely different world wherein we wouldn't sin, though that world wouldn't have had the sort of human beings in it that he created in our world."[24] But just who is the *we* here?

None of this is exactly clear, but clarity matters. Here is why: suppose that we have transworld identity, and indeed that we exist both in possible worlds in which "we" sin and in possible worlds in which "we" do not sin (Feinberg's use of "we" would seem to indicate this much).[25] If so, then, it turns out that God could have created *us* without sin. Perhaps this would mean that the line between superhuman and human is only artificial, or at least nonessential and accidental; it is not the kind of thing that threatens personal identity. If so, then the distinction does not do much work, for, call us what you will, *we* could exist without sin after

---
[22] Ibid., 173.
[23] Ibid., 176.
[24] Ibid., 183.
[25] I think that transworld identity is the only way forward for Feinberg, for counterpart theory would entail that all sinful humans are *necessarily* sinful; surely Feinberg would not affirm that.

all. Or perhaps Feinberg would insist that the line between superhuman and human is sharp and that the distinction is essential (where the "sort of humans" really refers to "sortals" in the sense of a natural kind that is distinct from the natural kind "superhuman"). But if so, then we should take Feinberg to mean that *we* can exist *sans* sin without being superhuman after all. Either way, it turns out that God could have created *us* in a possible world without sin after all. So just what is the basic distinction here, and precisely what is it supposed to be doing?

In addition, just what is "the sin nature" that is referred to so often? Surely we are not to take this to refer to some kind of substance that is inherently and essentially evil; assuming that God creates all substances, then this would entail the conclusion that God created evil. Feinberg flatly denies that God created evil, so we can safely rule out this option.[26] So is "the sin nature" a generic or kind-essence? Should we think of it as a complex property or set of properties "individually necessary and jointly sufficient" for inclusion in a natural kind?[27] This route does not look at all promising either (it would entail, among other things, that we all have at least two natures).

A better way, it seems, is to take Feinberg's language of "the sin nature" in the sense of *human*-nature-corrupted-by-sin. On this view, we do not have two natures. We have only one kind-essence: humanity. It has been corrupted by sin, and our humanity needs to be cleansed of it and renewed. But then it is not clear that the concept (of a sin nature) will do all that Feinberg intends for it to do. To eliminate evil in us, therefore, God would not have to "change our nature as human beings"—except to restore, cleanse, and sanctify it.[28] Eliminating evil, then, would not *threaten* the "integrity of humans."[29] To the contrary, it would *restore* this integrity.

SOME DEEPER WORRIES

In addition to the foregoing questions for clarification, several deeper concerns emerge from Feinberg's proposal. These are more directly *theological* in nature. Again, I do not present these as if they somehow contain fatal objections to his proposal; these are general concerns that at least

---
[26] Feinberg, *Many Faces of Evil*, 168–169.
[27] Thomas V. Morris (and others) have advocated the use of this metaphysics in Christology, e.g., *The Logic of God Incarnate* (Ithaca, NY: Cornell University Press, 1986).
[28] Feinberg, *Many Faces of Evil*, 178.
[29] As Feinberg refers to it in *No One Like Him*, 787ff.

might hamper the cogency of his case. At any rate, I do think that they are areas that deserve further attention.

Creation and Fall

Feinberg repeatedly uses the language of "eliminating," "removing," and even "eradicating" moral evil. He reflects at some length on what God might do to get rid of moral evil. But there is an important distinction between "getting rid of" or "eradicating" something and preventing it in the first place. Consider the gardener who sees the rows of carefully planted produce now intermingled and entangled with noxious weeds. She thinks of various ways that she might try to eliminate the weeds. She might douse the entire area with pesticides that would kill the weeds. But she realizes that the pesticide spray would also damage or kill many of the plants or render the produce unfit for consumption. She considers going through the garden on her hands and knees, pulling the weeds out. But she realizes that the weeds are so entangled (root and vine) that pulling them all out will likely uproot and severely damage her desired plants as well. Rather than take drastic measures and do great harm to her garden, the gardener decides to limit the damage as much as possible while awaiting the harvest. This gardener is in a very different position from that of the gardener who is able to create the truly ideal environment for the garden, one in which he can eliminate the very possibility of such infestation.

Much that Feinberg says presupposes the existence of moral evil and then addresses what God might have to do to remove it. He points out that various ways of rooting it out could be seriously disruptive and could damage the goodness that remains. But this does not exactly address the question (that Henry raised) of the origin of moral evil. And for the theological determinist (such as Feinberg), it seems that God is much more like the gardener who could have arranged things so as to avoid evil in the first instance.

The question of the origin of moral evil (what is sometimes referred to as "originating original sin") is deep and difficult for any theological system. For instance, the Free Will Defense (in the hands of either traditionalists or revisionist "open theists") appeals to mystery at some level, as it typically says that the "mystery of iniquity" is appropriately located at the level of the abuse of creaturely freedom (rather than locating it in the mysterious depths of the divine will). So no one—determinist or libertarian, classical or revisionist—has it easy when it comes to explanations of the origin of evil. But as Feinberg points out, various theological systems have the resources to deal with it. What those theological systems committed to classical orthodoxy have in common are these basic commitments: (a) God is not the "author" of evil, and (b) the creation itself is radically or fundamentally good rather than evil. Neither the goodness of God nor the primordial goodness of creation is negotiable. Feinberg agrees with both (a) and (b); he understands that the goodness of creation is not an optional Christian doctrine.

But for the determinist, there does not seem to be much room to work here. Affirmations of the genuine goodness of creation (as opposed to relative accounts of the goodness of creation, according to which the original creation was merely good "on balance" in that at the moment of creation the number of turps of evil in the world was outweighed by the amount of goodness) are not optional, but we begin to wonder if the creation has something "built into" it or "hardwired" into it so that moral evil is rendered inevitable.

So was the fall made inevitable by divine decree? Is the will of God finally and ultimately behind all moral evil, so that there would be no evil actions had God not willed that they happen? Do they all happen because *God* makes it impossible for them not to happen? If so, then it is not clear that Feinberg's defense does enough to show that God's goodness and glory are not besmirched by making God the ultimate causal agent. Or is there something about the creation of non-glorified (non-superhuman) humans that is just bound to go bad? Although humanity itself is not originally sinful, and even though desires themselves are not sinful, is there something about human nature itself that is hardwired for sin? So maybe the divine intention is not for humanity to go bad, but rather, if God was going to work with human nature, then this was all that could be expected. For on this account, if God is going to actualize a possible world with non-glorified humans, then some fall into sin (and resultant misery) just *will* occur. If God is going to work with regular, standard-issue, non-glorified humanity, then those humans just will sin and that humanity just will become sinful. Working with such materials, not even God can do anything about it. If so, then it is not clear how we are to affirm the goodness of creation. The former option calls into question

The Inevitability of Evil

This leads us to another concern: the inevitability of evil. Feinberg says that "the problem stems ultimately from us."[30] But what does this mean? Just what does it mean to say that "temptation to evil and the actual willing of evil stem not from God but from man?"[31] An indeterminist account can make sense of this; indeed, it is part and parcel of what an indeterminist says. Presumably Feinberg means that the human agents actually *will* the evil; God does not do it for us. But does not theological determinism entail that these humans will evil (and precisely as they do) because God wills that they will do so? God may indeed call us to "resist the temptation," but is it not true (according to theological determinism) that the divine decree has put us in situations where it is now impossible to resist? And if evil indeed is inevitable, then what does this do to moral responsibility? Are we not then failing to resist temptation because of God's all-determining decree—and then being held accountable for failing to do something that we could not do?

Henry has raised this worry: "if in fact man's fall into sin follows from the structure of human life as God created it, then Adam's fall was inevitable and Adam was not morally culpable."[32] The defender of Feinberg might be tempted to dismiss this as an "Arminian" concern, and might say further that such concerns do not affect the integrity of a determinist theological system. But Feinberg does not respond in this way; he seems to recognize that the moral culpability for sin is compromised if sin is inevitable. He offers two lines of response to Henry's criticism: first, he says that "there is nothing fatalistic about this arrangement, for God could have created a completely different world wherein we wouldn't sin, though that world wouldn't have had the sort of human beings in it that he created in our world." Second, he says that "sin isn't even inevitable in our world, for each person, though causally determined to do what she does, still has the ability and opportunity to choose otherwise than she has."[33]

---
[30] Feinberg, *Many Faces of Evil*, 172.
[31] Ibid., 171.
[32] Quoted in ibid., 183.
[33] Ibid.

Taking them in reverse order, let us take a closer look at these lines of response. It is immediately obvious that Feinberg is here adopting a "classical compatibilist" version of compatibilism (rather than the more recently popular Frankfurt-style versions or semi-compatibilism). He does not say a lot about this strategy here, but elsewhere he lists seven senses of "can" whereby the person who is determined to perform some action A could have performed not-A instead: there is the "ability" sense of can, the "opportunity" sense of can, the "rule consistent" sense of can, the "ill-consequence free" sense, the "authority" sense, the "reasonable" sense, and the "conditional" sense.[34] This is all very interesting, but the defender of compatibilism needs to do more than merely list these senses of "can" (and "could," "otherwise," etc.); he needs to show that they are sufficient (either individually or jointly) for freedom and responsibility, and he needs to show that the contra-causal sense of "can" is not necessary for freedom and responsibility. Without this additional work, Feinberg's defense merely inherits the problems of the conditional analysis approach.[35] Without such work, this strategy remains vulnerable to the criticisms that it really boils down to nothing more than the assertion that "well, S could do otherwise than A *if he were not determined to do A*" (which is, so far as I can see, only to repeat the tautology that "S could do otherwise than A if and only if he could do otherwise than A").

Feinberg's primary line of defense here is his assertion that we are not faced with inevitability or fatalism because *God* could have acted differently. As we have seen, Feinberg says that "there is nothing fatalistic about this arrangement, for God could have created a completely different world wherein we wouldn't sin, though that world wouldn't have had the sort of human beings in it that he created in our world."[36] While this statement is helpful, it is ambiguous in some important ways. Consider the statement that it "wouldn't have had the sort of human beings in it that he created in our world." What "sort of human beings" are we talking about? If Feinberg means "non-glorified" human beings, then it seems not unreasonable to conclude that "non-glorified humanity" entails sinfulness—for a world "wherein we would not sin" would be a world that did not have non-glorified humans. This would give us an

---

[34] Feinberg, *No One Like Him*, 722–724 (his emphasis removed).
[35] Many compatibilists are now convinced that this approach is doomed; e.g., Bernard Berofsky, "Compatibilism without Frankfurt: Dispositional Analyses of Free Will," in *The Oxford Handbook of Free Will*, 2nd ed., ed. Robert Kane (Oxford: Oxford University Press, 2011), 153–174.
[36] Feinberg, *Many Faces of Evil*, 183.

answer to the questions I have raised earlier (about the meaning of "non-glorified")—but such an answer could hardly be acceptable, for surely Jesus Christ is a non-glorified human who was, indeed, "tempted in all things as we are, *yet without sin*" (Heb. 4:15, NASB). On the other hand, perhaps "the sort of human beings" in mind is really *sinful* humanity. But this would contradict what Feinberg wants to say about the goodness of divine intention and action, and on his own account it cannot be true that God created humans as sinful. So neither reading should be satisfying to Feinberg—but then we are left to wonder just what we are to make of this statement.

Feinberg's claim that fatalism is avoided because God could have acted differently is a fairly typical move among theological determinists, and it is an important one. But I worry that it is imperiled by Feinberg's own arguments about divine omniscience.[37] Consider this common argument (CA) for the conclusion that exhaustive and definite divine foreknowledge entails determinism:

(1) If at t1 God knows what John will do at t2, then John is not free with respect to what John does at t2;

(2) If God is omniscient, then God knows at t1 what John will do at t2;

(3) God is omniscient;

(4) Therefore, God knows at t1 what John will do at t2 (from 2, 3);

(5) Therefore, John is not free with respect to what he does at t2 (from 1, 4).[38]

The lesson most commonly drawn from this familiar argument is that libertarian human freedom is not possible if God has exhaustive foreknowledge. Indeed, Feinberg appears very sympathetic to this argument and conclusion.[39] I do not think that the argument ultimately is successful, but for present purposes we should note something else. Consider a less common argument (CA*):

(1*) If at t1 God knows what God will do at t2, then God is not free with respect to what God does at t2;

---
[37] E.g., Feinberg, *No One Like Him*, 735–775.
[38] This particular formulation of the familiar problem comes from Keith E. Yandell, *Philosophy of Religion: A Contemporary Introduction* (New York: Routledge, 1999), 335.
[39] E.g., Feinberg, *No One Like Him*, 751–752, 759, 775.

(2*) If God is omniscient, then God knows at t1 what God will do at t2;
(3) God is omniscient;
(4*) Therefore, God knows at t1 what God will do at t2 (from 2*, 3);
(5*) Therefore, God is not free with respect to what God does at t2 (from 1*, 4*).

So on this argument, if foreknowledge cancels out human freedom, then it cancels out divine freedom as well.

Richard Swinburne sees this problem clearly, and he simply bites the metaphysical bullet. With characteristic clarity, he concludes that it is not possible for there to be a perfectly free person who is also omniscient (in the traditional sense of omniscience). And since God *is* a perfectly free person, the conclusion to be drawn is that God can "not have knowledge of his future free actions."[40] Thus God "will not know in advance what he will do."[41] Swinburne concludes that this places a "much larger limit on God's omniscience than the limit concerned with future free actions," and he concludes that God's "ignorance of the future must be vast."[42]

Swinburne bites the bullet and adopts what amounts to a radical version of open theism, but he is not alone. Some theological determinists bite the bullet too; of course they draw a very different conclusion. Paul Ramsey summarizes Jonathan Edwards's account of divine freedom: "it is obvious that Edwards (in saying that God in his volitional action is independent and self-moved yet motivated and inclined by what pleases him, while man chooses what pleases him yet is not self-moved) simply adds degrees and denies limits, and removes changeableness and other imperfections. Otherwise, what might be said of the divine will would be univocal with the account of human volition."[43] So, just as human actions are said to be free even though determined, so also are divine actions. But where the determination of human action might have its final explanation in the free decisions of God's will, the determination of divine action has its full and final explanation in God's nature.

Now with this in mind, let us return to the discussion of fatalism.

---

[40] Richard Swinburne, *The Coherence of Theism*, rev. ed. (Oxford: Oxford University Press, 1993), 179.
[41] Ibid., 181.
[42] Richard Swinburne, *The Christian God* (Oxford: Oxford University Press, 1994), 134.
[43] Paul Ramsey, "Editor's Introduction," in *The Works of Jonathan Edwards, Vol. 1: Freedom of the Will*, ed. Paul Ramsey (New Haven, CT: Yale University Press, 1957), 26–27.

Feinberg appears to endorse (CA), and there is good reason to think that if (CA) is successful then so too is (CA*). Against this view, Thomas P. Flint points out that it is not "plausible to think that internal factors (relating to his nature or character, say) over which he [God] has no control fully determine his creative activity. For if they did, then this world would be the only genuinely possible world, and all true distinctions between necessity and contingency would collapse, as would the gratuitousness both of God's creation and our existence."[44] Issues surrounding God's relation to modality are complicated and contentious, and this discussion deserves more attention, with hasty conclusions being somewhat risky.[45] Still, though, it is not hard to see the basic concern. Assume that God exists necessarily, which is to say that God exists in all possible worlds. Assume further (with Feinberg) that God is omniscient, thus God's performance of some action A at some time t is always foreknown by God. Then consider God's action of actualizing w^* (*this* possible world, the actual one), and let A stand for this w^*-actualizing action:

(6) If God foreknows that A, then God is not free to refrain from A (from (CA*));

(7) God foreknows that A (from omniscience);

(8) Therefore, God is not free to refrain from A (from 6, 7).

(9) If God is not free to refrain from A, then it is not possible that w^* not be actualized;

(10) Therefore, it is not possible that w^* not be actualized (from 8, 9);

(9) If it is not possible for w^* not to be actualized, then w^* is necessary;

(10) Therefore, w^* is both possible and necessary.

So only one possible world—one maximally consistent state of affairs—is possible. And this maximally consistent state of affairs is necessary. Thus we have modal collapse. And with modal collapse we seem to have regained fatalism (with either pantheism or panentheism likely thrown in for good measure).

If God's actions are all determined, the line between determinism and

---

[44] Thomas P. Flint, *Divine Providence: The Molinist Account* (Ithaca, NY: Cornell University Press, 1998), 30.
[45] Cf. Brian Leftow, *God and Necessity* (Oxford: Oxford University Press, 2012).

fatalism becomes perilously thin. In fact, there is good reason to think that it has disappeared entirely. For when faced with questions about whether or not things could have been different, theistic determinists (who, such as Feinberg, are compatibilists about human freedom) often respond that in fact things could have gone differently; the ultimate explanation is that if God had chosen to determine things differently, then of course things would have—and thus of course *could have*—turned out differently. But if God's own *all-determining choice* itself could not have been different, then surely Flint is correct to conclude that "all true distinctions between necessity and contingency would collapse." Modal collapse entails fatalism. For centuries, and with good reason, Christian theologians stoutly have resisted fatalism; whatever one's views on providence, predestination, and human responsibility, fatalism has been rejected as inconsistent with core Christian beliefs.[46] Modal collapse is widely held to be false—and so much the worse for any theological view that entails it.

Taking Stock

Again, I do not intend this to be taken as a refutation of Feinberg's work. It is far too soon to assume that these problems must be fatal for his proposal. There are various ways that one might avoid the conclusion of the foregoing argument: the defender of Feinberg might, for example, simply deny that God exists necessarily and adopt "plain theism" rather than "Anselmian theism."[47] Or one might back away from (CA). Indeed, perhaps there is a charitable reading of Feinberg's theology that lends itself to this; when he says that Ockhamism and Molinism suffer from the inability to account for *how* God knows future free actions, maybe he only means that Ockhamism and Molinism lack the explanatory power of compatibilism (rather than the stronger claim that they fail to show that foreknowledge might be consistent with libertarianism). This would be a welcome development, as many indeterminist theists would be cheered by a statement from Feinberg that libertarianism really is consistent with divine foreknowledge.

---

[46] Paul Helm recognizes that "a universe which is in some sense the inevitable outcome of God's choice which is in itself in some sense inevitable may conjure up the spectre of Spinozism" (*Eternal God: A Study of God without Time* [Oxford: Oxford University Press, 2011], 182).
[47] Cf. Keith E. Yandell, "Divine Necessity and Divine Goodness," in *Divine and Human Action: Essays in the Metaphysics of Theism*, ed. Thomas V. Morris (Ithaca, NY: Cornell University Press, 1988), 313–344.

More broadly and more drastically, Feinberg might look for a version of Calvinism that is consistent with indeterminism.[48] Or, more modestly, he might allow that Adam and Eve had libertarian freedom (even if the postlapsarian situation is different). And he can, of course, rightly insist that his is only a *defense*—and thus it needs only to be internally consistent. But while this much is true, it is also true that the defense will be considered successful by Christians only to the extent that it is consistent with other important Christian beliefs. So any work on the problem of evil must, for the Christian, avoid both the conclusion that creation itself is evil as such and the conclusion that humans are not really responsible for the moral evil that they perpetrate. And surely it must avoid the conclusion that God is the ultimate agent of moral evil.

Feinberg says that moral evil is a "concomitant of a world populated by non-glorified human beings."[49] The clarity of "concomitant" is less than crystal. Does this mean that to be a non-glorified human just is to be a sinner (perhaps at some point in the existence of the non-glorified human)? Are all possible worlds with non-glorified humans also worlds in which those non-glorified humans are also sinful humans? If the property *being sinful* is a necessary property of non-glorified humanity, then it is essential. Such a conclusion would be disastrous—not only metaphysically but theologically and Christologically as well (for then Jesus either is not a non-glorified human or is sinful). On the other hand, if *being sinful* is only an accidental property, then it seems that God could have actualized a world with sin-free non-glorified humans—but then it is hard to see how Feinberg might say that God *cannot* actualize such a world.

CONCLUSION

Fully three and a half decades after the publication of Alvin Plantinga's celebrated Free Will Defense, Richard Otte published an essay that exposed several potential problems with Plantinga's exposition and defense.[50]

---

[48] Richard A. Muller says that metaphysical determinism was "repugnant to the Reformed understanding of God and the world" in Reformed scholasticism (*Post-Reformation Reformed Dogmatics: The Rise and Development of Reformed Orthodoxy, ca. 1520–ca. 1725, Volume Three: The Divine Essence and Attributes* [Grand Rapids, MI: Baker Academic, 2003], 125).
[49] Feinberg, *Many Faces of Evil*, 190.
[50] Richard Otte, "Transworld Depravity and Unobtainable Worlds," *Philosophy and Phenomenological Research* (2009): 165–177.

Plantinga took up the challenge, and his response to Otte addressed the problems and ultimately strengthened the defense.[51] If the present essay can help in a similar way, I shall be grateful. In the meantime, I shall remain grateful indeed for John Feinberg's scholarship, friendship, and service to our Lord.

---

[51] Alvin Plantinga, "Transworld Depravity, Transworld Sanctity, and Uncooperative Essences," *Philosophy and Phenomenological Research* (2009): 178–191.

10

Evangelical Christology and Kenotic Influences: A "New" and "Better" Way?

STEPHEN J. WELLUM

Over a century ago, first on the Continent and later in the United Kingdom, a group of theologians attempted to reformulate Chalcedonian Christology in a "new" and "better" way, known as Kenotic Christology. Even though these theologians were dissatisfied with the "old" formulation, they did not entirely embrace the Enlightenment spirit. As a result, they offered a *via media* which most orthodox Christians, including later evangelical theology, rejected as lacking biblical and confessional fidelity.[1] Today, however, in evangelical Christology, even though the earlier kenoticism is not fully embraced, there is an unmistakable kenotic influence resulting in more diversity of thought than is often recognized.[2] In fact, broadly conceived, there is a spectrum of three viewpoints: the "newer" views known as ontological and functional kenotic Christology versus the "older" classical view.[3]

---

[1] See, e.g., David F. Wells, *The Person of Christ* (Westchester, IL: Crossway, 1984), 133–139.
[2] Contra John Macquarrie, *Jesus Christ in Modern Thought* (London: SCM Press, 1990), 250, who argued that kenotic Christologies "turned out to be no more than an episode in modern thinking about the person of Jesus Christ." As it turns out, the influence of kenoticism on nonevangelical and evangelical theology is huge. On this point, see Kevin J. Vanhoozer, *Remythologizing Theology: Divine Action, Passion, and Authorship* (Cambridge: Cambridge University Press, 2010), 105–177.
[3] For these categories, see Oliver D. Crisp, *Divinity and Humanity* (Cambridge: Cambridge University Press, 2007), 118–153.

In this chapter my intent is to sketch these "newer" Christological views, both of which incorporate some form of kenoticism, in order to offer some critical reflections and to support my conclusion that the "older, classical" way of theologizing about Christ is still to be preferred.

TWO FORMS OF EVANGELICAL KENOTICISM

Ontological Kenotic Christology (OKC)

In recent years, a small number of evangelical philosophers and theologians have rehabilitated some points of earlier nineteenth-century kenoticism.[4] Believing it was dismissed too hastily by orthodox and liberal theologians alike, they are now, once again, rethinking Jesus's deity and humanity in kenotic terms. Their aim, as C. Stephen Evans describes, is to provide "a viable kenotic theory" and to do so "within the boundaries of Christian orthodoxy, broadly and generously conceived."[5] Let me outline the view in five points.

First, what is the relationship of OKC to orthodoxy? Advocates of OKC insist that they are fully orthodox because they accept the church's confession of the Trinity, the Son's eternal preexistence, and the full deity and humanity of Christ. Additionally, in order to show that OKC is a species of orthodoxy, Stephen Davis asserts the following points: (1) Jesus really performed miracles, even though these miracles were not done by his own divine power but by the Spirit's power at work in him; (2) Jesus is essentially God and *not* a mere man who had his humanity enlarged by a few divine properties; and (3) the incarnate Son remained as the second person of the Trinity; he was *not* temporarily excluded from the Trinity as a result of his "setting aside" certain divine attributes.[6] Given these affirmations, OKC advocates insist that their view is consistent with Chalcedon, yet they argue that the Definition did not fully explain what a "nature" or "person" is; Chalcedon only established the broad

---

[4] See, e.g., C. Stephen Evans, ed., *Exploring Kenotic Christology: The Self-Emptying of God* (New York: Oxford University Press, 2006). Cf. Anna Marmodoro and Jonathan Hill, eds., *The Metaphysics of the Incarnation* (New York: Oxford University Press, 2011); Stephen T. Davis, *Christian Philosophical Theology* (New York: Oxford University Press, 2006); Stephen T. Davis, Daniel Kendall, and Gerald O'Collins, eds., *The Incarnation: An Interdisciplinary Symposium on the Incarnation of the Son of God* (New York: Oxford University Press, 2002); Ronald J. Feenstra and Cornelius Plantinga, Jr., eds., *Trinity, Incarnation, and Atonement: Philosophical and Theological Essays* (Notre Dame, IN: University of Notre Dame Press, 1989).
[5] C. Stephen Evans, "Introduction," in *Exploring Kenotic Christology*, 5.
[6] These points are taken from Stephen Davis, "Is Kenosis Orthodox?" in *Exploring Kenotic Christology*, 113.

parameters for Christological thought, and as such, we are free to "redefine" these concepts differently than the church did.[7]

Second, what is the overall view of OKC? OKC proposes that in the incarnation the divine Son "gave up" or "laid aside" certain divine attributes or properties normally belonging to deity, thus choosing to "fully enter into the life of a human being" and limiting himself to these experiences without completely relinquishing his divine nature.[8] Some OKC proponents view this divestment as temporary, only for the state of humiliation, and that after the Son's glorification he resumes possession of all the divine attributes.[9] Others view the divestment as permanent.[10]

Third, what are the perceived strengths of OKC? Over against the classical view, advocates suggest at least three advantages: (1) it helps reorient our thinking about God by giving us a God who is not distant, immutable, and impassible, but one "who can fully empathize with us";[11] (2) it avoids the classical view's tendency to overemphasize Christ's deity at the expense of his humanity in an effort to avoid Doceticism and Nestorianism;[12] and (3) it can better answer the charge of logical inconsistency because it does not resort to the perceived problematic features of the classical view—e.g., two wills and minds, reduplicative strategies, and the *extra*.[13]

Fourth, the real "novelty" of OKC centers on its understanding of Christ's divine nature. Before I discuss this point, let me first note that in current philosophical discussion regarding "natures," specifically a human nature, a contrast is often made between an abstract and a concrete nature.[14] For the most part, OKC opts for an abstract view that

---

[7] See Evans, "Introduction," 1–2, who views Chalcedon this way.
[8] See C. Stephen Evans, "Kenotic Christology and the Nature of God," 196; and Davis, "Is Kenosis Orthodox?," 113.
[9] See Davis, "Is Kenosis Orthodox?," 112–138; and Feenstra, "Reconsidering Kenotic Christology," in *Trinity, Incarnation, and Atonement*, 128–151.
[10] See C. Stephen Evans, "The Self-Emptying of Love," in *Incarnation: An Interdisciplinary Symposium*, 263–267; idem, "Kenotic Christology and the Nature of God," in *Exploring Kenotic Christology*, 200–202, who defends this possibility.
[11] Evans, "Introduction," 7.
[12] See ibid., 3, 7–8, for this charge.
[13] See John Hick, *The Metaphor of God Incarnate: Christology in a Pluralistic Age* (Louisville: Westminster John Knox, 1993), who charges classical Christology with rational incoherence. See Feenstra, "A Kenotic Christology of Divine Attributes," in *Exploring Kenotic Christology*, 144, who insists on the rational superiority of OKC. The *extra* refers to the church's affirmation that the incarnate Son's actions were not completely circumscribed by his human nature because the Son was able to continue to act in and through his divine nature and thus "outside" (*extra*) of his human nature in such activities as upholding the universe (Col. 1:17; Heb. 1:3). For an excellent discussion of the *extra*, see Paul Helm, *John Calvin's Ideas* (Oxford: Oxford University Press, 2004), 58–92.
[14] See Crisp, *Divinity and Humanity*, 34–71. A human nature which is *abstract* is a property or set of properties, necessary and sufficient, for being human. In contrast, a *concrete* human nature is a concrete

entails that, in the incarnation, the divine Son becomes human by assuming properties necessary and sufficient for being human while retaining what is *essential* to deity. In stressing the word *essential*, I am now able to discuss how OKC understands the divine nature.

Similar to earlier kenoticism, OKC rejects the classical view that *all* of God's attributes are *essential* to him; instead, it distinguishes between "essential and accidental" attributes.[15] Historically, orthodoxy affirmed that in the incarnation the Son retained *all* of his divine attributes and thus continued to be *homoousios* with the Father and Spirit, and, furthermore, the incarnation was an act of *addition*, not subtraction. This, however, is not the position of OKC. The challenge, then, is to explain how the Son remains *fully* God, given his divestiture of *some* of the divine attributes in the incarnation. By employing the essential-accidental distinction, OKC denies that the Son "gives up" his divine nature completely; instead, he only gives up its *accidental* attributes. But how does one decide which attributes are which? OKC's answer: By theologizing about the divine nature *in light of the incarnation*. So, for example, Scripture teaches that the incarnate Son is *fully* God yet lacking in knowledge. In order to make sense of this, we must rethink omniscience and omnipotence (indeed *all* of the divine attributes) in such a way as to affirm that the incarnate Son is divine *and* non-omniscient, non-omnipotent, etc. From this observation, we then conclude that the omni-attributes are *not* essential to deity.[16]

In their "redefining" the divine nature, it is not surprising that OKC advocates depart dramatically from classical theology, yet they insist their view is true to Chalcedon and is rationally coherent. How so? As long as we redefine omniscience (or any divine attribute that is inconsistent with being truly human) as x is *essential* to God "unless-freely-and-temporarily-choosing-to-be-otherwise,"[17] then it is logical to affirm that the incarnate Son is *truly* God because he retains all of the *essential* divine

---

particular, which means that it consists of a specific human nature which includes all essential human properties, such as a body and a soul. For a further discussion of the differences between an abstract and a concrete human nature, see Alvin Plantinga, "On Heresy, Mind, and Truth," *Faith and Philosophy* 16/2 (1999): 182–193; Hill, "Introduction," in *Metaphysics of the Incarnation*, 1–19; and William Hasker, *Metaphysics and the Tri-Personal God* (Oxford: Oxford University Press, 2013), 62–67.

[15] See Davis, "Is Kenosis Orthodox?," 115–116. Davis gives the following definitions: An *essential property* of x is an attribute that x has and cannot lose without ceasing to exist or to be x. An *accidental property* of x is an attribute that x has but can fail to have and still be x. For example, three-sidedness is an essential property of a triangle, while having hair or an arm is an accidental property of a human.

[16] On this point, see Feenstra, "A Kenotic Christology of the Divine Attributes," 158–164; and Evans, "Kenotic Christology and the Nature of God," 190–217.

[17] Davis, "Is Kenosis Orthodox?" 118.

attributes. After the Son's earthly work is finished, he can return to being with the Father and Spirit, "unchangeably and unalterably omniscient."[18] In this way OKC confesses that "Jesus Christ during his life on earth was both truly divine and, during his freely chosen, temporary, redemptive self-humiliation, not omniscient."[19]

Fifth, OKC is "novel" not merely in its redefinition of "nature" but also in its redefinition of "person," which entails some important Christological and Trinitarian implications.[20] For OKC, "person" is best defined as a "distinct center of knowledge, will, love, and action";[21] in Trinitarian theology, this idea requires an acceptance of three wills in God, and in Christology, the endorsement of monothelitism (because the will is located in the "person"). Historically, classical Christology rejected this understanding of person and instead, in the words of Boethius, defined person as an "individual substance of a rational nature."[22] Even though these two definitions seem similar, they are not. In the latter definition, the person is an "I" or an "active subject" that subsists in a nature, i.e., a subsistent individual who is the agent of his nature. The "rational nature" is best understood as a concrete particular consisting of a body-soul composite, and it is in the rational nature that the *capacities of will and mind* are placed. This is why classical Christology has always affirmed dyothelitism and that, in the incarnation, the divine Son subsists in two natures and *he*, as the Son, acts in and through the capacities of each nature. OKC theorists, however, locate the capacities of the rational nature, i.e., will and mind, in the person; hence, OKC's embrace of monothelitism. This redefinition of person is also seen in OKC's equation of "person" *and* "soul," so that in humans, the soul of the human nature is identified as the "person," and in Christology, the "person" of the Son replaces, or better, *becomes* the soul of the human body. In contrast, Chalcedon clearly distinguished the "person" from the "soul" in its confession that the Son assumed a human nature comprised of a body *and* a "rational soul."

This redefinition of "person" is evident in Thomas Thompson and

---

[18] Feenstra, "Kenotic Christology of Divine Attributes," 154.
[19] Ibid.
[20] See Thomas R. Thompson and Cornelius Plantinga, Jr., "Trinity and Kenosis," in *Exploring Kenotic Christology*, 165–189, for a helpful discussion of how OKC advocates redefine person along with its Trinitarian implications.
[21] See Cornelius Plantinga, Jr., "Social Trinity and Tritheism," in *Trinity, Incarnation, and Atonement*, 22. Cf. Hasker, *Metaphysics and the Tri-Personal God*, 19–25.
[22] Cited in Gilles Emery, "The Dignity of Being a Substance: Person, Subsistence, and Nature," *Nova et Vetera* 9/4 (2011): 994 (English edition). For the original source, see *Liber de Persona et Duabus Naturis*, chapter 3, "A Treatise against Eutychus and Nestorius," 85, *The Theological Tractates*.

Cornelius Plantinga. In discussing the kenotic strategy, they suggest that the Logos limited "his divine powers, prerogatives, attributes, and/or glory so as to be compatible with a humanity as animated by a human rational soul—that is, to be and live as a human person."[23] They make sense of this by positing "a strict identity between the Logos and Christ's human rational soul."[24] Given this strict identity, we can now think of the true nature of the Son's kenosis. In the incarnation the divine Son freely chose to assume the properties of a human nature by assuming a human body and *becoming* a human soul, and in this sense, a human person. In this choice, the divine Son "gives up" certain divine attributes which are incompatible with human existence and truly becomes a human person, even though he remains *fully* God, in the sense described above.[25] In other words, by an act of kenosis, the person of the Son becomes a human—a human soul by self-limitation—one unitive consciousness completely within the bounds of a human body.

At least two implications follow from OKC's understanding of "person." First, it must reject the reality of the *extra* as taught historically by the church. Why? Because for OKC, the *extra* is metaphysically impossible since *kenosis* entails that the Son is, at least temporarily, circumscribed by the limits of his human body. Second, it also requires an embrace of social Trinitarianism, the affirmation that in God there are three distinct centers of consciousness, will, mind, and agency.[26] The classical view, in contrast, argues that the three persons are distinct yet they also share the same capacity of will because they possess the same identical concrete nature. Thus, for OKC, the oneness of the Godhead is not found in the three persons sharing the same identical nature; instead, the divine persons are one because "God is like a community,"[27] a perichoretic unity of Trinitarian persons by which the divine persons have "unity of purpose, fellowship, communion, hospitality, transparency, self-deference, or just simply the love among Father, Son, and Spirit."[28] Furthermore, bound up with this social view, OKC advocates also reject a staple of pro-Nicene

---

[23] Thompson and Plantinga, "Trinity and Kenosis," 170.
[24] Ibid.
[25] See Richard Swinburne, "The Coherence of the Chalcedonian Definition of the Incarnation," in *Metaphysics of the Incarnation*, 156–160, who argues this point.
[26] On this point, see Richard Swinburne, *The Christian God* (Oxford: Oxford University Press, 1994), 182; and Thomas H. McCall, *Which Trinity? Whose Monotheism?: Philosophical and Systematic Theologians on the Metaphysics of Trinitarian Theology* (Grand Rapids, MI: Eerdmans, 2010), 12–19, 87–105.
[27] Stephen T. Davis, "Perichoretic Monotheism: A Defense of a Social Theory of the Trinity," in *The Trinity: East/West Dialogue*, ed. Melville Y. Stewart (Dordrecht: Kluwer Academic, 2003), 42.
[28] Thompson and Plantinga, "Trinity and Kenosis," 183–184.

theology, that is, the affirmation of the inseparable operations of the divine persons. As Thompson and Plantinga willingly concede, "To the objection that this sunders the *indivisa* of Trinitarian persons and their operations, we confess the transgression."[29]

Here, then, is OKC in a nutshell. Even though it confesses to function within the parameters of orthodoxy, almost at every point it redefines the terms and theological entailments of the Chalcedonian Definition. Below I will evaluate whether this "new" path is "better" than the old one, but before I do, let me now describe the functional kenotic viewpoint.

Functional Kenotic Christology (FKC)

Within evangelical theology, an FKC approach is more common and less radical. Not all who espouse this view would employ the "kenotic" label, given some of its connotations, but most would not object. Representative examples from biblical studies to systematic theology to philosophical theology, while differing at points, are: Gerald Hawthorne, Klaus Issler, Garrett DeWeese, and William Craig and J. P. Moreland.[30] Even though there are various nuances among FKC advocates, the view is best understood by setting it over against classical Christology and OKC in four steps.

First, in regard to the "divine nature," FKC agrees with classical Christology, over against OKC, that the "essential-accidental" distinction is illegitimate. As such, the incarnation is *not* a "giving up" of any of the divine attributes; instead, the incarnate Son is fully God and continues to possess *all* of the divine attributes as one who is *homoousios* with the Father and Spirit.[31]

Second, in regard to "person," FKC agrees with OKC, over against classical Christology, by defining "person" as a distinct center of knowledge, will, and action, thus locating will and mind in the person, hence its endorsement of monothelitism.[32] Additionally, many FKC theorists

---
[29] Ibid., 189.
[30] Gerald F. Hawthorne, *The Presence and the Power* (1991; repr., Eugene, OR: Wipf & Stock, 2003); Klaus Issler, *Living into the Life of Jesus* (Downers Grove, IL: InterVarsity Press, 2012); Garrett J. DeWeese, "One Person, Two Natures: Two Metaphysical Models of the Incarnation," in *Jesus in Trinitarian Perspective*, ed. Fred Sanders and Klaus Issler (Nashville: B&H, 2007), 114–153; William L. Craig and J. P. Moreland, *Philosophical Foundations for a Christian Worldview* (Downers Grove, IL: InterVarsity Press, 2003), 597–614.
[31] See Craig and Moreland, *Philosophical Foundations*, 607.
[32] DeWeese, "One Person, Two Natures," 144–149; Craig and Moreland, *Philosophical Foundations*, 611–612.

equate "person" with "soul"[33] so that in the incarnation, the person of the Son (which includes a distinct will and mind) now acts and functions through the limits of a human body, with the divine person/soul of the Son *becoming* the soul of the human body. For FKC, this is the most distinctive departure from classical thought, since Chalcedonian Christology always placed the capacity of will in the nature, not the person, hence its endorsement of dyothelitism. Also, classical Christology never equated the person with the soul. As I will note below, it is at this point that both OKC and FKC seem to face the difficult challenge of making sense of Christ's complete humanity, even though both views strongly affirm it. Both kenotic views insist that it is the classical view which cannot account for Christ's humanity. But, as I will note below, if Christ has only one *divine* will, then making sense of Christ's humanity apart from him possessing a distinct human will is difficult.[34] Furthermore, even though not all FKC theorists employ the categories of analytic philosophy, when they do, most think of Christ's human nature as abstract rather than concrete.[35] In so doing, the incarnation is understood as the Son assuming the properties of a human nature, including the property of being a human soul; hence the understanding that the Son *becomes* a human soul. On the surface this sounds rather Apollinarian, as some willingly admit; however, as Crisp helpfully explains, it is not necessarily so. Crisp clarifies the view: Technically, an FKC does not say "that the Word *replaces an existing human soul*. Instead the Word becomes the soul of the body of Christ."[36]

Third, FKC also differs from the classical view in regard to the incarnate Son's *exercise* or *functional* use of his divine attributes during the state of humiliation. Specifically, FKC denies that the incarnate Son *exercises his divine attributes* in upholding the universe and performing miracles, yet it must be admitted that within this view there is a spectrum of thought regarding the Son's use of his divine attributes. Some contend that the Son *never* uses his divine attributes; all of his "divine" acts are done by the power of the Spirit, in a way similar to but greater than previous Spirit-empowered men. Others modify this stance by acknowledging

---

[33] DeWeese, "One Person, Two Natures," 147–148; Craig and Moreland, *Philosophical Foundations*, 608–610.
[34] Crisp, *Divinity and Humanity*, 59, raises the challenge this way: "Possession of a will is constitutive of being either a human or a divine entity. So, if Christ is fully human he must have a distinct human will. And if he is fully divine he must have a distinct divine will." Yet, given OKC and FKC's definition of "person," it seems that Christ only has a distinct divine will and *not* a distinct human will.
[35] See e.g., Craig and Moreland, *Philosophical Foundations*, 597–614.
[36] Crisp, *Divinity and Humanity*, 50.

that the Son *occasionally* uses his divine attributes, but *predominantly* the Son lives his life as we do—not in his deity but in his humanity—dependent upon the Spirit, and through him the Spirit acts.[37] Here is another point where an FKC is *not* merely a species of the classical view.[38] Why? Because even though classical Christology unequivocally affirms that the Son lives a fully human life, it rejects the view that the incarnate Son is limited *only* or even *predominantly* to living a human life by the power of the Spirit. Given that the classical view places the capacities of will and mind in the natures, it is able to affirm the *extra*, which affirms that the incarnate Son is able to act in and through both natures and thus continue to live a fully human *and* divine life. FKC, on the other hand, given its view of one divine will and mind in the person, has a difficult time accounting for the *extra* and thus making sense of how Scripture says, for example, that the incarnate Son continued to uphold the universe by his own exercise of divine power (e.g., Col. 1:15–17; Heb. 1:3).[39] No doubt, similar to classical Christology, FKC affirms the full deity of Christ, yet it departs at significant points: its minimizing of Christ's *continuing exercise* of his divine attributes on earth, its commitment to monothelitism, and its difficulty in affirming or rejecting the *extra*.

Fourth, FKC is often associated with the term "Spirit-Christology." One reason for this association is its indebtedness to Gerald Hawthorne's conclusions in his important monograph, *The Presence and the Power*.[40] In this work, Hawthorne investigates the role of the Spirit in Jesus's life and ministry from conception to exaltation. He, along with many FKC advocates, is convinced that we have not done justice to the Spirit–incarnate Son relationship and, in fact, that this relationship is a missing

---

[37] Hawthorne represents the former view, while DeWeese and Issler represent the latter. In a similar way, Bruce A. Ware (*The Man Christ Jesus* [Wheaton, IL: Crossway, 2013]) argues for this understanding of the incarnate Son's exercise of his divine attributes. Yet, in private conversations with Bruce, he wants to distinguish his view from the monothelitism of Hawthorne, DeWeese, and Issler, and furthermore, he strongly endorses the *extra*. This entails that his view is slightly different than an FKC even though there are a lot of similarities. We await from him in print some further clarification of his view.

[38] Contra Peter Forrest, "The Incarnation: A Philosophical Case for Kenosis," *Religious Studies* 36 (2000): 127–140, who identifies the functional kenotic view as "quasi-kenotic" and then views it as a version of classical Christology.

[39] Making sense of the continuing cosmic functions of the incarnate Son separates the classical view from its kenotic variations. For example, Issler (*Living into the Life of Jesus*, 125n31) explains Colossians 1:17 and Hebrews 1:3 in this way: In a preincarnate decision the Son temporarily delegated his cosmic functions to the Father and Spirit, even though the text does *not* say this.

[40] For a helpful discussion and critique of Hawthorne, see Mark L. Strauss, "Jesus and the Spirit in Biblical and Theological Perspective: Messianic Empowering, Saving Wisdom, and the Limits of Biblical Theology," in *The Spirit and Christ in the New Testament and Christian Theology: Essays in Honor of Max Turner*, ed. I. Howard Marshall, Volker Rabens, and Cornelis Bennema (Grand Rapids, MI: Eerdmans, 2012), 266–284.

piece in our understanding of the incarnation. Following Hawthorne, FKC contends that the Son, in becoming a man, "willed to renounce the exercise of his divine powers, attributes, prerogatives, so that he might live fully within those limitations which inhere in being truly human."[41] In the incarnation, then, the divine attributes are not "given up"; instead, they become "potential or latent within this incarnate One—present in Jesus in all their fullness, but no longer in exercise,"[42] so that the incarnate Son chooses to live his life completely circumscribed by his human nature (or mostly so) and "within the bounds of human limitations."[43] Thus when it comes to how Jesus has supernatural knowledge and exercises supernatural power in his miracles, FKC insists that Jesus does so, *not* by the use of his divine attributes, but by the power of the Spirit. Thus, in all of the incarnate Son's actions, even actions traditionally viewed as *divine* actions (such as his miracles), Jesus performs them by the Spirit and in a similar way to other Spirit-empowered men and parallel to the Spirit's work in us. This is why Jesus can serve as our example, as he shows us how to live our lives in dependence upon the Spirit.

CRITICAL REFLECTIONS ON EVANGELICAL KENOTICISM
What should we think about these "new" Christological views? Much could be said; I offer four critical reflections with the goal of showing that the "classical" view is still to be preferred.

1. Evangelical Kenoticism, the Chalcedonian Definition, and the Burden of Proof
Even though both views claim formal adherence to the parameters of Chalcedon, they depart from it at significant points, especially in OKC's redefinition of the divine nature and in both of their redefinitions of "person," their equation of "person" with "soul," and their endorsement of monothelitism. Even though some try to downplay these differences,[44] one must legitimately ask: How far can we redefine our terms in ways that conflict with the Chalcedonian Definition before the Definition takes

---
[41] Hawthorne, *Presence and the Power*, 208.
[42] Ibid.
[43] Ibid., 212. As noted, Hawthorne thinks that the incarnate Son *never* exercised his divine attributes, while others, like DeWeese and Issler, think he *occasionally* did so, but rarely.
[44] See Feenstra, "Kenotic Christology of Divine Attributes," 156; and Evans, "Kenotic Christology and the Nature of God," 195n13.

on a different meaning? My point is *not* that confessions are equal to Scripture and can never be improved upon. Confessions are secondary standards and thus open to correction and, no doubt, adherents to either form of evangelical kenoticism insist that such rethinking is necessary. Nevertheless, given the consensus of pro-Nicene Trinitarianism and Chalcedonian Christology, one must exercise extreme care in such rethinking. One must demonstrate that classical Christology, properly understood, is, first, unbiblical, and second, theologically inadequate, before it is so easily dismissed. Oliver Crisp captures this point well: "It seems to me that someone dissenting from the findings of an ecumenical council of the church should have a very good reason—indeed, a very good *theological* reason—for doing so."[45] Once again, this is *not* to say that Christological reflection should cease; it is to say, especially for these "new" views, that they must demonstrate that they are more biblically and theologically faithful than the classical view—something not yet done.

2. Evangelical Kenoticism and the Redefinition of "Nature" and "Person"

In regard to the redefinition of the divine "nature," the main problem is with OKC over against classical Christology and FKC, and its difficulty in sustaining the deity of Christ.[46] There are at least two reasons to reject its proposal. First, OKC's view is not really an improvement on earlier kenotic views, in that it lacks serious *biblical* grounding. What David Wells says about earlier forms of kenoticism rightly applies to this one: "The only God of whom Scripture speaks is one who is all-powerful, knows everything, and is everywhere. By definition, a god who has diminished power and knowledge is not the biblical God."[47] Scripture simply does not allow an irreducible minimum for deity, and a God who lacks certain divine attributes is simply not God. OKC offers a logical way of speaking of Christ's deity, but *not* a biblical or traditional way.[48]

Second, OKC's view is arbitrary and inconsistent. As Craig and Moreland rightly assert, to say that God has "essential properties like being-

---
[45] Crisp, *Divinity and Humanity*, 35.
[46] See Davis, "Is Kenosis Orthodox?" 135–136, who acknowledges this problem.
[47] Wells, *Person of Christ*, 138.
[48] See Crisp, *Divinity and Humanity*, 126, who makes this point. Cf. the crucial discussion of what Scripture teaches about God's nature and attributes in John S. Feinberg, *No One Like Him: The Doctrine of God*, Foundations of Evangelical Theology, John S. Feinberg, gen. ed. (Wheaton, IL: Crossway, 2001), 233–374.

omniscient-except-when-kenotically-incarnate, which he never surrenders and which are sufficient for deity" is not only "explanatorily vacuous" but, ontologically speaking, "it is not clear that there even are such properties as being-omniscient-except-when-kenotically-incarnate."[49] Furthermore, as Crisp points out, such a view is arbitrary. He writes, "It is very difficult indeed to know where to draw the line demarcating contingent and essential properties. For if omniscience turns out to be a contingent rather than an essential divine property, then what are we to make of omnipotence, omnipresence, eternity or benevolence, to name four other divine attributes traditionally thought to be essential to the divine nature?"[50] Ultimately, the entire procedure looks ad hoc. In addition, why only stop at certain divine attributes? Why not, as Craig and Moreland suggest, consider the divine attributes of necessity, aseity, and eternality?[51] After all, how can we make sense of Christ's death unless he relinquishes these attributes? The very fact that OKC does not do so demonstrates something of its arbitrariness. Even more problematic is how this view can affirm that the incarnate Son is *homoousios* with the Father and Spirit, if the Father and Spirit retain *all* of the divine attributes while the Son does not, even temporarily. For the state of humiliation, the Son not only is *not* of the same substance as the Father and Spirit, but also the divine persons do not possess the divine nature equally, which smacks of a quasi-Arianism.[52]

What about both views' understanding of "person"? Even though FKC disagrees with OKC regarding the divine nature, in agreement with OKC over against classical thought, it redefines "person" in more contemporary terms: a distinct center of knowledge, will, and action, thus placing the capacities of will and mind in the person rather than the nature. The classical view, however, following Boethius's definition—"A person is an individual substance of a rational nature"[53]—does *not* place the capacities of will and mind in the person but in the nature. It views the "person" as an agent, or an "I" who subsists in a "rational nature." This is why the classical view insists that the divine Son, in assuming a concrete human nature, became human by adding to himself a human body *and*

---

[49] Craig and Moreland, *Philosophical Foundations*, 607.
[50] Crisp, *Divinity and Humanity*, 132.
[51] See Craig and Moreland, *Philosophical Foundations*, 608.
[52] See Crisp, *Divinity and Humanity*, 127n18, who makes this point.
[53] Cited in Emery, "The Dignity of Being a Substance," 994. See also Richard A. Muller, *Dictionary of Latin and Greek Theological Terms* (Grand Rapids, MI: Baker, 1985), 223–227.

soul (including a human will and mind), and as a result is now able to live a fully human life in and through the capacities of his human nature.[54] In addition, the classical view also affirmed that the incarnate Son is *not* limited to living his life merely through his human nature because, as the Son, *he* continues to possess the divine nature in relation to the Father and Spirit, and is thus able to continue to live a divine life (thus the *extra*).

It is important to stress, however, that this classical way of viewing Christ is *not* open to those who adopt the current understanding of person. Why? Because given that in Christ there is only one divine person (which includes in that person *one divine will and mind*), then how can we make sense of a Jesus who is truly human and exhibits limitations of knowledge if that one divine person is omniscient in the full sense of the word? This is why OKC proposes that in order to make sense of the incarnation, the divine Son must be able to "give up" certain divine attributes such as omniscience, because it is inconsistent with being human.[55] Or, from the FKC side, the rationale for kenosis is largely due to trying to

---

[54] Current discussion of "person" often misunderstands the classic view. Almost uniformly the charge is that the classic view is Nestorian, which is odd since the church consistently rejected Nestorianism. In addition, the current view of person tends to equate "person" with "soul," something the classic view never did. Probably the best way to distinguish the two views of person is via the topic of the *will*. It is not accidental that current views of person are monothelite while classical views are dyothelite. Why? William Hasker, in *Metaphysics and the Tri-Personal God*, helps answer this question by speaking of "will" in terms of three distinct applications: "it can refer to the *content* of one's will (the state of affairs that is willed), or to the *act* of willing, or to the *faculty or capacity* of willing" (206). In Trinitarian application, if "will" is used in terms of *content*, then all three persons will the same thing and hence have "one" will. But, argues Hasker, if we locate in the person the "will" in terms of "acts of will and faculties of willing" (207), then we must affirm that each divine person has a distinct will (thus three wills in the Godhead), and correspondingly, in Christology, Christ has only one will (monothelitism). What is perceptive about Hasker's discussion is how he distinguishes between (1) the *content* of one's will, (2) the *act* of willing, and (3) the *faculty* or *capacity* of willing, but what is unhelpful is how he conflates (2) and (3) and locates both of these in "person." He seems unaware that the classical view distinguished (2) and (3) in relation to the "person." A "person," classically, is an agent who *acts* in and through his "rational nature" so that (2) is identified with the person and (3) with the nature. Thus, in pro-Nicene Trinitarianism, the Father, Son, and Spirit, because they are distinct persons, *act* as persons according to their mode of subsistence. Thus the Father *acts* as the Father, the Son *acts* as the Son, and the Spirit *acts* as the Spirit; however, contrary to the current view, classical theology places the *faculty* or *capacity* of will in the nature (on this point, see Gilles Emery, *The Trinitarian Theology of St. Thomas Aquinas* [New York: Oxford University Press, 2007], 51–127, 338–412). This is why pro-Nicene theology affirmed that the three divine persons act inseparably, i.e., the Father, Son, and Spirit *act* according to their eternal relations (mode of subsistence) but in virtue of their common nature. Thus, the Father, Son, and Spirit all *act*, yet they *act* in and through the capacities of the one single divine nature that they equally possess and share. Because the nature is where the *capacity of willing* is found, we can say that the three persons *act* as distinct persons according to their eternal-immanent relations, in and through the *capacities* of the divine nature, which includes the same will. As this understanding is applied to Christology, the classical view affirms that the *one* person, the divine Son, given that he has two natures, also has two wills in terms of (3) and *not* (2). In Christ, then, the divine Son is the acting agent who acts in and through his natures, and now, as a result of the incarnation, is able to act *as a man according to his distinct human will*. This is why the divine Son can now live and experience a fully human life, even though he is not entirely circumscribed or limited by his human nature because he continues to subsist in the divine nature.

[55] See Stephen T. Davis, "The Metaphysics of Kenosis," in *Metaphysics of the Incarnation*, 129, who wrestles with this point.

make sense of how the Son's *one* divine mind can lack knowledge, given that the capacities of will and mind are located in the person.

On these points, it is crucial to note that classical Christology does *not* wrestle with these issues in exactly the same way as evangelical kenoticism does.[56] Why? Simply put, because of their differing conceptions of "person." For example, the classical view allows for the metaphysical possibility of there being two wills and minds in Christ because the *capacities* of will and mind are located in the nature and not the person. The divine Son, then, who is the agent of his natures, *acts* in and through both natures. This entails that the person of the Son, due to the incarnation, is able to live a fully divine life (as he has always done) and now a fully human life (because he assumes a concrete human nature, i.e., a body and a soul). This also allows for the employment of a proper sense of *communicatio idiomatum* along with the reduplication strategy so that what is true of the natures is predicated of the person. Thus, what is true of the divine nature (e.g., omniscience, omnipotence, omnipresence) may be predicated of the Son and likewise in relation to the human nature (e.g., growing in wisdom and knowledge, experiencing weakness, being tired). Yet, as the *extra* affirms, because the Son subsists in two natures, he is *not* limited or completely circumscribed by his human nature. The incarnate Son, in relation to the Father and Spirit, consistent with his mode of subsistence from all eternity, continues to act *as the Son* and now as the incarnate Son. But, once again, it is crucial to note that this classical understanding is *not* available to the kenotic viewpoints, given their redefinition of "person."

Where does this leave us? Obviously the classical and current views of "person" are different and, in truth, one of the main reasons for contemporary revisions of classical Christology is due to this difference. How, then, do we decide which view is correct? For sake of argument, I will assume that both views are rationally coherent, so ultimately we must decide in regard to their biblical-theological fit, namely, which view best accounts for *all* the data regarding Christ? In my final two reflections, I will question whether the "new" kenotic paths really meet this standard over against the "old" path of classical Christology.

---

[56] This is *not* to say that there is no mystery in the classical view! It acknowledges, rather, that OKC and FKC wrestle with different issues and provide different answers due to their specific view of person, while the classical view wrestles with similar issues but provides different answers due to its different view of person.

3. Evangelical Kenoticism and Various Trinitarian Implications

Both views of evangelical kenoticism affirm some form of social Trinitarianism given their understanding of person, yet not all social Trinitarians are equal, despite their family resemblances.[57] Given the major difference between OKC and FKC on the divine nature, I will address some of the Trinitarian implications of each view separately.

Some Trinitarian Implications of OKC

Even though there are numerous implications of OKC for Trinitarian-Christological theology, I will focus on three. First, as noted above, given OKC's redefinition of the divine nature, the divine persons are radically reconfigured in terms of their sharing of the divine attributes, especially in light of the incarnation. Not only does this create insurmountable problems for affirming that Christ is *homoousios* with the other divine persons (which makes it difficult to affirm Christ's deity), it also results in a triune God, who for a period of time looks more binitarian than Trinitarian—implications which are not acceptable.[58]

Second, OKC has great difficulty maintaining the continuity between the preexistent Son (*Logos asarkos*) and the incarnate Son (*Logos ensarkos*), thus implying huge disruptions in the internal relations of the triune persons. For example, in the incarnation, as the Son "gives up" his omniscience, even if it is only temporarily, his divine self-consciousness would be almost completely expunged. As Donald Macleod noted in regard to earlier kenotic views, such "a degree of amnesia" results in that "to which there can be no parallel."[59] On this issue, as difficult as it is for us to explain the psychology of the incarnate Son, the "older" path is better. Unlike OKC, classical Christology thinks of the divine Son as subsisting in two natures, which allows for the metaphysical possibility of two ranges of consciousness in Christ, given that mind and will are capacities of the natures. Even though we are left with plenty of mystery and unknowns, this explanation makes better sense of the biblical data that speaks of Christ's legitimate human growth without expunging the

---
[57] On this point, see Hasker, *Metaphysics and the Tri-Personal God*, 81–163.
[58] See Crisp, *Divinity and Humanity*, 127–131, for a discussion of these points.
[59] Donald Macleod, *The Person of Christ* (Downers Grove, IL: InterVarsity Press, 1998), 210.

Son's divine self-consciousness that was his from eternity. OKC simply cannot do justice to this full range of biblical data.

Third, OKC has difficulty accounting for the biblical teaching regarding the cosmic functions of Christ. Scripture attributes various cosmic functions to the *incarnate* Son (Col. 1:17; Heb. 1:3). Additionally, Scripture does not teach that the Son's sustaining of the universe temporarily ceased for a period of time. In fact, Scripture speaks of all three persons—Father, Son, and Spirit—acting together in every *ad extra* work, including that of providence. OKC, contrary to Scripture, proposes that the incarnate Son temporarily "set aside" those divine attributes necessary to carry out his cosmic activity, but in that case how do we explain these biblical texts? Evans, in a fairly typical way, suggests that normally all three persons are involved in these cosmic actions, but given the incarnation, the Father and Spirit carry out the work *without* the agency of the Son. He writes, "In some way the activity of each person of the Trinity must involve the activity of each of the others. I see no reason why, if the second person of the Trinity became incarnate and divested himself of omnipotence and omniscience, what we might call the sustaining work of this person in creation could not be carried on by the other persons."[60] Would this then lead to the incarnate Son being dependent on the Father and Spirit in ways that he was not before? Evans tackles this question by admitting that there are asymmetries in the relations of the persons, so it is not a problem to think of this occurring.[61]

The problem, however, with this explanation is twofold. First, Scripture does not teach it. Cosmic functions are directly attributed to the activity of the incarnate Son. Second, it makes the Trinitarian personal relations divided and lopsided. Not only do the divine persons not act together, which is a denial of pro-Nicene theology and tantamount to undermining Trinitarian monotheism; there is also an asymmetry among the persons that speaks of a fundamental inequality. On this understanding, it is not only difficult to make sense of how all three persons are *homoousios*, but nowhere does Scripture distinguish the divine persons in terms of their possession/nonpossession or use/nonuse of the divine attributes. Instead Scripture teaches that the divine persons equally possess the divine nature and act together in every divine action according

---
[60] Evans, "Self-Emptying of Love," 259. Cf. also Evans, "Kenotic Christology and the Nature of God," 213–214.
[61] See ibid., 259n28.

to the person's eternal relations. OKC, in the end, undercuts the biblical presentation of Trinitarian agency, and its "new" path is far too costly in regard to biblical-theological fidelity.

Some Trinitarian Implications of FKC

The approach of an FKC is much better than OKC. In the incarnation the Son does not set aside certain divine attributes; instead, the self-limitation of the Son is *functional*, as he chooses not to exercise his divine attributes. In his humanity, the Son relies on the power of the Spirit to live, act, and obey the Father's will for our salvation. Even though this view has a lot of strengths, there are at least two problems in Trinitarian terms.

First, FKC has difficulty accounting for how Scripture presents the deity of Christ in his life and ministry. In the Gospels, Jesus's inauguration of the kingdom, his teaching, and his miracles are not merely Spirit-empowered acts; they are ultimately acts identified with *YHWH*.[62] The Jesus of the Bible knows he is the eternal Son; he forgives sin and exercises divine power; he has divine authority and receives worship. How can this identification with *YHWH* be made? Because the very works of the incarnate Son testify to who he is (e.g., John 5:16–30). No doubt, all of these actions are done by one who is a man, yet one cannot simply explain Jesus in merely human terms, or even in terms that place him in the category of Spirit-empowered men of the past. His identity is thoroughly divine, and in everything he says and does, he demonstrates that he is God the Son incarnate. Scripture teaches this truth most clearly in those texts that attribute cosmic functions to the *incarnate* Son, not merely the Son prior to his incarnation or merely as glorified (Col. 1:17; Heb. 1:3). The only way we can make sense of these texts is to acknowledge that, in the state of humiliation, the Son *continues to exercise* his divine attributes *as the Son* in relation to and united with the Father and Spirit.

It is at this precise point, however, that the view of FKC stumbles. On one end of the spectrum, some claim that the Son *never* exercises his divine attributes while on earth, and on the other end, some claim that the Son *sometimes* does, yet *predominantly* the Son's unique actions are done by the power of the Spirit at work in him. But, contra classical

---

[62] See, e.g., Richard Bauckham, *Jesus and the God of Israel* (Grand Rapids, MI: Eerdmans, 2008); Wells, *Person of Christ*, 21–81.

Christology, no FKC advocate claims that the Son *continually* exercises his divine attributes—something that is necessary if the ongoing work of providence is to continue. Given FKC's redefinition of person, which entails a denial of two wills and minds in Christ, it is difficult to maintain the classical view of the *extra*. Classically, the *extra* has affirmed that the Son, in assuming a human nature, is not limited to it. As a result, the incarnate Son, in relation to the Father and Spirit, continues to carry out cosmic functions; furthermore, these divine actions are not viewed as a violation of Christ's humanity, because his divine attributes remain attributes of the divine nature alone and they are not shared with his human nature. The Son, then, as the acting agent, is able to act in and through both natures even while on earth, including upholding the universe *qua* his divine nature.

How, then, do proponents of FKC explain these cosmic functions attributed to the Son? Similar to OKC, Issler suggests that the Son in a preincarnate decision "temporarily delegated to the other members of the Trinity his usual divine duties, such as sustaining the universe (Col 1:17; Heb 1:3)."[63] But this explanation runs into the same problem as discussed above, namely, Scripture does not explicitly teach it, it potentially surrenders the unity of Trinitarian agency, and it results in a change in the content of the personal deity of the Son. In other words, FKC so changes the life of the divine Son that the self-identity of the Son, along with Trinitarian relations, is redefined.

The second Trinitarian problem FKC introduces is that it overemphasizes the Son-Spirit relationship and is not sufficiently Trinitarian in thinking through the Father-Son-Spirit relations. Due to the influence of Hawthorne, many FKC advocates believe that the role of the Spirit in the life of Christ is the key to making sense of the incarnation. As noted, their proposal is that the incarnate Son either *never* (e.g., Hawthorne) or *rarely* (e.g., DeWeese, Issler) exercises his divine attributes. Instead, the divine Son lives his life *solely* or *predominantly* in a human body with all of its corresponding limitations, *and* as one who is indwelt by, empowered by, and dependent upon the Holy Spirit. In regard to the supernatural activity of Christ, FKC argues that *all* or *most* of Christ's unique actions were done by the Spirit. There are, however, at least two problems with this view in regard to Trinitarian relations and agency.

---

[63] Issler, *Living into the Life of Jesus*, 125n31.

The first problem centers on the agency of the Son. In regard to his supernatural actions, it is as if the Son disappears and the acting agent is the Spirit. Think, for example, of Jesus's raising the dead or walking on the water or feeding the five thousand; FKC claims that *all* of these actions were done, *not* by the agency of the Son but by the Spirit. Given that the Son *never* or *rarely* exercises his divine attributes, these actions are not the Son's actions *as a man* (unless we affirm that humans can exercise omnipotence), but actions done by the Spirit. Similar to the Spirit's agency in other Spirit-empowered people, though admittedly greater, it is *not* the human who does the work (nor, in the case of Christ, the divine Son), but the Spirit who works through humans as instruments to accomplish his mighty power. If this is the case, however, then what has happened to the agency of the Son in all of his actions? Not only is the Spirit viewed as strangely "external" to the Son, which from a Trinitarian perspective is not so, but the divine Son as the person of the incarnation is also removed from the activity of his human nature, which renders problems for our understanding of the hypostatic union. Oliver Crisp points this out when he argues that such a view seems to assume that *God the Son*, as the person and acting agent of the natures, never acts directly "in" and "through" his human nature. Such action after the assumption of his human nature is only ever mediate, through the work of the Holy Spirit.[64] But surely, as Crisp insists, "[I]f the human nature of Christ is 'owned' by God the Son, it seems very strange that he is not the divine person *immediately* acting upon, or through, his human nature."[65] In fact, given the intimate relation between the Son and his assumed human nature, we must not remove the divine Son from his own human nature and replace it with the "external" action of the Spirit upon him.[66] Is there a better way of explaining this?

There is indeed a better way, and it leads to stating the second problem: the FKC model fails to be sufficiently Trinitarian. It rightly emphasizes the Son-Spirit relationship, which is obviously part of the biblical data; however, it does not satisfactorily think through the Father-Son-Spirit relations as a whole. After all, it is not enough to focus simply on the Son-Spirit relations; we must also account for John's Gospel,

---

[64] See Oliver D. Crisp, *Revisioning Christology: Theology in the Reformed Tradition* (Burlington, VT: Ashgate, 2011), 100–102.
[65] Ibid., 102.
[66] For a further development of this point, see ibid., 103–107.

for example, which stresses predominantly the Father-Son relations.[67] In other words, it is not enough to appeal to the Spirit's work without wrestling with how all three persons relate to each other. What is needed is a more robust appeal to Trinitarian agency that includes within it a classic understanding of the person-nature distinction and inseparable operations;[68] when this is done, I am convinced we can make better sense of all the biblical data. Think, for example, of John 5:19–30. Here we are told that Jesus can do *nothing* on his own initiative, but *only* what he sees the Father doing. And then Jesus quickly adds: he can do *everything* his Father does, i.e., create and sustain the universe, judge all people, give eternal life, and, in this context, heal on the Sabbath! The Son's personal, filial relation to his Father—a relation from all eternity—now explains why the Son obeys his Father's will, why he does not pursue his own initiative, why he is completely dependent upon his Father, and how he acts *as the Son* in relation to his Father. In truth, one can just as easily explain the Son's actions, dependency, lack of knowledge, and so on in terms of the Father-Son relationship, as FKC advocates attempt to do by appealing to the Son-Spirit relationship, yet to do so would be reductionistic. Instead, we must explain how all three persons relate *ad intra* and then carefully think through how these personal relations show themselves in the divine economy *ad extra*. When we do this, we can better make sense of the incarnation in terms of Trinitarian relations and agency, as classical Christology has always sought to do.[69]

4. Evangelical Kenoticism and the Humanity of Christ

One of the great strengths touted by evangelical kenoticism advocates over against classical Christology is its ability to account for Christ's humanity. However, given their redefinition of "person," it seems that it will be more difficult to uphold Christ's full humanity, first in making Christ's humanity unlike ours, and second, in making sense of how Christ

---

[67] See the excellent treatment of Trinitarian agency in Andreas J. Köstenberger and Scott R. Swain, *Father, Son, and Spirit: The Trinity and John's Gospel*, New Studies in Biblical Theology 24 (Downers Grove, IL: InterVarsity Press, 2008), 165–186.
[68] For a full account of pro-Nicene Trinitarian agency, see Gilles Emery, *Trinity, Church, and the Human Person: Thomistic Essays* (Naples, FL: Sapientia, 2007), 115–153; and Lewis Ayres, *Nicaea and Its Legacy* (New York: Oxford University Press, 2004).
[69] Due to space limitations I cannot develop this point here, but I have done so in my *The Person of Christ* (Wheaton, IL: Crossway, forthcoming).

either retains his humanity in the state of exaltation or is not permanently limited and thus changed in his ability to act as God the Son. Let us turn to each of these points.

Is Christ's Humanity Like Ours?

Scripture teaches that Christ's humanity is like ours in every way except sin (e.g., Heb. 2:14, 17; Rom. 8:3). This is not an insignificant point: If Christ is not fully human, he cannot represent us as our new covenant head. Our salvation requires not only that Jesus be fully God but also that he be fully human, and Scripture does *not* diminish his full humanity. Kenotic Christology makes much of this point and constantly charges classical Christology with docetic tendencies. We are told repeatedly that evangelicals stress Christ's deity more than they do his humanity,[70] yet given how OKC and FKC redefine "person," it is the kenotic views that seemingly face problems in regard to accounting for Christ's humanity being like our own.

For starters, both views seem to equate the "person" with the "soul," and thus, in the incarnation the Son *becomes* a human soul, or in the words of Craig and Moreland, "the Logos completes the individual human nature of Christ by furnishing it with a rational soul, which is the Logos himself."[71] But if this is so, then one cannot think of a distinct human soul that the Son assumes, contra the Chalcedonian Definition. Or think of how both views place the capacities of will and mind in the person, thus necessitating one will and mind in Christ, namely, the Son's *divine* will and mind. Similar to the problem with the soul, however, in Christ there is no *distinct* human will or mind, once again contrary to the classical affirmation of dyothelitism. The best that can be said is that the divine person of the Son has a will that in the incarnation has two aspects to it, but this is *not* the same as two distinct wills,[72] thus making it difficult to see how Christ's humanity is like ours. If the Son does not act, think, grow in wisdom and knowledge, express human emotions, and so on, in and through *the capacities of a human soul, will, and mind*, it is difficult to think how he is like us, and it is difficult to account for the biblical Jesus.

---

[70] For example, see this charge in Gordon D. Fee, "The New Testament and Kenosis Christology," in *Exploring Kenotic Christology*, 25.
[71] Craig and Moreland, *Philosophical Foundations*, 610.
[72] See Crisp, *Divinity and Humanity*, 57–61, who makes this point.

At this point, what both kenotic views often do is to assume some kind of "doubleness" in Christ, similar to classical Christology, yet without the metaphysical underpinning for it. So, for example, when it comes to consciousness, both views talk about a divine and human consciousness, or a divine subliminal knowledge and a human conscious knowledge. So, as Craig and Moreland suggest, in Jesus's conscious experience, he learns. "Even though the Logos possesses all knowledge about the world from quantum mechanics to auto mechanics, there is no reason to think that Jesus of Nazareth would have been able to answer questions about such subjects, so low had he stooped in condescending to take on the human condition."[73] Or, "the Logos allowed only those facets of his person to be part of Christ's waking consciousness which were compatible with typical human experience."[74] On the surface this explanation sounds plausible until we first remember, there is only *one* divine mind/soul in Christ, and second, how do we conceive of the *one divine mind* having levels of consciousness and knowledge? Even though the classical view has its challenges, at least it can make sense of how the divine Son, who now subsists in two natures, can continue to live a fully divine *and* fully human life, given that he has added to himself a concrete human nature comprised of a body *and* a distinct human soul.

The same may be said of how kenotic views speak of a divine and human willing in Christ, yet their view allows for only *one* divine will. For example, Craig and Moreland argue that Jesus possessed "a typical human consciousness,"[75] and as such, Jesus had "to struggle against fear, weakness and temptation in order to align his will with that of his heavenly Father."[76] In fact, "[t]he will of the Logos had in virtue of the Incarnation become the will of the man Jesus of Nazareth."[77] The implication of this view, then, is that "[i]n his conscious experience, we see Jesus genuinely tempted, even though he is, in fact, impeccable. The enticements of sin were really felt and could not be blown away like smoke; resisting temptation required spiritual discipline and moral resoluteness on Jesus' part."[78]

---
[73] Craig and Moreland, *Philosophical Foundations*, 612.
[74] Ibid., 611.
[75] Ibid.
[76] Ibid.
[77] Ibid.
[78] Ibid., 612. Gerald Hawthorne, *Presence and Power*, 136–140, 199–219, makes similar comments. He speaks of Christ having one divine will but then argues that Christ has a doubleness, not because the incarnate Son has a human will distinct from his divine will, but because the divine will functions in a divine and human way (213).

As far as it goes, all of this is fine, and in fact it agrees with classical Christology because it implicitly assumes some kind of "doubleness" in terms of the will. But given that FKC is committed to one will, how is the *divine* Son susceptible to human choices and resisting temptation in his humanity when there is no distinct human will and only a *divine* will? How does the Son act *as a man* if the capacities of will and mind are located in the person? Classical Christology, in its affirmation of two wills, can speak of the real temptation of the incarnate Son because the Son is able to live a fully human life *and will as a man*. It can make sense of the obedience of the Son *as a man*, which is so foundational to Christ serving as our Redeemer and new covenant head. This point is especially seen as Christ's obedience comes to a head in Gethsemane, where the incarnate Son, acting as our covenant head, aligns his human will with the will of his Father, as he chooses to forgo his rights and privileges and to lay down his life for us and thus accomplish our redemption.

Ultimately, every view of Christology must wrestle with Gregory of Nazianzus's famous maxim, "What is not assumed is not healed."[79] If the Son has not assumed a human nature like ours, that is, a human body *and* soul, then it is difficult to make sense of how the incarnate Son can serve as our new covenant head and mediator and obey *as a man* for our salvation. It seems that only if Christ possesses a distinct human will can he render obedience to God in *our* place. Even though kenotic views affirm in the strongest terms the humanity of Christ, their Christological formulation seemingly leaves us with a Christ whose humanity is *not* like *ours* in every way.[80]

Are Christ's Human Limitations Permanent?

Scripture and church tradition teach that the incarnation is not a temporary act but one in which the "Word became flesh" (John 1:14) now and forevermore. In addition, Scripture distinguishes between the states

---

[79] Gregory of Nazianzus, *Letter* 101, in *Nicene and Post-Nicene Fathers*, ed. Alexander Roberts, James Donaldson, Philip Schaff, and Henry Wace, 2nd ser., 14 vols. (Peabody, MA: Hendrickson, 1994), 7:440.
[80] There are other entailments as well. If mind is placed in person and there is no distinct human mind, then how can the Son grow in wisdom and knowledge if all he possesses is a divine mind? How does he serve as a role model for us if his humanity is not exactly like ours except for sin? What about Christ's death? If his soul is that of the person of the Son, then at death, when his body is placed in the grave, severed from his divine soul, what has happened to the hypostatic union? Do we still have an incarnation? Contrary to such a view, classical Christology insists that even in Christ's death, the incarnation continues because the person of the Son still continues to subsist in the divine nature *and* the human soul. On these points, kenotic Christology has problems affirming the full humanity of Christ.

of humiliation and exaltation. Even in the state of humiliation, "whatever the lowliness into which Christ stooped by his incarnation it was not such as to prevent his disciples seeing his glory (John 1:14). If it had been—if the earthly life had disclosed nothing but 'human likeness' (Phil. 2:7)—Christ would never have been worshipped and Christianity would never have been born."[81] Instead of the *kenosis* of the kenotic viewpoints, it is best to think of Christ's humiliation as *krypsis*, i.e., hiddenness or veiledness. In taking on a human nature, the Son not only accommodated himself to human weakness; he also veiled his glory, which is seen only by divine revelation.

As Jesus lived a fully human life, he had the ability to exercise his divine power and authority, but he chose to obey his Father's will for us and for our salvation. As the Son, he continued to live and act in Trinitarian relation to his Father and the Spirit as he had always done from eternity, but now as the *incarnate* Son he is able to live a fully human life in order to redeem us. During his life, acting as the last Adam, in filial obedience to his Father, sometimes Jesus denied himself the exercise of his divine might and energies for the sake of the mission. At other times, as the Father allowed, and in relation to the Spirit, he exercised those energies, and in the case of his cosmic functions, he continually exercised his divine power in relation to the Father and Spirit. Never once, though, did our Lord act in his own interest, because he always acted in light of who he is as the eternal Son. Even as he faced the cross, he willingly and gladly bore our sin and deployed no resources beyond those which his Father allowed *and* in relation to the Spirit. After his resurrection and ascension, the incarnate Son returned to his previous glory with the veil now removed, and presently the Lord Jesus rules at the right hand of the Father, interceding for his people, and from this posture of rule he will come again in glory to consummate what he inaugurated in his first advent. In his glorified state, of which we get a glimpse in his transfiguration (Matt. 17:1–13 par.), and more completely post–resurrection and ascension (John 20–21; Acts 1; 9:1–9; Rev. 1:9–20; 5:1–14; 19:11–18), our Lord Jesus Christ remains fully God and fully man, but the veil is now pulled back. In his glorified state, Jesus, as God the Son incarnate, continues to act through both natures as he relates to his people as the

---
[81] Macleod, *Person of Christ*, 211.

head and mediator of the new covenant, but it seems that the exercise of his deity is much more prevalent than during the state of humiliation.

Classical Christology, with its person-nature distinction, and affirmation of two natures, two wills, and two minds, is able to make better sense of the Son's asymmetrical acting and living through both natures, as well as the transition from earth to heaven, from humiliation to exaltation, and from *krypsis* to glorification. But can the kenotic views do so? Both OKC and FKC insist that *kenosis* is at the heart of the incarnation. To be sure, they affirm this truth differently, yet there is an overall similarity of approach, especially given their redefinition of person and their equation of person with soul. For both viewpoints, in Christ there is only one person and thus one *divine* mind and will, and, it seems, that in the Son adding to himself a human body and becoming a human soul, there are *necessary* and *permanent* limitations that result, almost as if the state of humiliation continues without a proper transition to the state of exaltation. In other words, in the Word becoming flesh, even if, as FKC advocates affirm, the Son continues to possess the divine nature in the robust understanding of it, the Son's ability to act as *God the Son* seems to be permanently limited.

For example, we see a glimpse of this in Hawthorne's unpacking of the incarnation. "In becoming a human being, the Son of God willed to renounce the exercise of his divine powers, attributes, prerogatives, so that he might live fully within those limitations which inhere in being truly human."[82] In fact, Hawthorne contends, unless this took place, we could not account for the unity of Christ's person as both human and divine, and it is very difficult "to think of Jesus as being in reality a genuinely human being."[83] In other words, in becoming a man, the divine Son necessarily covered himself with a created, limited, and finite human nature so that, even though Christ is fully God, he cannot express those divine attributes inconsistent with his humanity. While the Son's divine nature is fully present and intact, the manifestation of it is not allowed full expression, given the reality of the incarnation.

But a question must be asked: What about Christ's post-resurrection state? Are these limitations which are due to the incarnation now permanent? Given that the Son is now and forevermore the *incarnate* Son, can he now express only those divine attributes consistent with his humanity?

---

[82] Hawthorne, *Presence and Power*, 208. See also Issler, *Living into the Life of Jesus*, 109–129.
[83] Hawthorne, *Presence and Power*, 214.

Is his inability to express divine attributes inconsistent with his humanity only tied to the state of humiliation and a proper sense of *krypsis*, yet, even on earth the divine Son continues to uphold the universe, as Scripture teaches and the *extra* affirms, and furthermore, in glorification the veil is pulled back and the full glory of the Son is displayed? Or, is this inability to express his divine attributes bound up with the very nature of the Son's taking on a human nature so that now the Son *cannot* permanently express the full range of his divine attributes?

An affirmation of the permanent limitations of the incarnate Son seems consistent with the kenotic viewpoint, even though some advocates try to avoid this conclusion. The reason why it is consistent is due to how the kenotic view defines "person." From their equation of person with soul and their placing of will and mind in the person, it seems to follow that unless Christ's humanity is shed in his glorification, there are now permanent limitations on the Son in his expression and use of his divine attributes. Unlike the classical view, kenotic views do not affirm two wills and two minds in Christ, thus making it difficult to conceive how, in glorification, the Son can return to a full exercise of his divine attributes. Think for example of the Son's omniscience tied to his divine mind. If the adding of a human nature requires the necessary contraction of knowledge, or the divine consciousness becoming subliminal, then how does the Son return to a full, conscious, omniscient knowledge, given that he has only one mind and that it was the addition of his human body which brought about this contraction? In exaltation, if the glorified Christ returns to his previous state and can exercise all of his divine attributes, then how is he still truly human? On the other hand, if the glorified Christ can exercise all of his divine attributes and retain his humanity, then why cannot he do it in the state of humiliation as well, which, if admitted, seems to undercut the rationale for the kenotic view. It seems that a consistent kenoticism requires that either the Son must remove his humanity in order to return to the full exercise of his divine attributes, or there are permanent limitations entailed by the incarnation.[84] If those alternatives are not acceptable, then the other alternative would be to return to a classical Christology with its corresponding metaphysical commitments.

This is not a new challenge. Years ago, Donald Baillie raised this

---

[84] See Crisp, *Divinity and Humanity*, 135, who also raises this dilemma.

same problem and posed the same dilemma.[85] Denying that there were permanent limitations on the Son, Baillie pressed the kenotic view to account for how *kenosis* was merely temporary because it seemed to require some kind of permanent loss or the surrendering of Christ's humanity. If the logic of the position demands that it was necessary for the Son to give up certain divine attributes (or not to exercise them) in order to become incarnate because it was inconsistent with a truly human life, then the exalted Son either still lacks these attributes (or does not exercise them) or he is no longer truly human—options that Baillie, classical Christology, and Scripture find untenable. How do kenoticists respond? There are three responses.

First, a few deny the permanent humanity of Christ, which is nigh impossible to reconcile with Scripture and the historical confessions, and which ultimately robs us of our new covenant mediator now and forevermore.[86]

Second, more kenoticist supporters affirm that Christ's limitations are permanent. Evans, representing OKC, proposes that the glorified Christ remains fully human yet continues not "to possess all of the traditional divine properties."[87] This entails that the Son's preincarnate possessing and exercise of the divine attributes has changed beginning at the incarnation, and that change is now permanent. What this implies for the triune personal relations, Evans suggests, is that "[t]he resumption of the traditional divine properties can be understood as accomplished by the power of the Father and the Spirit, who bestow glorification on the Son, who merits it by virtue of his sacrificial life and death."[88] Concerned that this results in asymmetrical relations and inequality among the divine persons, Evans admits that everyone affirms some kind of "asymmetries in the relations enjoyed by the persons of the Trinity,"[89] but it is difficult to see how Evans can affirm that the Son is *homoousios* with the Father and Spirit because the Son does not possess the divine attributes in the same way. Historically, pro-Nicene orthodoxy has spoken of the ordering (*taxis*) among the divine persons according to their eternal, immanent re-

---

[85] See D. M. Baillie, *God Was in Christ* (New York: Charles Scribner's Sons, 1948), 97. Cf. Feenstra, "Reconsidering Kenotic Christology," 144, who acknowledges this problem and opts for Christ's limitations as only temporary.
[86] See David Brown, *The Divine Trinity* (London: Duckworth, 1985), 234, 257, who defends this option.
[87] Evans, "Kenotic Christology and the Nature of God," 200; cf. idem, "Self-Emptying of Love," 265–266.
[88] Evans, "Kenotic Christology and the Nature of God," 200.
[89] Evans, "Self-Emptying of Love," 267.

lations, but it has also consistently affirmed that all three persons equally possess the same identical concrete divine nature. On the other hand, Evans and those like him, in affirming permanent limitations of the incarnate Son, ultimately must reconfigure Trinitarian theology in unorthodox ways.[90] Within an FKC view, those who embrace permanent limitations will affirm that the incarnate Son continues to possess the divine nature equally, yet the Son-Spirit relation has now permanently changed from what it was prior to the incarnation, which now results in a different *taxis* from what it was in eternity past.

Third, probably the best response that fits with the Scriptural presentation of the glorified Christ is that the incarnate Son's limitations are temporary for the state of humiliation but *not* in the state of exaltation, even though Christ remains permanently the incarnate Son. From the OKC perspective, Feenstra argues this position by distinguishing between the incarnation, i.e., the Son's becoming human, which is permanent, and *kenosis*, i.e., the Son's emptying himself of certain divine attributes, which is temporary. Feenstra suggests, "The Incarnation need not involve his emptying himself of attributes such as omniscience. . . . The Incarnation does not, in itself, require the Son of God to lack attributes such as omniscience. The Son of God can *be*, and perhaps can even *become*, incarnate while possessing such attributes. The Incarnation simply is the Son's taking on human nature,"[91] while the *kenosis* is something different.

If this is the case, however, then why argue for an OKC, because this is precisely what a classical Christology has always affirmed? Feenstra responds by saying that *kenosis* is necessary in order to share our lot and to accomplish our redemption; it is not necessary in order to become human. But, once again, is it really necessary for the Son to set aside certain divine attributes in order to accomplish our salvation? If the Son can become truly human without *kenosis*, then it seems that Feenstra has undercut the very rationale for his view. Furthermore, classical Christology, which rejects *kenosis* but affirms incarnation and *krypsis*, can certainly account for Christ's full and complete humanity and his accomplishment

---

[90] In order to avoid permanent limitations on Christ, Evans suggests the possibility that Christ's glorified body may be compatible with "reacquiring and possessing the traditional divine attributes" ("Self-Emptying of Love," 265), and as such, in his glorified body he reassumes all the traditional theistic attributes. The problem, however, with such a view is that Christ's glorified human nature no longer looks human. What evidence is there that human nature, even in a glorified state, is able to be deified in the way that Evans proposes? Scripture gives no indication of this, and the church has carefully kept Christ's divine and human natures distinct, thus preserving the Creator-creature distinction even in the incarnation.
[91] Feenstra, "Reconsidering Kenotic Christology," 148.

of our redemption, and it can do so in ways that avoid the problematic features of kenotic Christology. Thus, on these two very crucial points, namely, whether evangelical kenoticism can make sense of Christ's complete humanity and whether Christ is now permanently limited, we find the "new" path problematic.

CONCLUDING EVALUATION

Christological reflection and formulation, whether ancient or contemporary, is not an easy task. Yet, in truth, it is probably our highest calling as Christians, as we seek to think God's thoughts after him, to bring our entire thought captive to Christ, and rightly to think about the glory and wonder of God the Son incarnate, our Lord and Redeemer. In such a task, there is a lot to think about, reflect on, and in prayer to ask our triune God for wisdom. Biblical, theological, historical, and philosophical data have to be weighed carefully. There are a lot of pitfalls to avoid, and given the importance of the subject matter, it requires our full attention, devotion, and care. Over the years, the church has wrestled with the identity of the Lord of glory and the wonder of the incarnation and, for the most part, it has spoken in a unified voice until recent days. Even though our theologizing about Christ is never complete, one must propose "newer" formulations with great trepidation, especially given the consistent Christological voice throughout the ages. "Newer" understandings are welcome, but they must always be tested in light of Scripture and the wisdom of the past. The verdict of this chapter is that the "old" Christological path, properly understood and explicated, is still the better way to theologize about our glorious Redeemer. In light of the overall biblical-theological data, the "newer" kenotic competitors are found wanting. Even though the "old" path leaves us with plenty of unknowns that lead us to further reflection and worship, I am convinced it is still the better road to travel for evangelical theology today.

11

Holy God and Holy People: Pneumatology and Ecclesiology in Intersection[1]

GREGG R. ALLISON

One of John Feinberg's most important gifts to evangelical scholarship is the Foundations of Evangelical Theology series that he is editing. Two contributions to this series are Graham Cole's *He Who Gives Life: The Doctrine of the Holy Spirit*[2] and my *Sojourners and Strangers: The Doctrine of the Church*.[3] Given that Graham's chapter in this Festschrift addresses the topic of Trinitarian theology and Christian sanctification, my contribution will combine his pneumatology and my ecclesiology in an appreciative essay in honor of John that explores the intersection of these two theological *loci*.

Concerning the ecclesiological aspect of this chapter, I am building on my book *Sojourners and Strangers* and the definition of the church offered therein:

---

[1] This chapter first appeared in modified form as a plenary address at the annual meeting of the Evangelical Theological Society in San Diego, November 20, 2014.
[2] Graham A. Cole, *He Who Gives Life: The Doctrine of the Holy Spirit*, Foundations of Evangelical Theology, John S. Feinberg, gen. ed. (Wheaton, IL: Crossway, 2007).
[3] Gregg R. Allison, *Sojourners and Strangers: The Doctrine of the Church*, Foundations of Evangelical Theology, John S. Feinberg, gen. ed. (Wheaton, IL: Crossway, 2012).

The church is the people of God who have been saved through repentance and faith in Jesus Christ and have been incorporated into his body through baptism with the Holy Spirit. It consists of two interrelated elements: the universal church is the fellowship of all Christians that extends from the day of Pentecost until the second coming, incorporating both the deceased believers who are presently in heaven and the living believers from all over the world. This universal church becomes manifested in local churches characterized by being doxological, logocentric, pneumadynamic, covenantal, confessional, missional, and spatio-temporal/eschatological. Local churches are led by pastors (also called elders) and served by deacons, possess and pursue purity and unity, exercise church discipline, develop strong connections with other churches, and celebrate the ordinances of baptism and the Lord's Supper. Equipped by the Holy Spirit with spiritual gifts for ministry, these communities regularly gather to worship the triune God, proclaim his Word, engage non-Christians with the gospel, disciple their members, care for people through prayer and giving, and stand both for and against the world.[4]

This definition of the church will be presupposed throughout this chapter.

As for the pneumatological aspect of this chapter, I do not offer a treatment of the personhood and deity of the Holy Spirit, nor do I present the various works of the Holy Spirit in the lives of individuals. These ministries include conviction of sin, (self-)righteousness, and (worldly) judgment (John 16:8–11) and regeneration (John 3:3–5; Titus 3:5–6) of unbelievers; sealing (Eph. 1:13), or marking out as the firstfruits (Rom. 8:23), or being the down payment/guarantee of salvation (2 Cor. 1:22; 5:5; Eph. 1:14) for believers; bearing witness for the assurance of salvation (Rom. 8:16); sanctification, empowerment for godly living, and transformation into Christlikeness (2 Cor. 3:18; Gal. 5:16–23; 1 Pet. 1:2); guidance in moral living (Rom. 8:4–8); prayer in desperate times (Rom. 8:26–27); the illumination of Scripture (1 Cor. 2:10–16); and resurrection from the dead (Rom. 8:11). While all of these works of the Holy Spirit are essential for becoming and living as Christians, Pannenberg reminds

---
[4] Ibid., 29–30.

us, "The gift of the Spirit is not just for individual believers but aims at the building up of the fellowship of believers, at the founding and the constant giving of new life to the church. . . . By the Spirit each is lifted above individual particularity in order, 'in Christ,' to form with all other believers the fellowship of the church."[5] Heeding Pannenberg's reminder, and in keeping with my intended focus, it will be on the works of the Holy Spirit in relationship to the church as a whole that this chapter concentrates.

The pneumatological characteristic of the church dare not be relegated to secondary status in contemporary theological formulation of the doctrine of the church or in contemporary efforts to plant, develop, shepherd, purify, unite, teach, pray for, multiply, and lead actual local churches.

THE ETERNAL BACKDROP: THE PROCESSION OF THE HOLY SPIRIT FROM BOTH THE FATHER AND THE SON

The Western church (i.e., the Roman Catholic Church and Protestant churches) confesses, with the Nicene-Constantinopolitan Creed (modified by the addition of the *filioque* clause from the Third Synod of Toledo [Spain] in 589), "I believe in the Holy Spirit, the Lord and giver of life, who proceeds from the Father and the Son." This eternal and double procession of the Spirit means (1) not that he was created; (2) not that he was eternally begotten or generated (rather, eternal begottenness or generation belongs to the Son of God);[6] (3) not that he derives his deity from the Father and the Son (as the Father and the Son are each *autotheos*, so too is the Spirit "God of himself"); but (4) that together both the Father and the Son eternally grant him his person-of-the-Spirit, thus marking him out as the third person of the Trinity, distinct from both the Father and the Son.

The warrant for this affirmation of the eternal and double procession of the Holy Spirit moves from the biblical basis for the temporal sending of the Holy Spirit by both the Father and the Son (the basis of which is to be set forth in the next main point) to make this claim: the eternal and double procession of the Spirit is a theological entailment of

---

[5] Wolfhart Pannenberg, *Systematic Theology*, trans. Geoffrey Bromiley, vol. 3 (Grand Rapids, MI: Eerdmans, 1998), 12–13.
[6] As well established by biblical affirmations such as John 5:26 and 1 John 5:18 and supported by a rich historical tradition.

the temporal sending of the Holy Spirit by both the Father and the Son, which is a truth clearly articulated by Scripture. Moreover, the *corpus theologicum* of the church has historically embraced this doctrine; accordingly, this claim is well supported by church tradition.[7]

THE TEMPORAL BACKDROP: THE SENDING OF THE HOLY SPIRIT BY THE FATHER AND THE SON TOGETHER

That both the Father and the Son sent the Holy Spirit on the day of Pentecost is a truth clearly articulated by Scripture, finding most of its support from Jesus's Upper Room Discourse in the Gospel of John (14–17). The key points that Jesus affirmed (articulated mostly in the future tense, as intended by Jesus when he presented them) are:

- Jesus will request from the Father, who will in turn give, the Holy Spirit as a gift for Jesus's disciples forever (John 14:16); this request came at the exaltation of Jesus to the right hand of the Father, from whom Jesus received the Spirit and poured him out on the disciples on the day of Pentecost (Acts 2:33–34)
- the Father will send the Holy Spirit in the name of Jesus (John 14:26)
- Jesus will send the Holy Spirit (John 16:7), specifically from the Father, from whom the Spirit proceeds (John 15:26)
- in a proleptic event, Jesus breathes and tells his disciples, "Receive the Holy Spirit" (John 20:22), thereby foreshadowing his sending, and their reception, of the Spirit on Pentecost
- in a genre other than the preceding narratives (John and Acts), Paul affirms the indwelling of the Spirit in Christians, referring to him as both "the Spirit of God" and "the Spirit of Christ" (Rom. 8:9)

Taken together, these passages provide the biblical basis for the Father and the Son sending the Holy Spirit on the day of Pentecost. As noted above in the previous section ("The Eternal Backdrop"), the church has historically found a theological entailment from this temporal sending of the Spirit, namely, his eternal and double procession from the Father and the Son: Because the Father and the Son together eternally grant to the

---

[7] For this rich tradition, see its development by the Cappadocian Fathers—Basil of Caesarea, Gregory of Nazianzus, and Gregory of Nyssa—and Augustine (especially his treatment of it in *On the Trinity*, book 5 (in *Nicene and Post-Nicene Fathers*, ed. Alexander Roberts, James Donaldson, Philip Schaff, and Henry Wace, 1st ser., 14 vols. [Peabody, MA: Hendrickson, 1994], vol. 3). For a summary, see Gregg R. Allison, *Historical Theology: An Introduction to Christian Doctrine* (Grand Rapids, MI: Zondervan, 2011), 436–438.

Spirit his person-of-the-Holy-Spirit, the two together sent the Holy Spirit on the day of Pentecost to inaugurate his new covenant mission.

But why should the sending of the Holy Spirit be emphasized as the temporal background (if not also the eternal and double procession of the Spirit as the eternal backdrop) for the intersection of pneumatology and ecclesiology? The purpose of the Father and the Son sending the Holy Spirit was, certainly, to launch him on his new covenant mission in the world, but importantly for our topic, the two sent the Spirit to inaugurate the new covenant people assembled together, that is, the church. The sending of the Spirit coincided with the institution—the birthday, if you please—of the church.

THE INITIAL FULFILLMENT: THE PROMISE OF THE HOLY SPIRIT, HIS DESCENT ON THE DAY OF PENTECOST, AND THE INAUGURATION OF THE CHURCH

This talk of inauguration of the new covenant mission of the Spirit and the institution of the church by the Spirit may mislead some to conclude that he was nonexistent, or at least inactive, prior to the day of Pentecost. Such would indeed be a misunderstanding, easily corrected by Old Testament affirmations of the Spirit's work in creating and sustaining the world (Gen. 1:2; Job 26:13; 33:4; Ps. 104:27–30); endowing human beings with understanding, discernment, wisdom, and craftsmanship (Gen. 41:38–39; Ex. 28:3; 31:3–5; 35:30–35; Job 32:8); stirring up judges and empowering them to deliver Israel from its oppressors (Judg. 3:10–11; 6:34; 11:29–33); coming upon Israel's kings and anointing them to rule (1 Sam. 16:13–14); speaking by the mouths of the prophets (2 Sam. 23:1–2; Ezek. 2:2; 8:3; Mic. 3:8); inspiring Scripture (2 Tim. 3:16–17; 2 Pet. 1:16–21); and the like.

Importantly, the Old Testament thematizes the anticipation of a fresh, new, unprecedented outpouring of the Holy Spirit in the future. Such an unparalleled movement is associated with the demise of the old covenant (established by God with his people, Israel) and the establishment of a new covenant. Jeremiah announced the impending obsolescence of the former covenant and the inauguration of a second, or new, covenant that would feature God situating his law within the hearts of his people, all of whom would know him as their Lord (Jer. 31:31–34). Ezekiel prophesied about an upcoming divine work consisting of sprinkling to cleanse people from sin, giving them a new heart and a new spirit, and putting the Holy Spirit within them so as to cause them to obey (Ezek. 36:25–27). Joel proclaimed that this Spirit would be poured out on all people—men and women, old and young, slave and free—who would in turn engage in prophesying, dreaming dreams, and seeing visions (Joel 2:28–32).

This Old Testament theme of anticipation was picked up by John the Baptist as he proclaimed, "I baptize you with water, but he who is mightier than I is coming, the strap of whose sandals I am not worthy to untie. He will baptize you with the Holy Spirit and fire" (Luke 3:16). Associating this Spirit baptism with the Messiah (who was already beginning his ministry), John continued and heightened the Old Testament's expectation of a fresh, new, unprecedented outpouring of the Holy Spirit.

Jesus did similarly. At the great Jewish Feast of Tabernacles, he announced, "If anyone thirsts, let him come to me and drink. Whoever believes in me, as the Scripture has said, 'Out of his heart will flow rivers of living water.'" The apostle John explained, "Now this he said about the Spirit, whom those who believed in him were to receive, for as yet the Spirit had not been given, because Jesus was not yet glorified" (John 7:37–39). Jesus pointed to the coming of the Spirit as a future event from the perspective of which he offered this hope of the fullness of the Spirit. Moreover, Jesus promised his disciples, "And I will ask the Father, and he will give you another Helper, to be with you forever, even the Spirit of truth, whom the world cannot receive, because it neither sees him nor knows him. You know him, for he dwells with you and will be in you" (14:16–17). Though his disciples were already familiar with and aided by the Spirit, Jesus promised them a more intimate relationship with the Spirit in the future. Jesus's announcement and his promise continued and heightened the Old Testament anticipation of a fresh, new, unprecedented outpouring of the Holy Spirit.

Furthermore, following his resurrection and prior to his ascension, Jesus gave final instructions to his disciples: "Thus it is written, that the Christ should suffer and on the third day rise from the dead, and that repentance and forgiveness of sins should be proclaimed in his name to all nations, beginning from Jerusalem. You are witnesses of these things. And behold, I am sending the promise of my Father upon you. But stay in the city until you are clothed with power from on high" (Luke 24:46–49). The sending of the Holy Spirit—the promise of God the Father—would equip Jesus's disciples for their mission of bearing witness to him, but that event required them to wait. More specifically, "And while staying with them he [Jesus] ordered them not to depart from Jerusalem, but to wait for the promise of the Father, which, he said, 'you heard from me; for John baptized with water, but you will be baptized with the Holy Spirit not many days from now'" (Acts 1:4–5). The fulfillment of the Old Testament expectation of a fresh, new, unprecedented outpouring of the Holy Spirit was imminent!

This anticipation promptly reached a climax: "When the day of Pentecost arrived, they [the 120 disciples, led by the (newly reconstituted) twelve apostles; Acts 1:15–26] were all together in one place. And suddenly there came from heaven a sound like a mighty rushing wind, and it filled the entire house where they were sitting. And divided tongues as of fire appeared to them and rested on each one of them. And they were all filled with the Holy Spirit and began to speak in other tongues as the Spirit gave them utterance" (Acts 2:1–4). The descent of the Holy Spirit on the day of Pentecost was the initial fulfillment of Old Testament prophecies, the initial fulfillment of the words of John the Baptist, and the initial fulfillment of Jesus's promises. Furthermore, it marked the outset of the new covenant work of the Holy Spirit, a ministry characterized by the giving of life and unfading glory, as opposed to the old covenant ministry of the letter that brought death and faded away (2 Cor. 3:1–11). Most importantly for our purposes, this descent of the Spirit inaugurated the church that, while anticipated and prepared by Jesus (by his building the apostles to be its leaders; by his teachings; by his establishment of baptism and the Lord's Supper as its new covenant rites), constitutes the new covenant people of God.

THE ONGOING FULFILLMENT: BAPTISM WITH THE HOLY SPIRIT AND HIS MISSIONAL IMPETUS TO EXPAND THE CHURCH

The descent of the Holy Spirit, brought about by the Father and the Son, who together sent him on the day of Pentecost, is in one sense a completely unique event: the inauguration of the church through the initiation of the Spirit's new covenant work cannot be repeated and is not ongoing. In another sense, the fulfillment of the Old Testament anticipation of a fresh, new, unprecedented outpouring of the Spirit, and the fulfillment of the correlative prophecies and promises of John the Baptist and Jesus himself regarding this expectation, was only initiated on Pentecost and, hence, continues today.

According to the apostle John, one of the descriptors of Jesus is "he who baptizes with the Holy Spirit" (John 1:33); that is, an ongoing ministry of Jesus in the lives of new believers today is Spirit-baptism. Just as Jesus did on the day of Pentecost for the 120 disciples (Acts 2:1–4), just as he did for the three thousand new Christians who responded to Peter's preaching of the gospel (with its accompanying challenge and promise: "Repent and be baptized every one of you in the name of Jesus Christ for the forgiveness of your sins, *and you will receive the gift of the Holy Spirit*"; Acts 2:38), and just as he did for Cornelius and his family and friends (upon whom, as hearers of the gospel, the Holy Spirit fell, amazing the onlookers "because the gift of the Holy Spirit was poured out even on the Gentiles" (Acts 10:44–45),[8] so Jesus continues to baptize new believers with the Holy Spirit, thereby incorporating them into his body, the church (1 Cor. 12:13).[9] Though this Spirit-baptism has obvious personal benefits for the individual Christians who receive it, importantly for our purposes this baptism with the Spirit is one of the ways that Jesus continues to fulfill his promise, "I will build my church" (Matt. 16:18), as he joins more and more believers to his people. Indeed, it must be seen as the ongoing fulfillment of the biblical anticipation of a fresh, new, unprecedented outpouring of the Spirit to cleanse from sin, intimately indwell those forgiven people, fill them abundantly, cause

---

[8] Confirmed by Peter's recollection of the event in the second account of the conversion of these Gentiles: "As I began to speak, the Holy Spirit fell on them just as on us at the beginning. And I remembered the word of the Lord, how he said, 'John baptized with water, but you will be baptized with the Holy Spirit.' If then God gave the same gift to them as he gave to us when we believed in the Lord Jesus Christ, who was I that I could stand in God's way?" (Acts 11:15–17). According to Peter, God gave the same gift of the Holy Spirit to the Gentiles when they became believers in Jesus Christ as he had given to Peter and the 120 disciples when they became believers on the day of Pentecost. But it would be a misnomer to call the outpouring of the Holy Spirit upon the Gentiles a "second Pentecost" or "Gentile Pentecost," because from the first preaching of the gospel to its preaching to Cornelius and his family, the Holy Spirit had been poured out on all those who had repented of their sins and embraced Jesus Christ by faith. And so the Spirit continues to be poured out today.

[9] This verse goes along with the other six passages—Matthew 3:11; Mark 1:8; Luke 3:16; John 1:33; Acts 1:5; 11:16—that address the baptism with the Holy Spirit, with this difference: Whereas the first four passages present Jesus as the one who baptizes with the Holy Spirit, and the last two passages specifically refer to the event on the day of Pentecost, 1 Corinthians 12:13 does not mention Jesus as the one who baptizes with the Spirit, nor does it point to the event on Pentecost. But this verse has all of the same elements as do the first six passages: the verb is "baptize" (*baptizō*) and the prepositional phrase is "with the Holy Spirit" or "in one Spirit" (*en . . . pneumati*). In every case, it is Jesus who baptizes with the Holy Spirit. First Corinthians 12:13 does not indicate that the Holy Spirit is the one who does the baptizing; rather, he is the element with which Jesus baptizes people. The only new element that this verse introduces is the purpose for which such Spirit-baptism occurs: Jesus baptizes new converts with the Holy Spirit for the purpose of incorporating them into his (Christ's) body, the church.

them to live obediently and faithfully, grant them knowledge of God through special revelation, and the like.

Accordingly, as the gift of the Holy Spirit is given to an increasing number of people as fruit of the mission of the gospel throughout the world, the church expands by the power of the same Spirit, again as Jesus promised his disciples: "But you will receive power when the Holy Spirit has come upon you, and you will be my witnesses in Jerusalem and in all Judea and Samaria, and to the end of the earth" (Acts 1:8). Spirit-baptized and empowered Christians bear witness to Jesus Christ by proclaiming his gospel, and to those who respond to the message with repentance and faith, the Holy Spirit is given for even more fruitful witness. Indeed, "no one can say 'Jesus is Lord' except in the Holy Spirit" (1 Cor. 12:3).

THE STRATEGIC PLAN(T): THE SPECIFIC GUIDANCE OF THE CHURCH BY THE HOLY SPIRIT

The presence and power of the Holy Spirit directs the expansion of the church from Jerusalem to Judea and Samaria and ultimately to all the corners of the globe (Acts 1:8), and this general direction is accompanied by his specific guidance of the church to encounter particular people and plant itself in particular places. Two biblical examples serve as illustrations. The first regards Philip, fresh off his fruitful evangelization of the Samaritans (8:4–25). "Now an angel of the Lord said to Philip, 'Rise and go toward the south to the road that goes down from Jerusalem to Gaza.' This is a desert place" (v. 26). As it so happened, a eunuch from Ethiopia, headed back to his homeland following a trip to worship in Jerusalem, was journeying along that road and reading from the prophet Isaiah. "And the Spirit said to Philip, 'Go over and join this chariot'" (v. 29). Explaining that Isaiah's prophecy referred to Jesus of Nazareth, Philip announced the gospel to the eunuch, who embraced it and was baptized (vv. 30–39). But the Spirit was not done with Philip, who "found himself at Azotus,[10] and as he passed through he preached the gospel to all the towns until he came to Caesarea" (v. 40). The specific guidance of the Spirit, rather than a chance meeting in the middle of nowhere, connected a witness of the gospel with a God-fearer and resulted in conversion.

---

[10] The expression "found himself" is probably a divine passive, indicating the movement of the Spirit to whisk Philip elsewhere.

The second example regards the small band of Paul, Silas, and Timothy (later joined by Luke) as they embarked on what is often referred to as Paul's second missionary journey. Though they were missionaries whose task and intention was to preach the gospel as they traveled, something unusual occurred: "And they went through the region of Phrygia and Galatia, having been forbidden by the Holy Spirit to speak the word in Asia" (Acts 16:6). A strange prohibition for a team of traveling evangelists! As if this ban were not enough, "And when they had come up to Mysia, they attempted to go into Bithynia, but the Spirit of Jesus did not allow them" (v. 7). Missionaries sent out to announce the good news of Jesus, now prevented by his Spirit from doing so? As the embargo against preaching the gospel continued, "a vision appeared to Paul in the night: a man of Macedonia was standing there, urging him and saying, 'Come over to Macedonia and help us.' And when Paul had seen the vision, immediately we sought to go on into Macedonia, concluding that God had called us to preach the gospel to them" (vv. 9–10). Paul and his gospel team journeyed for many weeks while obeying the specific guidance of the Holy Spirit not to preach the gospel. They finally arrived at "Philippi, which is a leading city of the district of Macedonia" (v. 12) and, finding a place of prayer alongside the river and halting their travel, they "sat down and spoke to the women who had come together. One who heard us was a woman named Lydia, from the city of Thyatira, a seller of purple goods, who was a worshiper of God. The Lord opened her heart to pay attention to what was said by Paul. And after [that] she was baptized, and her household as well" (vv. 13–15). For more than four hundred miles the Holy Spirit prohibited these missionaries from announcing the gospel—"Not here!" "No, not here!"—until they came to a particular place with a particular person to whom they told the good news—and through divine intervention she heeded it and was saved. Lydia's conversion was followed by the liberation of a demon-possessed fortune-teller (vv. 16–18) and the salvation of a jailer and his family (vv. 25–34); thus, the church of Philippi was planted, in exact accord with the specific guidance of the Holy Spirit.

This affirmation should not mask the difficulties that believers sometimes encounter in discerning the direction of the Holy Spirit. Even Scripture narrates such complicatedness. For example, Luke, in his narrative of Paul's ministry, highlights a tension among several presentations of the Spirit's guidance for Paul's future, a tension that apparently is never resolved. The first presentation is that of Paul's own Spirit-led determination to travel to Jerusalem: "Now after these events Paul resolved in the Spirit to pass through Macedonia and Achaia and go to Jerusalem, saying, 'After I have been there, I must also see Rome'" (Acts 19:21). Such personal resolution came about by the guidance of the Spirit.

The second presentation takes place as the apostle addresses the elders of the church of Ephesus: "And now, behold, I am going to Jerusalem, constrained by the Spirit, not knowing what will happen to me there, except that the Holy Spirit testifies to me in every city that imprisonment and afflictions await me. But I do not account my life of any value nor as precious to myself, if only I may finish my course and the ministry that I received from the Lord Jesus, to testify to the gospel of the grace of God" (Acts 20:22–24).[11] Importantly, though Paul senses a Spirit-given compulsion to go to Jerusalem and can articulate generally the Spirit-given testimony about upcoming persecutions in that city, he still sounds a note of vagueness in regard to this witness: "not knowing what will happen to me there." As John Miller explains, "The Spirit's testimony leaves Paul with an awareness that chains and suffering await him—an awareness that apparently lacks any detail. Paul's certainty that he understands the direction in which the Spirit leads is offset by an amorphous image of what he will find when he gets there."[12] Nonetheless, Paul is resolutely committed to finishing his gospel ministry, cost what it may cost.

The third presentation takes place during a final visit among the Christians in Tyre: "And having sought out the disciples, we stayed there for seven days. And through the Spirit they were telling Paul not to go on to Jerusalem. When our days there were ended, we departed and went on our journey . . ." (Acts 21:4–5). With unresolved tension—he makes no comment on the weeklong urging of the disciples of Tyre "through the Spirit"—Luke contrasts the apostle's Spirit-given conviction that he must travel to Jerusalem and these disciples' Spirit-given communication that he must not travel to Jerusalem. "The passage would be rather unremarkable

---

[11] "Constrained by the Spirit" is an expression found only here. Also, it should be noted that the same verb "testify" (*diamartureo*) is used three times in this passage, twice to describe Paul's announcement of the gospel and how it is appropriated, and once to describe the Spirit's announcement of the apostle's future persecution in Jerusalem. This same verb is also found in Acts 23:11 and 28:23 to refer to Paul's activity of preaching the gospel in Jerusalem and Rome.
[12] John B. F. Miller, "Not Knowing What Will Happen to Me There," in *The Unrelenting God: God's Action in Scripture: Essays in Honor of Beverly Roberts Gaventa*, ed. David J. Downs and Matthew L. Skinner (Grand Rapids, MI: Eerdmans, 2013), 55.

if it did not indicate a dramatic tension between characters who express two very different understandings of direction from the same Spirit."[13]

The fourth presentation of the Spirit's guidance comes as a prophetic warning about the dangers of a trip to Jerusalem, on the basis of which Paul's friends in Caesarea urge him to cease and desist from that trip:

> . . . a prophet named Agabus came down from Judea. And coming to us, he took Paul's belt and bound his own feet and hands and said, "Thus says the Holy Spirit, 'This is how the Jews at Jerusalem will bind the man who owns this belt and deliver him into the hands of the Gentiles.'" When we heard this, we and the people there urged him not to go up to Jerusalem. Then Paul answered, "What are you doing, weeping and breaking my heart? For I am ready not only to be imprisoned but even to die in Jerusalem for the name of the Lord Jesus." And since he would not be persuaded, we ceased and said, "Let the will of the Lord be done." (Acts 21:10–14)

Once again, the tension narrated in this passage is thick and remains unresolved: Agabus prophesies through the Spirit about Paul's upcoming seizure by the Jews in Jerusalem, and the Caesarean Christians, taking the prophet's message as a word from the Holy Spirit and expressing their deep love for the apostle, insist that he back off from his intention—stimulated, as narrated earlier, by the Spirit himself—to go to that city, so as to avoid capture.[14] Indeed, their display of love for him deeply moves Paul; still, a broken heart could not deter him from persisting in his travel. Finally, the group of friends capitulates to whatever the Lord has in store for Paul. "These passages feature anything but straightforward experiences of the Spirit. Different characters are guided by the same Spirit in different directions, with little or no explanation."[15]

Accordingly, not only does the Holy Spirit in a general sense propel the church on its missional movement; he also specifically guides the announcement of the gospel to particular people and the planting of the church in particular places. At the same time, such guidance may be interpreted differently by different people, without such tension necessar-

---
[13] Ibid., 56.
[14] Scholars debate about the accuracy of Agabus's prophecy. According to Acts 21:27–36, the Jews "laid hands on him [Paul]" (v. 27) and "seized Paul and dragged him out of the temple" (v. 30), while the Roman tribune, in company with his soldiers, "came up and arrested him and ordered him to be bound with two chains" (v. 33).
[15] Miller, "Not Knowing What Will Happen to Me There," 57.

ily being resolved. The church today is called to follow such Spirit-given guidance while being open to differing understandings of such direction.

THE REQUISITE RESOURCE: THE HOLY SPIRIT'S DISTRIBUTION OF SPIRITUAL GIFTS FOR THE BUILDING UP OF THE CHURCH

In whatever way he guides the church in its general and specific expansion, the Holy Spirit provides for its growth and development. One way that he does so is through distributing spiritual gifts to each and every member of the church. It is the Holy Spirit who "apportions [a gift or gifts] to each one individually as he wills" and empowers its/their use (1 Cor. 12:11), and "to each [church member] is given the manifestation of the Spirit for the common good" (1 Cor. 12:7). Thus, the Holy Spirit sovereignly distributes the gifts of teaching, leading, prophesying, speaking in tongues, faith, giving, mercy, and the like to the church and empowers their exercise by its members for its edification and expansion.

Sadly, this topic has become a point of debate and strong disagreement, with the church careening away from what should be a commitment on the part of all its members to use their Spirit-empowered gifts, to the neglect or near denial of spiritual gifts. Indeed, rather than a clash between cessationism and continuationism, a dispute over the necessity or nonnecessity of speaking in tongues as evidence of baptism with the Spirit, a conflict over whether or not Pentecostals and charismatics are genuine Christians, and an argument over whether or not dreams and visions of Jesus among Muslims are from God or the devil, the church is in desperate need of spiritual gifts that are exercised according to biblical instructions, employed in every one of its ministries, and empowered by the Holy Spirit coursing through the church in its missional endeavors, discipleship, worship, business meetings, pastoral care, elder council meetings, mercy ministries, and much more.

Practically speaking, as the steward of these Spirit-distributed gifts, the church bears the responsibility to (1) help its members identify their gift(s); (2) train and equip its members to employ their gift(s) for its edification and expansion; and (3) engage its members in specific ministries in which they are enabled and empowered by the Spirit to use their gift(s). In its first responsibility, the church may assess its members and their gifting using spiritual gift inventories[16] and/or by noting how its members engage in various ministries and encouraging those members who are particularly fruitful in their ministries to recognize the gift(s) that is/are on display. As for equipping its members in how to use their gift(s), the church may teach its teachers how to teach better (more accurate biblical teaching, more sound theological instruction, more clear explanation), its leaders how to lead better (without domination, to build consensus, more sensitive to the Spirit's leading), its members with the gift of mercy to be better in showing mercy (not running up to one who has just been excommunicated and reassuring her that "everything will be fine," until such time as repentance has been expressed and restitution made, at which point "everything will be fine" may indeed be shouted), and so forth. In its role of engaging its members in ministries in which their gift(s) is/are used, the church must fight the tendency to place its members as mere bodies to fill program slots and instead seek to match their giftedness with ministries that require the exercise of such gifts.

THE DIVINE CALLING: THE HOLY SPIRIT'S ESTABLISHMENT OF LEADERS FOR THE CHURCH

Moreover, the Spirit establishes some of these gifted people as leaders in the church. This work of the Holy Spirit rests on the victory of Christ over his enemies and his return to the Father (his ascension and its fruit):

> Therefore it says,
>
> > "When he [Jesus] ascended on high he led a host of captives, and he gave gifts to men."
>
> (In saying, "He ascended," what does it mean but that he had also descended into the lower regions, the earth? He who descended is the one who also ascended far above all the heavens, that he might fill all things.) And he gave the apostles, the prophets, the evangelists, the shepherds and teachers, to equip the saints for the work of ministry, for building up the body of Christ. (Eph. 4:8–12)

---

[16] Examples of such inventories include "Spiritual Gifts Survey," by LifeWay Christian Resources; "Team Ministry Spiritual Gifts Inventory," by Church Growth Institute; C. Peter Wagner's "Finding Your Spiritual Gifts"; Willow Creek's "Spiritual Gifts Discovery" (part of its Engage: Your Faith Journey); and "Gifted-2Serve," by BuildingChurch Ministries.

As noted earlier, the ascended Christ, exalted to the right hand of the Father, requested and received the Spirit from the Father and poured him out on the disciples on the day of Pentecost (Acts 2:33–34). From this initial outpouring, Christ through his Spirit continues to grant spiritual gifts to the members of his body and to appoint spiritually gifted leaders in it.

The office of apostle, held primarily by the twelve apostles[17] but including a few others as well,[18] was established "to proclaim the gospel and be the foundation of the church, to perform signs and wonders, to exercise peculiar authority in the first churches, and (in the case of some) to write what we now call the New Testament."[19] Prophets receive and communicate revelations from God (1 Cor. 14:26–32), not as supplemental to the Bible or bearing scriptural authority, but for the edification and guidance of the church. Evangelists announce the gospel of Jesus Christ and (probably) equip others to do the same. They are the key human agents in leading nonbelievers to repentance from sin and faith in Christ (Rom. 10:13–15; 1 Cor. 3:5).

"The shepherds and teachers"—an expression referring not to two groups of leaders but one—could also be called "pastors" or "elders" of the church. Their responsibilities, then, are twofold: First, they "shepherd the flock of God" by "exercising oversight" (1 Pet. 5:2) or being "over" church members (1 Thess. 5:12) at the highest level of human authority. This responsibility entails offering exemplary leadership, as Peter exhorts them: "shepherd the flock of God that is among you, exercising oversight, not under compulsion, but willingly, as God would have you; not for shameful gain, but eagerly; not domineering over those in your charge, but being examples to the flock" (1 Pet. 5:1–3). Imitation of their example and submission to their authority are the intended responses of the church to its shepherds (Heb. 13:7, 17).

Second, pastors teach, meaning that they are responsible for (1) understanding and embracing firmly the faith for themselves; (2) communicating this sound doctrine and the Christlike practices that flow from it; and (3) confronting those who deny or reject what they teach. As Paul

---

[17] Simon Peter, James (the son of Zebedee), John, Andrew, Philip, Bartholomew, Matthew, Thomas, James (the son of Alphaeus), Thaddaeus, Simon the Zealot, and Matthias (in place of Judas Iscariot) (Mark 3:16–19 with Acts 1:15–26). For further discussion, see Allison, *Sojourners and Strangers*, 205–206.
[18] Paul (Acts 26:12–18), Barnabas (Acts 14:14; 1 Cor. 9:6; Gal. 2:9), and James the brother of Jesus (Gal. 1:19; 2:9); possibly Silvanus/Silas and Timothy (1 Thess. 1:1; 2:6), Epaphroditus (Phil. 2:25–30), and Andronicus and Junia(s) (Rom. 16:7). See Allison, *Sojourners and Strangers*, 206–207.
[19] Ibid., 414.

underscores concerning an elder, "He must hold firm to the trustworthy word as taught, so that he may be able to give instruction in sound doctrine and also to rebuke those who contradict it" (Titus 1:9).

Accordingly, the shepherds and teachers of the church engage in providing wise direction and communicating sound doctrine; though not mentioned in this biblical passage, prayer (especially for the sick) is another responsibility enjoined on elders (James 5:13–15). These two responsibilities—shepherding and teaching—are elsewhere brought together and highlighted: "Let the elders who rule well be considered worthy of double honor, especially those who labor in preaching and teaching" (1 Tim. 5:17). In other words, all pastors must be able to teach (1 Tim. 3:2), but not all of them will have teaching as their primary ministry. Rather, while "labor[ing] in their ministries, some elders distinguish themselves through their outstanding leadership; this is specifically the case with those who dedicate themselves to the proclamation of the Word of God through preaching regularly and/or teaching extensively."[20]

Through such shepherding and teaching, the church is directed, discipled, nourished, cared for, protected, disciplined, edified, and expanded. Again, such progress is the fruit of the Holy Spirit's establishment, gifting, and empowering of leaders, as Paul underscored in his exhortation to the elders of the church of Ephesus: "Pay careful attention to yourselves and to all the flock, in which the Holy Spirit has made you overseers, to care for the church of God, which he obtained with his own blood" (Acts 20:28). An outstanding example of such appointment of leaders by the Spirit is the first largely Gentile church:

> Now there were in the church at Antioch prophets and teachers, Barnabas, Simeon who was called Niger, Lucius of Cyrene, Manaen a lifelong friend of Herod the tetrarch, and Saul. While they were worshiping the Lord and fasting, the Holy Spirit said, "Set apart for me Barnabas and Saul for the work to which I have called them." Then after fasting and praying they laid their hands on them and sent them off.
>
> So, being sent out by the Holy Spirit . . . they proclaimed the word of God. (Acts 13:1–5)

The Holy Spirit establishes leaders for the church.

---
[20] Ibid., 272.

THE SACRED PURPOSE: THE CHURCH AS THE TEMPLE OF THE HOLY SPIRIT

Such resourcing and empowering of the church has a clear and definite purpose: to build the church into a glorious temple of the Holy Spirit. As Paul reflected on the initiation of the church of Corinth—an endeavor that featured the apostle planting the church and Apollos watering the new plant—he instructed leaders how they should go about building their church:

> According to the grace of God given to me, like a skilled master builder I laid a foundation, and someone else is building upon it. Let each one take care how he builds upon it. For no one can lay a foundation other than that which is laid, which is Jesus Christ. Now if anyone builds on the foundation with gold, silver, precious stones, wood, hay, straw—each one's work will become manifest, for the Day will disclose it, because it will be revealed by fire, and the fire will test what sort of work each one has done. If the work that anyone has built on the foundation survives, he will receive a reward. If anyone's work is burned up, he will suffer loss, though he himself will be saved, but only as through fire. (1 Cor. 3:10–15)

With the foundation of the church firmly in place because of Jesus's grounding work, leaders are to build circumspectly on this one foundation. Two categories of building materials—two approaches to ministry—present themselves: gold, silver, and precious stones represent leadership efforts focused on salvation, truth, love, obedience, wisdom, hope, "a pure heart and a good conscience and a sincere faith" (1 Tim. 1:5), soundness, peace, unity, perseverance, hospitality, freedom, "simplicity and godly sincerity" (2 Cor. 1:12), assurance, beauty, multiplication—holy matters. Wood, hay, and straw represent leadership efforts bent toward deceitfulness, shipwreck in the faith, trickery, defiling/wounding of conscience, error, cunning and tampering with the Word of God (2 Cor. 4:2), timidity, fear, sensuality, legalism, debasement, divisiveness, hopelessness, carnality, depravity, idleness—unholy matters. Church leaders are urged to choose the former materials/approach to their ministry and to decry and avoid the latter materials/approach to it.

This sobering warning about the care with which church leaders should engage in their ministries leads up to a final apostolic threat: "Do you not know that you are God's temple and that God's Spirit dwells in you? If anyone destroys God's temple, God will destroy him. For God's temple is holy, and you are that temple" (1 Cor. 3:16–17). The church of Jesus Christ is the temple of the Holy Spirit and, as such, its leaders must employ holy materials—take a holy approach—in directing it toward even greater holiness—never oppositely. This essence of the church as the temple of the Holy Spirit is noted elsewhere in Paul's discussion of the uniting of both Jews and Gentiles into one new entity in Jesus Christ:

> For through him [Christ] we both have access in one Spirit to the Father. So then you are no longer strangers and aliens, but you are fellow citizens with the saints and members of the household of God, built on the foundation of the apostles and prophets, Christ Jesus himself being the cornerstone, in whom the whole structure, being joined together, grows into a holy temple in the Lord. In him you also are being built together into a dwelling place for God by the Spirit. (Eph. 2:18–22)

Jesus Christ is the cornerstone—"the principal stone of the building from which the rest of the edifice takes alignment"[21]—and thus at the center of the church. The apostles and prophets—not a reference to the New Testament apostles and Old Testaments prophets, but to those church leaders who were the initial heralds of the good news and communicators of divine revelation—constitute the foundation of the church. Members from all nationalities, ethnicities, races, socio-politico-economic backgrounds (Rev. 5:9; Acts 2:17–18) are the stones that are joined together as the materials for the building. And leaders, gifted by the Holy Spirit and established by him as those responsible for directing and teaching the church in a holy way, contribute to its development into "a holy temple," that is, "a dwelling place for God by the Spirit."

THE PROPER ATMOSPHERE: THE HOLY SPIRIT AS CREATOR AND SUSTAINER OF THE UNITY OF THE CHURCH

The last section introduced the topic of Jews and Gentiles, former enemies now brought into relationship through Jesus Christ and joined

---
[21] Ibid., 110–111.

together into one entity, the church. The reality of this Jewish-Gentile unity highlights another important point in our interface of pneumatology and ecclesiology, namely, the Holy Spirit as the one who creates and sustains church unity.

Such unity, of course, is grounded most fundamentally in the perichoretic harmony enjoyed by the triune God. Perichoresis is the mutual indwelling of each of the three distinct persons in the other two persons: the Father in the Son and the Son in the Father; the Father in the Spirit and the Spirit in the Father; the Son in the Spirit and the Spirit in the Son. That this perichoretic unity of the three distinct persons is the source and template of church unity is affirmed by the Son in his prayer to the Father for Christ-followers composing the church, "that they may be one, even as we are one" (John 17:11, 22), with the specific type of unity being further detailed: "that they may all be one, just as you, Father, are in me, and I in you" (v. 21). Because each of the divine persons is in the other two—the Father indwells the Son and the Spirit; the Son indwells the Father and the Spirit; the Spirit indwells the Father and the Son—the church is called to unity. This unity, however, is not that of all of its members mutually indwelling one another in Trinitarian, perichoretic fashion; that is impossible. Rather, as Miroslav Volf explains, "the indwelling of the Spirit common to everyone . . . makes the church into a communion corresponding to the Trinity."[22] This mutual indwelling of the three distinct persons in one another portrays and prompts a church unity that is not uniformity, nor union, but unity in diversity.[23]

This unity in diversity is fostered specifically by the Holy Spirit, who is the creator and sustainer of unity. Indeed, Paul urges the church "to walk in a manner worthy of the calling to which you have been called . . . eager to maintain the unity of the Spirit in the bond of peace" (Eph. 4:1, 3). Everett Ferguson explains this call for church members: "The human task is not to achieve unity among themselves, but to keep the unity already created. . . . 'United and pursuing unity' describes the situation of members of Christ's body, the church."[24] Accordingly, the church does not have to initiate its own unity; rather, it must work diligently to

---

[22] Miroslav Volf, *After Our Likeness: The Church as the Image of the Trinity* (Grand Rapids, MI: Eerdmans, 1998), 213.
[23] For further discussion, see Allison, *Sojourners and Strangers*, 168–169.
[24] Everett Ferguson, *The Church of Christ: A Biblical Ecclesiology for Today* (Grand Rapids, MI: Eerdmans, 1996), 406.

maintain the Holy Spirit's gift of unity because its members too readily corrupt and destroy his gifted harmony.

The church preserves this Spirit-given oneness while pursuing greater unity at the same time. Accordingly, unity is both a gift for and a goal of the church during its earthly pilgrimage; its members are to progress "until we all attain to the unity of the faith and of the knowledge of the Son of God" (Eph. 4:13). The vision of unity for the church is that its members "live in harmony with one another" (Rom. 12:16), "being of the same mind, having the same love, being in full accord and of one mind" (Phil. 2:2). To be strenuously avoided, therefore, are all obstacles to unity, including "enmity, strife, jealousy, fits of anger, rivalries, dissensions, divisions, envy" (Gal. 5:19–21). These attitudes and actions, eight of the fifteen "works of the flesh" listed by Paul, weaken or destroy the Spirit-given oneness of the church and are consequently condemned by the apostle.

Logically and biblically, then, church members must "walk by the Spirit" so as to avoid gratifying their sinful nature (Gal. 5:16) and thus wreaking havoc on unity, to enjoy and preserve his gift of harmony, and to increase in oneness. Unsurprisingly, then, Paul urges the church,

> And do not get drunk with wine, for that is debauchery, but be filled with the Spirit, addressing one another in psalms and hymns and spiritual songs, singing and making melody to the Lord with your heart, giving thanks always and for everything to God the Father in the name of our Lord Jesus Christ, submitting to one another out of reverence for Christ. (Eph. 5:18–21)

This instruction to "be filled with the Spirit" includes several key interpretive elements:[25]

- its mood is imperative; it is a command to be obeyed;
- its tense is present; it is an ongoing command: to paraphrase, "keep on being filled with the Spirit";
- its voice is passive; it is not an active-voice imperative ("fill yourselves"), calling for some action on the part of Christians, but a passive-voice imperative ("be filled"), calling for receptivity;
- the expected or intended response to this command is for Christians to yield to the Holy Spirit, to be controlled—pervaded or

---

[25] The following is adapted from Gregg R. Allison, "Baptism with and Filling of the Holy Spirit," *Southern Baptist Journal of Theology* 16/4 (2012): 15.

permeated—by the Spirit in all their ways, to consciously place themselves under the guidance of the Spirit moment by moment.

Such yieldedness to the Holy Spirit will be evidenced as together Christians experience genuine community, engage in powerful worship, express gratitude in every circumstance, and love one another through mutual submission (vv. 19–21). The four gerunds (participles in Greek)—speaking, singing, giving thanks, and submitting—not only indicate the results that flow from Christians obeying the Pauline command and thus being filled with the Spirit; they also absorb some of the imperatival force of the main verb ("be filled") and are thereby constituted concrete activities in which Christians filled with the Spirit are to be engaged. Accordingly, Spirit-filled Christians develop authentic community by rebuking, admonishing, correcting, encouraging, and edifying one another; worship the Lord together with great delight; live intentionally with gratitude; and show preference for and serve one another for Christ's sake.

When the church is characterized by members who, as they are being filled with the Spirit moment by moment, engage in genuine community life together, joyfully worship God, express thanksgiving in all things, and love and preferentially serve one another, it will experience a beautiful unity unlike that of any human family or human institution. Such oneness is fostered by the Holy Spirit, who is the creator and sustainer of church unity.

THE COORDINATE AGENCY: THE WORD OF GOD AND THE SPIRIT OF GOD IN THE CHURCH OF GOD

The church knows the call to unity in the Spirit, and it is instructed in how to maintain and further such unity through the Spirit, from the Bible. Beyond this clear point, it could be added that the church knows itself and the divine will for it—everything discussed so far in this chapter—through Scripture. Accordingly, the church lives and develops by the coordinate working of the divine agent, the Spirit of God, and the divine agency, the Word of God.

With regard to a fine balance between these two, Martin Luther insisted,[26]

---

[26] The section following the Luther quote is adapted from Allison, *Historical Theology*, 441–443.

> Because God has now permitted his holy gospel to go forth, he deals with us in two ways: First, outwardly, and second, inwardly. Outwardly he deals with us through the preached Word, or the gospel, and through the visible signs of baptism and the Lord's Supper. Inwardly he deals with us through the Holy Spirit and faith. But this always in such a way and in this order that the outward means must precede the inward means, and the inward means comes after through the outward means. So, then, God has willed that he will not give to anyone the inward gifts [of the Spirit and faith] except through the outward means [of the Word and the sacraments].[27]

Accordingly, the Spirit of God engages in his ministry to the church through the Word of God, never apart from it or in contradiction to it. Furthermore, the Spirit of God is absolutely essential for rightly interpreting the Word of God: "No one can correctly understand God or his Word unless he has received such understanding immediately from the Holy Spirit."[28]

Similarly, John Calvin closely linked Scripture and the Spirit, specifically criticizing the Catholic Church for boasting "of the Holy Spirit solely to commend with his name strange doctrines foreign to God's Word—while the Spirit wills to be conjoined with God's Word by an indissoluble bond."[29] This unbreakable link means "we are to expect nothing more from his [God's] Spirit than that he will illumine our minds to perceive the truth of his [Christ's] teachings."[30] In opposition to the fanatics or mystics, who claimed that the Spirit of God works independently of the Word of God, Calvin again insisted on the inseparable tie between the two: "For by a kind of mutual bond the Lord has joined together the certainty of his Word and of his Spirit."[31]

This Reformation legacy helps evangelical churches today to empha-

---

[27] Martin Luther, *Against the Heavenly Prophets in the Matter of Images and Sacraments*, in *Luther's Works*, ed. Jaroslav Pelikan, Hilton C. Oswald, and Helmut T. Lehmann, 55 vols. (St. Louis: Concordia, 1972), 40:83. Note that Luther closely associated the preaching of Scripture with the sacraments of baptism and the Lord's Supper, which he considered to be another form of preaching—not a verbal word, but an enacted word. This emphasis does not change or detract from the point that he closely linked the Word of God—in both its verbal form (preaching) and its enacted form (the sacraments)—and the Spirit of God.
[28] Martin Luther, *The Magnificat*, in *Luther's Works*, ed. Jaroslav Pelikan, Hilton C. Oswald, and Helmut T. Lehmann, 55 vols. (St. Louis: Concordia, 1972), 21:299.
[29] John Calvin, *Institutes of the Christian Religion*, ed. John T. McNeill, trans. Ford Lewis Battles (Philadelphia: Westminster, 1960), 4.8.14, in John Baillie, John T. McNeill, and Henry P. Van Dusen, gen. eds., Library of Christian Classics (LCC), 26 vols. (Philadelphia: Westminster, 1960), 21:1163.
[30] Ibid., 4.8.13; LCC 21:1162–1163.
[31] Ibid., 1.9.3.

size and rely upon both the Word of God and the Spirit of God. Sadly, many contemporary churches tend toward lopsidedness on this matter: Pentecostal and charismatic varieties often focus on the Spirit of God through their emphasis on the baptism of the Spirit as a post-conversion event, their enthusiastic yearning for Spirit-empowered gifts like speaking in tongues and miracles, their regard for the authority of immediate, prophetic messages over the preaching of divine revelation mediated through the Bible, and the like, while giving short shrift to the Word of God. Other evangelical churches often highlight the Word of God through their emphasis on preaching expository sermons and their appreciation for spiritual gifts like teaching and helps, while denying or refusing to practice the so-called sign gifts (like prophecy and healings) and while seemingly fearing to talk about, rely upon, and consciously submit to the Spirit of God. Such an imbalance contradicts both Scripture and the Reformation heritage.

Biblically, this Scripture-Spirit link is seen in the mighty works of God in salvation. Writing to the Thessalonian church, Paul emphasized that God's gracious choice of the elect becomes actualized as salvation through two essential means. "But we ought always to give thanks to God for you, brothers beloved by the Lord, because God chose you as the firstfruits to be saved, through sanctification by the Spirit and belief in the truth. To this he called you through our gospel, so that you may obtain the glory of our Lord Jesus Christ" (2 Thess. 2:13–14). For divine election to be realized in space and time, the Spirit of God must work powerfully, and the Word of God, preached as the gospel of truth, must be believed.

This preached word is associated with regeneration, as Peter explains: "you have been born again, not of perishable seed but of imperishable, through the living and abiding word of God; for 'All flesh is like grass and all its glory like the flower of grass. The grass withers, and the flower falls, but the word of the Lord remains forever' [Isa. 40:6, 8]. And this word is the good news that was preached to you" (1 Pet. 1:23–25). Although the divine agency of the Word of God in regeneration is highlighted here, elsewhere the divine agent of the Spirit of God is underscored for this work. As Jesus urged, "Truly, truly, I say to you, unless one is born of water and the Spirit, he cannot enter the kingdom of God. That which is born of the flesh is flesh, and that which is born of the Spirit is spirit. Do not marvel that I said to you, 'You must be born again.' The wind blows where it wishes, and you hear its sound, but you do not know where it comes from or where it goes. So it is with everyone who is born of the Spirit" (John 3:5–8). The Word of God and the Spirit of God are the divine agency and agent in regenerating nonbelievers.

Not to belabor the point, the divine work of sanctification is carried out by both the Word and the Spirit of God. Jesus highlights the role of Scripture when he prays for his disciples, "Sanctify them in the truth; your word is truth" (John 17:17). The Holy Spirit's role is emphasized in the expression "sanctification of/by the Spirit" (1 Pet. 1:2; 2 Thess. 2:13) and Paul's repeated insistence that Christians "walk by the Spirit," "be filled with the Spirit," and be "led by the Spirit" (Gal. 5:16–18; Eph. 5:18; Rom. 8:14) so as to grow in holiness.

Thus, the church lives and develops by the coordinate working of the divine agent—the Spirit of God—and the divine agency—the Word of God. It is to keep a fine balance between Scripture and the Spirit.

CONCLUSION: THE MISSIONAL GOD, THE MISSIONAL CHURCH, THE MISSION OF SALVATION, AND THE HOLY SPIRIT OF MISSION[32]

As Christopher Wright takes pains (rightly) to prove, the God and Father of the Lord Jesus Christ—the God whose people now exist as the church—is a missional God.[33] It was he who created the universe in general and human beings as his divine image in particular, thus initiating a missional reality (Genesis 1–2). It was God himself who announced the *protoevangelium*, promising the serpent, "I will put enmity between you and the woman, and between your offspring and her offspring; he shall bruise your head, and you shall bruise his heel" (3:15). It was he who called the pagan Abraham out of Ur, promising to make of him a great nation (eventually, the people of Israel) and through him to bless all the families of the earth (Genesis 12). It was God himself who liberated his people from enslavement, established covenants, raised up leaders (judges, kings, prophets) for his people, granted mercy to those who were not his people (Rahab; the Ninevites), cast his rebellious nation out of the Promised Land into exile, and reconstituted that nation. It was he

---
[32] The following is adapted from Gregg R. Allison, "North Star Theology," published by Sojourn Community Church, Louisville, KY.
[33] Christopher J. H. Wright, *The Mission of God: Unlocking the Bible's Grand Narrative* (Downers Grove, IL: InterVarsity Press, 2006).

who promised the Messiah who would ultimately renew and regather his people and reach out to the non-people: "It is too light a thing that you should be my servant to raise up the tribes of Jacob and to bring back the preserved of Israel; I will make you as a light for the nations, that my salvation may reach to the end of the earth" (Isa. 49:6):

> And I will have mercy on No Mercy,
> and I will say to Not My People, "You are my people";
> and he shall say, "You are my God."
> (Hosea 2:23; cf. 1 Pet. 2:10)

To actualize this mercy and peopling so as to be acknowledged and acclaimed as God throughout the world, the Father sent his own Son into the world: "The true light, which gives light to everyone, was coming into the world. He was in the world, and the world was made through him, yet the world did not know him. He came to his own, and his own people did not receive him. But to all who did receive him, who believed in his name, he gave the right to become children of God, who were born, not of blood nor of the will of the flesh nor of the will of man, but of God" (John 1:9–13). "During his earthly ministry, Jesus Christ intentionally engaged the Jewish people and not the Gentiles. 'He came to his own' (John 1:11), as evidenced by the narrative of Zacchaeus, about whom Jesus said, 'Today salvation has come to this house, since he also is a son of Abraham. For the Son of Man came to seek and to save the lost' (Luke 19:9–10)."[34]

In keeping with his own focus, Jesus commanded his disciples, "Go nowhere among the Gentiles and enter no town of the Samaritans, but go rather to the lost sheep of the house of Israel" (Matt. 10:5–6). Accordingly, the biblical narratives that recount Jesus's ministry to non-Jews— "the woman at the well (John 4:1–42), the demon-possessed Gerasene (Mark 5:1–20), the Roman centurion (Matt. 8:5–13), the Canaanite woman (Matt. 15:21–28), the Samaritan leper (Luke 17:11–19)"— should be understood "as unusual events that were harbingers of things to come. Unsurprisingly, then, the early church followed the pattern of their Lord in preaching the gospel and building disciples among the Jews first (Acts 1–11). But this pattern was not to continue for long."[35]

---

[34] Allison, *Sojourners and Strangers*, 438.
[35] Ibid.

Indeed, Jesus commissioned his disciples to "make disciples of all nations" (Matt. 28:19). Philip was the first to reach out with the gospel to the Samaritans (Acts 8:4–25), and he later led an Ethiopian eunuch to faith in Christ (vv. 26–40). Peter engaged the first Gentiles with the good news, grasping through a vision that "God shows no partiality, but in every nation anyone who fears him and does what is right is acceptable to him" (10:34–35). A bit later on were "men of Cyprus and Cyrene, who on coming to Antioch spoke to the Hellenists also, preaching the Lord Jesus. And the hand of the Lord was with them, and a great number who believed turned to the Lord" (11:20–21). Saul, later to be called Paul, was chosen to be the missionary to the Gentiles, sent "to open their eyes, so that they may turn from darkness to light and from the power of Satan to God, that they may receive forgiveness of sins and a place among those who are sanctified by faith in me" (26:16–18).

During their missionary journey, Paul and Barnabas encountered resistance from their Jewish listeners:

> And Paul and Barnabas spoke out boldly, saying, "It was necessary that the word of God be spoken first to you. Since you thrust it aside and judge yourselves unworthy of eternal life, behold, we are turning to the Gentiles. For so the Lord has commanded us, saying,
>
>> "'I have made you a light for the Gentiles,
>> that you may bring salvation to the ends of the earth'
>>   [Isa. 49:6]."
>
> And when the Gentiles heard this, they began rejoicing and glorifying the word of the Lord, and as many as were appointed to eternal life believed. And the word of the Lord was spreading throughout the whole region. (Acts 13:46–49)

As Wright notes, "Jesus' earthly ministry was launched by a movement that aimed at the restoration of *Israel*. But he himself launched a movement that aimed at the ingathering of the *nations* to the new messianic people of God. The *initial impetus* for his ministry was to call Israel back to their God. The *subsequent impact* of his ministry was a new community that called the nations to faith in the God of Israel."[36]

---

[36] Wright, *Mission of God*, 506.

God was from the beginning a missional God.

This missional God is now engaged in mission through his people, the missional church that is empowered by the Spirit of mission. The apostle John narrates one of Jesus's first post-resurrection appearances on the third day after the crucifixion:

> On the evening of that day, the first day of the week, the doors being locked where the disciples were for fear of the Jews, Jesus came and stood among them and said to them, "Peace be with you." When he had said this, he showed them his hands and his side. Then the disciples were glad when they saw the Lord. Jesus said to them again, "Peace be with you. As the Father has sent me, even so I am sending you." And when he had said this, he breathed on them and said to them, "Receive the Holy Spirit. If you forgive the sins of any, they are forgiven them; if you withhold forgiveness from any, it is withheld." (John 20:19–23)

The Father commissioned his Son with the mission of accomplishing salvation, and the Son in turn commissioned his people the church with the same mission, with this modification: the church's mission is not to accomplish salvation but to announce how to appropriate the salvation accomplished by the Son. For this missional task, the church is equipped by the Holy Spirit. Jesus proleptically breathed the Spirit—a foretaste or harbinger of his sending of the Spirit on the day of Pentecost—and commanded his disciples to receive the Spirit forwardly on that day.

The concrete terms of engagement for this upcoming mission are clearly noted: "There is no doubt from the context that the reference is to forgiving sins, or withholding forgiveness. But though this sounds stern and harsh, it is simply the result of the preaching of the gospel, which either brings men to repent as they hear of the ready and costly forgiveness of God, or leaves them unresponsive to the offer of forgiveness which is the gospel, and so they are left in their sins."[37] Accordingly, the missional God has sent the missional church to engage in the announcement of the gospel and its appropriation. To people who repent of their sins and embrace Jesus Christ by faith, the church proclaims, "you are forgiven of your sins and have eternal life." To those who refuse the offer

---
[37] John Marsh, *The Gospel of St. John* (Harmondsworth, UK: Penguin, 1968), 641–642; cited in D. A. Carson, *The Gospel According to John* (Grand Rapids, MI/Leicester, England: Eerdmans/Inter-Varsity, 1991), 656–657.

of salvation, the church proclaims, "you are still in your sins and primed for divine condemnation."

The missional God has equipped the missional church for its mission of salvation with the Holy Spirit of mission. Accordingly, this pneumadynamic characteristic of the church dare not be relegated to secondary status in contemporary theological formulation of the doctrine of the church or in contemporary efforts to plant, develop, shepherd, purify, unite, teach, pray for, multiply, and lead actual local churches.

12

God's Faithfulness, Human Suffering, and the Concluding Hallel Psalms (146–150): A Canonical Study

WILLEM VANGEMEREN

Faithfulness is one of the many admirable qualities of John S. Feinberg. It is evident that he has walked with his Savior for many years under the weight of great personal suffering. He models what he believes and is persuaded that the God of Abraham, Isaac, and Jacob is faithful. In his major volume on the doctrine of God, *No One like Him*,[1] he affirms the importance of God as truth, because "He knows the truth and only speaks the truth."[2] Reality as we know it corresponds and coheres, because it reflects God's being. Feinberg employs the correspondence theory of truth, according to which utterances "are true if what they assert about the world matches what we find in the world."[3] God is true, his words are true, and his actions are truthful.[4]

Feinberg treats God's faithfulness under the larger rubric of truthfulness:[5]

---

[1] John S. Feinberg, *No One Like Him: The Doctrine of God*, Foundations of Evangelical Theology, John S. Feinberg, gen. ed. (Wheaton, IL: Crossway, 2001).
[2] Ibid., 370.
[3] Ibid., 371.
[4] Ibid., 371–373.
[5] Ibid., 373–374.

God is truthful and dependable. Feinberg concludes, "what a comfort and encouragement to know that the God with all the power to meet our needs cares about us and is dependable at all times."[6] Feinberg additionally writes, "many passages that speak of God's truth are in psalms that extol God's virtues."[7] I agree with him and propose that the witness of the individual psalms be framed by and understood within the larger canonical and hermeneutical framework of the Psalter, especially considering the introductory psalms (Psalms 1–2) and the final hallelujah psalms (146–150).[8]

A CANONICAL APPROACH TO THE BOOK OF PSALMS[9]

The groundbreaking work of Brevard S. Childs opened a theological as well as hermeneutical trajectory in reading the Psalms. He reads the book from the wisdom frame provided by Psalm 1,[10] which opens with a beatitude promised to all who embrace Yahweh's instruction (*tōrā*) and who distinguish themselves by wisdom. This wisdom frame gives coherence to the book, as each psalm contributes to the development of the wisdom matrix. Childs's clarion call for reading the Psalter from a hermeneutical and theological matrix has made an impact on a generation of scholars.

Gerald T. Sheppard argues that in the final redaction of the Psalter, Psalms 1 and 2 encourage the reader to approach the whole book from the perspective of wisdom. The Psalter is God's Torah. He comments,

> Ps. 1 and 2 correlate the study of the Torah collection with the goal of attaining sacred wisdom like that found in the wisdom traditions, and perhaps in a set of biblical wisdom books. By his association with Ps. 2, David, who is, in canonical terms, the chief architect of the Psalter, is identified fully in accord with the ideals of Ps. 1. The entire Psalter, therefore, is made to stand theologically in association with David as a source book of guidance for the way of the

---
[6] Ibid., 374.
[7] Ibid., 371.
[8] For the canonical approach to the Psalms, see Willem A. VanGemeren, "Psalms," in *The Expositor's Bible Commentary*, Frank E. Gaebelein, gen. ed., vol. 5 (Grand Rapids, MI: Zondervan, 1991); idem, "Entering the Textual World of the Psalms: Literary Analysis," in *The Psalms: Language for All Seasons of the Soul*, ed. Andrew J. Schmutzer and David M. Howard, Jr. (Chicago: Moody, 2013), 29–48.
[9] For a survey of the recent study of Psalms, see David M. Howard, Jr., "The Psalms and Current Study," in *Interpreting the Psalms: Issues and Approaches*, ed. David Firth and Philip S. Johnston (Downers Grove, IL: InterVarsity Press, 2005), 23–40.
[10] Brevard S. Childs, *Introduction to the Old Testament as Scripture of the Church* (Philadelphia: Fortress, 1979), 504–525.

righteous. In this fashion, the Psalter has gained, among its other functions, the use as a source for Wisdom reflection and a model of prayers based on such a pious interpretation of the Torah.[11]

Gerald Wilson also advances the macrostructural approach to Psalms by paying attention to the doxological conclusions of the five collections in connection with the potentiality (Psalms 2; 72) and failure of the Davidic monarchy (Psalm 89) and the hope in Yahweh's kingship.[12] Similarly, J. L. Mays develops the kingship of Yahweh as the pattern for interpreting the Psalms in conjunction with the wisdom motif.[13] J. C. McCann looks at the genres of the psalms: they are for the purpose of teaching its readers how to praise, lament to, and confess their confidence in the Lord.[14] Nancy L. deClaissé-Walford adds a diachronic dimension to the synchronic reading of the Psalter by arguing that the Psalter as a whole be read in light of the postexilic world.[15] I am indebted to these and many other scholarly contributions for a holistic reading of the Psalms.[16]

In several recent articles I outlined an approach that encourages the entry into the textual world of the Psalms through the cultivation of a synoptic (poetic) vision.[17] In "Entering the Textual World of the Psalms," I wrote,[18] "These textual explorations encourage entering into a text in order to explore it from within ('emic'), to get lost in the world of the text, to undergo transformation, and to experience a textual world. Such imagination includes all aspects of human existence: intellectual, emotive, relational, theological, and spiritual. It is a way of knowing or epistemology that is not esoteric or Gnostic."[19]

---

[11] Gerald T. Sheppard, *Wisdom as a Hermeneutical Construct: A Study in the Sapientalizing of the Old Testament*, Beihefte zur Zeitschrift für die alttestamentliche Wissenschaft 151 (Berlin: de Gruyter, 1980), 142. See also David Firth, "The Teaching of the Psalms," in *Interpreting the Psalms*, 159–174.

[12] Gerald H. Wilson, "The Structure of the Psalter," in *Interpreting the Psalms*, 229–246.

[13] James L. Mays, *The Lord Reigns: A Theological Handbook to the Psalms* (Louisville: Westminster John Knox, 1994).

[14] See Firth, "Teaching of the Psalms"; J. C. McCann, *A Theological Introduction to the Book of Psalms* (Nashville: Abingdon, 1993).

[15] Nancy L. deClaissé-Walford, *Reading from the Beginning: The Shaping of the Hebrew Psalter* (Macon, GA: Mercer University Press, 1997).

[16] See my commentary on the Psalms in *The Expositor's Bible Commentary* (vol. 5; see note 8, above).

[17] Willem A. VanGemeren, "Our Missional God: Redemptive Historical Preaching and the *Missio Dei*," in Jason Van Vliet, ed., *Living Waters from Ancient Springs: Essays in Honor of Cornelis Van Dam* (Eugene, OR: Pickwick, 2011), 198–217; idem, "Entering the Textual World of the Psalms," 29–49.

[18] VanGemeren, "Entering the Textual World of the Psalms," 47.

[19] For example, Ryan P. O'Dowd links imagination and canonical interpretation in "Wisdom as Canonical Imagination: Pleasant Words for Tremper Longman," in *Canon and Biblical Interpretation*, ed. Craig G. Bartholomew et al., Scripture and Hermeneutics 7 (Grand Rapids, MI: Zondervan, 2006), 374. By paying attention to textual resonances, O'Dowd works out a theological hermeneutic from which he interprets texts (382–383).

Such holistic reading of the Psalter is much in keeping with the ancient church. Ronald Heine sets forth examples of its practices of praying through the psalms and of "living in the text," which he defines as living in the *story* of the text, not trying to live in the *ancient history* of the text."[20] One outstanding example is that of Gregory of Nyssa, who took the sequence of the Psalms seriously and wrote an entire treatise on the superscriptions of the Psalms.[21] He set forth the value of a sequential reading of the psalms in order to make progress in the beatific life.

In addition to singing the Psalms with the ancient church, Gregory developed an instructional approach to the book, as he wrote: "But so that we may more precisely understand the teaching about the virtues in which the Word instructs us through the total guidance of the psalm, it would be well for us first, by producing some systematic argument in a consequential orderly manner, to determine with reference to ourselves how the admirer of such a life can come to be in virtue. For in this way we would discover the progression of the teaching we pointed out previously."[22] According to Gregory, the psalms are to be read sequentially, to be integrated, and to mark the path of progression in wisdom and godliness. He conceived of the Christian life as the life of the Lord Jesus, who leads his followers on the path of the blessed life (Ps. 1:1). The aim of the blessed life is nothing less than the reflection of God, as "[l]ikeness to God . . . is a definition of human blessedness."[23]

The sequential (progressive) reading ends on the five final hallelujah psalms, on which Gregory comments, "praising God is appropriate for those who have arrived at the goal of the virtuous life and have been purified through the preceding sections (psalms) of the Psalms. . . . [O]ne can clearly perceive that the final section of the Psalms (Psalms 146–150), which consists for the most part of praise or exhortation to praise God, excels every lofty ascent through the Psalms."[24]

---

[20] Ronald E. Heine, *Reading the Old Testament with the Ancient Church* (Grand Rapids, MI: Baker Academic, 2007), 143–191.
[21] Ronald E. Heine, *Gregory of Nyssa's Treatise on the Inscriptions of the Psalms* (Oxford: Clarendon, 1995).
[22] Ibid., 85.
[23] Ibid., 84.
[24] Ibid., 142–143.

THE PROBLEM OF GOD'S FIDELITY IN THE PSALMS

One of the problems in reading individual psalms is the juxtaposition of genres, themes, and moods.[25] The variety is polyrhythmic in the sense that a number of melodies give rise to rhythms that continuously create surprises and at the same time open up the listeners to new dimensions of who God is: he is the Creator God, the God of the universe, the King. In the exercise of his dominion, he is faithful and sovereign (free) in his rule.[26] After all, he is God. The psalmists wrestle with the personal, communal, and cosmic dimensions of God's dominion. They expect their God to be with them and for them; however, they are often surprised by his action and inaction. The psalms force the readers to read a psalm in the light of the whole Psalter, and the book of Psalms demands the integration with all that is revealed of God: in creation, in the story of salvation, and in history.

Gregory of Nyssa understood this process of integration well. Describing the process in which the psalmists were in tune with God's creation, he observed, "For the concord of all creation with itself, which has been composed through opposites, is truly a hymn to the glory of the inaccessible and inexpressible God produced by such a rhythm."[27] Through the psalms, God both reveals and hides himself.

GOD'S FAITHFULNESS AND QUESTIONS IN THE PSALMS

God's faithfulness is at the heart of the Psalter. The opening two psalms raise expectations of God's faithfulness by affirming that God will care for the righteous who walk with him in wisdom and shun the way of folly (1:6). They are the "congregation of the righteous" (1:5), who are the "blessed" (1:1; 2:12b) and enjoy his protection (2:12b), but the wicked and the rebellious nations will perish (*'bd*; 1:6; 2:12a). The psalmists affirm and cling to the hope of God's faithfulness. David says in Psalm 18, "To the faithful you show yourself faithful, to the blameless you show yourself blameless, to the pure you show yourself pure, but to the devious you show yourself shrewd" (vv. 25–26, NIV).

Why, then, do the psalmists wrestle with God, asking questions and at

---

[25] Luther rightly commented, "Who would even dare to assert that anyone has completely understood one single psalm?" (Martin Luther, *Selected Psalms III*, in *Luther's Works*, ed. Jaroslav Pelikan, Hilton C. Oswald, and Helmut T. Lehmann, 55 vols. [St. Louis: Concordia, 1955–1986], 14:284).
[26] Willem A. VanGemeren, "Prophets, the Freedom of God, and Hermeneutics," *Westminster Theological Journal* 52 (1990): 79–99.
[27] Quoted in Heine, *Gregory*, 89.

times perhaps being perceived as impatient or even petulant? In their deep trust of Yahweh, the psalmists affirm God's "goodness," i.e., his righteousness, justice, equity, uprightness, faithfulness, commitment, love, compassion, and forgiveness. David's assertion is representative of the Psalter: "All the ways of the LORD are loving and faithful toward those who keep the demands of his covenant. For the sake of your name, LORD, forgive my iniquity, though it is great" (25:10–11, NIV). The godly wait for and hope in God. By faith they see the end of the wicked (1:6; 2:12; 145:20; 146:9; 147:6; 149) and the exaltation of the "horn" of the righteous (92:10; cf. 148:14). They rejoice in the unfolding of God's deeds (92:4) and reflect upon and speak about his faithfulness by day and by night (92:2; cf. 1:2; Lam. 3:22–24). They are likened to trees in God's sanctuary as they proclaim, in their advanced age, "The LORD is upright; he is my Rock, and there is no wickedness in him" (Ps. 92:15, NIV). They long for redemption as they grow in wisdom and understanding (107:43; cf. Psalm 73).

The sapiential theological perspective is not fideistic. The psalmists encourage the faithful to raise serious questions of God, as Marvin Sweeney, a Jewish Old Testament scholar, writes: "Psalms opens the way for the process of critical reflection on G-d and the world and the restoration of Jerusalem and Israel/Judah within the world that proceeds throughout the third major component [the Writings, or *Ketuvim*] of the [Hebrew] Bible."[28] Sweeney helps us to look at the Psalter as an entrée into a Jewish way of exploration: Jewish readers of the Psalms enter the prayers and laments of the psalmists to engage in a dialogue between God and themselves. Sweeney observes, "Fundamentally, the Tanak is an intertextual and dialogical book." The great issue in post-Holocaust Judaism is God's faithfulness. He writes, "The Shoah ('holocaust') constitutes a major and unanswerable challenge to claims about *YHWH*'s sovereignty and fidelity."[29]

In the Psalms we meet anonymous authors as well as composers such as David, the sons of Korah, and Asaph. They openly speak of their afflictions and incarnate a lifestyle of suffering.[30] They believe in Yahweh's

---

[28] Marvin A. Sweeney, *Tanak: A Theological and Critical Introduction to the Jewish Bible* (Minneapolis: Fortress, 2012), 375–376.
[29] Ibid., 10. See also Sweeney's definition of the task of Jewish biblical theology (20–36). Accordingly, biblical theology is dialogical as the results of exegesis are directly related to the *Nachleben* of the text throughout Jewish history so as to engage with Jewish concerns throughout the ages. He comments, "There is a continuous debate concerning G-d's actions on behalf of Israel and G-d's willingness and ability to protect the nation from threats" (488).
[30] Willem A. VanGemeren, "The Psalms as Wisdom Instruction: 'David' as Model, Teacher, and Critical Realist" (unpublished article, 2005).

faithfulness but do not presume to know when and how Yahweh will respond to their prayers. Rather, they invite others to become their disciples. The psalms of David particularly are full of invitations to enter into his experience as he draws close to Yahweh in the midst of adversity. David invites subsequent generations to join him in fearing the Lord, asking, "Who, then, are those who fear the LORD? He will instruct them in the ways they should choose. . . . The LORD confides in those who fear him; he makes his covenant known to them" (25:12, 14, NIV). Further, he prays vicariously for his people in his troubles, representing future generations who will enter into his same sufferings (25:16–21). He ends the psalm with, "Redeem Israel, O God, from all their troubles!" (25:22, NIV, 1984). The intensity of the lament psalms is fueled by the psalmists' trust in God's faithfulness. The psalmists question and trust, despair and hope, and know God and cannot comprehend him. They share the conviction of his faithfulness and dependability, but also his hiddenness. The tension is best illustrated by briefly looking at the argument at the seam of Books II (Psalm 72) and III (Psalm 73). Psalm 72 arches with Psalm 2, with its great expectations of a universal kingdom ruled by a Davidic king committed to justice and righteousness. The Davidic ruler is endowed with wisdom, divine favor, and power. He is like a father in his care for and vindication of the oppressed, but he crushes oppression and corruption. His reign brings peace on earth (cf. Isa. 9:6–7).

The great expectations of Psalm 72 are crushed in the following psalms. Book III opens and closes with the question of God's fidelity toward individuals (73:1–16; Psalm 88), the community (Psalms 74; 79; 80; 83; 89), and the Davidic dynasty (89:49). The opening words of Psalm 89 affirm God's dependability: the psalmist sings of God's faithfulness as evident in creation and in the story of redemption, particularly the election of David. He says, "I will sing of the LORD's great love forever; with my mouth I will make your faithfulness known through all generations. I will declare that your love stands firm forever, that you have established your faithfulness in heaven itself" (89:1–2, NIV). In the middle of celebrating Yahweh's goodness in the election of and commitment to the Davidic dynasty, the psalm turns the praise into a communal lament (vv. 38–51). At issue is God's faithfulness to David and, through David, to the people of God: "Lord, where is your former great love, which in your faithfulness you swore to David?" (v. 49, NIV).

Sweeney rightly interprets the placement of the royal psalm (Psalm 89) at the closure of Book III as having a typological significance: "Book III takes up the suffering of the entire nation in the king."[31] From its opening credo of God's goodness (73:1) till the concluding two psalms, Book III dialogically engages with attempts at understanding God's faithfulness. God defies any human attempts at comprehending him. Psalm 89 is preceded by the gloomiest psalm in the Psalter. The psalmist confesses that he belongs to God and seeks him, but is rejected by God and his people. He represents the (post-) exilic community with their questions (see Lamentations). Life without God is a "shady" existence, in that the psalmist is surrounded by darkness and experiences "death" while alive. He asks, "Is your love declared in the grave, your faithfulness in Destruction? Are your wonders known in the place of darkness, or your righteous deeds in the land of oblivion?" (88:11–12, NIV).

Gradually, lament changes to praise in Books IV and V as the issues and questions raised in Books I–III move the exilic and postexilic readers of the Psalms to a new theological awareness and understanding. The Psalms affirm that Yahweh is king of a universal kingdom (Psalms 93; 95–99), that he is good, and that his faithfulness is everlasting, "For the LORD is good and his love endures forever; his faithfulness continues through all generations" (100:5, NIV; cf. 106:1; 107:1; 118:1–4, 29; 136:1–26). Even when the present generation may not understand the divine ways, the psalmists pray for subsequent generations. They praise Yahweh's character, wisdom, reversal of fortunes, forgiveness, and constancy (Psalm 103; cf. 107).[32] They speak of the way of wisdom (Psalms 111–112; 127–128; cf. Psalm 1) that leads God's people back to God while in the throes of exile (Psalm 139), and they encourage the people to reflect on their past and to focus more on the uniqueness of their God in the praise (*hallel*) psalms. They have learned and now teach sapiential theology through the psalms as they lead subsequent generations from questions to the praise of God.[33] That is the purpose of the hallelujah psalms.

---

[31] Sweeney, *Tanak*, 389.
[32] I prefer the distinction found in the ESV, where "bless" is the rendering for the Hebrew *brk* as an expression of praise in distinction from "praise" (*hll*). The NIV does not distinguish between these two expressions and translates both as "praise."
[33] Walter Brueggemann was not the first, but he observed cogently how the Psalter moves from obedience to praise (see "Bounded by Obedience and Praise: The Psalms as Canon," *Journal for the Study of the Old Testament* 50 [1991]: 63–92).

GOD'S FAITHFULNESS IN THE CONCLUDING HALLELUJAH PSALMS (PSALMS 146–150)

The English translation "praise the Lord" gives the impression that praise is found throughout the Psalter. It is a fact that the Hebrew designation for the book of Psalms is *tᵉhillīm* ("praises," from *hll*, "praise"). We have already favored the interpretation that the Psalms is first and foremost a book of instruction (Torah). Praise is a movement within the Psalms that begins with wisdom (obedience) and gradually escalates to praise in Books IV and V. The imperatival usage of *hll* ("praise") in the expression "hallelujah" ("praise Yah") is limited to several collections of praise psalms in Books IV and V. The final two psalms of Book IV (105:45; 106:1) adumbrate Yahweh and his mysterious ways in the story of redemption from creation to exile.

In Book V "hallelujah" is found in three collections. In the Egyptian Hallel (113–118), "hallelujah" begins or ends the psalm (113:1; 115:18; 116:19; 117:2) and is bounded by wisdom. Two wisdom psalms open the *hallel* psalms (111:1; 112:1), and a lengthy alphabetic acrostic (119) confronts the reader with a focus on divine instruction (wisdom) that arches back to Psalm 1 but portrays the lostness of an individual representative of the exilic community, who cries out to the Lord but to little avail. The Songs of Ascent (120–134) that follow engage with issues raised in Psalm 119 and close on a *hallel* (135; 136).

Psalm 135 forms a closure with Psalm 111 and even goes back to Psalm 105. It is also the last *hallelujah* psalm before the concluding hallelujah psalms. The call to praise Yahweh ("hallelujah") is found three times: twice at the beginning and once at the end:

> Praise the Lord [*hallᵉlu yāh*]!
>   Praise [*hallᵉlu*] the name of the Lord,
>   give praise [*hallᵉlu*], O servants of the Lord,
> who stand in the house of the Lord,
>   in the courts of the house of our God!
> Praise the Lord [*hallᵉlu*], for the Lord is good;
>   sing to his name, for it is pleasant! . . .
> Blessed [*brk*] be the Lord from Zion,
>   he who dwells in Jerusalem!
> Praise the Lord [*hallᵉlu yāh*]! (135:1–3, 21)

The opening and close of Psalm 135, with the call to praise Yahweh (*hal-lᵉlu yāh*), anticipates the similar usage in the five concluding hallelujah psalms, but distinguishes itself from the prior usage, where the call to praise is found either at the beginning or at the end of the psalm. Psalm 136 also opens with a threefold call to give thanks (vv. 1–3) and closes on the same note. It distinguishes itself by its repetitive antiphonal response, "His love endures forever" (vv. 1–26, NIV). The reflections on God's faithfulness are severely interrupted by a deeply disturbing exilic lament (Psalm 137).

The concluding collection of Davidic psalms (138–145) also prepares the reader for the final five hallelujah psalms (146–150). David's final lament, while personal, also serves symbolically as his bearing the suffering of the people who await deliverance:

> Hear my prayer, O Lord;
>   give ear to my pleas for mercy!
> In your faithfulness answer me,
>   in your righteousness! . . .
> Teach me to do your will,
>   for you are my God!
> Let your good Spirit lead me
>   on level ground!
> For your name's sake, O Lord, preserve my life!
>   In your righteousness bring my soul out of trouble!
> And in your steadfast love you will cut off my enemies,
> and you will destroy all the adversaries of my soul,
>   for I am your servant. (143:1, 10–12)

David prays for his people (Psalm 144) and opens up a large vision of God's everlasting kingdom (Psalm 145).

Psalm 145

At the heart of the lament and praise of the psalmists is the veracity of God's character, to which David returns in his final psalm (145). It is in the form of an alphabetic acrostic and is the last acrostic in the Psalms.[34] The psalmist portrays a transcended world in which God is the great,

---
[34] See the alphabetic acrostic Psalm 111 for thematic and linguistic connections. It opens on *hallᵉlu yāh* and closes on *tᵉhillā* (v. 10).

powerful, beneficent king whose righteousness (vv. 7, 17), faithfulness (v. 13b), and grace and mercy (vv. 8–9) are widely celebrated in the world (vv. 9–10, 13–17). God is praised for his condescension, care, and particularly his restorative and retributive justice among his own (vv. 14–20). The hope of both Psalms 1 and 2 is realized by God's worldwide and everlasting kingdom giving protection to all who call on him in truth, fear him, and love him (145:18–20; cf. 1:5–6; 2:12b) and ridding his kingdom of all evil (v. 20b; cf. 1:5–6; 2:4–9). This restatement of God's character links with many such affirmations in the Psalms and receives no other such portrayal in the hallelujah psalms, except for images of God's condescension.

At the macrostructural level, Books IV and V are held together by the affirmations of Yahweh's universal reign of justice, righteousness, and mercy that brings in a new world for all who endure suffering and await his faithfulness (Book IV: 91:4; 92:2; 98:3; 100:5; 103; Book V: 108:4; 111:7; 115:1; 117:2; 119:75, 90; 143:1; 145).[35] The promise of God's faithfulness could be perceived as vacant, because of the delay in fulfillment; in the Psalms, however, it is linked to Yahweh's character and to the beatific experiences that confirm the realization of his promise of the end of the wicked and the vindication of the oppressed (Psalm 1) as part of the expected victory of God over the opposing forces (Psalm 2). The five concluding hallelujah psalms seal the promises with a vision of God that includes each one of these elements.

The psalmist leads creation in the praise of God. He sets the tone in the opening and close of the psalm (145:1–2, 6, 21).[36] The designation of praise ($t^ehillā$, v. 1; cf. v. 21) in the superscription[37] is unique, and the repetition of the word in verse 21 forms an *inclusio* and prepares the readers[38] for the following five praise (*hall^elu yāh*) psalms by the

---

[35] These verses affirm God's faithful reign. Many psalms celebrate Yahweh's kingship (93; 94–99; 101–106; 110; 138; 144–145) and celebrate it using other words, such as *justice, righteousness,* and *equity.*

[36] The first hallelujah psalm (146:1–2; cf. 104:33)) connects with the use of the first person singular (145:1–2, 5–6, 21) of the Davidic psalms. The final four psalms call for the praise without the composer's involvement of himself.

[37] On the problem of interpreting superscriptions, see Willem A. VanGemeren and Jason Stanghelle, "Psalms Superscriptions and Critical Realistic Interpretation of the Psalms," in *Do Historical Matters Matter to Faith?: A Critical Appraisal of Modern and Postmodern Approaches to Scripture*, ed. James K. Hoffmeier and Dennis R. Magary (Wheaton, IL: Crossway, 2012), 281–302.

[38] The identity of the audience is oblique. The designation of "saints" (lit., "faithful ones") may suggest a special group within God's people, but its syntagmatic parallel "works" favors a more generic understanding of godly people found in all humanity. See Frank-Lothar Hossfeld and Erich Zenger, *Psalms 3: A Commentary on Psalms 101–150*, Hermeneia: A Critical and Historical Commentary on the Bible (Minneapolis: Fortress, 2001), 599.

lexeme *hll* ("praise"). The praise of God consists of the exaltation of Yahweh's name (reputation, fame) in public and private proclamation, celebration, and reflection (vv. 1–6, 11–12, 21); in joyful exultation (v. 7); and in thanksgiving (v. 10). All[39] creation participates in thanksgiving (vv. 10–11), even when their words are not heard (19:1–5), for his mighty acts in the sustenance of creation, in human history, in his acts of retribution, and particularly in his ultimate deliverance and vindication of all who fear him (145:11–21). The evidence of his faithfulness is for all to see (vv. 7–13).[40] The psalmist expects the exaltation of the name of Yahweh to become more and more widespread throughout all generations, so that all humanity may join in the reflective praise of Yahweh's character, might, and glory (v. 12).

Psalms 146–150: The Concluding Hallelujah Psalms

The concluding hallelujah psalms function as the final "Amen" to the portrayals of God in Psalm 145, with its themes of God's universal kingdom, global praise, and retributive justice. The hallelujah psalms intersect with the wisdom theology of the Psalter, retrospectively reminding the readers of psalms that speak of the psalmists' desire to walk with Yahweh while finding themselves on the path of darkness, disappointment, distress, and even despair while waiting for Yahweh's help. Through instruction and lament, the readers are presented with God's intense and dynamic relationship with his "saints." The psalmists invite their readers to follow them as their "disciples"; their suffering becomes symbolic. The psalms instruct future generations on how to live in exile (diaspora) with the hope of salvation that is grounded in the very character of Yahweh. The path of righteousness (wisdom) leads through darkness, but Yahweh will deliver all who wait for his salvation. Yahweh is the object of praise in the final Hallel psalms as creation and the godly celebrate the fidelity of God, that is, his reliability, truthfulness, love, and constancy in the midst of their exilic suffering and dependency.

---

[39] The nineteen uses of *kol* ("all") in Psalm 145 are connected with God's deeds, words, ways (vv. 10, 13b, 17) in caring for all needy creatures (vv. 14–16, especially his beloved people [vv. 18, 20]) and in bringing in his everlasting kingdom (v. 13), to which the psalmist and all flesh respond in lasting praise (vv. 2, 21). The comprehensiveness of Yahweh's deeds, involvement, and lasting fame expresses his care for all, so that all "flesh" will "bless" his holy name (v. 21). In his righteous, good, and faithful vindication of his saints, he excludes "all the wicked" (v. 20; cf. 1:6). See also the tenfold use of *kol* in Psalm 148.

[40] The added *nun*-line of the LXX and Syriac (the last two lines of v. 13, included in the main text in the NIV and placed between brackets in the ESV), may be based on verse 17 (146:6–7; cf. 111:7). See note 46, below.

The final hallelujah psalms climactically present images of God's mighty faithfulness in creation and in redemption, in judgment and salvation, and in vengeance and vindication. First, the portrayal of Yahweh as the faithful Creator King, who stoops to all his creatures and delights himself in his children who await his help in their suffering, finds further development (146:5–10; 147:5–12; 148:1–14). Yahweh is the powerful and wise Creator King of the world, by whose word everything came into being (148:5, 13); the world of creation elevates the imagination of the psalmists to the Creator. Creation is more than an event in the past, however; it points to the Creator, who is confessed as "the Maker of heaven and earth, the sea, and everything in them" (146:6, NIV).[41] He is constantly involved with every aspect of his creation. He cares for and governs the whole of his creation (147:4, 8–9, 15–18; 148:2–13; 150:6; cf. Psalm 145). The psalmists unpack the confession of God as "the Maker of heaven and earth" (146:6) by combining creation and redemption themes in a holistic vision of creation that involves eschatology as well (Psalms 146–150). God, who spoke creation into being and upholds everything by his word (145:13b; 147:15, 18, 19; 148:5–6; 149:9; cf. Psalm 33), has also planned to renew his kingdom by vindicating the righteous and by ridding the earth of evildoers (1:6).

The tone for the concluding hallelujah psalms is set by Psalm 146.[42] In terms of composition, it is evidently an anthology of the book of Psalms, as evidenced by the many citations and allusions to many psalms by which the reader is reminded to go back to all parts of the Psalter in quiet reflection and say "Amen" to each of the propositions and images of Psalm 146.[43] Frank-Lothar Hossfeld and Erich Zenger list many of these connections and express their agreement with Egbert Ballhorn's observation that Psalm 146 is a "condensation of condensations" and gives "in

---

[41] The Nicene confession, "I believe in God Almighty, Maker of heaven and earth," moves the interest from the details of Genesis 1 to the theological concern with the nature of who God is. He is the Creator. See Christopher R. Seitz, "Our Help Is in the Name of the Lord, Maker of Heaven and Earth," in *Nicene Christianity: The Future of a New Ecumenism*, ed. Christopher R. Seitz (Grand Rapids, MI: Brazos, 2001), 19–34.

[42] See John S. Kselman, "Psalm 146 in Its Context," *Catholic Biblical Quarterly* 50 (1988): 587–599; Erich Zenger, "The Composition and Theology of the Fifth Book of Psalms," *Journal for the Study of the Old Testament* 80 (1998): 77–102.

[43] The anthological style of Psalms 144–145 is continued in Psalm 146. The composite portrayal of Yahweh encourages entering the textual world as the reader/listener of the psalms reflects on who God is in his manifold relationships, including creation. The language of these psalms opens up to the whole Psalter by repetition of phrases, lines, verses, and concepts. Sweeney's observation on Psalm 144 applies equally to Psalm 145, 146, and 147:1–11: "Psalm 144 is an anthological psalm . . . which draws on the language of other psalms in an effort to bless YHWH and to reflect on divine beneficence granted to mortal human beings" (Sweeney, *Tanak*, 394).

summary . . . the whole spectrum of the poetry previously found in the psalms."[44] They draw several conclusions from the intertextual connections. First, the call to praise God calls to mind the many perspectives the psalms present of Yahweh, especially his universal kingship (Psalm 104) and his grace to the needy (Psalm 103). Second, the rejection of power structures and the confidence in Yahweh's kingship confirm God's reliability, especially through the strong intertextual connections with Psalm 118:3, 21. Third, the hope in the end of the oppression of the needy is reminiscent of the exodus and shares features with the new exodus motif in Isaiah: Yahweh will inaugurate a kingdom of justice and righteousness within a corrupt world.[45] The second psalm introduced the motif of God's kingdom, and the last Davidic psalm (145) confirms the glory of God's kingdom. In Psalm 2 Yahweh offers the nations to the messianic ruler: "Ask of me, and I will make the nations your heritage, and the ends of the earth your possession" (2:8). In Psalm 145 David celebrates the righteous and faithful rule of God: "Your kingdom is an everlasting kingdom, and your dominion endures through all generations. The LORD is faithful to all his promises and loving toward all he has made" (145:13, NIV 1984; cf. vv. 7, 17).[46] Psalms 145 and 146 embrace Yahweh's faithfulness as a central tenet of his kingdom. The evidence of his constancy lies in the continuity of creation (creation continua).

Further, the patterning of Psalm 146 confirms and connects with the interpretive matrix suggested by the opening two psalms (Psalms 1, 2): the rejection of human (power) structures, the affirmation of Yahweh as the true hope and source of help, the assurance of the vindication of the righteous, the triumph over evildoers, and Yahweh's everlasting and global kingdom with its center in Zion. Each of these themes forms a motif throughout the Psalter and has its *telos* in the concluding hallelujah psalms. This *telos* serves to tie together the many aspects of God's being, character, and relationships. The psalmists believe that Yahweh is righteous as they long for the manifestation of Yahweh's glorious kingdom by

---

[44] Hossfeld and Zenger cite Ballhorn's study on the goal of the Psalter (*Zum Telos des Psalters* [Berlin: Philo, 2004], 304) in *Psalms 3*, 610.
[45] Ibid., 611.
[46] Psalm 145 is an alphabetic acrostic in which the line with the letter *nun* is missing (see note 40, above). Good arguments have been made for its inclusion from textual evidence (11QPsa; LXX, Syriac). The NIV includes it (see v. 13, above). Arguments have also been made against its inclusion, particularly its closeness in wording with Psalm 111:7b (see Hossfeld, *Psalms 3*, 592–593). Were verse 13b (NIV 1984) and the word "faithful" not authentic, the whole tenor of Psalm 145 would still affirm Yahweh's faithfulness. The themes and language are closely linked with Psalm 146.

his vindication of the righteous, thereby demonstrating his righteousness and faithfulness. The final verse comprehends both truths in the prayer, "May Yahweh reign."[47] Yahweh's reign will establish his everlasting sovereignty over creation, his care for the needy, and the future of Zion.[48]

The citizens of Zion separate themselves from power structures (146:3–4) in their search for the beatific life (v. 5; cf. 1:1, 5–6). Their hope and sustenance is God himself, to whom they look for help (146:5–6; 147:11), because he is like a father in his defense and restoration of the needy (146:6–8a). He is constant in his care and ultimate in his justice, because he is "the LORD his God, the Maker of heaven and earth" (vv. 5–6).[49]

Psalm 146 opens the final hallelujah collection and forms a bookend with the opening two psalms. The psalm affirms Yahweh's faithfulness and the beatific lives of the godly, reminiscent of Psalm 1: "Blessed are those whose help is the God of Jacob, whose hope is in the LORD their God. He is the Maker of heaven and earth, the sea, and everything in them—he remains faithful forever" (146:5–6, NIV; see 1:1, 5–6). This final beatitude ("blessed are those") connects with the first beatitude (1:1) and ties the whole book together. Psalm 146 portrays Yahweh as the Great King of Zion who is the hope and help of his people (vv. 5, 10; 147:1–20; 148:14; Psalm 149). He delights in his people and delivers them from affliction (147:11; 149:1–9).

The coalescence of the metaphors of Yahweh as the Creator and King binds Old Testament theology together. Jon Levenson has argued that creation, kingship, and temple form a triadic approach to the Tanakh (Old Testament).[50] Where, then, is the temple in the hallelujah psalms? It receives no mention. The word occurs in the first Davidic psalm in the final Davidic collection (Psalms 138–145): "I will bow down toward your holy temple and will praise your name for your unfailing love and your faithfulness, for you have so exalted your solemn decree that it surpasses your fame" (138:2, NIV). The spirit of Psalm 138 prepares for the vision of Yahweh's exaltation in his kingdom in Psalm 145, with its

---

[47] I agree with Zenger's argument that the verb be read as a jussive, contra NIV ("reigns") and ESV ("will reign"). See Hossfeld and Zenger, *Psalms 3*, 609.
[48] Zenger observes, "From this jussive perspective, v. 10 brings together the program of the final Hallel" (ibid.).
[49] Author's translation. The ESV shifts from present to past and again to present, "hope is in the LORD his God, who made heaven and earth, the sea, and all that is in them, who keeps faith forever." It is preferable to translate "who made heaven" as a noun, "Maker of heaven," as a confession of who God is. He is the Creator, rather than the one who created.
[50] Jon D. Levenson, *Sinai and Zion: An Entry into the Jewish Bible* (Minneapolis: Winston, 1985), 109.

broad perspective on creation. The triad creation, kingship, and temple are as much indissoluble in Genesis 1–2 as they are toward the end of the Psalter, where creation is the temple of God. The tabernacle/temple is temporal, whereas creation best represents God's kingship and temple, as Levenson writes: "In other words, the world is God's Temple and in it he finds rest, just as in the miniature man makes of it, the earthly Temple atop Mount Zion."[51]

Creation and kingship shape the hope of the final hallelujah psalms, as well as God's rule in and for the sake of Zion. Zion represents the symbolic presence of the Lord instead of the temple. The Creator of the world is seen as stooping down to bring justice to his needy children. In Psalm 145 the promise of reversal of fortunes extends to "all who call on him in truth. . . . who fear him; . . . [and] who love him" (vv. 18–20).

The hallelujah psalms also define the people in whom Yahweh delights. The Creator of the world pronounces happiness to all who look for his help and make him their hope; they are the objects of the beatitude, "Blessed is he whose help is the God of Jacob, whose hope is in the Lord his God, who made heaven and earth, the sea, and all that is in them, who keeps faith forever" (146:5–6). This final beatitude in the Psalms links up with the opening of the Psalter (1:1), which predicates happiness to all who walk on the path of wisdom, delighting themselves in God's word and avoiding the traps of human peer pressure (1:1–2). The righteous (146:8; cf. 1:5–6) may have experienced oppression, hunger, imprisonment, blindness, and affliction, but their ill fortunes will be reversed (146:7–8; cf. Psalm 107), because Yahweh delights himself in them (146:8), but the wicked "he brings to ruin" (v. 9; cf. 1:6). The inhabitants of Zion are healed, provided for, and secure in Zion (146:10; cf. Psalm 107; Isa. 33:19–24), because God is faithful. He sustains his people with his word of promise.

Similarly, Psalm 147 intertwines the themes of creation and the redemption of the people of God. The humble or humiliated people are portrayed as exiles—brokenhearted, wounded, and humble people (vv. 2–3, 6). Yahweh promises to be present with the exiles of Zion (vv. 2–7) by providing for them and protecting them (vv. 2–3, 6, 12–14), because he delights in them: "but the Lord takes pleasure in those who fear him, in those who hope in his steadfast love" (v. 11; cf. 146:5). He rewards

---
[51] Ibid., 145.

the "humble," but rejects the wicked (147:6; cf. 1:6). The Creator has consecrated Israel with his word (147:19–20) and sustains the order of creation and his relationship with his people by his word (vv. 15–20).

Psalm 147 develops God's reign as embracing his acts of creation (vv. 4–5, 8–9, 15–18) and redemption (vv. 2–3, 6, 10–14, 19–20). The psalmist weaves together the two strands of creation and redemption by going back and forth from the one theme to the other in order to portray Yahweh's concern with the restoration of his people in conjunction with his incomparable power and wisdom manifested in creation. He also connects these themes by suggesting many intertextual connections with all three parts of the Hebrew Old Testament: Law (Deuteronomy 4), the Prophets (Isaiah 40), and the Writings (Psalm 33; 104). The anthological manner of Psalms 144–147 also forms a connection between the words of David (Psalms 144–145) and the Hallel psalms. As God's word holds this world together by his mighty power (147:15–18), so it will be effective in shaping the people of God (vv. 19–20), in whom he delights (vv. 10–11).

Psalm 148 celebrates the praise of Yahweh throughout creation, both in heaven and on earth, because the Creator brought everything into being by his word (148:5; cf. Genesis 1; Psalm 33). The vision of the universal praise of Yahweh suggests Isaiah's vision of all creation anticipating redemption with codas of praise for God (Isa. 42:10–13; 44:23; 45:8; 48:20–21; 49:13; 51:13; 52:9–10; 54:1–3; 55:12–13).[52] In Isaiah 40–55, songs of praise close oracles of salvation and disputation speeches to meet Israel's objections and counter the attractiveness of the Babylonian way of life. In the Psalms, the call to praise serves in the concluding hallelujah psalms to confirm Yahweh's reliability and faithfulness to the whole of his creation and particularly to all who wait for Yahweh's salvation. Praise is a moment in time in which the godly peek into God's throne room, where he receives the praise due to him from every aspect of his creation: heaven, including angelic creatures, the sun, moon, and stars (Ps. 148:1–6); and the earth with its sea creatures, weather elements (lightning, hail, snow, rain, winds), geographical features, vegetation, animals, and human beings (vv. 7–12). Accordingly, God is exalted above his creation, over everything in heaven, on earth, and in the sea (v. 13).

The praise of God comes from every aspect of his creation; indeed,

---

[52] See Rikki E. Watts, "Consolation or Confrontation? Isaiah 40–55 and the Delay of the New Exodus," *Tyndale Bulletin* 41/1 (1990): 31–59.

the tenfold call to "praise" (*hall^elu; y^ehall^elu*) Yahweh, together with the twofold frame (hallelujah), suggests a completeness and a symbolic totality. The sense of wholeness is reinforced by the tenfold use of "all" (*kol*).[53] Psalm 148 also includes the narrower focus on Zion. While all creatures and created things will bring Yahweh praise (vv. 1–13), his favor rests on his faithful "people"—"all his saints, . . . the people of Israel who are near to him" (v. 14)—who will receive strength ("horn;" v. 14; cf. 75:10; 89:17; 92:10–11). The nature of the strength and of "saints" is further developed in Psalm 149.

In Psalm 149 "the saints" are members of the "assembly (*qāhāl*) of the godly"[54] (v. 1; cf. 1:5) and are further defined as "Israel," "the people of Zion," "his people," and "the humble" (149:2, 4, 5, 9). The "saints" rejoice in "their Maker" (v. 2). The Maker of heaven and earth (146:6) is also the Maker of Israel and the King of Zion (cf. 95:6–7). He will be their help (Psalm 121; 115:12–13, 15; 124:8). The "humble" (afflicted) are his people (*'ammo*) who will enjoy his victory over evil and will receive his glory, because he delights in them and endows them with victory and splendor (149:4–9).[55]

Psalm 150 celebrates the closure of the Psalter, the final hallelujah psalms, and all expressions of praise in the Psalter, with a greater sense of confidence in Yahweh's faithfulness. He will be victorious (Psalm 149). He will secure his kingdom and vindicate the saints. He will bestow on them honor (149:5, 9) and reward their perseverance with his lasting salvation (v. 4) as he brings the nations to submission (vv. 6–9). Joy will be theirs (v. 5), because Yahweh is the victorious King of Zion. They are witnesses to and participants in the execution of his "decree" to restore order to God's creation (v. 9). All humanity will praise the Lord at the end (150:6). The "Maker of heaven and earth" (146:6), whose sovereignty over all is without question, is the gracious "Maker" of Zion (149:2).

Some may be disappointed that God's program for the new creation in the final hallelujah psalms makes no mention of the future of David. The vision of the exaltation of the "horn" (148:14) has been interpreted as a

---

[53] See the nineteen uses of *kol* ("all") in Psalm 145.
[54] The ESV surprisingly changes the word translated as "saints" in 145:10 and 148:14 to "the godly" in 149:1, 5, 9.
[55] The mention of "Israel" (147:2, 19; 148:14; 149:2) reminds the readers that the promises also pertain to God's ancient people, who are still "loved on account of the patriarchs" (Rom. 11:28, NIV). Hope remains for ethnic Israel, because God is faithful. See Willem A. VanGemeren, "Israel as the Hermeneutical Crux in the Interpretation of Prophecy," Part I, *Westminster Theological Journal* 45 (1983): 132–145; Part II, *Westminster Theological Journal* 46 (1984): 254–297.

messianic allusion (cf. 89:24). Though it does not exclude the possibility of a Davidic hope, the reality of the postexilic era dims the messianic hope in favor of the survival of the people of God. Hope lies in God's relationship with wise people who are conformed to his righteousness (Psalm 1) and who find refuge in him (2:12). Yet, the very name of David is kept alive in all five books of Psalms by psalms associated with him. The Davidic collections open the Psalter proper (Psalms 3–41) after two introductory psalms and close it (Psalms 138–145) by launching the final hallelujah psalms. Underlying the Psalter is the hope that Yahweh will also be faithful to the messianic hope raised in its five Books (Psalms 2; 72; 89:1–38; 101; 110; cf. Isa. 9:6–7; ch. 11).

CONCLUSION

The final hallelujah psalms sustain the hope that Yahweh will bring an end to evil and oppression by vindicating his faithful children and by avenging himself on the wicked (146:9; 147:6; 149:6–9). In his faithfulness to the godly, their fortunes will be reversed (146:7–9; 147:3–6, 13–14), because he "delights" in them (147:11; 149:4). They are known as the "faithful" ones (NIV; ESV "saints" or "godly"; 148:14; 149:1, 5, 9). The Hallel psalms open the door to all who place their hope in him (146:5) and fear him (147:11; cf. 145:19; cf. 2:11). They are the people close to his heart (148:14, NIV). In the end, all humanity ("breath") will praise his holy name (150:6). There is no such future for the wicked, whether in or outside of Israel (146:9; 147:6; cf. 1:6).

HALLELUJAH IN THE NEW TESTAMENT

The Hebrew expression "hallelujah" ("praise the LORD") occurs four times in Revelation 19 and nowhere else in the New Testament. First, God/Jesus is the Creator-King over all creation (Rev. 3:14; cf. 10:6), the one to whom the saints in heaven and on earth sing hallelujahs (19:1–7). The scene is reminiscent of Psalm 148, in which God is praised by all creatures in heaven and on earth (Rev. 5:13; 7:11–12; 19:1–7; cf. Ps. 150:6). God's power extends to every part of his creation, and so do his judgments until he brings about a new creation, a new Jerusalem (Revelation 21–22). Second, the saints/martyrs in heaven long for the demonstration of God's power resulting in their vindication (6:10). They rejoice in his faithfulness and justice, in his "salvation and glory and power" (19:1), but they lament the delay of God's salvation (10:6). John portrays the coming of the end by the fall of Babylon and Christ's victory over the nations. The saints in heaven participate in singing hallelujah. It marks the end of their waiting, as they shout: "Hallelujah! Salvation and glory and power belong to our God, for his judgments are true and just; for he has judged the great prostitute who corrupted the earth with her immorality, and has avenged on her the blood of his servants" (19:1–2).[56] Their second "hallelujah" anticipates the end of evil in the world: "Hallelujah! The smoke from her goes up forever and ever" (v. 3). The perspective of the saints in heaven receives confirmation by the third hallelujah. The twenty-four elders and the four living creatures affirm the hallelujah of the saints by saying, "Amen. Hallelujah!" (v. 4; cf. 7:12). A heavenly voice calls on all people on earth to join in singing hallelujah, "Praise our God, all you his servants, you who fear him, small and great" (19:5). I agree with Grant Osborne that the translation "praise our God" is a contextualized form of hallelujah.[57] In response to the heavenly command, a "great multitude" on earth retorts in faith by shouting, "Hallelujah! For the Lord our God the Almighty reigns. Let us rejoice and exult and give him the glory, for the marriage of the Lamb has come, and his Bride has made herself ready" (vv. 6–7). John portrays Jesus riding into his creation as the victorious King, the rider on a white horse, and bearing many names: "Faithful and True" (v. 11), "The Word of God" (v. 13), and "King of kings and Lord of lords" (v. 16). God is faithful. Hallelujah!

Third, Jesus loves all who persevere. Revelation 19 sets a group of people apart; they are known as "his servants" (v. 2) and "his servants,

---

[56] Grant Osborne observes that the hallelujahs connect with the hymns in Revelation 4 and 5 as well as with the praises in Revelation 7:10–12; 11:15–18 (*Revelation* [Grand Rapids, MI: Baker Academic, 2002], 662). He cites favorably the study of W. H. Shea ("Revelation 5 and 19 as Literary Reciprocals," *Andrews University Seminary Studies* 22 [1984]: 249–257; see Osborne, *Revelation*, 662, 252–253), according to whom the four hallelujahs are associated with the four hymns in 5:8–14, but in reverse order. In 5:8–10 the four living creatures and the twenty-four elders prostrate themselves before the Lamb, singing a new song with the accompaniment of a harp and presenting "golden bowls full of incense," i.e., "the prayers of the saints." The praise focuses on the Lamb who "purchased men for God from every tribe and language and people and nation" and "made them to be a kingdom and priests to serve our God, and they will reign on the earth" (vv. 9–10, NIV). Angelic beings join in the praise, singing, "Worthy is the Lamb, who was slain, to receive power and wealth and wisdom and strength and honor and glory and praise!" (vv. 11–12, NIV). Every creature on earth joins in the praise, saying, "To him who sits on the throne and to the Lamb be praise and honor and glory and power, for ever and ever!" (v. 13, NIV). Their counterpart in heaven, the four living creatures, who are the counterpart to every creature on earth, join in the praise along with the elders (5:14). Evidently a major shift has taken place. Instead of the ambivalent position of the messianic expectation at the closure of the Psalter, the Lord Jesus Christ has taken center stage. He is the object of worship, because of his power, wisdom, and glory. The saints not only praise him for his wise and powerful rule; they will also rule with him.
[57] Osborne, *Revelation*, 667.

you who fear him" (v. 5; cf. 11:18). Theirs are the beatitudes (v. 9; cf. 1:3 [2x], 14:13; 16:15; 19:9; 20:6; 22:7, 14). As the psalmists qualify the true people of God, so does John in Revelation 19. The "great multitude" on earth walk on the path of wisdom by singing hallelujah as they long for his redemption and remain faithful to the one who is Faithful and True (19:11).

CONCLUSION

The final Hallel collection in Book V of the Psalms is a theological response to the questions and issues raised in the Psalter for the sake of subsequent generations.[58] In the affirmation of God's being "the Maker of heaven and earth," the godly have found a home in exile (the diaspora). They find him wherever they live. The whole creation is his temple. Jerusalem and the Promised Land are not trivialized, but they are no longer the sole focus of hope. Zion is transformed from being the city of David to the city of God. In the dialogue between God and the godly, Zion is democratized into a place where God meets with all the godly; the Infinite One meets with his people and assures them of the reality of his promises and of his faithfulness in Zion. He assures them that, in the working out of his mysterious purposes, they can count on him without being able to predict how and when he will be working out his purposes. His ways are mysterious and beyond human comprehension, and they evoke awe in the "saints."

The final Hallel psalms encourage hope and trust in God's words, acts, and ways by encouraging a lifestyle of wisdom, fear, and hope. They also assure of God's victory over evildoers, his care for his children living in "exile," and his vindication of the godly. They also permit questions, such as the Jewish problem with the Shoah and the Christian problem with the suffering of the saints and the persistence of evil.

As Christians we look at the Lord Jesus as the paradigm of God's faithfulness. Jesus fully submitted himself to the Father, learned obedience, and was perfected through suffering (Heb. 5:8–9). Jesus underwent the Shoah in his death. He experienced all that we experience (4:15), but was alone in his suffering unto death, so that "by the grace of God he

---

[58] See Gerald H. Wilson, "The Structure of the Psalter," in *Interpreting the Psalms*, 229–246. He comments, "Reading the psalms from beginning to end forces us to set aside our preconceptions and calls us to lay aside our own perceived needs as the driving force of our encounter with the psalms" (245).

might taste death for everyone" (2:9). Jesus walked on the path of the psalmists as he gave himself over to suffering, laments, tears, and questions (5:7). As he shared in our suffering, he also shares his glory with the saints. Jesus is "the" temple of God incarnate, and his followers have seen the glory of this latter temple (John 1:14; 2:19; cf. Hag. 2:9). Though the church still suffers and longs for victory, its delight in its Savior grows more intense as it finds its happiness in the triune God, who is "the Maker of heaven and earth." The church also longs for the Spirit's assurance that everything will work out for good (Rom. 8:28) and that its members are coheirs with the Lord Jesus—in the words of Paul, "if indeed we share in his sufferings in order that we may also share in his glory" (Rom. 8:17, NIV). With these assurances Christians discover order in the midst of the chaos when they follow the path of the psalmists and of our Lord, the apostles, and the saints of all ages. They suffer, long for, and pray for evidences of God's faithfulness. They grow in grace, virtue, and character. They learn obedience and cultivate hope in God's deliverance. Their perseverance is a witness to the reality of "the other world."

The present world is characterized by inhumanity, excruciating physical suffering, crippling diseases, mental anguish and depression, hatred and alienation, rejection and persecution, and mourning and suffering. Even so, the saints below can and must affirm God's faithfulness in the spirit and model of the Hallel psalms (Psalms 146–150) and of the saints on high (the "elders") and of the saints on earth (Rev. 19:1–7), by singing "hallelujah." Handel's "Hallelujah Chorus" ties together the fervent expectations of the Hallel psalms with Revelation 19: "And he shall reign. And he shall reign. And he shall reign. He shall reign. And he shall reign forever and ever. . . . Hallelujah! Hallelujah! Hallelujah! Hallelujah. Hallelujah." Yes, God is faithful, but not predictable. "Amen. Come, Lord Jesus!" (Rev. 22:20).

III

ERECTING THE SUPERSTRUCTURE OF EVANGELICAL THEOLOGY

13

Thinking Theologically in Public about Bioethics: Theological Formulation and Cultural Translation

JOHN F. KILNER

When the field of bioethics was gaining momentum in the 1960s, leading authors and speakers like Paul Ramsey worked out their theology based on a well-developed understanding of Scripture. Then they worked out the implications of that theology for issues in bioethics in books like *The Patient as Person*.[1] At that time the culture was friendlier to biblical values and language than it is today, so people could use a mix of biblical and secular language as the basis—the foundation—of their views. This state of affairs was not unique to bioethics. For instance, in the civil rights movement, the writings and speeches of Martin Luther King, Jr., were filled with language straight out of the Bible.

As the culture became more hostile to theological defenses of positions on issues in public, bioethicists began to discuss bioethics in purely secular language in the hope of maintaining a public voice. Many began not merely to speak secular language but also to think in secular terms. They gradually abandoned the time-consuming steps of developing biblically

---
[1] Paul Ramsey, *The Patient as Person* (New Haven, CT: Yale University Press, 1970).

and theologically sound views on issues and then translating those into language that a pluralistic public could understand and tolerate. Instead, they began to formulate their views directly in secular terms and categories, and that language began to shape them, rather than they—or the Bible—shaping the terms and categories of thinking and discourse.

There is a pressing need today for people who are adept at both theological formulation and cultural translation. People need to *begin* with theological formulation—i.e., with a good understanding of the Bible, a theological understanding grounded in the Bible, and the ability to formulate positions on bioethical issues based on such understandings. Then it is vital that people develop the ability to translate their biblically sound theological positions into language that is widely understood and accepted in the culture. Sadly, evidence of theological formulation is often lacking in bioethics today, even among Christians. Just as sadly, though, some Christians who succeed in theological formulation stumble over cultural translation. Today's Christians need to be bilingual—conversant in the language of the Bible and the language of the culture—and able to translate the one into the other. Otherwise, they either lose the genuinely Christian character of their bioethics—the salt loses its saltiness, to borrow a metaphor from Jesus—or they speak in a Christian language to which fewer and fewer will even listen.

Consider a recent issue of the *American Journal of Bioethics*, the journal of a secular national bioethics society. The lead essay argues that everything religious should fastidiously be eliminated from bioethics; "In Defense of Irreligious Bioethics" is its title.[2] The telling cover of the journal shows a physician listening to a Bible through a stethoscope. Not so subtly here, the question is not merely whether biblical language should be used in public discussion, but whether the Bible itself is still alive, i.e., relevant in today's world. If biblical language cannot be used to justify public arguments about bioethics, then for the Bible to be relevant, it must work in a less visible way. What is needed is the two-step process outlined above: formulating positions on bioethical issues that are biblically and theologically sound, and then translating them into language that is widely understood and accepted in the culture. This does not mean that there remains no place for biblically grounded theological language

---

[2] Timothy F. Murphy, "In Defense of Irreligious Bioethics," *The American Journal of Bioethics* 12/12 (2012): 3–10.

in public discussions. However, considering what that place looks like will have to wait until the end of this essay.

AN ILLUSTRATION FROM THE STEM CELL DEBATE

The widely publicized debate over stem cell research provides a helpful way to illustrate the process of theological formulation and cultural translation. Christians, first of all, need to put good biblical and theological understanding to work in formulating a sound approach to stem cell research. What would that look like? An adequate answer requires some background information about stem cells. A stem cell takes its name from the stem of a plant. Just as a stem produces leaves and flowers—things that a plant needs in order to live—so also a stem cell produces other cells that make up the blood, skin, muscles, nerves, and more—what our bodies need to live and to heal. However, there are different categories of stem cells. The cause of confusion in the so-called stem cell debate is a failure to consistently acknowledge this. One result is that many people wrongly think that a stem cell is basically one type of cell and that there are only two positions on stem cell research: *for* and *against*. This outlook fails to grasp that there have been at least two important categories all along. One is so-called adult stem cells, which are located in various parts of the human body and can essentially be obtained without harm. The other is so-called embryonic stem cells, which are obtained from a human embryo.

In contrast to the relatively harmless procedure for procuring adult stem cells from a human body, obtaining embryonic stem cells requires pulling apart a human embryo, killing the embryo in the process. Even where a particular experiment does not destroy embryos but instead uses cells from embryos previously destroyed by others, that experiment is inextricably tied to embryonic destruction in three ways. First, the experiment could not take place unless embryos had been destroyed. Second, the experiment implicitly encourages more research on a greater variety of embryonic stem cells, necessitating further destruction of embryos. Third, the experiment fosters a future in which embryos—genetically matched to patients—are produced by cloning and then destroyed for their stem cells. Thus embryonic stem cell research, as a practice, is inextricably tied to the destruction of embryos.

Virtually no one is against adult stem cell research, once they understand the difference between adult and embryonic stem cell research. The inherent ethical problems have to do with embryonic stem cell research alone. Proponents of embryonic stem cell research benefit from people failing to understand the difference between embryonic and adult stem cell research, because this failure leads people to oppose "stem cell research," by which they have in mind just embryonic stem cell research. Such people can then rightly be labeled "anti-science" because they are opposing the wonderful breakthroughs that are taking place today using adult stem cells. In the process, all opposition to stem cell research gets discredited, and embryonic stem cell research is the winner. Informed ethical opposition needs to focus more specifically on embryonic stem cell research.

Until relatively recently, supporting only adult stem cell research has been hard to do, because embryonic stem cells have one key attribute that adult stem cells don't have—they are "pluripotent." Pluripotent stem cells have the ability ("potent"-cy) to produce many ("plur"-al) different kinds of cells—in fact, all the kinds of cells that the human body requires. Adult stem cells just produce one kind of cell, and adult cells are not known to exist and be accessible for all types of body cells. To produce all types of cells, pluripotent stem cells appear to be necessary. As we will see shortly, a biblical outlook is concerned with developing treatments for all people with illnesses, not just those with certain types of illness. Is the destruction of human embryos necessary in order to produce all types of cells? It turns out that there now appear to be two other ways to produce all types of cells. One is producing pluripotent stem cells without destroying human embryos. The other is producing all kinds of cells without using pluripotent stem cells at all.

The first alternative, producing pluripotent stem cells without destroying human embryos, involves the production of so-called induced pluripotent stem cells. Researchers take a cell that is not a stem cell, such as a normal skin cell, and turn on the major portion of its genetic code that is normally turned off. This process converts it to a cell that is very similar to an embryonic stem cell and has the potential to do all that an embryonic stem cell can do without requiring the destruction of an embryo in the process.

Once produced, in 2006, induced pluripotent stem cells were soon heralded as a major breakthrough. Robert Lanza, the Chief Science Officer at Advanced Cell Technology in the United States, proclaimed their development to be "a tremendous scientific milestone—the biological equivalent of the Wright Brothers' first airplane."[3] Meanwhile, according to British news reports, Ian Wilmut, who produced the famous Dolly the sheep via cloning, was quick to proclaim that he was abandoning embryonic stem cell research to focus on induced pluripotent stem cell research instead.[4] By 2012 the significance of this breakthrough had become so clear that Dr. Shinya Yamanaka was awarded the Nobel Prize for Medicine that year for his pioneering work in developing induced pluripotent stem cells. His motivation, as reported in the *New York Times*, was powerful: "'When I saw the embryo, I suddenly realized there was such a small difference between it and my daughters. I thought, we can't keep destroying embryos for our research. There must be another way.'"[5]

Just the previous year a team of physicians at Mayo Clinic had published a comparative study of embryonic stem cell research and induced pluripotent stem cell research. They found both technologies likely to be scientifically viable, but they concluded that induced pluripotent stem cell research is preferable because embryos do not need to be destroyed—and a large supply of donated eggs is not required.[6] In 2012, there was some preliminary research questioning whether induced pluripotent stem cell research in humans is as safe as embryonic stem cell research; however, a new study published in the journal *Nature* in 2013 was reassuring on that score.[7] Later in 2013, researchers discovered a new way to generate induced pluripotent stem cells in mice using only chemicals rather than genetic manipulation, thereby increasing the likelihood that these cells will ultimately prove as safe to use as embryonic stem cells.[8]

As noted earlier, there is another type of research that has demonstrated a way to produce all types of cells without destroying embryos.

---

[3] "'Milestone' Stem Cell Advance Reported." Posted November 20, 2007 on cnn.com. See http://cr4.globalspec.com/blogentry/4036/Milestone-Stem-Cell-Advance-Reported.
[4] Roger Highfield, "Dolly Creator Prof Ian Wilmut Shuns Cloning," *The Telegraph*, November 16, 2007, sec. Science News, http://www.telegraph.co.uk/science/science-news/3314696/Dolly-creator-Prof-Ian-Wilmut-shuns-cloning.html.
[5] Martin Fackler, "Risk Taking Is in His Genes," *The New York Times*, December 11, 2007, sec. Science, http://www.nytimes.com/2007/12/11/science/11prof.html?_r=0&pagewanted=all.
[6] David G. Zacharias et al., "The Science and Ethics of Induced Pluripotency: What Will Become of Embryonic Stem Cells?" *Mayo Clinic Proceedings* 86/7 (July 2011): 634–640.
[7] Ryoko Araki et al., "Negligible Immunogenicity of Terminally Differentiated Cells Derived from Induced Pluripotent or Embryonic Stem Cells," *Nature* 494 (February 7, 2013): 100–104.
[8] Pingping Hou et al., "Pluripotent Stem Cells Induced from Mouse Somatic Cells by Small-Molecule Compounds," *Science* online (July 18, 2013), available at http://www.sciencemag.org/content/early/2013/07/17/science.1239278.

Called "transdifferentiation," it is most easily explained by comparing it with induced pluripotent stem cell research. Induced pluripotent stem cell research begins with single-type cells—for example, skin cells. These are called "differentiated" cells because the entire genetic code inside them has been turned off, except the part of the code with instructions to produce skin cells. That is why they are different from—or differentiated from—other types of cells. Induced pluripotent stem cell research turns virtually the entire genetic code back on—it "de-differentiates" these cells—so that they become pluripotent stem cells, just as embryonic stem cells are. The idea is that these pluripotent stem cells can then be directed to form any other type of cell, such as a nerve cell. Transdifferentiation simply cuts out the middle step. To use the same example, rather than turning most of the genetic code back on and then most of the code back off, it merely turns off the part of the code for producing skin cells and turns on the part of the code for producing nerve cells. No embryos are harmed. There have been a number of successes reported in recent years, ever since the report in *Nature* of the production of nerve cells from skin cells.[9] In fact, researchers have successfully transdifferentiated cells from urine into brain cells.[10] Needless to say, urine is a much more widely accessible source of cells—and a less ethically objectionable source than human eggs and human embryos are.

In summary, there now appear to be four viable ways to produce healthy human cells for treating a huge array of human illnesses and injuries: adult stem cells, embryonic stem cells, induced pluripotent stem cells, and transdifferentiation of cells. With that understanding, we are now in a position to engage in theological formulation—formulating a position on stem cell research that is biblically and theologically sound.

THEOLOGICAL FORMULATION

An important starting point is to acknowledge that no one group's interests settle the issue. Stem cell research is a matter of great importance for the future of humanity, and it is essential to consider carefully all who have a significant stake in this research. For biblically informed Christians, there will be a special sensitivity to those who are weakest

---

[9] Zhiping P. Pang et. al., "Induction of Human Neuronal Cells by Defined Transcription Factors," *Nature* 476 (May 26, 2011): 220–223.
[10] Lihui Wang et al., "Generation of Integration-free Neural Progenitor Cells from Cells in Human Urine," *Nature Methods* 10 (December 9, 2012): 84–89.

and most vulnerable—in biblical language, the "poor." Nowhere is this better stated than in Proverbs 14:31: "Whoever oppresses a poor man insults his Maker, but he who is generous to the needy honors him." In terms of defending the cause of poor and needy people, God himself asks, "Is not this to know me?" (Jer. 22:16). Likewise, in the New Testament, right after Jesus affirms that love is central to life (Luke 10:25–28; cf. Matt. 22:37–40), he illustrates love with the story of caring for a dying, marginalized person (Luke 10:30–35).

So in the context of stem cell research, in all its forms, who are the vulnerable people—those for whom Christians should have special regard? They would include: the potential *beneficiaries* of treatments to be developed from the research; those who serve as the *sources* of the biological materials used in the research; and the *subjects* of the research. More specifically for present purposes, the *beneficiaries* are patients who are ill or injured and are eagerly waiting for new stem cell treatments. The *sources* of the materials involved—in addition to already-existing embryos—are the people who donate eggs or somatic cells for the cloning process necessary to produce embryonic stem cells genetically matched to the patients using them. And the *subjects* include various groups. First of all, the subjects include patients on whom new stem cell treatments are tried (though the issues involved are the standard issues of research ethics and so, in light of space constraints, will not be rehearsed here). Another group of subjects includes those whom some have called the "invisible subjects"—the human embryos involved in embryonic stem cell research—because much greater controversy and confusion surround them.[11]

In other words, when beneficiaries, sources, and subjects are all considered, there are many vulnerable stakeholders connected with stem cell research. Christians need to be particularly careful not to miss the voices of the weakest and most vulnerable simply because they are the least accessible.[12] Moreover, it is insufficient and misleading to focus on just one vulnerable group, such as the patients *or* the embryos *or* the donors. Such a focus can easily happen if the technologies and the research become more important than the people affected by them. Research is for

---

[11] This three-part categorization of vulnerable people in stem cell research and some of the issues related to them are elaborated in John F. Kilner, "An Inclusive Framework for Stem Cell Research," in *The Blackwell Companion to Science and Christianity*, ed. J. B. Stump and Alan G. Padgett (West Sussex, UK: Wiley-Blackwell, 2012), 381–392.

[12] Traci C. West, *Disruptive Christian Ethics* (Louisville: Westminster John Knox, 2006).

people; people do not exist primarily to meet the needs of research. To hear some defenses of all possible forms that stem cell research can take, one would think that the activities of research are more important than the people who have a stake in what those activities involve and produce! One must reject such an idolatry of technology and hold every potential new technology accountable to the flourishing of the entire human community, including those who are most vulnerable.

In other words, it is important to distinguish two different ways to help vulnerable people. One, the admirable way, involves using ethically obtained resources to benefit as many people as possible. The other, dishonorable way involves harming some to benefit others. Christians need to recognize this latter approach for what it is: a dangerous utilitarian temptation. Utilitarian thinking says that if something will produce a lot of benefits, it must be right. "The greatest good for the greatest number" is the goal, and the rallying cry is "the end justifies the means." In other words, if the end achieved is beneficial enough, it can justify any means. One of the consequences is that anything can be done to a minority in order to benefit the majority.

The utilitarian temptation is as old as the human race. In fact, the Devil used it successfully to entice Adam and Eve in the very beginning. Consider Eve's encounter with the serpent in Genesis 3. After some initial discussion about all the trees in the garden, the conversation focuses on a particular tree: the tree of the knowledge of good and evil. The serpent focuses Eve's attention away from whether or not God has forbidden eating that tree's fruit (for some reason perhaps known only to God). Instead, he focuses on what the benefits and harms of eating the tree's fruit would be. Apparently, he "helps" Eve to think that there would be no harm—she would not die—and that there would be great benefits: food and wisdom. According to Genesis 3, "But the serpent said to the woman, 'You will not surely die.' . . . So when the woman saw that the tree was good for food, and that it was a delight to the eyes, and that the tree was to be desired to make one wise, she took of its fruit and ate, and she also gave some to her husband who was with her, and he ate" (Gen. 3:4, 6). Although the text does not elaborate, apparently Eve convinced Adam by making the same argument to him about the tree's benefits as the serpent had made to her. The human race has remained susceptible to this fatal temptation ever since.

Wise Christians will not be duped into accepting a utilitarian approach to stem cell research—i.e., harming some in order to benefit others. Such unethical behavior is too high a price to pay for trying to increase the benefits being produced. In the New Testament, Paul puts it this way: While Christians *are* to "do good" (Gal. 6:10), they are not to "do evil that good may come" (Rom. 3:8). Paul is building on a long biblical wisdom tradition here, which insists, "Better is a little with righteousness than great revenues with injustice" (Prov. 16:8). Rather than advocating harming some in order to benefit others, Christians should support using ethically obtained resources to benefit as many people as possible.

Consider what this would look like in relation to the three categories of stakeholders identified earlier. The first category is the beneficiaries of the treatment, i.e., the human beings who are ill or injured. Adult stem cell research is a wonderful means of using ethically obtained resources to benefit as many people as possible. These cells can be obtained without harming anyone in the process. And as early as 2006, there were already some seventy-three medical conditions that had been helped to some degree in some patients through the use of adult stem cells.[13] Many of the scientific studies documenting these developments—and more recent developments as well—are chronicled on the website www.stemcellresearch.org. It is important not to make too much or too little of this data. To conclude from it that adult stem cells are a magic bullet that will cure all diseases is to exaggerate greatly. However, to accept the idea promoted by some that adult stem cells have little to offer is also to succumb to slogans rather than to insist on careful evaluation. Those who are truly compassionate toward seriously ill or injured patients, but who still consider it unethical to harm human embryos in order to achieve those benefits, can take great encouragement from what adult stem cell research is accomplishing.

The second category of vulnerable people with a stake in stem cell research includes those who donate eggs or other cells. Christians must not condone allowing donors to be subjected to serious harm simply because the expected benefits of stem cell research for others are so great. One source of harm, when embryonic stem cell treatments are in view, is connected with the cloning process involved. To be widely effective,

---

[13] Michael Bellomo, *The Stem Cell Divide: The Facts, the Fiction, and the Fear Driving the Greatest Scientific, Political, and Religious Debate of Our Time* (New York: AMACOM, 2006).

embryonic stem cells likely will need to be genetically matched to the patients, so that the patient's bodies will not try to reject them. That means the embryonic stem cells would likely need to be produced through a cloning process, which involves placing the genetic material from a cell in a patient's body into a donated egg cell. Such cloning of humans was first documented in 2013.[14] Many people think that egg donation is no big deal; however, it has long been reported that up to ten percent of egg donors may experience severe ovarian hyperstimulation syndrome, which can cause pain and occasionally leads to hospitalization, renal failure, potential future infertility, and even death.[15] In addition to the immediate risks, there could also be a longer-term cancer risk.[16]

There are three different threats to the crucial ethical standard of informed consent that can all too easily arise with egg donors: *informational* coercion (risks may not be fully explained), *vocational* coercion (workers in labs can be urged by their boss to donate), and *financial* coercion (women can feel forced to accept payment for their eggs due to their financial need). It might seem that women should be able to assess what donating their eggs is worth to them. However, Debora Spar argues that this is not the case.[17] The normal protections of the market—information, competition, and transparency—are largely absent in this situation. Customers—researchers now, but ultimately very ill patients—are desperate; the norm of rational trade-offs does not apply. Enough money can induce poorer women to take risks they should not have to take—as human beings—simply to stay alive. "But we *have* to obtain those eggs," some will say, because developing the cures to help hurting people requires it. At the end of the day, there is one basic choice: give in to the utilitarian temptation to harm some to benefit others *or* insist on remaining ethical with regard to means as well as ends.

The final group of vulnerable people—the subjects of the research—must also not be victimized by an approach to stem cell research that harms some in order to benefit others. The most controversial members of this group, as previously noted, are those at the embryonic stage of

---

[14] Masahito Tachibana et al., "Human Embryonic Stem Cells Derived by Somatic Cell Nuclear Transfer," *Cell* 153 (May 15, 2013): 1228–1238.
[15] David Magnus and Mildred K. Cho, "Issues in Oocyte Donation for Stem Cell Research," *Science* 308 (June 17, 2005): 1747–1748.
[16] Helen Pearson, "Health Effects of Egg Donation May Take Decades to Emerge," *Nature* 442 (August 10, 2006): 607–608.
[17] Debora L. Spar, *The Baby Business: How Money, Science, and Politics Drive the Commerce of Conception* (Watertown, MA: Harvard Business Review Press, 2006).

development who must be killed in order to produce embryonic stem cells. For many in the world, they are "obviously" not persons, so there is no need to consider them seriously. However, Christians should resist the temptation to enter the debate on the world's terms, as explained previously. Rather, Christians should be looking first to Scripture for insight, then doing the necessary translation work.

What light does Scripture shed on the personhood of human embryos? Because the biblical authors lacked the genetic and biological knowledge of today, they do not speak of embryos with the precision that people use today. Nevertheless, they do make some references to humans in the womb—and to humanity as a category in contrast with nonhuman things. So it is appropriate to ask what view of the human embryo makes the most sense in light of those references. In other words, what view of the human embryo is in greatest harmony with what the Bible does say? The Bible's great themes include creation, corruption, *and* redemption, among others, and these themes constitute an appropriate framework for considering biblical teaching on a matter related to humanity.[18]

According to the *creation* account in Genesis 1, God created primarily according to categories rather than descriptive characteristics—ground, plants, creatures, etc. God's direct creation of all these things signals that they are all important and that people should treat them with respect. However, when God creates the category of humanity (vv. 26–27), there are some distinguishing features that mark people not only as different but also as warranting special protection. Among them is humanity's creation as God's image. The identical expression appears later in Genesis 9:6 to explain why human beings are so special, among all of creation, and are not to be killed. As is the case with nonhumans, humans most fundamentally constitute a category, not a set of varying characteristics. All humans are God's image because God says they are, without qualification.

The biblical texts that discuss the image of God never indicate that being God's image means having certain traits (though certain human capacities and functions do normally flow from being God's image). Who falls within this category of human beings, created as God's image? Who are so special that they should not be killed? All that the text of

---

[18] For a fuller account, see John F. Kilner, "Bioethics and a Better Birth," in *Why the Church Needs Bioethics: A Guide to Wise Engagement with Life's Challenges*, ed. John F. Kilner (Grand Rapids, MI: Zondervan, 2011), 79–97.

Genesis 1 indicates is that beings who are "human"—as opposed to nonhuman creatures, plants, and other things—are included. Human embryos fall into that category, as demonstrated by the scientific evidence. Accordingly, it is more plausible than not to include them among those whom others ought not kill, because they are created as God's image. While some of the characteristics of embryos, such as physical and mental abilities, differ temporarily from those of adults, that is not what defines God's image, according to the biblical texts.[19]

If there is reason in the context of *creation* to see human embryos as having the same moral status as adults, there is similar reason to do so in the context of *corruption*. Just as the creation of humanity as God's image means that all subsequent humans are God's image, so also Adam's rejection of God's way in favor of his own means that all subsequent humans share also in the corruption of sin and its consequence, death (Rom. 5:12). Sin may involve rejecting specific commands of God, as was the case with Adam and as has been the case with God's people ever since God gave them the written law through Moses. However, sin and thus death are also unavoidably connected with being human even apart from making a conscious choice to reject a command of God.

As Paul observes, "death reigned from the time of Adam to the time of Moses, even over those who did not sin by breaking a command" (Rom. 5:14, NIV). Sin simply is a hallmark trait of all who are human. If that is the case, then one's moral status and responsibility before God would not merely reflect a stage of development, such as whether one has developed a mental capacity to make choices. Instead, a biblical understanding of humanity would more plausibly support viewing children, fetuses, and embryos as defiled by sin, just as they are all God's image.

While the prescientific writings of the Bible do not say much about embryos specifically, there are several instances of references to the time when people first begin forming in their mothers' wombs (now called the embryonic stage of development). The biblical view of that period accords well with the biblical understanding of corrupted humanity in general, as just described.

For example, in Psalm 51, David recognizes that he has been a morally responsible human person (i.e., a person liable for his sinfulness) as

---

[19] For more detail on the image of God, see John F. Kilner, *Humanity as God's Image* (Grand Rapids, MI: Eerdmans, 2015).

long as he has existed, even in the womb. In his words, "Behold, I was brought forth in iniquity, and in sin did my mother conceive me" (v. 5). That he considers his time in the womb to be a part of his life in this world is also suggested elsewhere, such as Psalm 139, where he refers to his body as "his" (i.e., "my frame") and to himself as "I" when he was merely in an unformed state in his mother's womb (vv. 15–16). David, in Psalms 51 and 139, like others in Scripture such as Job (31:15), refers to himself as the same person—the same "I"—when he is developing in the womb and when he is an adult. He did not become the person David at some later point.

If it makes sense biblically to see embryos as persons created as God's image and as persons corrupted by sin, then it is also important to see what light the redeeming work of God can shed on the personhood of human embryos. The biblical theme of *redemption* centers around the earthly life, death, and resurrection of Jesus Christ—a series of events that begins with the incarnation. The incarnation could have involved Christ materializing directly as an adult man, much as he appeared decades later after his resurrection. Instead, the Gospel writer Luke describes this "becoming a human being" as beginning with Jesus as a newly conceived embryo.

According to Luke 1, after the conception of Jesus within Mary by the Spirit of God, she travels with haste, to visit her also pregnant relative Elizabeth (v. 39–40). The Bible knows no intermediate prehuman stage in which Christ is a mere clump of cells without the full moral status of a human being. Rather, the baby jumps in Elizabeth's womb in recognition of the presence of the woman carrying Jesus Christ as an early embryo in her womb (v. 41), and Elizabeth praises Mary—calling her now "the mother of my Lord" (v. 43). That makes sense: she truly already is a mother, because her son Jesus is already present.

Christ has not remained God only but has also become a human being. In fact, such language is not unique in relation to Jesus, for God's own messenger, the angel Gabriel, has just told Mary that Elizabeth has "conceived a son" (Luke 1:36). Elizabeth, like other women, conceives not a mere cell, but a son—not that which *will be* a son, but that which is appropriately called a son already. Keep in mind that Elizabeth's son in the womb is also referred to here as an infant child (*brephos*, vv. 41 and 44), the same term used six times elsewhere in the New Testament, always for one who is already born (e.g., the newborn children in Acts 7:19 and the child who knew the Scriptures in 2 Tim. 3:15). From a New Testament perspective, being a "child" is not a function of whether or not one has been born yet. There are strong biblical reasons, then, to consider embryos to be human beings who warrant the basic respect and protections accorded to other persons.

In light of the foregoing biblical-theological analysis, the difference between various approaches to producing healthy cells to heal the human body now becomes clearer. Whereas a utilitarian approach warrants harming some to benefit others, a theologically sound approach requires using ethically obtained resources to benefit as many people as possible. Embryonic stem cell research is a good example of the former approach. Adult stem cell research, induced pluripotent stem cell research, and transdifferentiation research are good examples of the latter.

CULTURAL TRANSLATION

The first task for Christians, then, is to develop their positions on issues through a process of biblically grounded theological formation. Once that is done, though, there remains the challenge of advocating those views effectively in a culture that is highly pluralistic—a culture in which many do not accept theological rationales for anything. Although Paul does not address this communication challenge explicitly in terms of ethics, he does address essentially the same issue in the context of speaking in tongues. He is happy for people to talk a "strange language" in private, but he is concerned if Christians do so in the presence of unbelievers without regard to its impact on them: "Unless you speak intelligible words with your tongue, how will anyone know what you are saying? You will just be speaking into the air.... Will they not say that you are out of your mind?" (1 Cor. 14:9, 23, NIV). This is indeed an apt description of the response of many non-Christians today when they hear Christians talking about *the* truth and *the* right way! Paul's alternative is to insist on translation. If Christians want to communicate the content of something they know through the Spirit of God, then they must use words and concepts that others can understand (1 Cor. 14:13, 27–28). There is a need, then, to be bilingual—to translate biblically grounded positions into publicly persuasive positions.

What might that look like in the context of stem cell research today?

A good place to begin is with the basic biblical outlook—that there should be special regard for those who are most vulnerable. This view can be grounded in concepts of human dignity and human rights, rather than biblical appeals. Admittedly, these concepts are sometimes attacked, particularly when people think that they are merely cover for smuggling religious commitments into public discussions. Nevertheless, the concept of human dignity, in particular, and the protections for all people that flow from that concept remain influential in today's world.[20] Respect for human dignity is an ethical mandate to which both sides of many bioethical debates do in fact appeal. For example, while the state of Oregon was legalizing physician-assisted suicide by passing the Death with Dignity Act, opponents were claiming that legalizing that practice would undermine the dignity of elderly, disabled, and dying patients.

The term "dignity" also surfaces frequently in important bioethical and other public documents. It has played a role in the constitutions of a politically diverse array of countries, including Afghanistan, Brazil, Canada, Costa Rica, Germany, Greece, Guatemala, Ireland, Italy, Nicaragua, Peru, Portugal, South Korea, Spain, Sweden, and Turkey. Even in countries where the term has not been influential in constitutional language, it has come to play an important role. The U.S. Supreme Court has employed the term in its deliberations over the meaning of the First, Fourth, Fifth, Sixth, Eighth, and Fourteenth Amendments to the Constitution. International documents relevant to issues in bioethics also have affirmed the critical importance of human dignity. For example, the United Nations, whose charter celebrates the "inherent dignity" of "all members of the human family," has issued a Universal Declaration of Human Rights whose preamble contains the same language. In other words, there is a public language for communicating the biblical-theological concern for carefully attending to the needs of all vulnerable people in deliberations over stem cell research.

As noted earlier, those people include the potential beneficiaries of treatments to be developed from the research, the people who serve as the sources of the biological materials used in the research, and the subjects of the research. However, some suggest that concern for one of the major groups of subjects, human embryos, can be defended only on overtly

---

[20] For a fuller account of human dignity, see John F. Kilner, "Human Dignity," in *The Encyclopedia of Bioethics*, ed. Stephen Garrard Post, 3rd ed. (New York: Macmillan, 2004); and Gilbert Meilaender, *Neither Beast nor God: The Dignity of the Human Person* (New York: Encounter, 2009).

biblical-theological grounds. Again it becomes evident how important it is to be bilingual—to be able to invoke nonreligious reasons for regarding human embryos as human beings—as persons—like all other people. Two of the best ways to do that are through appeals to science and appeals to logic.

In terms of science, genetics tells a powerful story. As early as the point of fertilization, when a new one-celled human being comes into existence, the entire human genetic code is present and active. The human genetic code contains 3 billion pairs of chemicals called nucleotides; that is like a code of 3 billion letters. With six letters in an average word, 250 words on an average page, and 250 pages in an average book, that is like 8,000 books of code already directing the life and growth of the initial single-cell embryo.

Those who think that an early fetus or even an early embryo is just an unsophisticated blob of material should think again. In light of these genetic considerations, it is no wonder that biology textbooks have long considered the beginning of a human being to be at conception, not sometime later such as birth. According to Ronan O'Rahilly's *Human Embryology and Teratology*, "'Embryo,' as currently used in human embryology, means 'an unborn human in the first 8 weeks.'"[21] Similarly, according to embryologist Bruce Carlson, "Fertilization represents the starting point in the life history, or ontogeny, of the individual."[22] To say that an embryo is a human being is to say that an embryo is human and is a being. That embryos are *human* is demonstrated by their genetics. That they are *beings*, as opposed to just piles of cells, is demonstrated by the fact that they are "organisms." Even the early embryo is not just "human life," as blood or skin cells are alive and human; rather, a human embryo is a human being/organism who, unless fatally disabled or injured, can typically develop through the human lifespan as long as suitable nurture and environment are provided. The same description is true of a child at any age.

Some people try to avoid this biological reality by changing the definitions of basic words, so that people who are concerned about human embryos are misled into thinking that embryos are not even involved. For example, the meaning of the word "embryo" has long been estab-

---

[21] Ronan R. O'Rahilly and Fabiola Müller, *Human Embryology and Teratology*, 3rd ed. (New York: Wiley-Liss, 2001), 87.
[22] Bruce M. Carlson, *Patten's Foundations of Embryology*, 6th ed. (New York: McGraw-Hill, 2003), 3.

lished, and mainline scientific sources are still clear regarding it. As the National Institutes of Health website suggests, a human embryo exists from the time of fertilization through the eighth week.[23] Accordingly, it is striking to see one of the strategies being used by some who want to convince others that embryonic stem cell research is morally acceptable. They simply assert that no embryos are harmed, because no embryos are involved. Consider this example from the book *Stem Cell Wars*: an embryo is defined as "a developing organism beginning about 2 weeks after conception."[24]

This is a clever tactic—moving the starting line for the human race. However, it is not fair play, or truthful play. Some of the leading embryonic stem cell researchers have seen right through this strategy. Johns Hopkins's John Gearhart has urged, "We should not be changing vocabulary at this point in time. It doesn't change some of the ethical issues involved."[25] Wisconsin's James Thomson puts it this way: "You're creating an embryo. If you try to define it away, you're being disingenuous."[26] What is lost in the process is the opportunity to have open and honest discussions of the core issues that are unavoidably at the heart of the matter. With embryonic stem cell research, the embryo is front and center—the subject of the research itself, the one being experimented upon. It is vital, as a matter of truth, to grapple with the actual concerns that people have regarding embryos, rather than to avoid them through word plays or false scientific reports.

In light of the biological evidence, it is more precise to see embryos as "persons with potential" than as "potential persons." A sperm, an egg, or a somatic cell is at most a *potential* person; it would have to be changed into something that it is not now in order to become a person. By contrast, embryos are actual persons already, who simply have not reached their full potential. Accordingly, they are persons with potential, rather than merely potential persons. In this understanding, the fact that human embryos have not yet manifested their full potential no more invalidates their personhood than adults' personhood is invalidated by the fact that

---

[23] See http://stemcells.nih.gov/info/pages/glossary.aspx#embryo.
[24] Eve Herold, *Stem Cell Wars: Inside Stories from the Frontlines* (New York: Palgrave Macmillan, 2007), 121.
[25] John Gearhart, "Stem Cells 1: Medical Promise of Embryonic Stem Cell Research (Present and Projected)," testimony before the U.S. President's Council on Bioethics, April 25, 2002. See http://bioethics.georgetown.edu/pcbe/transcripts/apr02/apr25session1.html.
[26] Alan Boyle, "Stem Cell Pioneer Does a Reality Check," News, *MSNBC*, June 25, 2005, http://www.nbcnews.com/id/8303756#.UYbDh7WG2So.

they have not yet manifested their full potential. Potential persons rightly do not receive the same protections as actual persons, but embryos are not potential persons: they are persons with potential.

The terms "person" and "human being" are being used here interchangeably, as most people use them in common speech. Some, however, would distinguish the two terms, maintaining that a human being becomes a person at some point in development when a certain human characteristic emerges, and only the lives of persons need to be protected. In other words, they identify some human characteristic and assert that having it is what it means to be a person—and that, because embryos do not have it, they are not persons. However, that claim does not make good logical sense if one compares how adults are treated with what is being said about embryos. Here is where not just science but also logic comes into play.

There are at least six major contenders for when personhood begins: (1) Some have said that personhood begins during infancy, when a baby develops self-consciousness. Yet adults can lose consciousness—not to mention self-consciousness—and they are not called nonpersons for that reason. (2) Some have said that personhood begins at birth, when a baby is no longer connected to and totally dependent on another. Yet adults can become connected to and totally dependent on a ventilator in the same way, and they are not called nonpersons on that basis. (3) Some have said that personhood begins at viability, when the fetus is at least capable of independence. Yet Siamese twins or persons dependent on pacemakers are not capable of independence, and they are not called nonpersons for that reason. (4) Some have said that personhood begins at quickening or motility, when the fetus is capable of motion. Yet adults can become paralyzed, and they are not called nonpersons on that basis. (5) Some have said that personhood begins at about six weeks after fertilization, when brain activity is detectable—or even earlier when the so-called primitive streak (the bodily basis for the brain) first appears. These are points when the potential for self-consciousness is evident. Yet when adults develop severe dementias or lose consciousness near the end of life, they can also lose the potential for self-consciousness, and they are not called nonpersons for that reason. (Moreover, the *potential* for self-consciousness is present as early as fertilization, because the genetic basis for it is already in place at that point.) (6) Some have said that personhood begins at implantation, when the embryo attaches to the wall of the uterus, because without that attachment the embryo cannot live. Yet when adults lose the capacity to breathe on their own and are in desperate need of becoming attached to a ventilator in order to live, they are not called nonpersons until they are attached.

In other words, there is no point later than fertilization after which a human being is more like an adult, in a definitive sense, than already is the case at fertilization. There is no capability or potential that makes one more definitively a person than what genetics has already established at fertilization. Thus a strong case can be made for considering human embryos to be persons who warrant the same protections as all other persons—on grounds other than the Bible.

Once the importance of all three of the vulnerable stakeholder groups is established, then it is time to consider whether or not it is ethically acceptable to harm some in order to benefit others. As noted above, such utilitarian thinking, though widely influential in contemporary culture, is unethical on biblical grounds. However, is it possible to translate that concern into language that communicates more effectively in a pluralistic public? Yes, it is.

By no means are embryos the first vulnerable group in society who have been abused—even fatally abused—because society considered that the benefits to others would warrant such treatment. There was a time when using black slaves as property was so economically beneficial that people advocated doing it. That made some people uncomfortable unless slaves could be defined as less than full human beings, which was not hard to do. There were obvious visual differences between these black slaves and their white owners. Even the Supreme Court conveniently ruled in the Dred Scott case that black slaves were mere property from which to profit, rather than human beings sharing in the basic equality of all human beings. As the Court saw it, it was "too clear for dispute" that Dred Scott was not a human being.[27] What unsettles many today is that it was as clear to the Court then that Dred Scott was not a full human being—a person—as it is clear to others today that an embryo is not a person.

It is quite easy to underestimate what people can mentally justify, many worry, if the economic or medical benefits are attractive enough. The dangers of this thinking—especially the inadequate protections for

---
[27] *Dred Scott v. Sandford* 60 U.S. (19 How. 1857), 393.

certain groups of people that can follow—are quite substantial in the realm of medical research. Some point to the Tuskegee Syphilis Study, conducted in Alabama from 1933 to 1972 by the U.S. Public Health Service, involving 399 poor African-American men in Alabama with latent syphilis.[28] These researchers wanted to learn how the disease would progress if left untreated. The goal was to learn whether various medical interventions would genuinely be beneficial. They knew that if the men learned about treatment options, those patients might get treated, and their value to the study would be lost; therefore, the men were not told, nor were they treated, and many were seriously harmed in the process. As many as one hundred men who might have been helped died of syphilis-related complications, with many more subjected to increased suffering.[29] Others note that another forty wives plus nineteen babies may have been unnecessarily contaminated in the process.[30]

According to the official panel convened years later to investigate, no informed consent requirements were observed even after the men received legal status following the formulation of the Nuremburg Code for the protection of research subjects.[31] The Tuskegee researchers likely had the same good motives as embryonic stem cell researchers today: to be able to more effectively treat suffering patients in the future. What worries many people is that such motives can become disengaged from a commitment to caring for all vulnerable groups involved—as they did in the Tuskegee Study (according to a senior investigator's official critique).[32] When that happens, if there appears to be no other way to obtain certain medical benefits, then seriously harming some to benefit a greater number of others who are suffering can be justified. The challenge here is not to forget the lesson of the tragic Tuskegee experience: "Doing Bad in the Name of Good" is a temptation that society today must fastidiously resist.[33]

---

[28] Allen Brandt, "Racism and Research: The Case of the Tuskegee Syphilis Experiment," in *Tuskegee's Truths: Rethinking the Tuskegee Syphilis Study*, ed. Susan M. Reverby (Chapel Hill: University of North Carolina Press, 2000), 15–33.
[29] James H. Jones, *Bad Blood: The Tuskegee Syphilis Experiment* (New York: Simon & Schuster, 1993); James H. Jones, "The Tuskegee Syphilis Experiment: 'A Moral Astigmatism'," in *The "Racial" Economy of Science: Toward a Democratic Future*, ed. Sandra Harding (Bloomington: Indiana University Press, 1993), 275–286.
[30] Matthieu Ricard and Trinh Xuan Thuan, *The Quantum and the Lotus: A Journey to the Frontiers where Science and Buddhism Meet* (New York: Three Rivers, 2009), 17. For both sides of the debate over the extent of the harm done here, see Kilner, "Inclusive Framework for Stem Cell Research," 381–392.
[31] Jay Katz, "Addendum to the Final Report of the Tuskegee Syphilis Study Ad Hoc Advisory Panel" (submitted to the U.S. Department of Health, Education, and Welfare on April 28, 1973), 14.
[32] Ibid.
[33] "Doing Bad in the Name of Good" was the name of a symposium about the Tuskegee Syphilis Study, convened at the University of Virginia, February 23, 1994. http://exhibits.hsl.virginia.edu/badblood/symposium/.

The point here is not that the Tuskegee research and embryonic stem cell research are similar in all respects—only that utilitarian thinking has often been operative in the justification of both. This experience is a part of a larger pattern of susceptibility to utilitarian thinking in the United States and elsewhere, as chronicled in the book *Useful Bodies*.[34] While regulations are currently in place to constrain abuse of research subjects, the experiences in this book document how persistent the tendency is to look at the bodies of human beings—especially the weakest and most vulnerable—and justify using them more as property than viewing them as human beings. In other words, the utilitarian mind-set driving much of embryonic stem cell research can be powerfully critiqued on other than biblical grounds. That recognition has led to the following observation in *Wired* magazine, a secular technology publication: "The stem cell argument isn't exclusively a religious debate anymore. Right-to-life advocates aren't the only ones who believe stem cell research could threaten moral integrity.... Now, even stem cell researchers themselves, and patients who could be cured as a result of stem cell studies, are opposing them. Mary Jane Owen is one of them. She is blind, has partial hearing loss, and uses a wheelchair because of a spinal cord injury. [As she puts it:] 'I think we've lost our sense of morality.... We've become so utilitarian.'"[35]

Publicly rejecting a utilitarian outlook that can justify harming some to benefit others, and favoring approaches to producing body cells that use ethically obtained resources to benefit as many people as possible, need not depend on overtly theological appeals. Cultural translation enables Christians to communicate biblically grounded theological positions using publicly understandable and acceptable language in today's pluralistic world. For such translation to remain authentically Christian, however, like everything else for the Christian, it must be marked by love—love of God and love of people. As Jesus explains in Matthew 22:37–40, all that God calls on people to do boils down to this.

Consider first what loving people entails. When Christians address a bioethical challenge like stem cell research in public language, they need to be careful that they are not just telling people what *not* to do. Christians ought to be known by what they are *for*, not just by what they are

---

[34] Jordan Goodman, Anthony McElligott, and Lara Marks, eds., *Useful Bodies: Humans in the Service of Medical Science in the Twentieth Century* (Baltimore: Johns Hopkins University Press, 2003).
[35] Kristen Philipkoski, "Embryonic Cell Debate Is On," *Wired*, August 24, 2000. See http://www.wired.com/science/discoveries/news/2000/08/38401.

against. Love requires that. There are usually hurting people intimately involved in bioethical debates, such as infertile couples, pregnant women who cannot afford a child, terminally ill patients, or sick and injured people needing stem cell treatments. If a Christian is accurately translating a biblical-theological outlook on an issue into secular language, it *must* include attention to how the needs of all the vulnerable people involved can best be met.

In the context of stem cell research, the needs of suffering patients can be met through alternatives to embryonic stem cell research, including adult stem cell research, induced pluripotent stem cell research, and transdifferentiation research. Vulnerable egg donors can be protected by pursuing these same alternatives rather than creating a huge need for eggs through embryonic stem cell research. Embryos themselves can be protected in the same way. Because so many excess embryos are produced and frozen as part of in vitro fertilization procedures, though, this claim to protection of embryos rings hollow if embryos not used in embryonic stem cell research are just going to be thrown away anyway. An often-cited RAND Corporation study identified 400,000 embryos in frozen storage in the United States in 2003.[36] Why not at least get the benefit of more research knowledge, if the embryos will perish whether or not they are used for embryonic stem cell research?

Christians should first subject such objections to biblical scrutiny. They will find that the obligation not to kill innocent people is not conditional—not dependent upon whether or not those people are going to die soon anyway. The timing of death, as Paul acknowledges in Philippians 1, is rightfully in God's hands, not humans'. Humans are instead responsible for nurturing innocent people, not destroying them—period. King David, "a man after God's own heart," illustrated this priority well shortly after the death of his predecessor, King Saul. In 2 Samuel 1, David severely punishes the man who claims to have killed Saul. The fact that Saul had been mortally wounded and was already in the process of dying was *not* a legitimate consideration, according to David. Intentionally ending the lives of people is wrong, for people are God's image (Gen. 9:6).

Christians, then, do well to oppose the destruction of human embryos in embryonic stem cell research, regardless of the eventual fate

---

[36] RAND Corporation, "How Many Frozen Human Embryos Are Available for Research?" *Law and Health Research Brief* (Santa Monica, CA: RAND Institute for Civil Justice/RAND Health, 2003).

of those embryos. Moreover, cultural translation requires providing a nontheological warrant for that position and a constructive alternative that demonstrates love.

An effective way to provide a nontheological warrant is to point to other settings in contemporary public life where essentially the same issue has been debated regarding groups of people other than embryos. For example, some have proposed that it should be acceptable to kill people who are dying soon in order to obtain their organs for transplant. Because they are dying soon anyway, the argument goes, why not allow other people who are suffering to gain some benefit from their bodily materials? This question has been addressed at length in public forums. The U.S. Department of Health and Human Services has considered it with regard to removing vital organs from dying patients.[37] The U.S. United Network for Organ Sharing has given similar consideration to removing vital organs from prisoners on death row.[38] Both institutions have concluded that the fact that people are dying is an insufficient justification for killing them even earlier in order to benefit others medically. Public decision makers have rejected the utilitarian appeal.

Returning to the context of human embryos: the parallel with the mindset of the investigators during the Tuskegee Syphilis experiments is again quite striking. Some people today say that many frozen embryos will, realistically, never be born—just like Tuskegee researchers said that those poor enslaved African-Americans with syphilis would never seek out medical treatment anyway, and so should be allowed to die in the Tuskegee syphilis experiments instead.[39] Was the likely fate of those men a reason to facilitate the experimentation or, rather, to protest it? Everything possible should have been done to help those people avoid such a fate, and many are saying the same today regarding the fate of frozen embryos.

Refraining from killing embryos for research accomplishes little for these embryos if they are just going to remain in frozen storage and eventually be discarded. Love requires more—a constructive alternative. Though unwanted by their biological parents, such embryos are not truly unwanted. They are extremely wanted—by women yearning to adopt them and carry them to term in their own wombs. There are now more

---

[37] U.S. Department of Health and Human Services, "Minimum Procurement Standards." Available at http://www.organdonor.gov (accessed May 1, 2009).
[38] United Network for Organ Sharing, "White Papers." Available at http://www.unos.org/Resources/Bioethics.asp (accessed May 1, 2009).
[39] Katz, "Addendum to the Final Report," 14.

than 200 agencies facilitating such adoptions—and some have waiting lists. One of them—California's Snowflakes agency—has provided thousands of embryos for adoption already.[40]

It might seem a stretch to think that all of the 400,000 frozen embryos documented by the RAND study could be adopted through such channels. However, a closer look at that study reveals that more than 88 percent of those embryos are actually very wanted by the people who produced them; those people are planning to implant them in the future. Of the remaining 11.8 percent, only two-thirds of those are likely to survive thawing, so this leaves only some 30,000 frozen embryos that are likely to be both viable *and* unwanted by those who produced them. It is realistic to think that parents could be found for this number of embryos, especially because it often takes more than one embryo to achieve a pregnancy. A Christian translation of theologically grounded positions into secular language, then, can and must be marked by love of people by advocating ways that the most vulnerable subjects—human embryos—can survive and flourish.

At the same time, as noted earlier, cultural translation must also be marked by love of God. This final point provides an opportunity to circle back to a comment made near the outset of this essay. The importance of translating biblical language into secular language by no means suggests that there is no place in public for explicit appeals to God's Word to justify positions on issues in bioethics. There are at least three public situations where explicitly biblical justifications for bioethical positions on issues are warranted.

First, there are sometimes occasions when a governing body or another organization wants to know what biblically based Christians think about a particular issue in bioethics. In such a situation, it is important to describe and document what the Scriptures say, so that others cannot claim that the Bible (and those who take the Bible seriously) supports positions on bioethical issues that are not genuinely biblical.

Second, there are other occasions when an audience contains a substantial number of people known to be biblically based Christians, in addition to many others who have no particular interest in what the Bible has to say. In such a situation, it is important to explain multiple separate rationales for whatever bioethical position one is espousing. Rationales

---

[40] For Snowflakes, a directory of agencies, and another example, see http://www.nightlight.org/programs_SnowflakesFrozenEmbryoFaqs.html#General, and http://www.miracleswaiting.org/clinics.html, and http://www.embryodonation.org/about.html.

rooted in the Bible have their place, as do rationales involving no explicit reliance on theological considerations. Purely secular language will be unconvincing by itself to many biblically based Christians, and purely biblical language will be unconvincing by itself to most other people. However, it is crucial to make it clear why biblical rationales are being included. It is to show why the bioethical position in view is—and should be—attractive to those who take the Bible seriously. At the same time, biblical rationales are not being included merely because holding the position *depends* on taking the Bible seriously, and it must be made clear that the position is well warranted ethically, whether or not one has any interest in what the Bible says on the matter.

Finally, there is a third type of occasion when it is warranted in public to give biblical rationales for positions on bioethical issues. Christians in all walks of life have the responsibility to bear witness to Christ before the watching world. Christians can do a great job in their work and can effectively communicate by using exclusively secular language. Yet that alone brings glory only to oneself and not necessarily to God. It does not take seriously Jesus's admonition to "let your light shine before others, so that they may see your good works and give glory to your Father who is in heaven" (Matt. 5:16).

When will people know to glorify God? It will be when people see that something attractive in the work someone does, or in the position someone takes on an issue, is because of God. When is the right time to do that in public? That time is when the Spirit leads—not meaning by that simply "when I feel like it." Rather, it is at the time that *God* directs. That is the case in one's personal life as a Christian and in one's professional life as well. There is no simple formula here, but it is surely the case that Christians are not prompting people to glorify their Father in heaven if they never say anything in public about the connection between their bioethical views and God.

The challenge here is faithfulness versus effectiveness. It is a never-ending tension that Christians will not ever resolve fully, either in bioethics or in the rest of life. However, as long as Christians do the tough work of developing effectiveness within the bounds of faithfulness, they will be headed in the right direction. Similarly, as long as Christians settle for neither theological formulation nor secular communication alone, but insist on a process of cultural translation after formulating views theologically, God will indeed be glorified.

14

The Trinity, Imitation, and the Christian Moral Life

GRAHAM A. COLE

An outstanding aspect of theological thought over the past century has been the retrieval of the doctrine of the Trinity as the core of a Christian understanding of God.[1] Two names in particular stand out in this retrieval. On the Protestant side stands the towering figure of Karl Barth (1886–1968), whose accent on the Trinity in his massive *Church Dogmatics* stands in marked contrast to that of Friedrich Schleiermacher (1768–1834), for whom the Trinity was worth only a brief chapter at the end of his seminal *The Christian Faith*. On the Roman Catholic side, it is Karl Rahner (1904–1984) who saw the need for the recovery of an explicitly Trinitarian construal of God to combat the practical unitarianism he witnessed in the churches of his day.

Evangelicals too have contributed to this revival of Trinitarian theology. In particular, some evangelicals have seen the relevance of the doctrine to matters of morality, especially to those that concern gender relations. For example, Wayne Grudem maintains that there is a parallel relationship between the persons of the Trinity and a human family. The

---

[1] For an excellent survey of the history of Trinitarian theology including its twentieth-century revival, see Stephen R. Holmes, *The Quest for the Trinity: The Doctrine of God in Scripture, History, and Modernity* (Downers Grove, IL: IVP Academic, 2012). Holmes argues that, in the light of classical Trinitarian theology as found through the first seventeen hundred years of church history, more recent Trinitarian theologies are not so much retrievals or revivals as they are departures (xv–xvi).

Father is analogous to the husband, the Son is analogous to the wife, and the Holy Spirit is analogous to a child of the parents.[2] However, there are an increasing number of theologians who, though appreciating the revival of Trinitarian theology, see some dangers in it. Gerald Bray, for instance, argues that "Modeling human relationships on the Trinity is a recipe for failure, because those relationships are different—even though the concept of relationship is one shared between them."[3] Are there limits, then, to applying the doctrine of the Trinity to life? Is doing so simply wrongheaded?

This chapter examines some of the recent attempts to apply the doctrine of the Trinity to the moral life. The contrasting approaches of Jürgen Moltmann and D. Broughton Knox will be examined. Both see the importance and relevance of the doctrine but with very different understandings of how the doctrine is to shape the moral life. Having expounded their respective views, albeit briefly, we shall bring the biblical witness into play. Special revelation is the touchstone of any doctrinal or ethical claim that calls itself Christian. To deepen the discussion, an important distinction drawn from the work of ethicist Oliver O'Donovan will be explored and then employed before the study is brought to a conclusion.

IMITATING THE ESSENTIAL TRINITY'S INNER LIFE

In recent years it has become more and more popular to appeal to the inner life of the essential Trinity as paradigmatic for the moral choices of the Christian. Brian Edgar, for example, writes, "The Trinity is also the Christian's paradigm for *social and political life*."[4] The works of D. Broughton Knox and the much more famous Jürgen Moltmann illustrate the point.[5]

Knox contends that Paul's words in 1 Corinthians 11:3 ("the head

---

[2] Wayne Grudem, *Systematic Theology: An Introduction to Biblical Doctrine* (Grand Rapids, MI/Leicester, England: Zondervan/Inter-Varsity, 1994), 257.
[3] Gerald Bray, "The Trinity: Where Do We Go from Here?" in *Always Reforming: Explorations in Systematic Theology*, ed. A. T. B. McGowan (Downers Grove, IL: IVP Academic, 2006), 35. Another theologian who sees the danger is Geoffrey Wainwright. The danger he sees lies in developing the doctrine in one-sided ways. He cites the work of Amos Yong as a case in point. See Wainwright's foreword to Keith E. Johnson, *Rethinking the Trinity and Religious Pluralism: An Augustinian Reassessment* (Downers Grove, IL: IVP Academic, 2011), 9. Johnson's work itself is first-rate.
[4] Brian Edgar, *The Message of the Trinity* (Leicester, England: Inter-Varsity, 2004), 29 (emphasis his). Edgar, though, is aware of the difficulty of "connecting fundamental theological principles to large-scale social outcomes" (277).
[5] Knox was the longest-serving principal of Moore Theological College in Sydney, Australia, and my theological teacher. His theology is influential in Australia and Britain, especially but not exclusively in Anglican circles, and increasingly among evangelicals in the United States.

314 *Graham A. Cole*

of Christ is God") provide a window into the very Trinitarian nature of God. He sees in this language a pattern of headship and response that the Christian and the church are to emulate. The Father is the eternal head of the Son. It is important to observe, though, that the headship Knox recommends is defined in terms of taking the initiative in service. He maintains, "Headship implies responsibility and initiative in welfare, and if this is to be discharged properly all must acknowledge that God has created order in relationship in humanity, and it will be a help to see that this reflects the order eternally subsisting in the Trinity."[6] Knox rejects any idea of a headship that involves "lording over" the other. The order he speaks of is based in the first instance in the very nature of God as Trinity, and subsequently in the creation of male and female as images of God. Thus, this style of headship ought to be reflected in the way men and women relate to one another in a pattern of headship and response in the home, in the church, and in society. He argues, "Our homes and our society, as well as our congregations, should reflect the order which is part of their constituent created nature and is an image of the order in the Trinity."[7]

Knox's position is a species of complementarianism,[8] a position arguing that in the divine plan, men and women are equal in value but differ in function in terms of headship and response; they are equal but different. As we saw above, Knox believed that this order with its pattern of headship and response ought to be seen not only in the family and the church but also in wider society. Indeed, if this order is in the very nature of God, and human beings bear God's image, then it would appear to follow that this view should apply to the public square and not only to the home and the church. The logic of Knox's view is hierarchical, and he

---

[6] D. Broughton Knox, "God in Trinity," in Tony Payne, ed., *D. Broughton Knox, Selected Works, Vol. 1: The Doctrine of God* (Kingsford, NSW: Matthias Media, 2000), 93. Curiously, Knox argues, "The Father is greater than the Son, but not as we evaluate greatness; for according to the real values of God, the servant is the greatest" (92). Given that logic, then, the Father serves the Son. Knox would not have embraced this implication.
[7] Ibid.
[8] Logically speaking, there are at least three levels of complementarianism. Level-one complementarianism argues that there is a complementarity between husbands and wives in the home as indicated by the head (male) and body (female) language in the Pauline letters. Level-two complementarianism argues that there is a complementarity between husbands and wives in the home as indicated by the head (male) and body (female) language in the Pauline letters, and between males and females in the church, as Paul indicates in 1 Corinthians 11, 14 and 1 Timothy 2. Level-three complementarianism argues that there is a complementarity between husbands and wives in the home as indicated by the head (male) and body (female) language in the Pauline letters, and between males and females in the church as Paul indicates in 1 Corinthians 11, 14 and 1 Timothy 2, and between males and females outside the church in the wider society because of the creation-based argument of 1 Timothy 2. Knox was a level-three complementarian.

was comfortable with such language.[9] He was also very comfortable with the language of the eternal subordination of the Son to the Father within the Trinity *ad intra*. However, once more it is important to note that he did not subscribe to any kind of domineering of men over women.[10]

Other social Trinitarians take a very different course than the one described above. Jürgen Moltmann also sees the Trinity as our social program, but unlike for Knox, for Moltmann the Trinity is the model of egalitarianism rather than complementarianism. Given the divine nature with its eternal, internal freedom and equality, the God who is Father, Son, and Holy Spirit stands opposed to all hierarchical uses of power whether in the church or the wider world. Moreover, simple non-Trinitarian monotheisms can be and have been historically agents of oppression. So he argues. On Moltmann's more radical proposal, the social program that Trinitarian theology ought logically to underwrite is one of "social personalism or personalistic socialism."[11] Men and women, on this view, are equal in value and, excepting functions tied to biology, there is no necessary difference in function between them, whether in the family, in the church, or in wider society. In his theology, the equality of the sexes flows from his model of the Trinity. He argues, "We have said that it is not the monarchy of a ruler that corresponds to the triune God; it is the community of men and women, without privileges and without subjugation."[12] And again, "The Christian doctrine of the Trinity provides the intellectual means whereby to harmonize personality and sociality in the community of men and women without sacrificing the one to the other."[13] According to Moltmann, in such a model, "The trinitarian principle replaces the principle of power by the principle of concord."[14]

In a witty fashion, Keith E. Johnson raises precisely the right question in relation to Moltmann's project and ones like it:

> First, apart from explicit scriptural warrant, how do we know what implications follow from specific metaphysical features of God's

---

[9] Knox, "The Ordination of Women," in *D. Broughton Knox, Selected Works, Vol. 2: Church and Ministry*, ed. Tony Payne (Kingsford, NSW: Matthias Media, 2003), 207–209.
[10] For the bulk of this paragraph see D. Broughton Knox, *The Everlasting God* (Homebush: Lancer, 1988), 69–75 and 129–146. In other places, Knox seems to restrict the pattern to family and church life, excluding wider social life. See D. Broughton Knox, *Sent by Jesus* (Edinburgh/Carlisle: Banner of Truth, 1992), 46–47.
[11] See Jürgen Moltmann, *The Trinity and the Kingdom of God* (London: SCM, 1981), 199. See also his *Experiences in Theology* (London: SCM, 2000), 332, where the heading is "The Trinity is our social programme."
[12] Moltmann, *Trinity*, 198.
[13] Ibid., 199.
[14] Ibid., 202.

immanent life? Consider the triunity of God. Theologians like Moltmann frequently argue that hierarchical political and ecclesial structures are incompatible with the perichoretic unity and equality of the three divine persons. But why not argue that the threeness of God constitutes the blueprint for governmental structures with three "equal" yet "distinct" branches of authority: an executive branch (corresponding to the Father), a legislative branch (corresponding to the Word) and a judicial branch (corresponding to the Spirit, who is described in John's Gospel as "Counselor")? On this basis we could claim that the American government is in the image of the Trinity.[15]

The great danger is that of projection, namely, reading back into eternity and into divine triune life what is found in human social life.[16] Xenophanes (c. 570–c. 475 BC) comes to mind: "Ethiopians say that their gods are snub-nosed and black; Thracians that theirs are blue-eyed and red-haired."[17]

What are we to make of these very divergent applications of Trinitarian theology? The divergence begs both methodological questions and substantive ones concerning the shape of a given application.[18] At the very least, the divergence of opinion between a Knox and a Moltmann underscores the difficulty of moving from describing a model of the Trinity to prescribing the shape of human social life.[19] Precisely which model is to be followed is the issue.[20]

THE BIBLICAL WITNESS

For those who hold a high view of biblical authority, as John Feinberg does, Scripture serves as the touchstone of any theological proposal.[21] So the key question is whether either Moltmann or Knox has good biblical

---
[15] Johnson, *Rethinking*, 201. Johnson and I share many of the same arguments and conclusions, although arrived at quite independently.
[16] A point well made by Johnson, *Rethinking*, 202–204.
[17] "Xenophanes," http://plato.stanford.edu/entries/xenophanes/ (accessed January 7, 2013).
[18] I owe this point to Johnson, who read an earlier draft of this essay and made many helpful comments.
[19] The *Catechism of the Catholic Church* appears to appreciate this difficulty when it states, vaguely, "There is a certain semblance between the union of the divine persons and the fraternity that men are to establish among themselves in truth and love" (*Catechism of the Catholic Church* 1878). In fact, in this massive work of some 800 pages and 2,865 numbered paragraphs, the Trinity per se is hardly ever appealed to as an ethical paradigm.
[20] Which model to follow becomes even more complicated if the *filioque* dispute is factored into the discussion. Is the Eastern *taxis* to be followed, or the Western one? See Kathryn Tanner, *Christ the Key* (Cambridge, U.K.: Cambridge University Press, 2010), 180 and 187. I am grateful to Johnson for drawing her work to my attention.
[21] This may be an appropriate point at which to express my appreciation for John Feinberg's theological and philosophical acumen as well as his warm friendship.

warrant for their move from the essential Trinity to the moral life of the Christian. What do the relevant Scriptures say concerning imitation?

A handy way to sum up what Scripture—both Old Testament and New—says concerning imitation is that imitation involves primarily walking in God's ways and walking in Christ's ways, respectively. Imitation means secondarily walking in the ways of someone who walks in Christ's ways. St. Paul comes to mind here (1 Cor. 11:1).

THE OLD TESTAMENT ACCENTS: THE IMITATION OF GOD

At the very beginning of the biblical story, we find the Creator creating a creature in the divine image (Gen. 1:27): "So God created man in his own image, in the image of God he created him; male and female he created them." As to what that image means, theologians differ. Are human beings, as images of God, like the image of President Lincoln stamped on an American coin? Is the image ontological or, put another way, substantial? On this view, we bear the stamp of rationality, volition, and moral sense. Or, are human beings, as images of God, like the image we see of ourselves in a mirror? What we do, so the image does; if I scratch my ear, so too does my image. So is the image functional? Or is it neither, but rather is it a relational idea? Just as male and female are the image of God, so there is something relational about God on the inside (*ad intra*). Ultimately, on this view, the doctrine of the Trinity lies behind human beings being the images of God. C. John Collins rightly sees the complexity in the debate and wisely suggests, "Scholars will advocate one of these three over the others, but we will note that they need not be mutually exclusive. Perhaps none is right, or some combination is right, or maybe we simply cannot come to a firm conclusion."[22]

The reason for the debate is a simple one. Nowhere in Scripture is the image defined. Even so, J. I. Packer helpfully contributes to our understanding of the image:

> The statement at the start of the Bible (Gen. 1:26–27, echoed in 5:1; 9:6; 1 Cor. 11:7; James 3:9) that God made man in his own image, so that humans are like God as no other earthly creatures are, tells

---
[22] C. John Collins, *Genesis 1–4: A Linguistic, Literary, and Theological Commentary* (Phillipsburg, NJ: P&R, 2006), 63.

us that the special dignity of being human is that, as humans, we may reflect and *reproduce at our own creaturely level the holy ways of God*, and thus act as his direct representatives on earth. This is what humans are made to do, and in one sense we are human only to the extent that we are doing it.[23]

Packer is correct to draw attention to the ways of God, because walking in God's ways is a consistent biblical theme, as we shall see. More than that, as James Muilenburg suggests, "The primary image to express conduct or behavior in the Old Testament is the 'way' or 'road' (*derek*)."[24]

Tragically, the unfolding biblical narrative makes it plain that God's son Adam fails to image God as he should (Genesis 3); thus, Adam and Eve are expelled from Eden. But God has not abandoned his project to have a creature that images his character and ways in the world. Abraham is called into covenant relationship with God and becomes a pivotal character in the divine plan to reclaim and restore the creation order (Gen. 12:1–3; 15:1–21). Later, in the Torah's unfolding story, we find that God's corporate son Israel—composed of the children of Abraham—is rescued from Egyptian bondage to become "a display-people, a showcase to the world of how being in covenant with Yahweh changes a people."[25] Accordingly, imaging God involves walking in God's ways: "The LORD will establish you as his holy people, as he promised you on oath, if you keep the commands of the LORD your God and *walk in his ways*. Then all the peoples on earth will see that you are called by the name of the LORD, and they will fear you" (Deut. 28:9–10, NIV 1984).[26] Leviticus 19:2 gives greater specificity as to what walking in God's ways looks like. In general terms, Israel is to "be holy because I, the LORD your God, am holy" (NIV 1984). More generally, Israel is to be morally different from the surrounding nations, different from the Egypt that Israel left behind at the exodus (18:1–5) and different from the nations to which they were headed (20:22–23). Israel is to be set apart from the nations around about her (20:24).

---

[23] J. I. Packer, *Concise Theology: A Guide to Historic Christian Beliefs* (Australia/Singapore/U.K.: Anzea/Campus Crusade Asia/Inter-Varsity, 1993), 71 (emphasis mine).
[24] Quoted in Charles H. H. Scobie, *The Ways of Our God: An Approach to Biblical Theology* (Grand Rapids, MI: Eerdmans, 2003), 98.
[25] J. I. Durham, *Exodus*, Word Biblical Commentary, vol. 3 (Dallas: Word, 2002), comment on Exodus 19:6, CD-Rom version.
[26] Walking in God's revealed ways is frequently emphasized in Deuteronomy (e.g., Deut. 5:33; 8:6; 10:12; 11:22; 19:9; 26:17; 30:16).

THE NEW TESTAMENT ACCENTS: THE IMITATION OF CHRIST

In the New Testament we find both continuity and discontinuity with the Old Testament revelation. An example of continuity is found in the way Jesus instructs his disciples in the famous Sermon on the Mount to exhibit the divine character, which is to say, to be like God:

> You have heard that it was said, "You shall love your neighbor and hate your enemy." But I say to you, Love your enemies and pray for those who persecute you, so that you may be sons of your Father who is in heaven. For he makes his sun rise on the evil and on the good, and sends rain on the just and on the unjust. For if you love those who love you, what reward do you have? Do not even the tax collectors do the same? And if you greet only your brothers, what more are you doing than others? Do not even the Gentiles do the same? You therefore must be perfect, as your heavenly Father is perfect. (Matt. 5:43–48)

"Perfection" in this setting does not refer to some Platonic ideal but to concrete behavior on the human plane that is informed by the character of God. A similar passage in Luke's account makes that clear, as Jesus puts the point more concretely: "Be merciful, even as your Father is merciful" (Luke 6:36).

Another example of continuity is that both the corporate imaging of God and the walking in God's ways are accentuated. First Peter reaffirms the moral stance of Leviticus: "As obedient children, do not be conformed to the passions of your former ignorance, but as he who called you is holy, you also be holy in all your conduct, since it is written, 'You shall be holy, for I am holy'" (1 Pet. 1:14–16). This New Testament letter also reaffirms that God's new covenant people, like Israel of old, are to be a "display-people." Indeed 1 Peter 2:9 clearly uses the categories of Exodus 19:5–6 to describe the church: "a chosen people, a royal priesthood, a holy nation, a people belonging to God" (NIV 1984). Significantly, the *imitatio dei* of 1 Peter 1 becomes the *imitatio Christi* of 1 Peter 2. This is particularly emphasized when the issue of the Christian slave and the oppressive master come into view; it is now the individual who is in mind, not the group:

> Servants, be subject to your masters with all respect, not only to the good and gentle but also to the unjust. For this is a gracious thing, when, mindful of God, one endures sorrows while suffering unjustly. For what credit is it if, when you sin and are beaten for it, you endure? But if when you do good and suffer for it you endure, this is a gracious thing in the sight of God. For to this you have been called, because Christ also suffered for you, leaving you an example, so that you might follow in his steps. He committed no sin, neither was deceit found in his mouth. When he was reviled, he did not revile in return; when he suffered, he did not threaten, but continued entrusting himself to him who judges justly. (1 Pet. 2:18–23)

This Petrine application of the gospel is especially interesting because the walking in Christ's ways is clearly prominent: "Christ also suffered for you, leaving you an example, so that you might follow in his steps" (1 Pet. 2:21).

In fact, the *imitatio Christi* motif pervades the New Testament literature, as Richard A. Burridge so persuasively demonstrates.[27] For example, moving from the Pauline and Petrine witness to the Johannine one, we find God's people are instructed, "Whoever claims to live in him must walk as Jesus did" (1 John 2:6, NIV 1984).[28] John 13 provides an abiding example of what walking in his ways looks like. This famous story, set in the upper room during the Passion Week, presents Jesus as the servant who takes the humble role in an other-person-centered way: he provides the hospitality to others that should have been accorded to him. Jesus draws the moral:

> You call me "Teacher" and "Lord," and rightly so, for that is what I am. Now that I, your Lord and Teacher, have washed your feet, you also should wash one another's feet. I have set you an example

---

[27] Richard A. Burridge, *Imitating Jesus: An Inclusive Approach to New Testament Ethics* (Grand Rapids, MI/Cambridge: Eerdmans, 2007). Importantly Burridge shows, by drawing on the parallels between the imitation motif (*mimesis*) in ancient pagan biography writing (*bioi*), the rabbinic accent on the imitation of the teacher (*ma'aseh*, 'precedent'), and the four canonical Gospels, that the imitation theme is something held in common by all three bodies of literature (esp. 73–78). Such imitation included actions. Kyle D. Fedler, *Exploring Christian Ethics: Biblical Foundations for Morality* (Louisville: Westminster John Knox, 2006), 175–176, takes a different view. He argues that Jesus did not command the imitating of him but the following of him. If we are to imitate Christ, it is the imitation of his virtues and emotions and not his actions. Useful though Fedler's text is, I find Burridge more convincing. An important recent study of the *imitatio Christi* motif is Jason B. Hood, *Imitating God in Christ: Recapturing a Biblical Pattern* (Downers Grove, IL: IVP Academic, 2013).
[28] The NIV version here is more a faithful paraphrase than a translation (lit., "The one claiming to abide in him [Jesus] ought to walk as that one walked").

that you should do as I have done for you. I tell you the truth, no servant is greater than his master, nor is a messenger greater than the one who sent him. Now that you know these things, you will be blessed if you do them. (John 13:13–17, NIV 1984)

Three caveats are in order, though. First, not all of Jesus's actions are imitable. The wise reader of Scripture discerns the difference between the imitable and the unique. John 13 presents the imitable, as we have seen. However, Jesus as the mediator between God and human beings has a unique vocation: "For there is one God and one mediator between God and men, the man Christ Jesus, who gave himself as a ransom for all men—the testimony given in its proper time" (1 Tim. 2:5–6, NIV 1984). Second, Christology must not be reduced to a merely exemplarist one. John Webster points out this danger: "the language of imitation often appears to envisage Jesus Christ as simply an exemplar whose work is the revelation of the perfect love of God for men and the demonstration of a perfect response to that love."[29] Christ is that, but so much more. The last caveat is that this present account, to be more complete, would need to explore the promise of the Paraclete in John 14–16. A Christlike life is a life lived in union with Christ (a branch on the vine, as in John 15) through the enablement provided by the Spirit of Pentecost.[30]

The famous hymnic passage in Philippians 2:5–11 is instructive here. Despite many virtues as a church, the Philippians needed encouragement to be other-person-centered. Paul exhorts them, "Let each of you look not only to his own interests, but also to the interests of others" (v. 4). Significantly, for our purposes, Paul's next theological move is not to draw attention to the eternal relation of the Father and the Son with some imperative along the lines of, "Be like the Son always has been in his centering not on himself but on the Father!" Rather, Paul rehearses the great stooping of the Son in his incarnation and atonement:

> Have this mind among yourselves, which is yours in Christ Jesus, who, though he was in the form of God, did not count equality with God a thing to be grasped, but emptied himself, by taking the form of a servant, being born in the likeness of men. And being found in

---
[29] Quoted in Scobie, *Ways of Our God*, 796.
[30] The pneumatological aspect of the *imitatio Christi*—and *imitatio Pauli*, for that matter—is well discussed in Rodney Reeves, *Spirituality according to Paul: Imitating the Apostle of Christ* (Downers Grove, IL: IVP Academic, 2011), 13–18.

human form, he humbled himself by becoming obedient to the point of death, even death on a cross. Therefore God has highly exalted him and bestowed on him the name that is above every name, so that at the name of Jesus every knee should bow, in heaven and on earth and under the earth, and every tongue confess that Jesus Christ is Lord, to the glory of God the Father. (Phil. 2:5–11)

What is on view is Christ's other-person-centeredness as exhibited in the evangel. Paul's ethic is shaped in this letter, not by some notion of eternal divine relations but by gospel ones. It truly is an evangelical ethic.

Paul has another important contribution to make to this study. Both the imitation of God and the imitation of Christ are brought together by Paul in his Ephesians letter: "Be kind to one another, tenderhearted, forgiving one another, as God in Christ forgave you. Therefore be imitators of God, as beloved children. And walk in love, as Christ loved us and gave himself up for us, a fragrant offering and sacrifice to God" (Eph. 4:32–5:2). God's forgiveness is to be imitated in our own forgiving of others.[31] But it is not forgiveness as a general principle that is thematized; rather, it is the forgiveness that comes through the gospel of Christ. Christology is the key to understanding the nature of this forgiveness. The apostle does not leave it there, but goes on to draw a conclusion about the shape of the Christian's moral life. It is walking in Christ's ways.[32]

Secondarily, though importantly, the imitation of Christ informed Paul's own understanding of the shape of apostolic life. He writes to the Corinthians, "I urge you, then, be imitators of me. That is why I sent you Timothy, my beloved and faithful child in the Lord, to remind you of my ways in Christ, *as I teach them everywhere in every church*" (1 Cor. 4:16–17). Clearly, the Corinthians were not a special case. Later, in the same letter, the Christological paradigm is even more clearly in view. Paul instructs the Corinthians in the following way: "So, whether you eat or drink, or whatever you do, do all to the glory of God. Give no offense to Jews or to Greeks or to the church of God, just as I try to please everyone in everything I do, not seeking my own advantage, but that of many, that

---

[31] I owe this insight to Keith Johnson and a paper he gave at the annual meeting of the Evangelical Theological Society in Milwaukee, November 16, 2012. He has also written astutely on the question of the relevance of the Trinitarian paradigm in Johnson, *Rethinking the Trinity*, esp. chapter 6. Burridge, *Imitating Jesus*, 145, points out that this bringing together of the imitation of God and the imitation of Christ is unique in the Pauline corpus.

[32] The ESV serves us better here than the NIV, which renders the idea with the bland "live a life of love" (1984) or "walk in the way of love" (2011), which loses the Old Testament resonances.

they may be saved. Be imitators of me, as I am of Christ" (10:31–11:1). Paul appears to have the model of Christ before him. Christ lived to the glory of God, not his own. He lived a life of other-person-centeredness. He did not set out to give offense, although people took offense at his teaching and claims. Accordingly, Paul sought to minister in the same way, and he counsels the Corinthians to adopt his ways insofar as they were reflective of Christ's own.[33]

It is important to note, however, that in other letters Paul calls on his readers to imitate him but does not in any explicit way draw on the Christ story in so doing. To the Thessalonians he writes,

> Now we command you, brothers, in the name of our Lord Jesus Christ, that you keep away from any brother who is walking in idleness and not in accord with the tradition that you received from us. For you yourselves know how you ought to imitate us, because we were not idle when we were with you, nor did we eat anyone's bread without paying for it, but with toil and labor we worked night and day, that we might not be a burden to any of you. It was not because we do not have that right, but to give you in ourselves an example to imitate. For even when we were with you, we would give you this command: If anyone is not willing to work, let him not eat. (2 Thess. 3:6–10)

The Pauline example of hard work is to inform the behavior of these Thessalonian Christians; thus, he rebukes some there who had embraced idleness, for idleness is not an option. Paul's language is strong: "For you yourselves know how you ought [*dei*, "it is necessary"] to imitate [*mimeisthai*] us" (v. 7). This is not an afterthought on Paul's part; it was his intention all along: "It was not because we do not have that right, but to give you in ourselves an example to imitate" (v. 9). He left them a pattern (*tupos*) of behavior to be imitated (*mimeisthai*). Similarly he offered his example to the Philippians: "Brothers, join in imitating [*summimētai*] me and keep your eyes on those who walk according to the example [*tupos*] you have in us" (Phil. 3:17).

What is of great significance is that Paul makes no appeal to the inner life of the Father, Son, and Holy Spirit in their intradeical relations when

---

[33] Another way Christians imitate Christ is every time the Lord's Supper is performed. The fourfold action of Christ is imitated: e.g., the taking of bread, the giving of thanks, the breaking of the bread, and the giving it out (cf. Luke 22:19 and 1 Cor. 11:23–24).

giving moral instruction. Neither does any other New Testament writer, as far as I can see.[34]

IMITATING THE ESSENTIAL TRINITY?

What is not found in the biblical witness is any moral imperative that is grounded on a clear appeal to the inner life of the essential Trinity. Both Moltmann and Knox have run far ahead of any biblical evidence in claiming otherwise. Some might suggest that Jesus's prayer in John 17 is a counterexample to what I am arguing:

> I do not ask for these only, but also for those who will believe in me through their word, that they may all be one, just as you, Father, are in me, and I in you, that they also may be in us, so that the world may believe that you have sent me. The glory that you have given me I have given to them, that they may be one even as we are one, I in them and you in me, that they may become perfectly one, so that the world may know that you sent me and loved them even as you loved me. Father, I desire that they also, whom you have given me, may be with me where I am, to see my glory that you have given me because you loved me before the foundation of the world. O righteous Father, even though the world does not know you, I know you, and these know that you have sent me. I made known to them your name, and I will continue to make it known, that the love with which you have loved me may be in them, and I in them. (John 17:20–26)

However, in this wonderful High Priestly Prayer of Jesus, there is much description of the essential relationship between the Father and the Son, and the love that has always been between them, and of the divine love with which Jesus desires his disciples to be loved. Even so, description is not prescription. There is no moral imperative in the text based on that relationship. In fact, when Jesus does command love, he does so informed by his own example: "A new commandment I give to you, that you love one another: just as I have loved you, you also are to love one another" (13:34). Christian love is Christomorphic.

Another possible counterexample is found in Paul's discussion of male

---

[34] Interestingly, John S. Feinberg and Paul D. Feinberg's widely used text, *Ethics for a Brave New World*, 2nd ed. (Wheaton, IL: Crossway, 2010) contains no reference to the Trinity per se. This work is over eight hundred pages in length. It is therefore no mere primer.

and female decorum in the context of a worshiping congregation: "But I want you to understand that the head of every man is Christ, the head of a wife is her husband, and the head of Christ is God. Every man who prays or prophesies with his head covered dishonors his head, but every wife who prays or prophesies with her head uncovered dishonors her head, since it is the same as if her head were shaven" (1 Cor. 11:3–5). However, the text does not argue that the head of the Son is the Father, but that the head of Christ (lit., "the Christ") is God. That the reference is to the Trinity operating economically rather than the essential Trinity per se makes better sense of the text (contra Knox's view, discussed earlier).[35] Both John Calvin and Charles Hodge argued this point in terms of Christ's mediatorial role as the incarnate one.[36] If so, once more the imitation of Christ *qua* Christ is on view.[37]

THE TRINITY, MORAL REFLECTION, AND MORAL DELIBERATION

Eminent ethicist Oliver O'Donovan suggests a distinction, with debts to Aristotle, between moral reflection and moral deliberation: Moral reflection asks what the reality is; moral deliberation asks what is to be done in the light of that reality. For the Christian, God's revelation defines what is real. So O'Donovan argues, "In the first place, we reflect upon the history

---

[35] I prefer to speak of the *essential Trinity* and the *essential Trinity operating economically* rather than the usual distinction between the essential (or immanent) Trinity and the economic Trinity. This distinction can give the misleading impression, albeit unintentional on the part of those who employ it, that there are two different Trinities. Johnson, *Rethinking The Trinity*, 65n2, makes the same point: "One of the disadvantages of speaking of the 'economic Trinity' and the 'immanent Trinity' is that this language may offer a mistaken impression that there are two trinities."

[36] Calvin argues that in 1 Corinthians 11:3 it is Christ as the incarnate mediator who is on view. See John Calvin, *Commentary on the First Epistle to the Corinthians*, trans. William Pringle (Eugene, OR: Ages Software, 1998), 299. Charles Hodge, in the tradition of Calvin, maintains regarding 1 Corinthians 11:3 that on display is the economic subordination of the Christ to God. This he describes as follows: "economical" subordination is the Son's "official subjection" to the Father as the *theanthropos* (lit., "God-human") in his roles as redeemer and head of the church. See Hodge's comments on 1 Corinthians 11:3 in any edition of his commentary.

[37] In my view, the only way that more can be said of the essential Trinity is if a strict reading of Rahner's Rule is adopted, namely, that the immanent Trinity is the economic Trinity means that one can argue from the narrative of Christ's life back into the eternal state. However, this plays havoc with the two states of Christ Christology. It argues *de facto* that the state of glory and the state of humiliation are the same. The New Testament argues otherwise (e.g., John 17:5; 2 Cor. 8:9; Phil. 2:5–11; Heb. 5:8). For a discussion of loose versus tight readings of Rahner's Rule, see Fred Sanders, "Entangled in the Trinity: Economic and Immanent Trinity in Recent Theology," *Dialog* 4:3 (Fall 2001), 175–182. Randal Rauser suggests three possible readings of the rule—strict realist, loose realist, and anti-realist—in "'Rahner's Rule:' An Emperor without Clothes?" *International Journal of Systematic Theology* 7/1 (January 2005): 81–94. For an excellent treatment of Rahner's Rule in the light of careful exegesis of the New Testament, see Scott Harrower, *Trinitarian Self and Salvation: An Evangelical Engagement with Rahner's Rule* (Eugene, OR: Pickwick, 2012). For the rule itself, see Alister E. McGrath, ed., *Theology: The Basic Readings* (Malden, MA: Blackwell, 2008), 51: "the Trinity of the economy is the immanent Trinity and vice versa."

of God's dealings with the world: in creation, in the coming of Christ and in the promised fulfillment."[38]

In the light of O'Donovan's distinction, one might argue that moral reflection on the biblical revelation of the triune God yields a number of important values that should inform any ethic that calls itself a Christian one. These values include—and this list is indicative rather than exhaustive—love, righteousness, reciprocity, and other-person-centeredness. These are values that have always been true of the God who is the essential Trinity. Each of these values is relational. Love has its object, righteousness is behavior appropriate to a relationship, reciprocity speaks of mutuality, and other-person-centeredness presupposes the other. However, embracing these values in order to be like the God we worship and the Christ we follow does not tell us how to act morally in a given situation. Moral deliberation, one might argue, takes such values and assesses what the moral agent ought to do in a given moral situation in the light of them.[39] At this juncture it would be useful to turn our attention to an actual moral situation to see if this is a workable idea.

Life outside of Eden poses difficult moral questions. It raises the questions that come under the heading of "the ethics of quandary." Think of the moral problems posed by a patient in a hospital bed who by every test is brain-dead. Ought heroic measures be abandoned and all life support withdrawn?[40] What ought the relatives to be advised? Moral deliberation explores what ought to be done. What ought love to do?[41] It is not easy to see how working from a putative reconstruction of the inner life of the Trinity helps much here. General guidance maybe, but more concrete guidance? Kathryn Tanner is right to argue in relation to such Trinitarian visions, "A treasure is dangled before us with no clue as to how we might get to it from the desperate straits of social relations marked by violent conflict, loss and suffering."[42] In the case of the brain-dead patient, one

---

[38] Oliver M. T. O'Donovan, "Christian Moral Reasoning," in *New Dictionary of Christian Ethics and Pastoral Theology*, ed. David J. Atkinson and David H. Field (Leicester, England/Downers Grove, IL: InterVarsity Press, 1995), 123.
[39] A moral situation is one in which the language of right and wrong, praise and blame applies. For example, a good night's sleep is not a moral situation. A good night's sleep while on watch on the front lines in a war zone is.
[40] A heroic measure is one adopted as a last resort that poses considerable risk and danger to the patient's well-being or carries little, if any, prospect of success.
[41] A fuller account would draw on virtue ethics and ask questions about the person who is acting in the situation. A biblical ethic is interested in the moral agent (virtue ethics), the moral action (deontological ethics), and the aftermath (consequentialist ethics). It is holistic.
[42] Tanner, *Christ*, 229. She points out how, after appealing to the essential Trinity, "one is still left with very vague recommendations" (223).

could modify Tanner's observation as follows: a treasure is dangled before us with no clue as to how we might get *from* it (a Trinitarian vision) *to* the desperate straits of social relations marked by violent conflict, loss, and suffering.

If appealing to the inner life of the essential Trinity does not help with the ethics of quandary, what does? Here the example of Christ may more helpfully come into play. In Luke 6:6–11, Jesus is confronted in the synagogue by a man with a withered right hand. Scribes and Pharisees are watching. Jesus poses a question: "I ask you, is it lawful on the Sabbath to do good or to do harm, to save life or to destroy it?" (v. 9). He heals the man. This Lukan story presents a principle of doing good versus doing harm. The saving of life is doing good and the destroying of life is doing evil. When Jesus did not have an Old Testament precedent to consider—unlike the story of the disciples plucking ears of corn on the Sabbath (vv. 1–5)—he dug deep down into moral principle.

In our case in point, we do not have "chapter and verse" (unlike that first Lukan story; vv. 1–5); therefore, I would argue that to find a way forward, one needs to dig down into principle (the second Lukan story; vv. 6–11). What ought love to do? Love ought to prolong life. Love ought not necessarily postpone death. And other-person-centeredness takes into account not only the patient but the relatives and the matters of triage, if there is another person with a greater need for that particular life-support equipment. All things considered, I would argue that the life support be shut off. The life is already destroyed as far as life in this world is concerned.

The attentive reader will have noticed that I have tackled this admittedly difficult moral problematic with an appeal to *imitatio Christi* (his words and deeds) and not to the Trinity per se. The reason is simple. Values such as love and other-person regard can be derived from moral reflection on the Christological story—or on the revealed character of God, for that matter—without the need to refer to the inner life of the essential Trinity. If I may adapt some words of Kathryn Tanner, appealing to the Trinity "does not tell anyone anything one did not know" from reflecting on the life of Christ.[43] As the title of her book suggests, "Christ [is] the Key."

---

[43] Ibid., 230. Tanner rejects any attempt to model oneself on the Trinity per se; rather, she argues for our participation in the triune God through union with Christ as the clue to how to close the gap she perceives between the life of the Trinity and our own. Her argument is very sophisticated. However, her chapter that tackles the issue barely contains any reference to Scripture (see 212n8 as a rare exception). The lack of exegetical grounding is the great weakness in this otherwise wonderfully stimulating work.

CONCLUSION

I deeply appreciate the revival of Trinitarian theology. The Holy Trinity is the only God there is. It is a nonnegotiable element in Christian doctrine; after all, we are baptized in the one name of the Father, Son, and Holy Spirit. We pray to the Father through the Son in the Spirit. Our doxology is "Glory be to the Father and to the Son and to the Holy Spirit." However, be that as it may, the thrust of the foregoing argument is that the attempt to move from reconstructions of the inner life of the essential Trinity to the Christian moral life is burdened with immense difficulties. These difficulties were evident in the work of both Knox and Moltmann. Different reconstructions of the *taxis* (order) within the essential Trinity lead to very different applications of the doctrine, raising acute methodological concerns.[44] The chief difficulty is that the biblical writers give no evidence that this is how the Christian moral life is to be construed. Instead, we find the accent in the Old Testament falls on the imitation of God (Yahweh) per se; and in the New Testament, although that emphasis continues, much more to the fore is the imitation of Christ. Where the doctrine of the essential Trinity may play a role is in providing values derived by way of moral reflection that informs moral deliberation. Even so, it is hard to see how moral reflection on the Trinity operating economically, with Christ at the center, is not sufficient. More pointedly, moral deliberation ought not bypass the Christological story. Bypassing the gospel is the danger that attends moving too facilely from reconstructions of the inner relations of the essential Trinity to the Christian moral life. That life is to be Christomorphic. What an irony if evangelicals in pursuit of the relevance of the doctrine of the Trinity end up with an ethic that leaves the evangel behind!

---

[44] It needs to be noted that although Knox's and Moltmann's proposals are not justified in my view by an appeal to the inner life of the Trinity, their truth value is not overturned thereby. Their proposals on gender relations, for example, may find justification on other grounds. That, however, is another matter and beyond the brief of this essay. What is clear is that they both cannot be right, given their very different views about hierarchy.

15

Christian Apologetics in a Globalizing and Religiously Diverse World

HAROLD A. NETLAND

In the Gospel of John, we have a fascinating encounter between Jesus and some Greeks in Jerusalem for the Passover. The Greeks, probably "God-fearers," approach Philip with a request: "Sir, we wish to see Jesus" (12:21). Presumably Philip and Andrew led them to Jesus and they engaged in conversation, although the text is silent on this. John is not concerned with the content of their conversation. Rather, he uses this encounter between Jesus and some Gentiles to point to the coming climax of Jesus's ministry: no longer does Jesus belong merely to the Jews, for he is the Savior of the world, of Jews and Gentiles alike.

The Greeks in John's Gospel were interested in more than simply observing what Jesus looked like physically. They wished to experience for themselves what they had heard about him and to learn more about who Jesus really is. Similarly, in the church's witness to others today, our concern should be that we enable others to see Jesus, encountering him as the risen Christ and thereby coming to acknowledge him as Lord and Savior.

But which Jesus will people see? There are multiple images of Jesus available today, as symbolically Jesus has gone global. Thus, part of our task in witness is to clarify who Jesus really is and to provide reasons for accepting the biblical portrait rather than these distorted alternatives.

Jesus appears today in some surprising places. Despite the small number of Christians in Japan, for example, there is an intriguing story of Jesus's tomb in northern Japan.[1] Local legend maintains that, after growing up in Galilee, Jesus lived in Japan before beginning his public ministry in Galilee at the age of thirty-three. Facing opposition from the Jewish leaders, Jesus returned to Japan, settling in the town of Shingo near beautiful Lake Towada in northern Japan. Jesus's brother, Isukuri, was crucified in Jesus's place on the cross, and Jesus actually lived on in northern Japan until his death at age 106. How did this fascinating distortion of the gospel story become embedded in local narratives in a remote mountain area of northern Japan, far from any known centers of Christianity? Many believe that this is a confused version of an account about Jesus from the early Roman Catholic presence in Japan in the sixteenth and seventeenth centuries.

The West has its own alternative pictures of Jesus. With the rise of critical biblical scholarship during the past three centuries, we have witnessed an astonishing variety of "Jesuses" crafted by critics, each supposedly embedded within the layers of the New Testament.[2] Within popular culture, the astonishing success a decade ago of Dan Brown's novel *The Da Vinci Code*—translated into over forty-four languages—demonstrates not only the continuing fascination people have with Jesus but also a widespread willingness to consider revisionist perspectives with no historical support.[3] Jesus has had enormous appeal in American popular culture over the past two centuries, as a bewildering multiplicity of images of Jesus—most at odds with the biblical witness—have been put forward by diverse groups.[4]

Jesus has also become adopted by many of the religions of the world.[5] According to Islam, the second largest religion today, Jesus is a highly revered prophet, although he is in no way to be identified with God.[6] Many Hindus regard Jesus as an avatar, or a manifestation, of a Hindu deity. Mahatma Gandhi had enormous respect for Jesus as a great moral

---

[1] John Koedyker, "Another Jesus," *The Japan Christian Quarterly* 52/2 (1986): 167–169.
[2] Ben Witherington III, *The Jesus Quest: The Third Search for the Jew of Nazareth*, 2nd ed. (Downers Grove, IL: InterVarsity Press, 1997); and Craig A. Evans, *Fabricating Jesus: How Modern Scholars Distort the Gospels* (Downers Grove, IL: InterVarsity Press, 2006).
[3] Patrick T. Reardon, "'The Da Vinci Code' Unscrambled," *Chicago Tribune*, February 5, 2004.
[4] See Stephen Prothero, *American Jesus: How the Son of God Became a National Icon* (New York: Farrar, Straus, & Giroux, 2003).
[5] For a helpful source of texts from Judaism, Islam, Hinduism, and Buddhism on Jesus, see Gregory A. Barker and Stephen E. Gregg, eds., *Jesus beyond Christianity: The Classic Texts* (New York: Oxford University Press, 2010).
[6] See Geoffrey Parrinder, *Jesus in the Qur'an* (New York: Oxford University Press, 1977); and Kenneth Cragg, *Jesus and the Muslim: An Exploration* (Oxford: Oneworld, 1999).

and spiritual leader, but he rejected the orthodox view of Jesus as God incarnate, the one Lord and Savior for all humankind. Gandhi stated, "I regard Jesus as a great teacher of humanity, but I do not regard him as the only begotten son of God."[7] Buddhists also find a place for Jesus within their system. The Dalai Lama, for example, states, "As a Buddhist, my attitude toward Jesus Christ is that he was either a fully enlightened being or a bodhisattva of a very high spiritual realization."[8] Jesus is also one of many divine manifestations or messengers of God in Baha'i.[9] And, of course, Jesus has a prominent, if unorthodox, place in the remarkably successful new religion of Mormonism, or the Church of Jesus Christ of Latter-Day Saints.[10]

All of this complicates the task of Christian witness today. In earlier times it was easy to assume that most people in the West were already familiar with the biblical teaching on Jesus and that those in Africa and Asia had not yet heard his name. But this is clearly not the case now. Many in the West have little understanding of the biblical Jesus, and those in other cultures often have some awareness of Jesus, although it is shaped by their particular religious and cultural traditions. The gospel of Jesus Christ comes into these contexts not as something entirely new but rather as a rival perspective on an already familiar religious symbol. A pressing question then is, why should one accept this new, biblically faithful picture of Jesus instead of the view of Jesus already embedded within one's own cultural and religious framework?

The challenges to Christian witness in the early twenty-first century go well beyond the issue of competing Christologies. Questions about Jesus's identity are framed from within particular religious or nonreligious worldviews, reflecting very different ways of understanding the cosmos and different sources of religious knowledge. Thus, questions about the existence and nature of God—not all religions believe in a Creator God—or the authority of the Bible are inescapable. The endeavor to respond to these challenges and to commend the case for accepting the Christian claims as true has traditionally been known as apologetics. Properly understood and conducted, apologetics is an important component of

---

[7] As quoted in Robert Ellsberg, ed., *Gandhi on Christianity* (Maryknoll, NY: Orbis, 1991), 26.
[8] His Holiness the Dalai Lama, *The Good Heart: A Buddhist Perspective on the Teachings of Jesus*, ed. Robert Kiely (Boston: Wisdom, 1996), 83. See also Rita M. Gross and Terry Muck, eds., *Buddhists Talk about Jesus, Christians Talk about the Buddha* (New York: Continuum, 2000).
[9] Peter Smith, *An Introduction to the Baha'i Faith* (New York: Cambridge University Press, 2008), 107.
[10] Claudia L. Bushman, *Contemporary Mormonism* (New York: Rowman & Littlefield, 2008).

Christian witness. But apologetics always occurs within particular historical and social contexts, and the profound transformations of the past half century have significant implications for how we should engage in apologetics in the twenty-first century. In this chapter I will focus on some of the implications for apologetics that flow from our increasing awareness of globalization and religious diversity.

APOLOGETICS AND CHRISTIAN FAITH

The term "apologetics," derived from the Greek *apologia*, refers to the activity of defending the Christian faith against particular criticisms concerning the truth or plausibility of central Christian claims. The Christian faith includes some audacious and controversial truth claims. Christian apologetics is the attempt to respond to critiques of such claims in a biblically faithful, intellectually sound, and culturally appropriate manner. Moreover, apologetics is concerned with persuasion; it actively seeks to persuade those who are skeptical to accept Christian beliefs.[11]

But apologetics has always been somewhat controversial within the Christian community.[12] Some Christians insist that any attempt to provide reasons for faith commitments is illegitimate because doing so entails resting one's faith on human reason rather than God's authority or the power of the Holy Spirit. Others acknowledge a modest place for apologetics in refuting the errors of critics but resist any attempt to go beyond this to provide positive reasons for believing the claims of the Christian faith. Still others maintain that it is essential that Christians provide compelling reasons for belief if they are to be rational in their faith, but they disagree over the strength of the case that can be made for Christian theism. I will not attempt to sort through the maze of theological and philosophical issues in this internal debate, but will make some brief comments on the relation between faith and reason.

First, much depends here upon how we understand key terms such as "faith" and "reason";[13] properly understood, the two concepts are not

---

[11] Although I am discussing apologetics in reference to those who are not (yet) believers, apologetics also has a crucial role in helping Christian believers to understand their faith commitments better and to have greater confidence in the truth of Christian claims.
[12] For some different approaches to the nature and role of apologetics, see John S. Feinberg, *Can You Believe It's True? Christian Apologetics in a Modern and Postmodern Era* (Wheaton, IL: Crossway, 2013), chapters 7–9; and Steve B. Cowan, ed., *Five Views on Apologetics* (Grand Rapids, MI: Zondervan, 2000).
[13] For a helpful philosophical exploration of the relation between faith, reason, and evidence, see Paul Helm, *Faith with Reason* (Oxford: Oxford University Press, 2000); and Kelly James Clark and Raymond J. VanArragon, eds., *Evidence and Religious Belief* (New York: Oxford University Press, 2011).

incompatible. The term "faith" is ambiguous, as it can refer to intellectual assent to what God has revealed (belief that; *fides* or *assensus*) or to an attitude or disposition of trust in God (belief in; *fiducia*). Faith as *fides* includes assent to certain beliefs or propositions, or accepting certain beliefs as true. "I believe in God" in this sense is equivalent to "I believe that there is a God." Faith as *fiducia* involves more than mere intellectual assent to a particular belief; it includes a volitional response of trust in the object of faith. "I believe in God" in this sense includes entrusting oneself to God and acting upon this trust in God. Drawing on both elements, we can think of Christian faith as a general orientation or disposition toward God and what he has revealed, which includes acceptance of certain beliefs or propositions about God, trust in God, and obedience to God.

What about reason? In a general sense, reason is the God-given faculty or capacity through which we recognize truth. More specifically, it is the set of faculties through which we identify relationships between things, draw inferences from (often implicit) premises, engage in critical reflection, and apprehend truth. Christian philosopher J. P. Moreland states, "By 'reason' I mean all our faculties relevant to gaining knowledge and justifying our beliefs about different things."[14] In this sense, reason is a gift from God and is something we use regularly every day, for we could not understand anything in any domain without employing reason. We could not even understand the gospel or the claims of Scripture without using reason, for reason is that faculty which helps us to "make sense" of the semantic and syntactic patterns that communicate meaning in any given language. Properly understood, then, there is nothing about reason itself that is inimical to the exercise of Christian faith, and acting responsibly as disciples of Jesus Christ requires the appropriate use of reason in distinguishing what is epistemically acceptable from what is not.[15]

We must also acknowledge that saving faith is always a gift from God, and that it is the supernatural work of the Holy Spirit that brings about the conviction of sin (John 16:8–11) and liberates the spiritually blind person from the grasp of the adversary, resulting in new birth in Christ

---

[14] J. P. Moreland, *Love Your God with All Your Mind: The Role of Reason in the Life of the Soul* (Colorado Springs: NavPress, 1997), 43.
[15] To be sure, the effects of sin on the human mind, and thus on our use of reason, must be acknowledged. The mind, just as all other dimensions of the human person, has been affected by sin. But the noetic effects of sin should not be exaggerated; sin does not totally vitiate reason, although it does affect how it is used. Even after the fall it is still possible for people (regenerate and unregenerate alike) to know many things, including God's reality (Rom. 1:19–21, 28, 32). See Feinberg, *Can You Believe It's True?*, 282–296.

(John 3:5; 1 Cor. 2:14–16; Titus 3:5). But this does not make apologetics unnecessary, any more than it renders evangelism optional. Both evangelism and apologetics must be carried out with prayer and conscious dependence upon the power of God.

Appropriate forms of apologetics are necessary as part of a comprehensive Christian witness today. Many evangelicals acknowledge that Christian witness in our pluralistic, relativistic world demands a fresh appreciation of Christian apologetics. When John Stott, for example—the architect of the Lausanne Movement—reflected back upon the twenty years since the first Congress on World Evangelization at Lausanne in 1974, he made a clear link between apologetics and effective evangelism:

> We evangelical people need to repent of every occasion on which we have divorced evangelism from apologetics, as the apostles never did. We have to argue the Gospel we proclaim. We need to be able to say confidently to our hearers what Paul said to Festus: "What I am saying is true and reasonable" (Acts 26:25). We cannot possibly surrender to the current understanding of "pluralism" as an ideology that affirms the independent validity of every religion. Our task, rather, is to establish the criteria by which truth claims can be evaluated and then to demonstrate the uniqueness and finality of Jesus Christ.[16]

It is significant that The Cape Town Commitment, from the Third Lausanne Congress on World Evangelization, held in Cape Town in October 2010, calls for a robust apologetics emphasis in our witness. The Commitment rightly sees skepticism about religious truth as a central issue for Christian witness today. In the section "Bearing Witness to the Truth of Christ in a Pluralistic, Globalized World," the Commitment states, "We long to see greater commitment to the hard work of robust apologetics." Responsible apologetics must involve both "those who can engage at the highest intellectual and public level in arguing for and defending biblical truth in the public arena" and pastors and other Christian leaders who can equip ordinary believers so that they are confident in their faith.[17] For too long, evangelical approaches to Christian

---

[16] John Stott, "Twenty Years after Lausanne: Some Personal Reflections," *International Bulletin of Missionary Research* (April 1995): 54.
[17] *The Cape Town Commitment*, II.A.2.A (Peabody, MA: Hendrickson and The Lausanne Movement, 2011), 34.

witness—especially in multireligious contexts—have been dominated by a pervasive pragmatism and anti-intellectualism that ignores difficult issues about the plausibility of the Christian faith in a pluralistic world. Apologetics can take many forms and should be adapted to fit varying contexts and levels of intellectual rigor. But whatever its form, apologetics should always be faithful to the biblical witness, intellectually responsible, and culturally appropriate.

GLOBALIZATION, SECULARIZATION, AND RELIGIOUS DIVERSITY

Christian apologetics in the West during the past three centuries has focused primarily on challenges arising from religious skepticism or atheism. Secular atheism is a significant movement worldwide, and critiques from atheists must be taken seriously by Christian apologists. A particularly aggressive form of atheism in the twenty-first century, which has had significant influence in some places outside the West, asserts not only that religion is false but that it is socially destructive and morally repugnant.[18]

Traditional issues that Christian apologists have been addressing for years in the West—the existence of God, the reliability of the Bible, the historicity of the resurrection of Jesus Christ—will continue to demand thoughtful response. But secular atheists remain a minority among humankind. Despite the growing numbers of those who are explicitly nonreligious, the overwhelming majority of people today worldwide regard themselves as followers of some religious tradition; indeed, roughly 80 percent of people worldwide profess some religious affiliation.[19] Without ignoring challenges from secular atheists, Christian apologetics in the days ahead must contend with some new questions, including sophisticated challenges from adherents of other religions and a pluralistic ethos that rejects any particular religion as distinctively true. We will consider briefly secularization, globalization, and the growing awareness of religious diversity, then draw some implications from these transformations for apologetics today.

---

[18] See, for example, Christopher Hitchens, *God Is Not Great: How Religion Poisons Everything* (New York: Twelve, 2007); Richard Dawkins, *The God Delusion* (New York: Houghton Mifflin, 2006); and Sam Harris, *The End of Faith: Religion, Terror, and the Future of Reason* (New York: W. W. Norton, 2004).
[19] Joanne O'Brien and Martin Palmer, *The Atlas of Religion* (Berkeley: University of California Press, 2007), 14.

Secularization

Few subjects are as complex or controversial as secularization theory.[20] There is no need to rehearse here the often convoluted debates over secularization in Europe and North America, but in order to appreciate the context in which apologetics takes place today, it will be helpful to look briefly at the recent work of philosopher and social theorist Charles Taylor.

In *A Secular Age* (2007), Taylor traces the intellectual and social developments of the past four centuries in the West resulting in significant changes in the conditions of religious belief. Whereas classical secularization theory had maintained that modernization (inevitably?) results in the decline of religion, Taylor presents a far more nuanced and subtle thesis that acknowledges that in many cases, religious expression continues even with high modernization, but that the nature of religious belief and the conditions within which it is manifest are transformed. What emerges, then, is a kind of secularism—even among those who remain religious. The heart of secularism, for Taylor, is expressed in the following question: "why was it virtually impossible not to believe in God in, say, 1500 in our Western society, while in 2000 many of us find this not only easy, but even inescapable?"[21] Taylor's contention is that, in Europe and North America, modernization has brought about a profound change in the conditions of belief so that what was once taken for granted is now contested.

Taylor suggests that we think of secularization in terms of three fundamental transformations.[22] First, there are changes in public institutions and practices, so that "whereas the political organization of all premodern societies was in some way connected to, based on, guaranteed by some faith in, or adherence to God, or some notion of ultimate reality, the modern Western state is free from this connection." The second change consists in the decline in the numbers of those who continue to embrace traditional religious beliefs and participate in traditional religious practices. This decline is evident much more in parts of Europe than in the United States. But the third transformation acknowledges that religion continues to be significant for many people in modern societies, including the United States, although the way in which people "are religious" changes. The shift here "consists, among other things, of a move from a

---

[20] A helpful summary and analysis of the debate is found in Rob Warner, *Secularization and Its Discontents* (New York: Continuum, 2010).
[21] Charles Taylor, *A Secular Age* (Cambridge, MA: Harvard University Press, 2007), 26.
[22] Ibid., 1–3.

society where belief in God is unchallenged and indeed unproblematic, to one in which it is understood to be one option among others, and frequently not the easiest to embrace." Secularization involves the change that "takes us from a society in which it was virtually impossible not to believe in God, to one in which faith, even for the staunchest believer, is one human possibility among others.... Belief in God is no longer axiomatic. There are alternatives."[23] In modern Western societies "belief in God, or in the transcendent in any form, is contested; it is an option among many; it is therefore fragile; for some people in some milieus, it is very difficult, even 'weird'. Five hundred years ago in Western civilization, this wasn't so."[24] Secularization in this sense can be observed to some extent in some modernizing societies in Asia as well, although the very different social and religious histories of Asian societies means that secularization there looks somewhat different than it does in Europe and North America.[25]

Taylor's comments echo a prominent theme in the later writings of sociologist Peter Berger, who maintains that "Modernity pluralizes the lifeworlds of individuals and consequently undermines all taken-for-granted certainties."[26] Modern urban centers in particular are characterized by increasing diversity in ethnicity, class, religions, lifestyles, and worldviews. Berger observes, "We do have a problem of belief, and it not only raises the question of why we should believe in God but why we should believe in *this* God. There are others, after all, and today they are made available in an unprecedented way through the religious supermarket of modern pluralism."[27]

Globalization

Secularization in this sense is related to globalization, at the heart of which is the awareness that local patterns are shaped in significant ways

---
[23] Ibid., 3.
[24] Charles Taylor, "Western Secularity," in *Rethinking Secularism*, ed. Craig Calhoun, Mark Juergensmeyer, and Jonathan Van Antwerpen (New York: Oxford University Press, 2011), 49.
[25] See Madsen, "Secularism, Religious Change, and Social Conflict in Asia," and Peter Van der Veer, "Smash Temples, Burn Books: Comparing Secularist Projects in India and China," in *Rethinking Secularism*, 248–269 and 270–279, respectively. Also helpful are Rajeev Bhargava, ed., *Secularism and Its Critics* (Oxford: Oxford University Press, 1998); and Ian Reader, "Secularisation, R.I.P.? Nonsense! The 'Rush Hour away from the Gods' and the Decline of Religion in Contemporary Japan," in *Journal of Religion in Japan* 1 (2012): 7–36.
[26] Peter Berger, "Reflections on the Sociology of Religion Today," in *Sociology of Religion* 62 (2001): 449.
[27] Peter Berger, *A Far Glory: The Quest for Faith in an Age of Credulity* (New York: Anchor, 1992), 146–147.

by developments elsewhere. Malcolm Waters characterizes globalization as "a social process in which the constraints of geography on economic, political, social and cultural arrangements recede, in which people become increasingly aware that they are receding, and in which people act accordingly."[28] Globalization is a process involving increased interrelatedness across traditional boundaries in multiple dimensions, including politics, economics, culture, and religion.

On one level, of course, global connections are not new. Trade, war, and migrations of people linked people throughout the ancient world, and since the European voyages of discovery in the fifteenth and sixteenth centuries, cultures around the globe have been increasingly interconnected. But the late twentieth century introduced something new. Nayan Chanda states, "The big differences that mark the globalization of the early years with that of the present are in the *velocity* with which products and ideas are transferred, the ever-growing *volume* of consumers and products and their *variety*, and the resultant increase in the *visibility* of the process."[29] Recent globalization has been driven by the staggering technological innovations in the computer and telecommunications industries.

Globalization affects religion in profound ways. Mark Juergensmeyer reminds us that religion has always been global, as "religious communities and traditions have always maintained permeable boundaries. They have moved, shifted, and interacted with one another around the globe.... Religion is global in that it is related to the global transportation of peoples, and of ideas."[30] Some religions in particular have moved intentionally across boundaries, becoming part of new cultural settings. Religions such as Christianity, Islam, and Buddhism are what Juergensmeyer calls transnational religions, or "religious traditions with universal pretensions and global ambitions." In these religions, "at the core of their faith is the notion that their religion is greater than any local group and cannot be confined to the cultural boundaries of any particular region."[31] Islam and Buddhism are today genuinely global religions, with large numbers of adherents in Europe and North America.

---

[28] Malcolm Waters, *Globalization*, 2nd ed. (New York: Routledge, 2001), 5.
[29] Nayan Chanda, *Bound Together: How Traders, Preachers, Adventurers, and Warriors Shaped Globalization* (New Haven, CT: Yale University Press, 2007), xiii (emphasis his).
[30] Mark Juergensmeyer, "Thinking Globally about Religion," in *The Oxford Handbook of Global Religions*, ed. Mark Juergensmeyer (New York: Oxford University Press, 2006), 4–5.
[31] Ibid., 7.

Religious Diversity

Given globalization, people today are aware of religious diversity and disagreement as never before, and this can foster a kind of skepticism or relativism about religious claims. Religious skepticism has been a significant force in the West since the sixteenth century, and it is today often reinforced through the modern research university with its worldwide influence. Thus, Berger speaks of the globalizing effects of the "faculty club culture," which involves the "internationalization of the Western intelligentsia, its values and ideologies." This class of international intellectuals "spreads its beliefs and values through the educational system, the legal system, various therapeutic institutions, think tanks, and at least some of the media of mass communication."[32] Influences from Western academia—including the methodologies and assumptions of higher criticism regarding the Bible—thus shape the educational elite in other parts of the world, thereby spreading secular values and assumptions.

Thus, the challenges to Christian faith today come not only from secular atheists but also from those who are deeply religious. Religious diversity and disagreement raise perplexing questions, both for followers of Jesus Christ and for those still considering the gospel message. With the many alternatives available today, why should one become or remain a Christian? Given the widespread disagreement among religions, can one reasonably suppose that one's own particular religious tradition is true and all others are false? Does not the fact of widespread disagreement undermine the plausibility of any particular claim to distinctive truth? Interreligious apologetics is concerned with challenges arising from the fact of religious diversity and disagreement. Two questions in particular are significant: (1) Given the many sophisticated alternative religious systems in our world today, why should we accept the claim that the core teachings of the Christian faith, and not those of any rival religion, are true? Why Jesus and not the Buddha? (2) Why should we insist that the Christian faith is uniquely true and salvific instead of affirming that all major religions are more or less equally acceptable human responses to the religious ultimate? Why not pluralism?[33]

---
[32] Peter Berger, "Four Faces of Global Culture," *National Interest* 49 (Fall 1997): 24–25.
[33] It is an encouraging development that recent works in apologetics are including discussions of religious diversity/religious pluralism in the list of issues addressed. See Feinberg, *Can You Believe It's True?* chapter 13; and Douglas Groothuis, *Christian Apologetics* (Downers Grove, IL: InterVarsity Press, 2011), 567–598.

INTERRELIGIOUS APOLOGETICS IN HISTORY

Christian apologetics is often perceived as a modern Western response to the various challenges posed by the European Enlightenment. Thus, it is claimed, while there may be a place for apologetics in the modern West, there is no place for it in encounters with other religions. Interreligious apologetics is at best a Western, theistic concern that is not shared by Asian religious traditions, and it is inappropriate in Christian witness among religious others.

But this common assumption is seriously misleading. Apologetics, understood as providing reasons for one's own religious commitments and raising questions about the beliefs of religious others, is not a modern innovation but can be traced back to the early church fathers and has been practiced by adherents of Asian religious traditions as well as Christians. During the second and third centuries, Christian apologists such as Justin Martyr, Claudius Apollinaris, Athenagoras, Tatian, Theophilus of Antioch, Clement of Alexandria, Tertullian, and Origen responded to critics with important defenses of Christian belief and practice. Some addressed attacks from pagan Greco-Roman thinkers; others tried to persuade Jews to accept the claims of the New Testament.[34]

Whereas during the first four centuries Christian apologists addressed issues arising from Judaism or the surrounding Greco-Roman world, by the eighth century attention was directed to challenges from Islam. With the rapid rise of Islam, Christians in Damascus and Baghdad were forced to respond to Islamic religious claims. John of Damascus (d. 749), who lived all his life among Muslims and even held an administrative post under the Umayyad caliphs, wrote the *Fount of Knowledge*, arguably the first systematic theology. But the book was also a "response to the commanding intellectual challenge of Islam" and was intended "to discredit the religious and intellectual claims of Islam in the eyes of inquiring Christians."[35] John also wrote *A Dialogue between a Saracen and a Christian*, a work explicitly devoted to apologetics in the Islamic context. Theodore Abu Qurrah (d. 830) wrote *God and the True Religion* in Arabic, a work that confronts the problem of choosing among Zoroastrian

---
[34] See Robert M. Grant, *Greek Apologists of the Second Century* (Philadelphia: Westminster, 1988); and Mark Edwards, Martin Goodman, and Simon Price, eds., *Apologetics in the Roman Empire* (Oxford: Oxford University Press, 1999).
[35] Sidney H. Griffith, *The Church in the Shadow of the Mosque: Christians and Muslims in the World of Islam* (Princeton, NJ: Princeton University Press, 2008), 42.

religion, Samaritan religion, Judaism, Christianity, Manichaeism, and Islam—all of which claim divine revelation. Abu Qurrah attempted to demonstrate "that Christianity presents the most plausible idea of God, exhibits the fullest understanding of man's actual religious needs, and prescribes what appear to be the most appropriate remedies."[36]

The introduction of Christianity to Asian cultures was regarded by Hindus, Muslims, and Buddhists as a direct threat to their teachings and ways of life. Proclamation of the Christian gospel often was met with hard-hitting intellectual responses by Hindus, Muslims, and Buddhists, who attempted to demonstrate the falsity or irrationality of Christian claims.[37]

One of the earliest accounts of a Christian engagement with Buddhism is found in the diaries of William of Rubruck, a Franciscan friar who reached the Mongol court in 1253. William gives us a fascinating look at a debate between a Buddhist and himself in 1254 before Mongke Khan, the grandson of the notorious Mongol ruler Genghis Khan. William and the Buddhist engaged in a vigorous exchange, with the Buddhist pressing hard on the problem of evil, an issue that Buddhists regard as devastating for monotheism. "If your God is as you say, why does he make the half of things evil?" When William insisted that all that proceeds from God is good, the Buddhist demanded, "Whence then comes evil?"[38]

Ippolito Desideri (d. 1733), an Italian Jesuit missionary to Tibet, made a careful study of Tibetan Buddhism and wrote in Tibetan a major work, *Inquiry into the Doctrines of Previous Lives and of Emptiness, Offered to Scholars of Tibet by the White Lama Called Ippolito*. He treated Buddhist teachings as serious philosophical claims and employed forms of argumentation accepted by the Buddhist community in raising questions about the truth of two central doctrines of Buddhism—teachings on rebirth and emptiness (*sunyata*). The distinguished scholar of Buddhism Donald Lopez calls this "the most sophisticated work ever written in the Tibetan language by a European," a book that "reveals

---

[36] Avery Dulles, *A History of Apologetics* (Philadelphia: Westminster, 1971), 74.
[37] See Richard Fox Young, *Resistant Hinduism: Sanskrit Sources on Anti-Christian Apologetics in Early Nineteenth Century India* (Vienna: Institut für Indologie der Universität Wien, 1981); R. F. Young and S. Jebanesan, *The Bible Trembled: The Hindu-Christian Controversies of Nineteenth Century Ceylon* (Vienna: Institut für Indologie der Universität Wien, 1995); Kenneth W. Jones, ed., *Religious Controversy in British India* (Albany: State University of New York Press, 1992); and Harold Coward, ed., *Hindu-Christian Dialogue: Perspectives and Encounters* (Maryknoll, NY: Orbis, 1989).
[38] Richard Fox Young, "*Deus Unus* or *Dei Plures Sunt*? The Function of Inclusivism in the Buddhist Defense of Mongol Folk Religion against William of Rubruck (1254)," *Journal of Ecumenical Studies* 26/1 (1989): 115.

a deep and nuanced understanding of Tibetan Buddhist doctrine and philosophy."[39] Desideri addressed Buddhist scholars respectfully "in their own language and on their own terms," for he saw in Tibetan Buddhism "a commitment both to rational philosophy and to ethical practice."[40]

In the sixteenth century another Jesuit missionary scholar, Matteo Ricci (d. 1610), journeyed to the imperial court in China and embarked upon a serious study of early Chinese religious and intellectual traditions.[41] Ricci mastered classical Chinese and became convinced that early Confucianism had been monotheistic and that Chinese Christians could adopt much of the Confucian terminology and conceptual categories, although he believed that Daoism and Buddhism were incompatible with Christian teachings. In 1603 Ricci published *On the True Meaning of the Lord of Heaven*, an impressive work that attempts to establish the existence of a personal Creator God and thus show the inadequacy of Daoist and Buddhist conceptions of religious ultimacy.[42] Ricci had a significant impact on the Chinese cultured elite, and a number of Confucian literati became Christians through his ministry.

Francis Xavier (d. 1552) introduced Christianity to Japan in 1549, and in the next decades the number of Christians grew dramatically. The Jesuit missionary presence provoked a vigorous response by Japanese Buddhists, who argued that Christianity not only was unreasonable but would be harmful for the Japanese people.[43] There were numerous debates between Christians and Japanese Buddhists during this time, as well as many polemical writings intended to demonstrate the falsity of Christianity and the superiority of Japanese religious traditions. Much later, when Protestant missionaries entered Japan in the nineteenth century, Buddhists launched a sharp anti-Christian campaign that criticized the idea of a personal Creator, the divine inspiration of the Bible and—due to the recent influence of German religious and scientific scholarship on

---

[39] Donald S. Lopez, *From Stone to Flesh: A Short History of the Buddha* (Chicago: University of Chicago Press, 2013), 108. See also Trent Pomplun, *Jesuit on the Top of the World: Ippolito Desideri's Mission to Tibet* (New York: Oxford University Press, 2010).
[40] Lopez, *From Stone to Flesh*, 110.
[41] See Andrew Ross, *A Vision Betrayed: The Jesuits in Japan and China, 1542–1742* (Maryknoll, NY: Orbis, 1994); Jonathan Spence, *The Memory Palace of Matteo Ricci* (New York: Viking, Penguin, 1984); and Liam Matthew Brockey, *Journey to the East: The Jesuit Mission to China, 1579–1724* (Cambridge, MA: Harvard University Press, 2007).
[42] Matteo Ricci, *The True Meaning of the Lord of Heaven*, trans. Douglas Lancashire and Peter Hu Kuo-chen (St. Louis: Institute of Jesuit Sources, 1985).
[43] See George Elison, *Deus Destroyed: The Image of Christianity in Early Modern Japan* (Cambridge, MA: Harvard University Press, 1973).

Japanese education—the alleged incompatibility of the biblical account of creation with Darwinian science.[44]

There were also significant debates among Asian religious traditions, as each tradition attempted to defend the truth of its own claims and to discredit the views of others through reason and argument. While it is true that some traditions within Hinduism, Buddhism, and Daoism minimize the role of reason in favor of direct, intuitive experiences of the religious ultimate that allegedly transcend reason, many others (such as Tibetan Buddhism, noted above) historically have made use of rigorous rational analysis in supporting religious claims. There were vigorous debates among competing schools within Hinduism and Buddhism, for example, as well as between adherents of religions such as Jainism, Hinduism, Buddhism, Daoism, and Confucianism. Speaking of Hinduism, Richard Fox Young observes,

> [P]roponents of the great *darsanas*, philosophical views or systems, endeavored to brace their own ideas or doctrines by exposing the fallacies of others. To cite only one instance, Sankara's commentary on the Brahmasutras refuted, in turn, each of the major theories, cosmological, metaphysical, soteriological, etc., to which other Hindu thinkers, Buddhists, Jains, and materialists subscribed. Apologetics was so much a part of classical works on religion and philosophy that a text without at least an adumbration of the standard criticisms of its rivals would surely seem incomplete.[45]

There were ongoing disputes over whether there are enduring substantial souls (Hindus and Jains said yes, Buddhists denied this) or whether a Creator God exists (some Hindus said yes, Jains and Buddhists denied this).[46]

---

[44] See Notto Thelle, *Buddhism and Christianity in Japan: From Conflict to Dialogue, 1854–1899* (Honolulu: University of Hawaii Press, 1987), chapter 2.
[45] Young, *Resistant Hinduism*, 13.
[46] For Buddhist critiques of the existence of God, see Parimal G. Patil, *Against a Hindu God: Buddhist Philosophy of Religion in India* (New York: Columbia University Press, 2009); Arvind Sharma, *The Philosophy of Religion: A Buddhist Perspective* (Delhi: Oxford University Press, 1995); and Gunapala Dharmasiri, *A Buddhist Critique of the Christian Concept of God* (Antioch, CA: Golden Leaves, 1988). For analysis of such critiques, see Paul Williams, "Aquinas Meets the Buddhists: Prolegomena to an Authentically Thomas-ist Basis for Dialogue," in *Aquinas in Dialogue: Thomas for the Twenty-First Century*, ed. Jim Fodor and Christian Bauerschmidt (Oxford: Blackwell, 2004), 87–117; and Keith Yandell and Harold Netland, *Buddhism: A Christian Exploration and Appraisal* (Downers Grove, IL: InterVarsity Press, 2009), 180–192.

INTERRELIGIOUS APOLOGETICS AND WORLDVIEW ANALYSIS

It is clear, then, that even prior to the modern era there was a long tradition of interreligious apologetics. This is hardly surprising, for religious leaders have characteristically understood their religious claims to be of great significance, and those within a particular tradition are expected to accept these teachings as true and to live accordingly.

While they include much more than merely doctrines, religions characteristically make far-reaching assertions about the nature of reality. Religions offer particular perspectives on what is of ultimate significance, the nature of the predicament confronting humankind, and the way to overcome this predicament and realize a much more desirable state. Religions hold that realization of the desired state—whether salvation or liberation or enlightenment—depends in part on accepting the central teachings of the religion as true and acting appropriately on them.

But the religions notoriously disagree about the nature of the religious ultimate, the diagnosis of the problem afflicting humankind, and the cure. Thus, it has traditionally been maintained that not all of the religions can be correct in their claims. Buddhists, for example, insist that there is no Creator God, whereas Muslims teach that the universe was created by God. Christians maintain that Jesus of Nazareth was God incarnate, fully God and fully man; Muslims deny this. Theravada Buddhists deny the ontological reality of an enduring soul, whereas Advaita Vedantin Hindus not only affirm the reality of the soul but hold that the soul is (somehow) to be identified with Brahman (whose existence Buddhists also reject). Not all of these claims can be true. It is accepted across religions that counterassertions from other traditions, which implicitly call into question one's own commitments, must be addressed and shown to be unwarranted.

But interreligious apologetics strikes many today as distasteful and inappropriate in our pluralistic world. For many today, interreligious encounters should be marked instead by the search for mutual understanding, respect, and common ground, objectives said to be incompatible with apologetics. There is a kind of orthodoxy among many in religious studies and interreligious dialogue that insists that mutual understanding is the primary objective of interreligious encounters, that criticism of the claims of others is inappropriate, and that actively defending one's own religious commitments and trying to persuade religious others to change their views must be rejected.

Paul Griffiths, an analytic philosopher and Christian theologian who is also an authority on Tibetan Buddhism, provides a trenchant critique of the view that apologetics has no place in interreligious dialogue.[47] He argues that, in certain circumstances, religious communities actually have an obligation to engage in interreligious apologetics. If intellectual leaders of a specific religious community believe that some or all of their own central teachings are incompatible with some claims made by another religious community, then they have an obligation to respond to the rival religious claims by attempting to show that they are unwarranted or that their own beliefs are not threatened by such claims.[48]

Griffiths maintains that there is both an epistemic and a moral component to this obligation.[49] Religious communities hold their own religious beliefs to be true, thus when a particular community is confronted by other claims challenging these beliefs, it has an epistemic duty to consider whether the challenge does make it improper (epistemically) for the community to continue believing as it does. Moreover, most religious traditions hold not only that their teachings are true but also that there is great salvific value in accepting and acting on these beliefs as true. If a religious community believes that humankind suffers from a general malady (sin, ignorance), that its central religious claims are true, and that accepting and acting appropriately upon these beliefs can bring about deliverance from the malady, then the community has an ethical obligation to share this good news with those outside the tradition, trying, in appropriate ways, to persuade them of the truth of the community's beliefs.

Similarly, Ninian Smart, an analytic philosopher and phenomenologist of religions who was one of the major figures in the development of religious studies in the twentieth century, took very seriously the issues of competing truth claims across religions. Smart understood religions as complex, multidimensional phenomena, with each religious tradition manifesting a particular worldview or set of core beliefs in terms of which it interprets humanity, the cosmos, and the religious ultimate. Smart called for "worldview analysis," by which he meant both the analysis

---

[47] Paul Griffiths, *An Apology for Apologetics: A Study in the Logic of Interreligious Dialogue* (Maryknoll, NY: Orbis, 1991).
[48] Ibid., 3.
[49] Ibid., 15–16.

of the ways beliefs function internally within a system and the relation between core beliefs of diverse worldviews. Smart contended that such analysis was incomplete unless it included assessment of the truth or rationality of different worldviews; thus, a primary task for "cross-cultural philosophy of religion" is "to clarify the criteria for determining the truth as between worldviews."[50] Although it should include much more than just philosophical inquiry, interreligious apologetics should be informed by what Smart calls cross-cultural philosophy of religion or worldview analysis.

SOME ISSUES IN INTERRELIGIOUS APOLOGETICS

The kind of worldview analysis that Smart advocated and that is presupposed by interreligious apologetics goes against three widely accepted assumptions, which we might call the relativism thesis, the incommensurability thesis, and the epistemic parity thesis. There are sophisticated versions of each thesis, and if any of these positions is sound, then interreligious apologetics is impossible.[51]

"Relativism" is a term referring to a group of perspectives that claims that truth and rationality must be understood relative to particular contexts, whether these be social, historical, linguistic, cultural, or religious contexts. There is no truth, and there are no principles for rationality that are somehow independent of particular contexts and, thus, can be used in a nonarbitrary manner for assessing two or more contexts. With respect to worldviews, this perspective maintains that truth and rationality norms are all internal to particular worldviews, and there are no worldview-independent criteria by which to evaluate the truth or rationality of competing worldviews. Interreligious apologetics is pointless, then, for there are no nonarbitrary criteria on the basis of which we might conclude that one religious perspective is more likely to be true than others.[52]

---

[50] Ninian Smart, "The Philosophy of Worldviews, or the Philosophy of Religion Transformed," in Thomas Dean, ed., *Religious Pluralism and Truth: Essays on Cross-Cultural Philosophy of Religion* (Albany: State University of New York Press, 1995), 24. See also idem, *Reasons and Faiths: An Investigation of Religious Discourse, Christian and Non-Christian* (London: Routledge & Kegan Paul, 1958); idem, "Soft Natural Theology," in Eugene Thomas Long, ed., *Prospects for Natural Theology: Studies in Philosophy and the History of Philosophy*, vol. 25 (Washington, D.C.: Catholic University of America Press, 1992), 198–206; and idem, *Worldviews: Crosscultural Explorations of Human Beliefs*, 2nd ed. (Englewood Cliffs: Prentice-Hall, 1995).
[51] John Feinberg provides a helpful discussion of a variety of issues associated with religious skepticism and relativism in *Can You Believe It's True?*, chapters 1–6.
[52] See Joseph Runzo, "Pluralism and Relativism," in Chad Meister, ed., *The Oxford Handbook of Religious Diversity* (New York: Oxford University Press, 2011), 62–76.

If religious relativism is true, then we should accept the consequences and simply abandon all talk of non–contextually restricted truth or rationality in religion; any judgments about truth or rationality would be simply the product of principles or criteria strictly internal to a particular religious worldview and thus would have no validity when applied to other worldviews. All we could say would be, "From within my particular worldview and based upon criteria within my worldview, I make the judgment that religion X is unsatisfactory." But it is unclear why anyone who does not already embrace a particular worldview should be bothered by this judgment. Although advocated as a way of respecting the integrity of the religions, religious relativism not only fails to take religions seriously on their own terms, but it results in intellectual suicide.

Interreligious apologetics also presupposes the falsity of what is sometimes called the incommensurability thesis. As applied to religions, the incommensurability thesis maintains that religions are discrete, self-contained, and comprehensive wholes that are so different from each other that they can be understood only from within particular religious systems. A non-Buddhist, for example, cannot really understand what Buddhism is about; thus, it is inappropriate for a non-Buddhist outsider to try to assess the truth or rationality of Buddhism. The incommensurability thesis, then, is a sophisticated form of relativism applied to understanding religious worldviews: while one can from within a particular religious worldview understand and speak meaningfully of the "truth" of that worldview, one who is not an insider to the worldview can neither really understand it nor make responsible judgments about its truth or reasonableness.

If either religions relativism or the incommensurability thesis is true, then interreligious apologetics is impossible. The issues here are complex, but there are good reasons for rejecting both theses.[53] Understanding is not a matter of all or nothing; it is a matter of degrees. There is no reason to suppose that an adherent of one religion (or of no religion) cannot attain a sufficiently accurate and deep understanding of another religious worldview to make responsible judgments about its truth. Nor is there

---

[53] See Harold Netland, *Encountering Religious Pluralism* (Downers Grove, IL: InterVarsity Press, 2001), 284–307; Keith Yandell, *Christianity and Philosophy* (Grand Rapids, MI: Eerdmans, 1984), 272–285; Smart, *Reasons and Faiths*; idem, "The Philosophy of Worldviews," in Eliot Deutsch, ed., *Culture and Modernity: East-West Philosophic Perspectives* (Honolulu: University of Hawaii Press, 1991); and Michael Peterson et al., *Reason and Religious Belief*, 5th ed. (New York: Oxford University Press, 2013), 337–340.

any good reason to hold that there are no criteria for assessing truth or rationality that apply across religious worldviews.

The epistemic parity thesis is the view that evidential and rational considerations relevant to religious belief are such that no particular religious tradition can be said to be rationally superior to others; the data are sufficiently ambiguous that the major religions enjoy more or less epistemic parity. Unlike relativism, this view acknowledges that there are truths and criteria for rational assessment of religions that are not arbitrary or strictly internal to particular frameworks, but it maintains that when applied to religious worldviews, the results are ambiguous. This is a popular perspective and has been defended by Robert McKim, who claims, "To say that the world is religiously ambiguous is to say that it is open to being read in various ways, both religious and secular, by intelligent, honest people. . . . In particular, disagreement in the area of religion suggests that this is an area in which the available evidence does not point clearly in one direction rather than another, and it suggests that the matters about which religions purport to speak are matters about which it is unclear what we ought to believe."[54] If McKim is correct, then interreligious apologetics should be abandoned and replaced by a modest skepticism or religious agnosticism.

But it is far from obvious that the epistemic parity thesis is the best way to understand implications of religious diversity and disagreement. Is it really the case that the proposition "God exists" has no greater evidential or rational support than its denial? Or is it really true that the central claims of Theravada Buddhism or Jainism have the same degree of rational support as those of orthodox Christianity? To the contrary, I think that there are good reasons for accepting theism rather than nontheistic worldviews, and for Christian theism in particular.[55]

Assuming the inadequacy of these three perspectives and that, in principle, interreligious apologetics could be a viable endeavor, what should it look like? What should we expect from interreligious apologetics? Should

---

[54] Robert McKim, *Religious Ambiguity and Religious Diversity* (New York: Oxford University Press, 2001), 25, 181–182. The notion of religious ambiguity is central to the work of John Hick, including his influential treatment of religious pluralism (John Hick, *Arguments for the Existence of God* [London: Macmillan, 1970]; and idem, *An Interpretation of Religion*, 2nd ed. [New Haven, CT: Yale University Press, 2004], chapters 5–13).

[55] The literature here is vast, but helpful introductions to the issues can be found in J. P. Moreland, Chad Meister, and Khaldoun A. Sweis, eds., *Debating Christian Theism* (New York: Oxford University Press, 2013); Keith Yandell, *Philosophy of Religion: A Contemporary Introduction* (London: Routledge, 1999); and William Lane Craig and J. P. Moreland, eds., *The Blackwell Companion to Natural Theology* (Oxford: Blackwell, 2009).

we try to present a conclusive case for Christian theism that definitively demonstrates that Christianity is the one true religion once and for all?[56]

Religious worldviews are complex and sophisticated, and questions about their truth or rationality very quickly become complicated. One way to approach matters is to focus on the epistemic credentials of a few particular beliefs central to certain religious worldviews. If, for example, it can be established that an eternal Creator God exists, this provides strong reasons for rejecting the claims of religions such as Theravada Buddhism, which are generally regarded as incompatible with theism. How then do we establish God's existence? Through sound deductive arguments? While classical theistic arguments should continue to be explored, in light of the prohibitively high expectations that accompany deductive theistic arguments[57] and the lack of consensus after centuries of debate, this is probably not the most fruitful approach. There is no reason to expect that an appropriate apologetic in contexts of religious diversity requires a simple algorithmic procedure for testing worldviews, or even that it should seek a conclusive deductive argument for theism. Nor should we suppose that all reasonable persons, when presented with the relevant evidence and arguments, will be readily convinced. Few issues of any real significance meet these expectations, and persuasion involves much more than simply compelling arguments.

A more promising approach is the cumulative case or inference to the best explanation argument, which maintains that a strong (but not conclusive) case for Christian theism can be established through the careful accumulation and analysis of a wide variety of data from various dimensions of our experience and the world.[58] While none of the phenomena, either individually or collectively, entails the truth of Christian theism, the argument claims that Christian theism provides a more plausible

---

[56] On the idea of Christianity as the true religion, see Robert B. Stewart, ed., *Can Only One Religion Be True? Paul Knitter and Harold Netland in Dialogue* (Minneapolis: Fortress, 2013).
[57] Because deductive arguments are intended to establish conclusively, or to entail, the truth of the conclusion, for a deductive argument for God's existence to be effective in apologetics, the following conditions must be met: (1) the argument form must be valid; (2) all its premises must be true; (3) the premises must be known to be true, or the apologist must be able to persuade the skeptic that they are true; (4) the skeptic must have greater confidence in the truth of the premises than in the truth of the conclusion (otherwise there is no point to the argument); and (5) there must be a clear and relevant connection between the premises and the conclusion. The conclusion is only as strong as the weakest premise, and reasonable doubt about a premise results in reasonable doubt about the conclusion.
[58] On cumulative case arguments, see Basil Mitchell, *The Justification of Religious Belief* (Oxford: Oxford University Press, 1981); William J. Abraham, "Cumulative Case Arguments for Christian Theism," in *The Rationality of Religious Belief: Essays in Honour of Basil Mitchell*, ed. William J. Abraham and Steven W. Holtzer (Oxford: Clarendon, 1989); and Paul Feinberg, "Cumulative Case Apologetics," in *Five Views on Apologetics*, 147–172.

explanation for the data than other alternatives. There is of course an inescapable measure of personal judgment in such arguments, but this does not mean that such judgments are necessarily arbitrary. As William Abraham puts it, "Personal judgment simply means the ability to weigh evidence without using some sort of formal calculus."[59]

Interreligious apologetics can also provide a critique of particular claims made by other perspectives. We might consider the claims that are based on certain kinds of introspective experiences in Hinduism, Buddhism, and Daoism. Is it really reasonable to accept as veridical purported experiences of Nirguna Brahman among Hindus? Or of Emptiness among Buddhists? Keith Yandell, among others, has persuasively argued that certain introspective enlightenment experiences at the heart of Advaita Vedanta Hinduism and Buddhism *cannot* be veridical.[60] If he is correct, this has significant implications for religious claims based on such experiences. Similarly, if the notion of *anattta* (no self) in classical Buddhism is indeed incoherent, as many argue, then this provides positive reason for rejecting a central tenet of many Buddhist traditions.[61] And so on.

Some questions addressed in interreligious apologetics will be similar to those dealt with traditionally in apologetics in the West. The questions of God's existence and of the problem of evil, for example, will be important with Buddhists and Jains as well as with secular agnostics and atheists. Questions about the deity of Jesus Christ are relevant for secular atheists, Muslims, Hindus, and Buddhists. But the manner in which these familiar issues are framed will be somewhat different in Muslim, Hindu, and Buddhist contexts, for critiques by these religious communities, and not just by secular atheists, will need to be taken seriously and given appropriate response.

Other issues take on special urgency in an interreligious context. Many religions have sacred authoritative texts; how is one to know which, if any, sacred scriptures are indeed divinely inspired?[62] Why accept the Bible as God's Word but not the Qur'an or the Gita? This question has received

---

[59] Abraham, "Cumulative Case Arguments for Christian Theism," 34.
[60] See Yandell, *Philosophy of Religion*, chapters 12–13; idem, *The Epistemology of Religious Experience* (New York: Cambridge University Press, 1993), chapters 8–9, 13–14.
[61] See Yandell, *Philosophy of Religion*, chapter 12; and Yandell and Netland, *Buddhism*, chapters 4–5.
[62] Frederick M. Denny and Rodney L. Taylor, eds., *The Holy Book in Comparative Perspective* (Columbia: University of South Carolina Press, 1985); John Bowker, *The Message and the Book: Sacred Texts of the World's Religions* (New Haven, CT: Yale University Press, 2011). See also Charles Taliaferro, "Recognizing Divine Revelation," in *God Is Good, God Is Great*, ed. William Lane Craig and Chad Meister (Downers Grove, IL: InterVarsity Press, 2009, 169–186.

surprisingly little attention by Christian apologists and theologians. Similarly, many religions include miracle claims.[63] Are they all to be accepted as true? If not, why should we accept the miracle claims in the Bible but not those in other religious texts? All kinds of claims are based on religious experiences. Do certain mystical states provide direct access to ultimate reality? If not, why not? How should we assess reports of religious experiences in the many religions? Are they all veridical? How do we distinguish those that are veridical from those that are not? And so on.

Those engaging in interreligious apologetics must take the time to study other religious traditions carefully, so that they understand other religious worldviews accurately and do not respond to simplistic caricatures. This demands rigorous study of the relevant materials, mastering the necessary languages for the study of authoritative texts, as well as producing ethnographic studies of religious communities and listening carefully to the perspectives of religious others. Responsible interreligious apologetics will be fair in its treatment of other religious worldviews, willingly acknowledging what is true and good in them even as it points out what is false or otherwise problematic. The objective is not to score easy points at the expense of the other but to understand the other's position adequately so that one can provide compelling reasons for considering what the Scriptures say about Jesus Christ.

Interreligious apologetics today occurs in a world marked by deep ethnic, cultural, and religious tensions that often erupt into acts of religious violence. Sadly, Christian evangelism and apologetics are often viewed as contributing to interreligious tensions. Discussions about the reasons for Christian faith do not occur in a historical or cultural vacuum; both sides of the encounter bring with them the accumulated heritage of the past as well as the potential for misunderstandings in the present. Deeply rooted attitudes shaped by centuries of past conflicts often obscure the case for the gospel. Those engaging in apologetics in contexts of religious and ethnic diversity need to be especially sensitive to potential misunderstandings and negative attitudes toward Christians based on past injustices. They must conduct themselves with genuine humility and grace, showing

---

[63] See Kenneth L. Woodward, *The Book of Miracles: The Meaning of the Miracle Stories in Christianity, Judaism, Buddhism, Hinduism, and Islam* (New York: Touchstone, 2000); David K. Clark, "Miracles in the World Religions," in *In Defense of Miracles*, ed. R. Douglas Geivett and Gary Habermas (Downers Grove, IL: InterVarsity Press, 1997), 199–213; and Graham H. Twelftree, ed., *The Cambridge Companion to Miracles* (Cambridge: Cambridge University Press, 2011), part 4, which has essays addressing miracles in non-Christian religions.

respect for the other. Furthermore, they must adopt culturally appropriate means of persuasion. Public debate and aggressive argumentation are more acceptable in some cultures than in others. In some cultures indirect means of communication and persuasion, making effective use of carefully framed questions, will be more effective than tight arguments.

Christian apologists must be especially sensitive to the place of symbolic power within interreligious encounters. The attempt to persuade religious others that they should change their fundamental beliefs and accept core Christian claims as true can easily be perceived as an inappropriate assertion of power, especially if the Christian is an American and thus associated with significant cultural, economic, political, or military frameworks of power. Any activity that is manipulative or coercive, or otherwise infringes upon the dignity of the other, must be rejected. Christians should be especially careful about apologetics encounters with religious communities that have suffered in the past at the hands of Christendom. Apologists in interreligious contexts must be not only skilled at defending the truth of the Christian message but also winsome and gracious, serving as peacemakers and instruments of reconciliation as appropriate. All of this makes effective interreligious apologetics particularly challenging. But when conducted by informed men and women who understand both the Christian message and the religious context in which they minister, and who are guided and empowered by the Holy Spirit, interreligious apologetics can help to reduce barriers to faith and enable those within other religious frameworks to see the truth of the Christian gospel.

16

Ethics from the Margins:
A Conversation with Womanist Thought

BRUCE L. FIELDS

> Come to Bethel, and transgress;
> to Gilgal, and multiply transgression;
> bring your sacrifices every morning,
> your tithes every three days;
> offer a sacrifice of thanksgiving of that which is leavened,
> and proclaim freewill offerings, publish them;
> for so you love to do, O people of Israel! (Amos 4:4–5)

I therefore, a prisoner for the Lord, urge you to walk in a manner worthy of the calling to which you have been called, with all humility and gentleness, with patience, bearing with one another in love, eager to maintain the unity of the Spirit in the bond of peace. (Ephesians 4:1–3)

Under the auspices of their covenantal relationship, the people of God were blessed in pervasive ways through communion with the one true God (Deut. 7:9–11; Heb. 9:13–15). This communion would be enhanced through the approach of purified hearts and with particular demonstrations of obedience as instructed by the revealed word of God. Relevant for this short reflection in Christian ethics is the possibility that in a given religious, sociocultural setting, much can appear to be in order, but such order may render hidden the matter of divided hearts toward God and the need for other elements of decay to be named, with accompanying correction. Charles Feinberg summarizes his study on the Amos text above:

> The words are meant to convey that everything was outwardly in order and done according to law, yet in the doing of them they were multiplying transgression. Why? Because at the same time they were steeped in all the debasing forms of idol worship. . . . Thus, though they were going through the rounds of worship, they were sinning because their hearts were not wholly unto the Lord.[1]

Christopher Wright makes a more immediate connection between the observance of mere ritual that Amos confronts and the ethical implications of such hypocrisy, as he comments that "the rampant social injustice made a blasphemous mockery of it."[2]

M. Daniel Carroll R., because he has engaged multiple readings of the book of Amos by members of various racial, ethnic, and gender groups, argues that, for many, "The book of Amos has always held an attraction for approaches seeking theological warrant for significant socio-political, economic, and cultural change."[3] Though it is not my primary concern in this essay, I would concur with his observation as it relates not only to Amos but also to the Old Testament prophetic writings in general. The prophetic writings often express God's demand that manifestations of an authentic relationship with him also incorporate concerns for sociopolitical and economic justice. One of the groups with whom Carroll interacts in his study is the Womanist ethical community, a community that focuses much attention on issues of justice.[4] It is this community I will draw into dialogue throughout this work.

Paul, as a New Testament voice, does not bring the dire warning to God's people that Amos delivers in the Old Testament, but he does establish a bridge between authentic faith (having the "calling") and the way members of the church of Jesus Christ were to "walk" (*peripatēsai*; Eph. 4:1). Out of the context of God's saving work in Christ, Paul exhorts believers to live every aspect of their lives identifying certain ideals

---
[1] Charles L. Feinberg, *The Minor Prophets* (1948; repr., Chicago, IL: Moody, 1990), 100.
[2] Christopher J. H. Wright, *Old Testament Ethics for the People of God* (Downers Grove, IL: InterVarsity Press, 2004), 374.
[3] M. Daniel Carroll R., *Amos: The Prophet and His Oracles* (Louisville: Westminster John Knox, 2002), 53.
[4] Ibid., 61–64.

of attitude and behavior. Peter O'Brien describes well the determinative nature of Ephesians 4:1 for what then follows in the rest of the epistle:

> Within Ephesians the apostle has already used the language of "walking" to describe the readers' former lifestyle in sin and death (2:1–2; cf. v. 3) and then, by contrast, in relation to the good works God has prepared for them to *walk* in (v. 10). Now, at the beginning of the exhortatory material in chapters 4–6, this significant motif appears again, as the readers are admonished to lead a life that is in conformity with the calling they have received, and it continues like a scarlet thread through the next two chapters (4:17; 5:2, 8, 15).[5]

In continuity with O'Brien's development of the relational significance of Ephesians 4:1, E. K. Simpson argues that, in light of what God has accomplished in Jesus Christ, believers should commune with one another "magnanimously and genially" as they walk in the pathway of their mutual heavenly journey.[6]

Because of who God is and what he has accomplished in Jesus Christ in particular, God's people are granted covenantal relationship with the one, true, and living God. As a result, they must commune with him with pure hearts and pure intentions, because this is only fitting to their status in the covenant forged by the incomprehensible grace of God. Certain theological realities provide the rationale for particular attitudes and behaviors. The additional blessing for believers is that the Lord provides power through the Holy Spirit to facilitate this "walk" (Eph. 5:18). It is the conjunction of relationships and behaviors assessed as appropriate that provides opportunities for explorations and evaluations in the realm of ethics.

SOME REFLECTIONS ON THE THEOLOGICAL ETHICS OF JOHN S. FEINBERG

John S. Feinberg, in conjunction with his brother, Paul, now deceased, has produced a substantive work on ethics to aid the church's formulation

---

[5] Peter T. O'Brien, *The Letter to the Ephesians* (Grand Rapids, MI: Eerdmans, 1999), 275.
[6] E. K. Simpson and F. F. Bruce, *The Epistles to the Ephesians and Colossians* (Grand Rapids, MI: Eerdmans, 1980), 89. See O'Brien's exploration of the relational implications of the "calling" (*Letter to the Ephesians*, 275–280).

of responses to contemporary challenges.[7] My intent is to facilitate a cross-pollination between his reflections on methodology and the specific area of "The Christian and the Secular State" (chapter 15), with some discussions within the realm of Womanist ethical formulation. Womanist thought engages much of the historical and sociocultural background of a setting that in turn generates the laws, policies, and practices of said setting. An essential element of any setting is that which can be identified as the state. My primary concern encompasses the church's relationship to political power when forms of injustice persist through the mechanism of sociopolitical structures. Feinberg demonstrates an awareness of these dynamics biblically and theologically, but Womanist thought shines a brighter light on arenas of normally hidden structures. These hidden structures remain hidden to some because of background influences such as race, ethnicity, gender, theological and philosophical stances, and socioeconomic class. These factors shape a network of life experiences that affect all of life, many times in ways of which we are unaware.[8]

My dialogue begins with a presentation of Feinberg's determinative conclusions on the matter of the Christian church and the secular state. These observations have much to contribute to any discussion on the matter of justice in a given sociocultural construct. I will then offer a critique from the perspective of "Womanist ethics" to probe more fully the call for greater particularity in Feinberg's argument. He offers solid biblical parameters for engaging the issues of the Christian church and the secular state with a concomitant concern for law and its implications. More questions can emerge, nevertheless, as a function of the perspective and the burdens demanding address, based on the experiential perspective of the formulator, i.e., Womanist. Finally, precautionary comments will flesh out some mutually beneficial emphases.

Feinberg shows noteworthy consistency in the development of his argument for a proper understanding of the relationship between the church and the secular state. In his methodological section (chapter 1), he states his conviction on the centrality of Scripture:

---

[7] John S. Feinberg and Paul D. Feinberg. *Ethics for a Brave New World*, 2nd ed. (Wheaton, IL: Crossway, 2010). Paul Feinberg passed away in February 2004.
[8] This networking of influential life experiences is comparable to the framework that Michael Emerson and Christian Smith refer to as a "racialized society": ". . . a society wherein race matters profoundly for differences in life experiences, life opportunities, and social relationships" (Michael O. Emerson and Christian Smith, *Divided by Faith: Evangelical Religion and the Problem of Race in America* [New York: Oxford University Press, 2000], 7).

Ethics from the Margins: A Conversation with Womanist Thought 357

We take our ethical norms from Scripture. Since we believe Scripture is God's word, we hold a form of divine command theory. Contrary to some divine command theories, we think God's commands are neither arbitrary nor irrational, because we think they stem from and reflect his nature.[9]

Feinberg identifies and discusses relevant Old Testament and New Testament passages.[10] From his exegetical work some fundamental conclusions are drawn informing his treatment of the church's relationship to the secular state. I will not identify all of them, but some observations dominate his study. First, Feinberg suggests that, from the perspective of the Old Testament, the people of Israel were never commanded to overthrow a foreign power once that foreign power had established control over the land. Second, God would be the climactic ruler over all things at his appointed time. The people of God should continually cultivate a trust in God that would at times require a quality of faith that empowered a conviction that God was accomplishing his will even under the occasional domination of foreign powers.[11] Jesus believed that human government has the right to demand certain responsibilities from its citizens, including his followers. However, Jesus did not absolutize the state (Matt. 22:15–20). Believers were to give both to the state (Caesar) what was due to the state and to God what was indeed due to God.[12] Feinberg further argues that apostolic teaching was in congruity with both Old Testament instruction and Jesus's teaching and example. A stream of submission would exist in the hearts and minds of believers because they could believe that God was ultimately in control. Third and finally, Feinberg insists, in light of the danger of granting the state an absolute status, that submission

> does not force one to ignore God-given tasks or divine principles of morality, nor does it remove the believer's right and responsibility to speak on the moral and spiritual issues confronting society.[13]

There are three further observations arising from Feinberg's exegetical and theological analyses that provide the opportunity for Womanist

---
[9] Feinberg and Feinberg, *Ethics for a Brave New World*, 37.
[10] Ibid., 700–707.
[11] Ibid., 701.
[12] Ibid., 704–705.
[13] Ibid., 707.

ethical inquiry. That is to say that, even from sound biblical and theological engagement, a pressing for definition and application can be forthcoming affected by the assumptions and concerns of the inquirers, in this case, Womanist ethicists.

First, beginning with an Old Testament framework, there is a need to reflect on the role and mission of the prophet. Even if there is agreement that, "The prophet's role was simply to call the king and his people back to righteousness,"[14] there may still be questions remaining on the meaning and proper manifestation of "righteousness." No doubt the nature of God and the guidance of law provide a framework for an understanding and implementation of righteousness. The situation deemed righteous could be somewhat conditional, i.e., conditioned on matters such as the spirituality of the agents and the situation of need existing at the time.

Second, what exactly constitutes the things "rendered to Caesar" and the things rendered to God? The resolution of this question is not easily achieved because of a network of influential considerations that come to bear on definitions and applications, sometimes temporarily hidden from inquirers. These influential considerations can be constructed by various theological and sociocultural factors.

Third, and finally, there is simply a lack of specific commands from Scripture to provide the inspired, authoritative resolution to every situation that may confront God's people in relation to the state. Feinberg notes this fact as he studies the biblical material. "For many of these issues, the only scriptural help will come inferentially from general biblical principles whose applications to concrete problems are not spelled out."[15] This is not to argue that there are some matters that simply cannot be addressed with scriptural authority because of a lack of direct instruction. It is to suggest, rather, that in the construction of biblical guidelines, the determination of what can be inferred legitimately from the biblical texts may not be shared by all inquirers. Disagreement can emerge with something as simple as the varying degrees of awareness existing in the church regarding what issues should be pursued, in what ways, and the timing of when they should be pursued. In the end, any offered analysis of an issue inextricably impacts any offered solution.

---

[14] Ibid., 701.
[15] Ibid., 707. A similar comment was made earlier, on the need to distinguish descriptive and prescriptive texts: "Unfortunately, this means there is little direct biblical instruction on many of the matters before us" (700).

REFLECTIONS FROM THE MARGINS:
WOMANIST THEOLOGICAL ETHICS

My heading, "Reflections from the Margins," is not intended to communicate that Womanist ethical thought is marginal in an absolute sense, i.e., in relationship to the entire theological ethics community.[16] Instead, I mean "marginal" in terms of the type of formulations that are done in Feinberg's evangelical community. The construction of an ethical system with what are regarded as foundational elements (Scripture, orthodox theological stances, etc.) has some strengths that I will identify below, but the sociocultural framework can facilitate a certain selectivity of who is engaged and who is not, and the accompanying rationale for each pathway. Some issues may not be deemed sufficiently critical. Womanist theological ethics is still a fresh arena for such study, analysis, and evaluation. For comparison and evaluation purposes, I will briefly discuss the nature of ethics and its purpose in Womanist thought. I will also discuss sources for Womanist theological ethics and how they can contribute to an ethical system in comparison to that represented by Feinberg. I am convinced, however, that Feinberg's ethical formulations can concurrently make contributions to Womanist thought. Some concluding thoughts will comprise the final part of this presentation.

The Nature and Purpose of Theological Ethics

Ethics, for Feinberg, encompasses both a theory of value and a theory of obligation. As such, Feinberg seeks to determine more emphatically what "one is morally obligated to do or refrain from doing."[17] He then applies his overall ethics theory to some extremely conflicted areas in

---

[16] Though having some common characteristics and objectives, Womanist thought is not one and the same with Feminist thought. Delores S. Williams, "Black Theology and Womanist Theology," in *The Cambridge Companion to Black Theology*, ed., Dwight N. Hopkins and Edward P. Antonio (New York: Cambridge University Press, 2012), 61–62, delineates the call for Womanist uniqueness: (1) "Black sociologists such as Elsa Barkley Brown criticized certain white feminists for not wanting to include black women's racial experience as women's experience and for not wanting to include race among women's issues" (61); (2) "Some black women had reservations about white feminist definitions of patriarchy as the primary cause of *all* the oppression *all* women experience. . . . Black women needed additional language to name and describe the ways of 'master and mistress' rule they had experienced over the years" (61); (3) The need for its own theological voice, using Ruether's "full-humanity of women": "Womanist theologians, in asserting 'the full humanity of women' are resisting and denying a negative idea about all black humanity that prevails in the USA even to this day, in addition to resisting the contention that women are not in the image of God" (62); (4) Womanist among poor women: "They tried to produce theology whose construction, vocabulary, and issues took seriously the everyday experience, language, and spirituality of women. This kind of struggle needed its own theological ideas, framework, and vocabulary" (62); (5) The emphasis on survival: "Black people's survival was at risk, but no Christian theology (feminist and black liberation theologies included) had made survival one of its primary issues" (62).

[17] Feinberg and Feinberg, *Ethics for a Brave New World*, 22.

contemporary society, admittedly from an evangelical perspective—to such issues as abortion, euthanasia, capital punishment, and genetic engineering, to name a few examples. By contrast, Womanist theological ethics does not ignore these kinds of issues but it differs from Feinberg in its fundamental attitude of deconstruction. This is to say, Womanist thought adopts a critical distancing from the ethical constructs of the dominant culture because of its potential for various forms of oppression that may be cloaked in the formation and implementation of such constructs.[18] Emilie Townes, for example, calls for some critical reflection on the search for "universal" principles to be applied to various communities. Womanist theological ethics takes the particularity of black women's existence as its starting point:

> Rather than argue for universals, womanist ethics begins with particularity. It does so with the knowledge that claims about universalities often evolve out of particular communities and ideologies that have been dominant, yet unacknowledged for being so. What is dominant is seen as the norm and therefore neutral.[19]

Germane to Womanist ethics is the concern, not only for justice, but for wholeness as well. Ethics must be applied in a way that impacts every facet of life, for the individual but also for the community. Wholeness of community bears intense attention. Individualism, ideally, is expressed within a healthy communal awareness, with appropriate responsibilities to be exercised. Womanist critical distancing facilitates the demand that the dominant white society cease placing "obligations and duties" on the ethical formulations and applications of the African-American community.[20]

As noted above, the purpose of theological ethics within a Womanist framework is not only to deconstruct theological and ethical systems of

---

[18] Assuming a connection between theology and ethics, Jacquelyn Grant, for example, calls for an investigation of the relationship between theological symbols and the oppression of women. See "A Womanist Christology," in *Walk Together Children: Black and Womanist Theologies, Church, and Theological Education*, ed. Dwight N. Hopkins and Linda E. Thomas (Eugene, OR: Cascade, 2010), 177.
[19] Emilie M. Townes, "Ethics as an Art of Doing the Work Our Souls Must Have," in *Womanist Theological Ethics: A Reader*, ed. Katie Geneva Cannon, Emilie M. Townes, and Angela D. Sims (Louisville: Westminster John Knox, 2011), 36–37. Traci C. West, *Disruptive Christian Ethics: When Racism and Women's Lives Matter* (Louisville: Westminster/John Knox, 2006), 7, can express the same concern in her criticism of Reinhold Niebuhr's concern for "universals": "For him, particular historical and empirical circumstances served as examples for ethical principles, exemplifying, for instance, a universal human proclivity toward pride and a 'will to power.'" West was not denying the validity of Niebuhr's concern. Her focus was on his lack of specificity on some issues that affected the African-American community.
[20] Townes, "Ethics as an Art of Doing the Work Our Souls Must Have," 37.

the dominant culture but also to develop an ethic of "wholeness": in the words of Katie Cannon, "Our bottom-line, common denominator is a passionate commitment to survival and wholeness of entire people, male and female."[21] This ethic must provide teaching on every area of life, including political and economic systems, while being sensitive to racial and ethnic perspectives. The call for this kind of sensitivity, as measured by members of the Womanist community, is needed because inherent power relationships between the dominant members of a capitalist system and people of color hinders the naming of inequities. Cannon incorporates the work of social theorist Oliver C. Cox to help foster an awareness of such potentially hidden power constructs.

Cox, for example, argues that "racism must be viewed as an inherent part of the basic political economy—the capitalist system."[22] Furthermore, the evils of the system were verified by the fact that it was under the auspices of this system that the labor power of slavery itself became an indispensable institution to Whites.[23] Cannon would then insist that the capitalist system and its institutions have perpetuated a lingering, destructive view of people of color: "The hatred and fear of people of color now has developed into a global system of ideological subjugation, justifying the legitimacy of control of Third World countries through massive debt, monopoly industry, and direct military imperialism."[24]

To a community that has experienced oppression in the spheres of race, class, and gender, awareness of the conforming power of attitudes, policies, and institutions of various sorts would be at an intense and suspicious level. Womanists make every effort to maintain a critical distance from the dominant sociocultural constructs in order to identify, name, and confront endemic manifestations of oppression. The humanity and health of the marginalized community are at stake. This community is made up not only of black females and males but of any minority population experiencing oppression in the dominant culture, with its standards and values held as normative and right. Such standards and values have been shaped often without contact and consultation with the marginalized. In addition, there is the need to process the fact, identified by some

---

[21] Katie Geneva Cannon, "Racism and Economics: The Perspective of Oliver C. Cox," in *Womanist Theological Ethics*, xvi.
[22] Ibid., 7.
[23] Ibid. In this work Cannon consults Cox's work, "The Modern Caste School of Race Relations," *Social Forces* 21 (1942): 218–226.
[24] Ibid., 21.

such as Malcolm X, that those who are in possession of the reins of power and influence do not simply divest themselves of power and influence.[25] Strategies for confronting and correcting systems of abusive power must be formulated and implemented. Such strategies cannot be forged easily by those who are enslaved to identity structures imposed by the dominant culture—structures that are often accompanied by the suppression of the type of hope that empowers a vision of what should and could be at the individual and community levels. Strategies must be formed for pervasive engagement in all spheres of life. Such spheres extend to the laws made and enforced in a given national or international setting. Such spheres requiring scrutiny and analysis include those of theology and ethics.

Womanists insist that the task of ethical formulation not only encompasses guidelines by which individuals and communities demonstrate similar values and behaviors among themselves; such formulations must also aid in identifying, confronting, and correcting people and human-constructed structures of dehumanization and injustice. A concomitant burden for Womanists engaged in ethical formulations is the incorporation and maintenance of their distinctive characteristics as African-American women. There is then a twofold focus to Womanist ethics. The first focus, as mentioned above, is deconstructing dominant structures of formulation and implementation to uncover implicit and explicit forms of oppression. The second focus is on the development of strategies for individual and communal survival and flourishing. The strategies are admittedly shaped from the perspective of African-American women. There are consultations with perspectives and system that are considered helpful, but there is a foundational commitment to Womanist interpretations of life experience.

Sources for Womanist Theological Ethics

Ethical reflections flow from interpretations of life experience, but these reflections also flow from biblical and theological systems often chosen from groups on the margins of the systems constructed by members of the dominant community. Biblical passages are incorporated, theological

---

[25] In one of his speeches, for example ("The Ballot or the Bullet," in *Malcolm X Speaks*, ed. George Breitman [New York: Grove, 1990], 38), Malcolm X speaks about the perspective of Black Nationalism: "Black people are fed up with the dillydallying, pussyfooting, compromising approach that we've been using toward getting our freedom. We want freedom *now*, but we're not going to get it saying 'We Shall Overcome.' We've got to fight until we overcome" (emphasis his).

Ethics from the Margins: A Conversation with Womanist Thought 363

categories are mined and reformulated, if need be, to provide deconstruction lenses and strategies for survival. Such sources may also provide another essential ingredient for deriving an effective ethical system, namely, inspiration. Inspiration drives the hope and motivation to overcome systems of oppression. It is one thing to name a power of oppression; it is another thing to decide to stand and confront it. It takes another level of inspiration to work to accomplish needed changes because of the pervasive effects of powers of opposition, often hidden from the uninformed. A certain frustration and hopelessness can set in when the marginalized uncover the depth of what must be accomplished for the formulation and implementation of a sensitized system of theology and ethics. Instruction and modeling must be drawn from consulted voices. Some examples of theological consultation, along with some biblical engagement, will be presented in the course of the rest of this presentation.

Structural considerations, justifying the Womanist theological and ethical project, abound in all discussions. Some representative offerings legitimating this structural focus will be informative. Marcia Riggs, for example, believes that lessons on processing the effects of racism can be learned from African-American women living during the 1800s. The Woman's Mutual Improvement Club, begun in 1895, was comprised of African-American women who "were determined not to allow class, education, profession, or religious affiliation as criteria for exclusion from a movement that was intrinsically concerned about alleviating race-gender-class oppression."[26] This kind of commitment is an important ingredient for contemporary African-American women who seek to facilitate the development of an effective ethical strategy to confront the negative social stratification that many African-American women have had to face. Riggs, after historical and contemporary social analyses, calls for a "mediating ethic" that is theologically affected:

> The vision of God's justice, intragroup social responsibility, and the logic of interstructured oppression deriving from the ethic of the black club women are the basis for a socioreligious mediating ethical process for black liberation that may truly be the way to overcome the depth of race-gender-class oppression.[27]

---
[26] Marcia Riggs, "What Do Nineteenth-Century Reformers Have to Say to Twentieth-Century Liberationists?" in *Womanist Theological Ethics*, 24.
[27] Ibid., 34.

Characteristics of Womanist ethical reflection are present in this statement: the awareness of God and his concern for justice, the critical recognition of the structural nature of oppression, and the burden for the well-being of the community. The overcoming of oppression is a multifaceted endeavor calling for theologically driven vision and motivation.[28]

Renita J. Weems engages another fundamental structural matter related to Womanist theological ethics, the question of biblical hermeneutics. Biblical and theological reflection requires engagement with numerous disciplines, including history, philosophy, sociology, and anthropology. Weems, however, expresses solidarity with the voices that may be marginalized in these related discussions, particularly in the realm of biblical interpretation, because, for whatever reason, or reasons, they are regarded as "other": "Ultimately, reading the Bible for liberation is grounded in the acknowledgement and respect for the otherness of those whose otherness is silenced and marginalized by those in power."[29] Not only should the biblical hermeneutics of the dominant culture be challenged, but she argues that the Bible itself must be confronted for some of its "misogynistic" tendencies.[30] There emerges a type of "canon within the canon" when she insists that the reader must be "ready to take a stand against those texts whose worldview runs counter to one's own vision of God's liberation activity in the world."[31] This "canon within the canon" is legitimated by what is regarded as a primary task of Womanist theology, that which contributes to authentic ethical reflection. According to Jacquelyn Grant, "we must read and hear the Bible and engage it within the context of our own experience. This is the only way that it can make sense to people who are oppressed."[32] An immediate question could be posed: is it then "experience" or the rest of

---

[28] Riggs envisions a role for the Black church, but it is a role exemplifying "renunciation," i.e., the giving up of a privileged position. The church must work in conjunction with the community "in coalitions within the community who do not share certain theological points of view" (ibid., 33). Riggs is not clear, however, on what are the nonnegotiables in terms of doctrinal confessions and acceptable courses of action for the church in light of said confessions.
[29] Renita J. Weems, "Re-Reading for Liberation: African American Women and the Bible," in *Womanist Theological Ethics*, 54.
[30] Concerning the narratives of Dinah (Genesis 34), Tamar (Genesis 38), the concubine of Judges 19, and the prostitute anointing the feet of Jesus in Luke 7:36–50, Weems argues that, in the Bible itself, there is insufficient condemnation of the oppressive conditions involved in these stories: "Their story of women's abuse and subjugation may be too costly to hold on to and too hopelessly misogynistic to try saving" (in *Womanist Theological Ethics*, 59).
[31] Ibid., 61.
[32] Jacquelyn Grant, "Womanist Theology: Black Women's Experience as a Source for Doing Theology, with Special Reference to Christology" in *Black Theology: A Documentary History, Volume Two: 1980–1992* (Maryknoll, NY: Orbis, 1993), 281.

the Canon that aids the liberative reader in the identification of "God's liberation activity in the world"?

These representative emphases on both structural oppression and biblical hermeneutics contribute to, and arise from, a theological construct. All aspects of what can be understood as "experience" contribute to the task of theological formulation and the derived system of ethics. It is beyond the scope of this essay to discuss all elements appropriate to the exposition of Womanist theological categories. I will survey only a few, with brief treatments of each. The danger in the brevity of my approach is that it might do an injustice to the sophistication of particular biblical and theological treatments by specific Womanist thinkers. My desire is to provide exposure to some slants reflected in some theological categories. This is not to suggest that all members of the Womanist community share the exact same slants. The emphases presented, however, do appear among some Womanist theologians and ethicists. I will offer brief comments in the areas of theology proper, Christology, humanity, and the church.

Theology Proper

The God of Womanist theology is a God of liberation and justice similar to what is often portrayed in Black theology.[33] Liberation and justice are required not only of individuals but also of nations within their sociopolitical systems. In much of Black theology the exodus has been embraced as a liberation paradigm. Womanist theologians and ethicists, however, call for more nuancing in the understanding of God and his work when referring to the exodus. Wholeness of existence is a matter of God's care, touching every area of life, encompassing the individual and the community with all the complexities of relationships that exist in interconnected ways. In order to accomplish this kind of wholistic view of God, Womanist theology insists that multiple traditions are to be consulted and allowed their voice in order to provide a challenge and correction to current thought. Josiah U. Young focuses on the meaning of the exodus and observes that Native American theologians, for example, do not interpret this event in the same way that many Black theologians and black churchpeople do.[34] Other voices can

---
[33] For an expanded treatment on the God of liberation in Black theology, see James H. Cone, *God of the Oppressed*, rev. ed. (Maryknoll, NY: Orbis, 1997).
[34] Josiah U. Young, "Survival and the Quality of Life: Notes on a 'Womanist Hermeneutic of Identification-Ascertainment'," in *Walk Together Children*, 52. Young cites the work of George E. Tinker concerning

have a sensitizing impact on the emerging Womanist view of God, and enhance the development of principles that should be demonstrated in all facets of life.

Christology

In terms of Christology, Jesus is a focal figure in Womanist theology. Some attention is drawn to the meaning and significance of Christ's deity, but a greater emphasis is on Jesus's capacity to identify with black women because of the common ground of his unjust suffering. Grant, for example, establishes this interconnectedness beginning with the experiences of slave women:

> For Christian Black women in the past, Jesus was their central frame of reference. They identified with Jesus because they believed that Jesus identifies with them. As Jesus was persecuted and made to suffer undeservedly, so were they. His suffering culminated in the crucifixion. Their crucifixion included rapes, and husbands being castrated (literally and metaphorically), babies begin sold, and other cruel and often murderous treatments. But Jesus' suffering was not the suffering of a mere human, for Jesus was understood to be God incarnate.[35]

Grant also affirms that many in the Black/Womanist community believe that the Jesus of history, a Jewish person experiencing oppression under Roman rule, is also the Christ, God incarnate.[36] Because Jesus was Jewish and suffered under Roman power as well as under Jewish religious opposition, Jesus was "Black."[37] He identifies with the lowly of his day and the lowly of today. In speaking of Jesus's solidarity with the marginalized, including African-American women, Grant exercises needed caution by

---

Native American reflections on the exodus in Tinker, *Spirit and Resistance: Political Theology and American Indian Liberation* (Minneapolis: Fortress, 2004), 90.

[35] Grant, "Womanist Theology: Black Women's Experience," 281.
[36] Ibid., 283.
[37] Ibid., 284. Here Grant is drawing from the work of James H. Cone, *God of the Oppressed* (New York: Seabury, 1975), 134. On the matter of the validity of the "blackness" of Jesus, Cone argues, "Of course, I realize that 'blackness' as a christological title may not be appropriate in the distant future or even in every human context in our present. This was no less true of the New Testament titles, such as 'Son of God' and 'Son of David,' and of various descriptions of Jesus throughout the Christian tradition. But the validity of any Christological title in any period of history is not decided by its universality but by this: whether in the particularity of its time it points to God's universal will to liberate particular oppressed people from inhumanity. This is exactly what blackness does in the contemporary social existence of America" (135). The universality of certain titles of Christ gain universal scope because they are found in the inspired Scriptures (2 Tim. 3:16), as in the case of "Son of God" and "Son of David."

disallowing any understanding of this solidarity that would lead to passivity. Rather, Jesus "inspires active hope in the struggle for resurrected, liberated existence."[38]

Anthropology

Womanists certainly view humans as image-bearers of God but, more importantly, as victims and victimizers. We, as humans, are capable of awe-inspiring demonstrations of generosity and sacrifice, while also demonstrating incomprehensible inhumanity to one another. Though the victimizers, the dehumanizers, are themselves dehumanized by their attitudes toward and oppression of other human beings, Womanist theological reflections and subsequent ethical principles give more attention to the inspiration of liberative activities by the victims against unjust suffering. M. Shawn Copeland offers a definition of "suffering": "As a working definition, I understand suffering as the disturbance of our inner tranquillity caused by physical, mental, emotional, and spiritual forces that we grasp as jeopardizing our lives, our very existence."[39] Womanist ethics derives its motivation and content from an insistence that human beings are agents of their own destiny. This is not to dismiss the will of God in the determination of said "destiny," but because we are his image-bearers, God's will for us is release from suffering, and image-bearing human agency demands active involvement in the fulfilment of God's will. Copeland is one of many voices in the Womanist theological community who adamantly insists that, both in the determination of God's will and in the development of the theological/ethical system to actualize said destiny, we are ultimately accountable only to ourselves.[40]

Ecclesiology

Many traditional confessions that have existed a long time within the Black church are also found in the Womanist theological community,

---
[38] Ibid., 285.
[39] M. Shawn Copeland, "'Wading through Many Sorrows': Toward a Theology of Suffering in a Womanist Perspective," in *Womanist Theological Ethics*, 136.
[40] Though Copeland is addressing the particular development of a theology of suffering, this self-accountability is evident: Copeland writes, "A theology of suffering in womanist perspective grows in the dark soil of the African-American religious tradition and is intimate with the root paradigms of African-American culture, in general, and African-American women's culture, in particular. Such a theology of suffering attends critically and carefully to the differentiated range of Black women's experiences. It holds itself accountable to Black women's self-understanding, self-judgment, and self-evaluation" (ibid., 152).

regardless of denominational affiliations. The church is precious, but it too houses much that is good and much that is problematic. The deconstruction project pervasive in Womanist theology is also applied to the church, specifically in the realm of perpetuating systems of oppression toward black women. Copeland calls for rejection of *aesthetics of submission* "through which the central images, symbols, metaphors, narrative interpretations, traditions, and rituals of Christian practice, explicitly and implicitly, coach tame women to surrender to patriarchal and kyriarchal prerogatives and privilege."[41] Agents of needed transformation within the church can identify pervasive structures of oppression even extending to the preaching of sermons that do not manifest critical sensitivities:

> If the sermon is to heal and to nourish imagination toward decolonization of mind and living, then its message must be rooted in exegetical and theological content that projects a reality worthy of black Christianity. Given the failure of the churches to take women seriously and given society's proclivity to reduce black women to body parts and to tolerate sexual and physical violence against women, the preacher's theological attitude toward personhood, toward the humanity of women, is of paramount concern.[42]

Copeland does offer some guidelines on how something so foundational to the liturgy of the Black church, namely the sermon, can be used as a channel of justice and needed transformation.[43]

This brief exposure to Womanist theological categories is intended only to provide some awareness of an emerging body of reflection that gives rise to ethical formulations. These are representative voices and perspectives. The volume of writings on Womanist thought comprises a world of thought in and of itself. My hope is that there has been sufficient material presented to pursue ways in which a representative of a more dominant movement, evangelicalism, can engage in a mutually beneficial conversation with representative members of the Womanist theological ethics community.

---

[41] M. Shawn Copeland, "Body, Representation, and Black Religious Discourse," in *Womanist Theological Ethics*, 109.
[42] Ibid., 109.
[43] See ibid., 110–112.

SUMMARY: MUTUAL INFORMING

Dr. John S. Feinberg is one of the most compassionate people I know. He has the gift of hearing the stories and burdens of colleagues and students, then offering comfort tempered with wisdom. I advance my view of him in this way because I find it difficult to treat him as merely a member of the "dominant theological/ethical community." Nevertheless, while I incorporate him as a dialogue partner with Womanist thought, I realize that I may be on the pathway of radical unfairness to him. As a participant in evangelical theological and ethical systemization accomplished by members of the dominant culture, often without consultation with such marginalized communities as Womanists, he can be addressed by, and can offer address to, Womanist thinkers.

Womanists, through their insistence on the validity of their particular experience and its subsequent effects on their theological/ethical reflections, would intensely challenge the seemingly normative aura generated by members of the dominant theological/ethical community. The particularity of African-American women's experience may move some members of the dominant evangelical community to dismiss the validity of observations and formulations arising from the Womanist community. The evangelical community would then miss the opportunity to learn of the systemic nature of racism, sexism, and classism.

Evangelicals have great sensitivity to manifestations of personal, or individual, sin. Feinberg demonstrates this great sensitivity to people and the various problems they face in life. It is another thing, however, to be moved by the systems that mold people, often in ways of which they are unaware, that can still perpetuate situations that humiliate and disrespect members of marginal communities. It is one thing to demonstrate sensitivity to the particular problems that people face in various arenas of life. It is another thing to write in such a way that reflects an awareness and concern for the sinful effects pervasive in systems, whether they are systems of government, philosophy, business policies, attitudes on race and ethnicity, and even biblical and theological studies.

Feinberg has done impressive work in apologetics, particularly in confronting elements of postmodern thought.[44] I focus here on postmodernism because, with its rejection of metanarratives and its insistence on

---

[44] Here I am assuming that Christian apologetics is the defense of the Christian worldview, or a defense of the Christian understanding of reality.

truth recognized only within a particular community, it shares a common thread with Womanist thought on the matter of the proper sphere of accountability for the determination of truth and its proper expression. Womanists insist that such recognition can take place only within the sphere of black women's experience and the representative Womanist community. Feinberg presents helpful strategies for effective conversation with participants in postmodern thought, showing the problematic results of certain postmodern ways of engaging truth. For example, Feinberg confronts postmodernists who feel that they need not be concerned with being "logical."[45] Before harmfully labeling Womanist theologians, against the backdrop of their autonomous accountability claims, as members of the dominant theological/ethical sphere, it would be wise to consider another related matter.

Distrust, claims of autonomy, anger, and resentment, can arise from any community that experiences humiliation and pain. From Womanist perspectives, it is erroneous to think that such experiences come only at the hands of insensitive individuals. This wrong thinking neglects needed analyses of networks that perpetuate such experiences. Why would a member, or members, of such a marginalized community listen to members of the dominant culture on anything? Such people may not even be aware of how their normal activities, even in disciplines associated with theological and ethical formulations, can keep forces of negative dominance in play. Unfortunately, Womanist thinkers can be crippled in the fulfilment of their intentions for their communities as the expression of their distrust for the dominant culture's theological/ethical contributions leads them to miss needed considerations. Though such distrust and disrespect exists on both sides, and may seem to be an insurmountable problem, these conditions actually generate a reason for hope.

The simple lesson for the dominant evangelical community is the willingness to listen in on various conversations. Argumentation, analyses of data, questions, etc., are not to be excluded in said conversations. Hearing the stories of Womanist thinkers is absolutely critical, if there is any desire to demonstrate authentic concern for the communities from which they have come. Hear the pain, hear the anger, know and begin to understand their resolution to survive and to name their own experiences. For

---

[45] See Feinberg's treatment, "Answers to Postmodern Skepticism (I)" (chapter 3) in *Can You Believe It's True: Christian Apologetics in a Modern and Postmodern Era* (Wheaton, IL: Crossway, 2013).

many in the dominant culture—including evangelicals—such encounters may not appear worthwhile. For anyone who would seriously entertain this point of view, it is wise to remember that members of the Womanist community do come from Bible-believing, gospel-believing churches, and if dominant-culture theological and ethical reflections are for the church, then there is the need to remember that the Black church is every bit as much the church as any other racial-ethnic group. A powerful demonstration of authenticity is simply listening first, before attempts are made at analysis and debate.

A statement by Emilie Townes on the development of an "ethic of justice" provides a platform for analyses of its meaning and hope for implementation. This is certainly a section where some of Feinberg's methodology for ethical formulation can propose some critical contributions:

> As a womanist ethic of justice emerges, it must be radically rooted in the truth-tradition and history of African-American life and witness. It cannot succumb to a praxeological framework in which all the women are white and all the Blacks are men. . . . An ethic of justice must be based on the community from which it emerges, for it can degenerate into flaccid ideology if it does not espouse a future vision that calls the community beyond itself into a wider and more inclusive circle. This circle is neither tight nor fixed.[46]

An overarching challenge for Womanist theological ethics is the identification of some needed particularities. Through questions and comments, I will probe the following: the particularity of authority in Womanist thought, the particularity of behavior, and the particularity of a vision for a community of justice.

Townes's statements assume some network of authority, or that which facilitates the emergence of models and standards. How else can one identify what "justice" is? How does the systematician separate the "'truth-tradition' . . . in African-American life and witness"? In the synthesis of an ethic of justice, how does one determine what to draw from the community from which such an ethic "must be based"? If the community is to move into a "wider and more inclusive circle," how are the bounds that make the community what it is to be recognized and maintained? At what point does the community become something other than what it

---
[46] Townes, "Ethics as an Art of Doing the Work Our Souls Must Have," 38.

was? If the circle of consultation is "neither tight nor fixed," then what defines it? Townes's convictions are oriented, not only for the benefit of African-American women with special application to theological ethicists, but also to the community. Authoritative standards must be named and implemented to aid each other in the meeting of community needs.

Feinberg is appropriately insistent that Scripture is the foundation for authority in ethical formulations. The Womanist community often emphasizes the determinative nature of "experience" as a standard of evaluation in biblical and theological analyses. Is this a stable standard, given that "experience" is by nature diverse? If experience must remain in focus, then the components of "experience" must be named and the foundational elements of such naming must gain some normative status. Such normative status is critical to achieving the recognition and propagation of standards embraced by the community for appropriate attitudes and behavior in the community.

It is the wholistic concern for the community that moves Womanist ethical constructs beyond the task of deconstructing dominant systems, but the issues confronting the community demand greater specificity. What defines an African-American and the nature of the African-American community, since self-definition is a right demanded by many in the Black/Womanist theological community? What is, or what should be the relationship between Black churches and the government at local and national levels? What of family relationships, particularly when a large percentage of our children are born out of wedlock? Related to this is the expression of the hopes and dreams of individual members in the families who are concurrently members of the larger community. Personal freedom, however conceived, and pursuit of dreams must be limited at times to give the time, attention, and resources required for children to grow and flourish. What of relationships with other minority groups who must live in the same political sphere? To what extent should there be allowances for compromise, and even sacrifices made, to benefit the larger political construct?

Admittedly, these are rambling questions. I offer them only to encourage specific responses on these matters because these areas, and others, affect the community at a foundational level.

What standards must be adopted to inspire and to provide a vision for the future? Vision is so important on many levels, but it is critical for the growth and development of young people. They must be able to affirm themselves and others as having great worth and potential despite the pervasive presence of racism and its possible effects. What would a "just" society look like? Can it be achieved in the present time-space continuum, or is there a supernaturally achieved climactic establishment of justice that only God can actualize? Is the answer somewhere in between? The authoritative structures of evaluation in Womanist formulations should offer answers.

The prophets were powerful voices calling individuals and power institutions to a conformity to God's will and ways. The church as God's people has a similar burden. The primary call of accountability is to Jesus Christ as Lord and Savior. Not far beyond this call is the command to "walk in a manner worthy of the calling to which you have been called" (Eph. 4:1). This walking may involve confronting individuals who violate God's standards for divine and human interaction, but it may also involve confrontation with laws, policies, and practices in a given sociocultural setting. This setting shapes individuals. When attempting to construct a prophetic, corrective structure, addressing God's people first, then the surrounding society, we need to hear each other in the community of Christian faith.

Those engaged in evangelical theological/ethical reflection must consider the realm of *experience* if they want to be heard by minority communities such as Womanist thinkers. Womanist thinkers, in turn, must consider the benefits derived from a consideration of authoritative structures that could provide needed light on "experience." We need each other to expand the pool of recognized particular violations of God's will and ways. We need constant biblical engagement to determine commonalities, embrace the transcendent perspective, prioritize problematic manifestation of human sin, and underscore the common hope of divine liberation that only the Lord himself can actualize.

Response by John Feinberg

On an occasion like the publication of this Festschrift, it is very tempting to offer a response to explain why I don't deserve this honor. However, I'm going to resist that temptation so that I can do something more important: thank those involved in making this project happen.

Before turning directly to that, I'd like to say just a word about my teaching ministry. Throughout the many years of teaching, I have been driven by various passions. But two in particular have been especially significant.

First, there is a strong passion for truth. This actually goes back to my childhood and upbringing. My parents made it very clear that we had to tell the truth. In some cases, we were told, lives actually depend on it. If people don't tell the truth, they cannot be depended on, and if that is so of everyone, society will collapse. The importance of telling the truth was underscored by my parents telling me that no matter what I might do wrong, I would make things enormously worse if I didn't tell the truth about it. This wasn't mere idle talk, as I learned that punishments varied not only in terms of what wrong I had done but also in terms of whether I told the truth about it or not.

With this strong emphasis on truth in general, I also learned the importance of Christian truth and the need for people to be grounded in the truth. Though some people act at times with seemingly little thought beforehand, much of the time people do what they are thinking. So, I concluded, it is important to help people know and understand the truth so that they can live it. During my years of teaching, then, it always seemed paramount that I teach what I understand to be biblical truth. Of course, one cannot make one's students agree with everything one teaches, but the thought that a student might graduate, get into ministry, teach something that is not true, and then be called on the carpet because of teaching error has always haunted me. If I could have taught that student something to keep him or her from error, then hopefully, such an unpleasant situation could have been avoided. I realize that such a singular focus on what is true does not always make one the most popular. It would be much easier to tell students that they are right, regardless of what views they espouse. A passion for truth has made it very difficult for me to sit quietly when I hear something I believe is not true.

On the other hand, my second great passion in teaching has been and still is a passion for students. As my dad would sometimes say, "What is a teacher without students?" Of course, teaching as a ministry means preparing people to serve the Lord, but I have always cared greatly about the people God has placed in my classroom. Before I started teaching, I probably was thinking mostly about the chance to help students understand and defend the great concepts of the faith. That would be exciting; and perhaps along the way, I would get to know a few students on a more personal level, but that wasn't my main focus. Much to my delight, the Lord has given me students who are not only extremely gifted intellectually but are also among the nicest people I have ever known. Over the years I have found myself caring not only about my students' intellectual growth but very much about them personally as well. I guess I hadn't expected to get so close to so many personally, but that is what has happened, and I am so very glad it did!

So, these two things, a passion for truth and a passion for my students, are what has driven my teaching ministry. Sadly, there have been times when my passion for the truth has gotten in the way of my passion for my students. Thankfully, over the past fifteen-plus years, I have done better at emphasizing the importance of truth without letting that get in the way of my strong, positive feelings for my students. This Festschrift tells me that everyone involved "got it." That is, perhaps better than I understood it along the way, the contributors saw that I cared enormously not only about truth, but about them as well!

Now let me turn to offer specific words of thanks. First and foremost, all of my praise for this honor must go to the Lord. No matter what the circumstances of our lives and ministries, no one can accomplish anything positive without God's hand in and on their life. That is especially so when you are called to minister in circumstances that, humanly speaking, seem to make it impossible to accomplish anything. I know that there would be nothing to celebrate about me if not for the Lord's involvement and enablement in my life! Beyond that, what the contributors have done in producing this Festschrift is an enormously gracious thing for them to do. And, I know who moved them to do it and enabled them to carry it out. It is not even close to overstatement for me to say that God's hand has been in my life and ministry and in their generous honor at every step along the way! So, first and foremost this event is a celebration of the Lord and his ability to turn even the most difficult of situations into something very positive.

Next, I must thank my wife, Pat. This Festschrift is a celebration of her as much as of me. All along the way, she has been there with all of her love and support. She has always been encouraging about anything I ever wanted to do. Even if I had doubts about my ability to complete or even start some ministry project, she never did. Pat told me some years ago that she would have preferred being a pastor's wife. But she has been a great professor's wife, and has always recognized and supported my calling both to teach and to preach. Even more, though, despite her illness, she has made it her mission never to let her disease get in the way of anything any family member wanted to do. And she never has! No one has ever heard even one word of complaint from her about her disease. And God has honored her desire that her disease wouldn't get in the way of ministry or anything else a family member wanted to do. In many respects, she is far more deserving of this honor than I could ever be!

Next, I thank the contributors to this Festschrift, which would have been incomplete without each of you as part of it! To my former and current colleagues, thank you so very much for your friendship, your encouragement, your enormous faith in me and grace to me, and your participation in this Festschrift. Additionally, in God's providence, I've been blessed to help train others who have gone into teaching ministry. To my former students, I am very proud of what you have done and are accomplishing. I am so thankful for your friendship and involvement in this project.

Last, but certainly not least, I must thank Crossway and everyone on staff there over the many years I've worked with them. My relationship with Crossway began thanks to Chuck Phelps, whom I met while in Portland at Western Seminary. A few years later, after both Chuck and I had "migrated" to Chicago, I got in touch with him again. By that time he was working for Crossway, and he strongly encouraged me to come to the press and meet Lane and Jan Dennis.

Making that connection with Crossway and the Dennis family was, I believe, providential. I have been enormously blessed to know the Dennis family and all those who have served in editorial for Crossway over the past thirty-plus years. What has developed beyond the friendships is a mutual bond of respect and trust between me and Crossway.

In all my dealings with Crossway, it has been clear that the paramount questions in regard to a book proposal are, what is the message of the book, who needs to hear this message, and how will it minister to them? Nothing is said about how much money might be made from the sale of the book. That is because the people at Crossway see it first and foremost as a ministry, not a business. That should be the approach of every Christian publisher and of every Christian author!

It is one thing, however, to say such things; it is another actually to conduct a publishing company in that way. But that is, in fact, the policy at Crossway. I know this because Crossway has published some works I've written that we knew at the outset wouldn't likely be "best sellers." But Crossway believed in the importance of the message and printed the books anyway. But that is not all. Something just as important is also true of Crossway. Put simply, no press I've ever worked with gives a book it publishes a "longer leash" than Crossway does. That is, if Crossway publishes your book, they will promote it and leave it in print a very long time so that everyone who could benefit from the book can have a reasonable chance to read it. That makes sense only if you publish a book for the sake of its message, not its sales potential.

As every academic knows, upon beginning your career it's exciting just to see something you wrote in print. But it is far more important for your work to have longevity. Who wants to invest five to ten years of their productive academic life to produce a work that gets published and then is out of print in twelve to sixteen months? It is better to have a publisher who believes in your message than to have a publisher with perhaps a more prestigious name who abandons your work as soon as sales decrease.

That's why Crossway is my publisher of first choice. But can a publisher that operates this way stay in business? Thankfully, the answer is that it not only can stay in business; it can thrive. Crossway sees book publishing as a ministry and a way to honor God. And, in response, God has seen to it that books and Bibles that are very good sellers come to Crossway. And, so, the press thrives.

So, have my own books published by Crossway gotten wide circulation and stayed in print a long time? Absolutely yes. In fact, of all the books I have published with Crossway, only one is out of print—and only after enjoying a very long print life. As to wide circulation, yes as well. In 2001 Crossway released my book *No One Like Him*. About a year or so later, I received an interesting and encouraging e-mail from a layperson in a church. He told me that his adult Sunday school class was using *No One Like Him* for their Bible study each Sunday. He said the class was enjoying it but had some questions about what they were reading. Would I be open to answering some of their questions?

Needless to say, I was happy to do so, but also very thankful that the book was being used that way in the local church. What absolutely floored me, however, is that the e-mail came from New Zealand! I immediately thought, "how would people so far away even know about this book, let alone purchase it?" Very quickly, I answered my own question: "There you go, that's the difference having a really good publisher makes!"

For all these reasons and so many more, I thank the Dennis family and everyone at Crossway for the relationship we've had over the years. And I am deeply honored by Crossway's publication of this Festschrift.

Chronological List of John Feinberg's Publications

Theologies and Evil. Washington, D.C.: University Press of America, 1979.

"Luther on Vocation: Some Problems in Interpretation and Application." *Fides et Historia* 12 (Fall 1979): 50–67.

"Review of David Wells' *The Search for Salvation*." *Eternity* 30 (November 1979): 50–52.

"Review of *Hearing and Doing*, edited by Kraay and Tol." *Journal of the Evangelical Theological Society* 23 (September 1980): 279–281.

"And the Atheist Shall Lie Down with the Calvinist: Atheism, Calvinism, and the Free Will Defence." *Trinity Journal* 1NS (Fall 1980): 142–152.

"Review of *Perspectives on Evangelical Theology*, edited by Kantzer and Gundry." *Themelios* 6 (April 1981): 30–31.

"Noncognitivism: Wittgenstein." In *Biblical Errancy: An Analysis of Its Philosophical Roots*. Edited by Norman Geisler. Grand Rapids, MI: Zondervan, 1981.

Tradition and Testament: Essays in Honor of Charles L. Feinberg. Edited by John S. Feinberg and Paul D. Feinberg. Chicago: Moody, 1981.

"Salvation in the Old Testament." In *Tradition and Testament: Essays in Honor of Charles L. Feinberg*. Chicago: Moody, 1981.

"Why Christians Should Support Israel." *Fundamentalist Journal* 1 (September 1982): 1017.

"Adultery without Sin?" *Fundamentalist Journal* 2 (March 1983): 18–21, 29.

"Truth, Meaning, and Inerrancy in Contemporary Evangelical Thought." *Journal of the Evangelical Theological Society* 26 (March 1983): 17–30.

"An Undershepherd or a Hireling?" *Fundamentalist Journal* 2 (October 1983): 16–18.

"Keeping the Pastorate in Perspective." *Fundamentalist Journal* 3 (June 1984): 31–33, 48.

"Truth: Relationship of Theories of Truth to Hermeneutics." In *Hermeneutics, Inerrancy, and the Bible*. Edited by Earl Radmacher and Robert Preus. Grand Rapids, MI: Zondervan, 1984.

"Doubt, Religious," "Evil, the Problem of," "Pain," "Theism," and "Theodicy." Dictionary articles in *Evangelical Dictionary of Theology*. Edited by Walter Elwell. Grand Rapids, MI: Baker, 1984.

Review of *Christian Theology*, Vol. 1, by Millard Erickson. *Trinity Journal* 5NS (Autumn, 1984): 208–217.

"God Ordains All Things." In *Predestination and Free Will*. Edited by Randall Basinger and David Basinger. Downers Grove, IL: Intervarsity Press, 1986.

Responses to other three participants in *Predestination and Free Will*. Edited by Randall Basinger and David Basinger. Downers Grove, IL: Intervarsity Press, 1986.

"I Peter 3:18–20, Ancient Mythology, and the Intermediate State." *Westminster Theological Journal* 48 (Fall, 1986): 303–336.

"Getting Smart about Smut." *Voices of Trinity Evangelical Divinity School* 13 (1987): 3–6.

"Divine Causality and Evil: Is There Anything Which God Does Not Do?" *Christian Scholar's Review* 16 (July 1987): 394–402.

Continuity and Discontinuity: Perspectives on the Relationship between the Old and New Testaments: Essays in Honor of S. Lewis Johnson, Jr. Edited by John S. Feinberg. Westchester, IL: Crossway, 1988. Reprinted 2000.

"Systems of Discontinuity." In *Continuity and Discontinuity: Perspectives on the Relationship between the Old and New Testaments: Essays in Honor of S. Lewis Johnson, Jr*. Edited by John S. Feinberg. Westchester, IL: Crossway, 1988.

"Rationality, Objectivity, and Doing Theology: Review and Critique of Wentzel Van Huysteen's *Theology and the Justification of Faith*." *Trinity Journal* 10NS (Fall 1989): 161–184.

"Process Theology." *Evangelical Review of Theology* 14/4 (October 1990): 291–334.

Ethics for a Brave New World. Coauthored with Paul D. Feinberg. Wheaton, IL: Crossway, 1993.

The Many Faces of Evil: Theological Systems and the Problems of Evil. Grand Rapids, MI: Zondervan, 1994.

Contemporary Theology 1: From Hegel to the Death of God Theologies. Institute of Theological Studies Course. Available, 1994.

"A Baby at Any Cost and by Any Means? The Morality of *In Vitro* Fertilization and Frozen Embryos." *Trinity Journal* 14.2 (Fall 1993).

"Literary Forms and Inspiration." In D. Brent Sandy and Ronald L. Giese, Jr., *Cracking Old Testament Codes* (Nashville: Broadman & Holman, 1995), 45–67.

"Arguing about the Rapture: Who Must Prove What and How?" In *When the Trumpet Sounds*. Edited by Thomas Ice and Timothy Demy. Eugene, OR: Harvest House, 1995.

"God, Freedom, and Evil in Calvinist Thinking." In *The Grace of God, the Bondage of the Will*, Vol. 2. Edited by Bruce Ware and Thomas Schreiner. Grand Rapids, MI: Baker, 1995.

"Sistemas de Discontinuidad" (primera de dos partes), *Kairos* 18 (Enero-Junio 1996): 7–26.

"Sistemas de Discontinuidad" (segundo de dos partes), *Kairos* 19 (Julio-Diciembre 1996): 7–34.

Deceived by God? A Journey through Suffering. Wheaton, IL: Crossway, 1997.

"The Incarnation of Jesus." In *In Defense of Miracles: Has God Acted in History?* Edited by Gary R. Habermas and R. Douglas Geivett. Downers Grove, IL: Intervarsity Press, 1997.

"A Theological Basis for Genetic Intervention." In *Genetic Ethics: Do the Ends Justify the Genes?* Edited by John F. Kilner, Rebecca D. Pentz, and Frank E. Young. Grand Rapids, MI: Eerdmans/Paternoster, 1997.

GENERAL EDITOR, FOUNDATIONS OF
EVANGELICAL THEOLOGY SERIES. WHEATON,
IL: CROSSWAY. TITLES IN PRINT:

Bruce Demarest, *The Cross and Salvation: The Doctrine of Salvation*, 1997.

John S. Feinberg, *No One Like Him: The Doctrine of God*, 2001.

David K. Clark, *To Know and Love God: Method for Theology*, 2003.

Graham A. Cole, *He Who Gives Life: The Doctrine of the Holy Spirit*, 2007.

Gregg R. Allison, *Sojourners and Strangers: The Doctrine of the Church*, 2012.

Contemporary Theology II: From Theology of Hope to Postmodernism. Institute of Theological Studies Course. Available, 1998.

"Euthanasia: An Overview." In *Suicide: A Christian Response*. Edited by Timothy J. Demy and Gary P. Stewart. Grand Rapids, MI: Kregel, 1998. Reprint of chapter 4 of *Ethics for a Brave New World*.

"New Dimensions in the Doctrine of God." In *New Dimensions in Evangelical Thought: Essays in Honor of Millard J. Erickson*. Edited by David S. Dockery. Downers Grove, IL: InterVarsity Press, 1998.

"Why I Still Believe in Christ, in Spite of Evil and Suffering." In *Why I Am a Christian*. Edited by Norman Geisler and Paul Hoffman. Grand Rapids, MI: Baker, 2001.

No One Like Him: The Doctrine of God. Foundations of Evangelical Theology Series. Wheaton, IL: Crossway, 2001.

The Many Faces of Evil: Theological Systems and the Problems of Evil. Rev. and expanded ed. Wheaton, IL: Crossway, 2004.

Where Is God? A Personal Story of Finding God in Grief and Suffering. Nashville: Broadman & Holman, 2004.

"A Journey in Suffering: Personal Reflections on the Religious Problem of Evil." In *Suffering and the Goodness of God*. Edited by Christopher W. Morgan and Robert A. Peterson. Wheaton, IL: Crossway, 2008.

Ethics for a Brave New World, 2nd ed., updated and expanded. Wheaton, IL: Crossway, 2010.

"Dispensationalism and Support for the State of Israel." In *The Land Cries Out*. Edited by Salim Munayer and Lisa Loden. Eugene, OR: Cascade, 2011.

"Postmodern Themes from Isaiah 53." In *The Gospel according to Isaiah 53*. Edited by Darrell L. Bock and Mitch Glaser. Grand Rapids, MI: Kregel, 2012.

Can You Believe It's True? Christian Apologetics in a Modern and Postmodern Era. Wheaton, IL: Crossway, 2013.

"Israel in the Land as an Eschatological Necessity?" In *The People, the Land, and the Future of Israel*. Edited by Darrell L. Bock and Mitch Glaser. Grand Rapids, MI: Kregel, 2014.

PUBLICATIONS IN PRESS

"Inerrancy of the Bible: Christianity," for a multivolume, multi-edited work entitled, *Encyclopedia of the Bible and Its Reception*. DeGruyter.

PUBLICATIONS IN PROCESS

The volume on Scripture for Crossway's Foundations of Evangelical Theology series

A revision and update for reprinting *Where Is God?* Kregel.

General Index

Abraham, William J., 349n58, 350
Abu Qurrah, Theodore, 340–341
Ackroyd, Peter R., 69
Acts, book of, on the word of God, 40
Aepinus, John, 20
Alden, Robert L., 73n17
Alexander, Joseph Addison, 72n14
Allison, Gregg R., 238n7, 253n23, 254n25, 255n26, 258n32
Ames, William, 51–52
apologetics: apologetics and Christian faith, 332–335; and the critique of particular claims made by other perspectives, 350; and the cumulative case or inference to the best explanation argument, 349–350; definition of, 332; and the epistemic parity thesis, 348; and globalization, 337–338; and the incommensurability thesis, 347; interreligious apologetics in history, 340–343; interreligious apologetics and worldview analysis, 344–346; and miracle claims, 351; and the multiple images of Jesus in the world today, 329–332; and reason, 333; and the relativism thesis, 346–347; and religious diversity, 339; and sacred authoritative texts, 350–351; and secularism, 336–337; and the study of religious traditions, 351; and the term "faith," 333; value of to Christian believers, 332n11
apostles, in the New Testament, 249, 249nn17–18
Apostles' Creed, 20; Rufinius's version of, 20n15
Aquinas, Thomas, 20, 98
Athanasius, 36
atheism, 335; secular atheism, 335
Athenagoras, 340
atonement, 22; doctrine of, 22n28
Audi, Robert, 96n13
Augustine, 23, 185
Austin, J. L., 186
Ayres, Lewis, 225n68

Baha'i, view of Jesus, 331
Baillie, Donald, 231–232
Bakhtin, Mikhail, on creative understanding, 41–43
Ballhorn, Egbert, 275–276
Balthasar, Hans Urs von, 20–21, 21n22
Barker, Gregory A., 330n5
Barrett, C. K., 87n54, 113n54

Barth, Karl, 64, 141, 180, 187, 312; Christocentricity of, 187; commentary of on the book of Romans, 64; on Scripture, 187n25
Basil of Caesarea, 18, 19, 30, 36, 238n7
Basinger, David, 114, 117; on "divine action patterns," 116, 125, 128, 129
Bauckham, Richard, 222n62
Bavinck, Herman, 35n84, 36–37
Beardsley, Monroe, on the "intentional fallacy," 53
Bebbington, David, 22
Begg, Christopher T., 69n5
Beilby, James, 103, 103n37, 106, 106n42; on Plantinga's epistemic model, 97–102, 97n16
Beker, J. C., 76
Bell, Richard H., 72n9
Benson, Bruce Ellis, 43n113
Berger, Peter, 337; on the "faculty club culture," 339
Bergmann, Michael, 193n20
Berofsky, Bernard, 199n35
Betti, Emilio, 56
Bhargava, Rajeev, 337n25
biblical theology: definition of, 60; foundational principles for, 61–63; and hermeneutics, 60–63; meanings of, 16
bioethics, 287–289; public situations where explicitly biblical justifications for positions on issues are warranted, 310–311. *See also* stem cell research
Black theology, 365
Bloesch, Donald, on Scripture, 179–180, 182, 185, 187
Blomberg, Craig, 55
Bockmühl, Klaus, 176n9
Boethius, 210; definition of "person," 217
Borg, Marcus J., 118, 120, 124, 130
Bowker, John, 350n62
Bray, Gerald, 313
Brockey, Liam Matthew, 342n41
Bromiley, Geoffrey, 187n25
Brown, Dan, 330
Brown, David, 232n86
Brown, Elsa Barkley, 359n16
Brown, Jeannine, 32
Brown, Raymond E., on *sensus plenior*, 59
Brueggemann, Walter, 270n33
Buber, Martin, 171, 175
Buddhism, 343, 350; denial of a Creator God, 344; as a global religion, 338; introspective experiences in, 350; minimization of the role

of reason, 343; response to the introduction of Christianity to Asian cultures, 341, 342–343; Theravada Buddhists' denial of an enduring soul, 344; as a transnational religion, 338; view of Jesus, 331
Bultmann, Rudolf, 176–177, 178
Burridge Richard A., 322n31; on imitating Jesus, 320, 320n27
Byrd, Randolph B., 127n42

Calvin, John, 30, 40, 72, 98; on the Apostles' Creed's "he descended into hell," 21–22; on Christ's mediatorial role as the incarnate one, 325, 325n36; on Scripture and the Holy Spirit, 256
Cannon, Katie Geneva, 161
canonicity, 45–46
Carlson, Bruce M., 302
Carroll, M. Daniel, on the book of Amos, 354
Casdorph, H. Richard, 125n38
Catechism of the Catholic Church, 23, 316n19
catholicity, 36, 46–50
Chalcedon Creed, 19
Chanda, Nayan, 338
Childs, Brevard, 78n29; on the "Canonical Approach" to Scripture, 64; on the Psalms, 264
Christianity: as a transnational religion, 338; view of Jesus, 344
church, the: the Holy Spirit as creator and sustainer of the unity of the church, 252–255; as the temple of the Holy Spirit, 251–252; the Word of God and the Spirit of God in the church of God, 255–258
Church of Jesus Christ of Latter-Day Saints. *See* Mormonism, view of Jesus
civil rights movement, 287
Clark, David K., 351n63
Clark, Kelly James, 332n13
Claudius Apollinaris, 340
Clayton, Charles, 55
Clement of Alexandria, 340
Clements, Ronald E., on the book of Deuteronomy, 78
Collins, C. John, 317
complementarianism, 314; level-one complementarianism, 314n8; level-two complementarianism, 314n8; level-three complementarianism, 314n8
Cone, James H., 365n33; on the "blackness" of Jesus, 366n37
Confucianism, 343
Connell, Martin F., 20n17
contextuality, 46
Cooper, David E., 106n43
Copeland, M. Shawn: on an "aesthetics of submission," 368; on a theology of suffering, 367, 367n40
Council of Constantinople (381), 19
Council of Nicaea (325), 18, 48
Cowan, Steve B., 332n12
Cox, Oliver C., 361
Cragg, Kenneth, 330n6
Craig, William L., 348n55; on kenotic Christology, 212, 213n35, 216–217, 217n51, 226, 227

Cranfield, C. E. B., 67n2, 74, 74n18, 76, 76n21, 77, 82, 82n33, 84n44
Crisp, Oliver D., 30n62; on kenotic Christology, 206n3, 208n14, 213, 213n34, 216, 216n48, 217, 217n52, 220n58, 224, 226n72, 231n84
Critique of Pure Reason, The (Kant), 174
Cunningham, William, 32n70
Cutrofello, Andrew, 31n66

Da Vinci Code, The (Dan Brown), 330
Dahl, Nils, 87, 87n53
Dalai Lama, 331
Daoism: introspective experiences in, 350; minimization of the role of reason, 343
Davis, Stephen T., 207, 208n9, 209, 209n15, 211, 216n46, 218n55
Dawkins, Richard, 335n18
Dead Sea Scrolls, 58; and the "Teacher of Righteousness," 58
deClaissé-Walford, Nancy L., 265
Denny, Frederick M., 250n62
Derrida, Jacques, 171
Descartes, René, 166, 170, 173; his *cogito, ergo sum* ("I think, therefore I am"), 173
Desideri, Ippolito, 341–342
Deuteronomy, book of: assumption in that Israel is a nation, 78; emphasis on walking in God's revealed ways in, 318n26
DeWeese, Garrett J., 212, 214n37, 223
DeYoung, James, 54–55
Dharmasiri, Gunapala, 343n46
Dialogue between a Saracen and a Christian, A (John of Damascus), 340
dispensation, 16
dispensationalism, 16–17
Docetism, 20
doctrinal development, 16; and the analytic/hermeneutic distinction, 29–32; and the identity of doctrines, 17; maximal doctrinal development, 18; minimal doctrinal development, 18; and the problem of continuity and discontinuity, 16, 18; the right development of doctrine as an entailment of the gospel of the triune God, 17. *See also* doctrinal development, criteria for discerning right doctrinal development; doctrinal development, as missiological improvisation; doctrinal development, recent evangelical accounts of; doctrinal development, theories of; doctrinal development, three case studies
doctrinal development, criteria for discerning right doctrinal development: canonicity, 45–46; catholicity, 46–50; contextuality, 46
doctrinal development, as missiological improvisation, 38–49, 44nn114–115; dialogization, 40–43; evangelization, 39–40; improvisation, 43–45
doctrinal development, recent evangelical accounts of, 32; Alister E. McGrath, 33–34; Malcolm B. Yarnell, III, 35–38; Peter Toon, 32–33
doctrinal development, theories of: the balanced dynamic approach: organic development (*ipse* identity), 28–29; the conservative approach: logical development (*idem* identity),

26–27; the liberal approach: "free radical" development (non-identity), 27–28
doctrinal development, three case studies: the deity of the Holy Spirit, 18–20; "he descended into hell," 20–22; the salvation of unbaptized infants, 22–24
doctrine, 17, 20n14, 24. *See also* doctrinal development; doctrine, levels of
doctrine, levels of: correspondence with the universal, translocal, and local manifestations of the church, 49n125; level 1, 19–20, 49; level 2, 22, 24, 49; level 3, 24, 49
dogma, 20, 20n14
dogmatics, 25
"Doing Bad in the Name of Good" symposium (February 23, 1994), 306n33
Donaldson, Terence L., 80
Dred Scott v. Sandford (1857), 305
dualism, modern Western, 169–171; evangelical theology and modern dualism, 179–183; the rise of modernity's destructive dualisms (Newton and Kant), 171–175; the separation of God's Word from history and text, 175–179; Spinoza's separation of the Word of God from Scripture, 171–172
Dulles, Avery, 180, 343
Dunn, James D. G., 67nn2–3, 77, 81n32, 84, 130
Durham, J. I., 318n25

Edgar, Brian, 313, 313n4
Edwards, Jonathan, 201
Edwards, Mark, 340n34
Einstein, Albert, 174, 187; criticism of Newton's view of the universe, 173n7
eisegesis, 55
Elison, George, 342n43
Emerson, Caryl, 42
Emerson, Michael O., 356n8
Emery, Gilles, 210n22, 218n54, 225n68
Erickson, Millard, 22
Essay on the Development of Christian Doctrine, An (Newman), 28
Evans, C. Stephen, 207, 208nn7–8, 208n10, 208n12, 208n16, 215n44, 221, 232, 233n90
explication, 30

Fackre, Gabriel, on Scripture, 180–181, 182, 187
faith: as belief in (*fiducia*), 333; as belief that (*fides* or *assensus*), 333; saving faith, 333–334
Fedler, Kyle D., 320n27
Fee, Gordon D., 226n70
Feenstra, Ronald J., 208n9, 208n13, 209–210, 209n16, 215n44, 232n85; on the incarnation, 233
Feinberg, Charles L., 354
Feinberg, John S., 112n53, 135, 138, 216n48, 263–264, 316, 332n12, 333n15, 339n33, 346n51, 372; on church and state, 355–358; confrontation with postmodern thought, 369–370, 370n45; critique of Plantinga's epistemic model, 91–92; on the doctrine of the Trinity, 151–152, 153, 154, 156. *See also* Feinberg, John S., on the problem of evil

Feinberg, John S., on the problem of evil, 189–190, 203–205; and creation and fall, 196–198; his "integrity of humanity" defense, 190–192; and the inevitability of evil, 198–203; questions for clarification, 192–195
Feinberg, Paul D., 349n58; on church and state, 355–358
Ferguson, Everett, 253
Fernandez, Andre F., on *sensus plenior*, 59
Fiddes, Paul S., 37, 38nn97–98
Firth, David, 265n11, 265n14
Flew, Antony, 115–116, 115n5, 115–116n7, 117, 125n35
Flint, Thomas P., 202, 203
Forrest, Peter, 214n38
Fount of Knowledge (John of Damascus), 340
Frame, John M., 184, 184n21
Francis Xavier, 342
functional kenotic Christology (FKC), 212–215; association with the term "Spirit-Christology," 214–215; Trinitarian implications of, 222–225; understanding of the "divine nature," 212; understanding of the incarnate Son's exercise or functional use of his divine attributes, 213–214; understanding of "person," 212–213

Gadamer, Hans-Georg, 34; on the "fusion of horizons," 31, 41
Galot, Jean, 23
Gandhi, Mahatma, 330–331
Gardner, Rex, 125n28
Gavrilyuk, Paul, 27n49
Gearhart, John, 303
George, Timothy, 37n95
globalization, 337–338
God: the central expression of the divine transcendence in the self-sufficiency of God, 139–142; a deductive argument for God's existence, 349n57; glorifying God, 150; glorification of, 146–147; glory of, 146–147; implications from the divine transcendent self-sufficiency of God for the glory of God, 142–145; love of, 147–149; obedience to, 149; the priority and centrality of the divine transcendence in the doctrine of God, 137–139; serving God, 149
God and the True Religion (Abu Qurrah), 340–341
Goldsworthy, Graeme, 63
Goodman, Martin, 340n70
Gowan, Donald E., 78n28
Grant, Jacquelyn, 360n18, 364; on Jesus's capacity to identify with black women, 366–367
Grant, Robert M., 340n34
Gregg, Stephen E., 330n5
Gregory of Nazianzus, 19n9, 228, 238n7
Gregory of Nyssa, 238n7; on the Psalms, 266, 267
Greiner, Clemens, 37n93
Griffith, Sidney H., 340
Griffiths, Paul, on apologetics, 345
Grogan, Geoffrey W., 72n14
Groothuis, Douglas, 339n33

Grudem, Wayne, 21, 21n21, 312–313
Guarino, Thomas G., 27

Habermas, Gary R., 114n2, 115–116n7, 121n25, 124–125n35, 126n38, 130n55
Hafemann, Scott, 67nn2–3
Haldane, Robert, 82
"hallelujah," in the New Testament, 281–283, 282n56
Harnack, Adolf von, 26, 32
Harris, Sam, 335n18
Harris, W. S., 127n42
Harrison, Everett, 77n25, 83n42
Harrower, Scott, 325n37
Hartshorne, Charles, 142, 142n14
Hasker, William, 209n14, 210n21, 220n57; on the will, 218n54
Hawthorne, Gerald F., 212, 214–215, 214n37, 215n43, 223, 227n78; on the incarnation, 230
Heidegger, Martin, 177
Heine, Ronald E., 266
Helm, Paul, 203n46, 208n13, 332n13
Henry, Carl F. H., 169, 181, 194, 198
hermeneutics, 51; and biblical theology, 60–63; early study of, 51–52; evangelicals and the principle of the single meaning of the text, 53–56; and New Criticism, 53; and Second Temple exegetical methods, 57–58; and *sensus plenior* interpretation, 59–60; and the theological interpretation of Scripture, 63–65
Herold, Eve, 303
Hick, John, 27, 348n54
Hinduism, 343, 350; Advaita Vedantin Hindus' view of the soul, 344; introspective experiences in, 350; minimization of the role of reason, 343; response to the introduction of Christianity to Asian cultures, 341; view of Jesus, 330
Hirsch, E. D., Jr., 64; on validity in interpretation, 55–56
Hitchens, Christopher, 335n18
Hodge, Charles: on Christ's mediatorial role as the incarnate one, 325, 325n36; on doctrinal development, 33
Hofius, Otfried, 68n3, 85n49, 87
Holmes, Stephen R., 312n1
Holy Spirit: baptism with the Holy Spirit and his missional impetus to expand the church, 241–243, 242n9; the church as the temple of the Holy Spirit, 251–252; as creator and sustainer of the unity of the church, 252–255; deity of, 18–20; distribution of spiritual gifts for the building up of the church by, 247–248; establishment of leaders for the church by, 248–250; procession of from both the Father and the Son, 237–238; the promise of the Holy Spirit, his descent on the day of Pentecost, and the inauguration of the church, 239–241; the relationship between the internal instigation of the Holy Spirit and a person's native cognitive faculties (relational causality), 104, 107; sending of by the Father and the Son together, 238–239; specific guidance of the early church by, 243–247; the Word of God and the Spirit of God in the church of God, 255–258; works of in the lives of individuals, 236–237
Hood, Jason B., 320n27
Hossfeld, Frank-Lothar, 273n38, 275–276, 276n46
Howard, David M., Jr., 264n9
Hubbard, Robert L., Jr., 55
Hübner, Hans, 85
Hultgren, Arland J., 67n3
Hume, David, 174
humility, 143–144
Hurty, Sarah, 54–55
Hyde, Daniel R., 22n26

image of God, 317–318
Inquiry into the Doctrines of Previous Lives and of Emptiness, Offered to Scholars of Tibet by the White Lama Called Ippolito (Desideri), 341–342
International Council on Biblical Inerrancy, "Articles of Affirmation and Denial," 54
International Theological Commission, 23n35
Islam, 350; as a global religion, 338; and non-Trinitarian monotheism, 160; response to the introduction of Christianity to Asian cultures, 341; as a transnational religion, 338; view of creation, 344; view of Jesus, 330, 344
Israel: "calling" of, 77; creation of to be a nation, not just a spiritual people, 77–78; special role of in God's plan of salvation (a "kingdom of priests"), 78; and territory (national land), 78
Issler, Klaus, 212, 214nn37–38, 223

Jacobson, Stephen Robert, 95n11
Jainism, 343, 350
Japan, the legend of Jesus's tomb in, 330
Jebanesan, S., 341n37
Jesus: acts of identified with *YHWH*, 222; descent of into hell, 20–22; humiliation of as *krypsis*, 229, 231, 233; miracles of in the Synoptic Gospels, 118–124; on the salvation of the Gentiles, 74–75; as the Word of God, 169, 187–188
Jewett, Robert, 67n2, 67–68n3, 82
John, Gospel of, emphasis of on the Father-Son relations, 224–225
John of Damascus, 340
Johnson, Keith E., 315–316, 316nn15–16, 322n31, 325n35
Jones, Kenneth W., 341n37
Journet, Charles, 83, 84
Judaism, and non-Trinitarian monotheism, 160
Juergensmeyer, Mark, 338
Justin Martyr, 340

Kant, Immanuel, 172, 173, 174–175; as "Newton's philosopher," 170
Kasemann, Ernst, 67n2
Keener, Craig S.: on contemporary miracles, 126–129; on miracles in the Synoptic Gospels, 119–120, 120n23, 125, 135n36

Keil, Carl Friedrich, 73
Kelly, J. N. D., 20
kenotic Christology, 206–207; recent evangelical philosophers and theologians who have rehabilitated some points of nineteenth-century kenoticism, 207n4. *See also* functional kenotic Christology (FKC); kenotic Christology, critical reflections on; ontological kenotic Christology (OKC)
kenotic Christology, critical reflections on, 234; evangelical kenoticism, the Chalcedonian Definition, and the burden of proof, 215–216; evangelical kenoticism and the humanity of Christ, 225–234; evangelical kenoticism and the redefinition of "nature" and "person," 216–219
Kidner, Derek, 72–73, 72n14
Kilner, John F., 293n11, 297n18, 298n19, 301n20, 306n30
King, Martin Luther, Jr., 287
Klann, Richard, 20n18
Klein, William W., 55
Knox, D. Broughton, 313, 313n5; on the Trinity, 313–316, 314n6, 315n10, 324
Kodell, Jerome, 40n105
kol (Hebrew: "all"), in the Psalms, 274n19, 280, 280n53
Köstenberger, Andreas J., 225n67
Krauth, C. P., 23n36
Kselman, John S., 275n42
Kuhn, Thomas, on "normal science," 33

Lanza, Robert, 290–291
Larmer, Robert A., 126n38
Lash, Nicholas, 46n119
Lauber, David, 21n19
Leibniz, Gottfried Wilhelm von, Principle of the Identity of Indiscernibles of, 164, 165
Letow, Brian, 202n45
Levenson, Jon D., 277, 278
Lewis, C. S., 109–110, 140, 147, 148, 149
Licona, Michael, 121–122n27
Longenecker, Bruce W., 79n30
Lopez, Donald S., 341–342
Lord's Supper, and the imitation of Christ, 323n33
Luther, Martin, 20, 64, 72, 267n25; on Scripture and the Holy Spirit, 255–256, 256n27

Mackie, J. L., 115, 117, 125
Macleod, Donald, 220, 229
Macquarrie, John, 206n2
Madsen, Richard, 337n25
Malcolm X, 362; on Black Nationalism, 362n25
Marcion, 57
Marrow of Theology, The (Ames), 51–52
Marsh, John, 261
Marshall, I. Howard, 123
Maxwell, J. Clerk, 174, 187
Mays, James L., 265
McCall, Thomas H., 192n16, 211n26
McCann, J. C., 265, 265n14
McCartney, Dan, 55
McCormack, Bruce L., 187n25
McGrath, Alister, 16n3, 38, 325n37; on doctrinal development, 33–34, 34n82

McKim, Robert, 348
McNicol, Allan J., 70, 89, 89nn55–56; on the "key texts" of the Old Testament prophets concerning the salvation of the nations, 70n7
Meier, John P., 118–119
Meister, Chad, 348n55
Merrill, Eugene, 72
Miller, John B. F., 245–246, 246
miracles, 114–115; definition of "miracle," 114; divine action patterns in contemporary miracle claims, 125–130, 130–131; divine action patterns in the Synoptic Gospel miracles, 118–124, 130; the philosophical requirements for, 115–118; recent critical scholars who hold that Jesus thought that his miracles confirmed both his person and his message, 123n29; the resurrection of Jesus, 115, 117, 130
mission, 258–262; and dialogization, 40–43; and evangelization, 39–40; and improvisation, 43–45
Mitchell, Basil, 349n58
Models of Revelation (Dulles), 180
Mohler, Al, 19n13
Molinism, 203
Moltmann, Jürgen, 181, 313; on the Trinity, 315–316, 324
Moo, Douglas, 67, 77n23, 81n32, 82n39, 83n40, 84, 85–86
Moreland, J. P., 212, 213n25, 216–217, 217n51, 226, 227, 348n55; on reason, 333
Mormonism, view of Jesus, 331
Morris, Thomas V., 109n48, 195n27
Morrison, John Douglas, 170, 188n26
Morson, Gary Saul, 42
Moser, Paul K., 93n7, 106–107n44
Motyer, J. Alec, 72n14, 73
Muilenburg, John, 318
Mulder, Dwayne H., 93n7
Muller, Richard A., 204n48, 217n53
Murphy, Timothy F., 288
Murray, Andrew, on humility, 144
Murray, John, 82, 83

Nägelsbach, Carl Wilhelm Eduard, 72n14
Neill, Stephen, 124, 124n34, 131
Netland, Harold, 343n46, 347n53, 350n61
New Criticism, 53, 57; and the intentional fallacy, 53
New Hermeneutic, 57
Newman, John Henry, 28–29; criteria for judging doctrinal developments, 29n59
Newton, Isaac, 170, 172, 173–174
Nicene Creed, 19n12; and the *homoousion* term, 188
Nicene-Constantinopolitan Creed, 19, 19n12, 237
Niebuhr, Reinhold, 360n19
Noth, Martin, 78

O'Brien, Peter, 355
Ockhamism, 203
O'Donovan, Oliver M. T., 313, 325–326
O'Dowd, Ryan P., 265n19
oikonomia (Greek: "dispensation"), 16

Oldham, Steven L., 34n80
Oliver, Simon, 31n66
Olson, Roger, 183
On the True Meaning of the Lord of Heaven (Ricci), 342
ontological kenotic Christology (OKC), 207–212; overall view of, 208; perceived strengths of, 208; relationship of to orthodoxy, 207–208; Trinitarian implications of, 220–222; understanding of Christ's divine nature, 208–210; understanding of "person," 210–212
O'Rahilly, Ronan R., 302
Origen, 340
Orr, James, 32
Osborne, Grant, 282, 282n56
Otte, Richard, 204

Packer, J. I., 181, 184n21; on the image of God, 317–318
Pannenberg, Wolfhart, 20, 236–237
Parrinder, Geoffrey, 330n6
Pascal, Blaise, 109
Patil, Parimal G., 343n46
Pelikan, Jaroslav, 15, 17n6, 18, 25n40; on dogma, 20n14
Peterson, Michael, 347n53
Philastrius of Brescia, 20n17
Philipkoski, Kristen, 307
Philosophia Christi, on "Ramified Natural Theology," 125n35
philosophy: analytic philosophy, 30; Continental philosophy, 30
Pinnock, Clark H., on Scripture, 181–183, 187; and "the Scripture Principle," 182
Piper, John, 76n20
Pitstick, Alyssa Lyra, 21n19
Plantinga, Alvin, 190, 209n14; Free Will Defense of, 204–205. *See also* Plantinga, Alvin, epistemic model of
Plantinga, Alvin, epistemic model of, 91–94, 95, 96n14, 100n25, 105–106, 107; distinction between the A/C and the extended A/C models, 98–102; distinction between the typical believer and the paradigmatic believer, 97–102; and indexing a person's depth of ingression, 105–106; notion of warrant, 92, 93, 97–98, 99, 101–102, 106; and the variability of belief and affective evidence, 97–102
Plantinga, Cornelius, Jr., 210–211, 210nn20–21, 212
Pneumatomachians (lit., "enemies of the Spirit"), 18–19
Pöhler, Rolf J., 25n44, 28n54
Pollock, John L., 95
Pope Innocent III, 23n33
Porter, Steven L., 94n8
postmodernism, 369–370
Power, William L., 111n52
Prado, C. G., 30
Price, Simon, 340n34
Provenzola, Thomas A., epistemic model of, 93–94, 112–113; and epistemic charity, 111–112; and the eucatastrophe of the implicit, 108–112; and evidence and the affective capacities, 102–108; and rationalization, justification, and truth, 94–97
Psalms, book of: Book III, 270; Book IV, 271; Book V, 271; Books I–III, 270; Books IV–V, 270, 271, 273; a canonical approach to, 264–266, 264n8; God's faithfulness in Books IV–V, 271–274; God's faithfulness and questions in the Psalms, 267–270; as God's Torah, 264–265, 271; Hebrew designation for (*tehillim*, "praises"), 271; the problem of God's fidelity in the Psalms, 267; the seam of Books II and III, 269. *See also* Psalms, book of, the concluding hallelujah psalms (Psalms 146–150)
Psalms, book of, the concluding hallelujah psalms (Psalms 146–150), 274–281, 283–284; creation and kingship in, 278; definition of the people in whom Yahweh delights in, 278; images of God's mighty faithfulness in, 275; lack of mention of the future of David in, 280–281; lack of mention of the temple in, 277–278; Psalm 146 as a bookend with Psalms 1–2, 275–277; *telos* of the book of Psalms in, 276–277

Quinn, Philip L., critique of Plantinga's epistemic model, 92

Rabbi Eliezer ben Jose, 58
Rabbi Hillel, 58
Rabbi Ishmael ben Elisha, 58
Rahner, Karl, 312; Rahner's Rule, 325n37
Rainey, Robert, 32n70
Ramm, Bernard, 54
Ramsey, Paul, 201, 287
Rauser, Randal, 325n37
Rea, Michael C., 30n62
Reader, Ian, 337n25
reason, 333; effects of sin on, 333n15
Reeves, Rodney, 321n30
relativism, 346–347
Revelation, book of: allusions in to the Old Testament, 89; the Hebrew expression "hallelujah" in, 281–283; the salvation of the nations in, 88–90
Ricci, Matteo, 342
Riggs, Marcia, 363; on the Black church's role of "renunciation," 364n28; on a "mediating ethic," 363
Risser, James, 40n104
Ross, Andrew, 342n41
Runzo, Joseph, 346n52
Ryle, J. C., 52

Sakdapolrak, Patrick, 37n93
salvation, of Israel and the nations, 66; the issue, 67–68; the overall eschatological salvation history pattern, 74; the salvation of the nations in the book of Revelation, 88–90; the teaching of the Gospels on, 74–75. *See also* salvation, of Israel and the nations, the Old Testament teaching on; salvation, of Israel and the nations, Paul's teaching in Romans 9–11 on

salvation, of Israel and the nations, the Old Testament teaching on: the dominant theme of the salvation of the nations when Israel is restored, 68–70, 71; the minor theme of the salvation of the nations when Israel is in disobedience, 70–75

salvation, of Israel and the nations, Paul's teaching in Romans 9–11 on, 67, 75; "all Israel," 68, 71, 81, 85, 85n49, 86; the future blessing of the world, 81–85; Israel's rejection and hardening have not voided the "covenants" and "promises," 76–78; the nature of Israel's salvation, 85–88; the present salvation of Gentiles is not the final fulfillment of the prophesied salvation of the Gentiles, 79–80

Sanders, Fred, 17–18n7, 48–49n123, 325n37

Sanneh, Lamin, 40n103

Schaff, Philip, 45

Schleiermacher, F. D. E., 175–176, 178, 185, 312

science: "normal science," 33; and paradigm shifts, 33

Scobie, Charles H. H., 318n24

Scripture: and the adequacy of human language, 183–185; and "bibliological adoptianism," 179–183; the centrality of the divine authority of, 169; and God as a human language user, 184–185; as God's illocutionary "speech act," 185–187; as God's written Word to us, 187–188; and the "identity thesis," 179; inerrancy of, 169; inspiration of, 169; resources for renewed affirmation of Scripture's divine authority, 183–187; the Word of God and the Spirit of God in the church of God, 255–256

Searle, John, 186

Second Temple exegetical methods, 57–58; and *gematria*, 58; and *middoth*, 58; as the "Midrashic" or "Pesher" methods, 58; and *notrikon*, 58

secularization, 337–338

Seifrid, Mark A., 72n11

Seitz, Christopher R., 275n41

Sharma, Arvind, 343n46

Shea, W. H., 282n56

Sheppard, Gerald T., 264–265

Simpson, E. K., 355

Smart, Ninian, 347n53, on "worldview analysis," 345–346

Smith, Christian, 356n8

Smith, Morton, 119–120

Snowflakes agency, 310

Spar, Debora L., 296

speech act theory, 185–186; and God as a "Trinitarian" communicative agent, 186; the illocutionary act, 186; the locutionary act, 186; the perlocutionary act, 186

Spence, Jonathan, 342n41

Spinoza, Baruch, 170; his Cartesian separation of the Word of God from Scripture, 171–172

spiritual gift inventories, 248, 248n16

Stamm, J. J., 86

Stanghelle, Jason, 273n37

stem cell research, 289–292; and adult stem cells, 289; categorization of vulnerable people in, 293, 293n11; and embryonic stem cells, 289; and induced pluripotent stem cells, 290–292; and transdifferentiation of cells, 292. *See also* stem cell research, advocacy of a biblically grounded theological formation in a highly pluralistic culture; stem cell research, theological formation of a position on

stem cell research, advocacy of a biblically grounded theological formation in a highly pluralistic culture, 300–312; through appeals to logic, 304–305; through appeals to science, 302–304; viewing embryos as "persons with potential" rather than as "potential persons," 303–304

stem cell research, theological formation of a position on, 292–300; and corruption, 298–299; and creation, 297–298; and redemption, 299–300

Stewart, Robert B., 349n56

Stott, John, 82, 83, 83n42, 334

Strauss, Mark L., 214n40

Sullivan, Francis A., 23n35

Swain, Scott R., 225n67

Sweeney, Marvin A.: definition of Jewish biblical theology, 268n29; on the Psalms, 268, 270, 275n43

Sweis, Khaldoun A., 348n55

Swinburne, Richard, 95nn10–11, 114, 117, 121, 124n33, 125, 125n35, 211nn25–26; on God's omniscience, 201; on transgressing a law of nature, 116, 116n11

Taliaferro, Charles, 350n62

Tanner, Kathryn, 316n20, 326, 326n42, 327, 327n43

Tatian, 340

Taylor, Charles, on secularization, 336–337

Taylor, Rodney L., 350n62

Terry, Milton S., 53–54

Tertullian, 340

The Cape Town Commitment, 334

Thelle, Notto, 343n44

theology: and the "analogy of faith" method, 61; analytic theology, 29–32; as biblical reasoning, 25; hermeneutic theology, 29–32; process theology, 141–142; systematic theology, 61. *See also* biblical theology

Theophilus of Antioch, 340

Thiselton, Anthony, 34n81, 34–35n82

Thompson, Thomas R., 210–211, 210n20, 212

Thomson, James, 303

Tillich, Paul, 177–179, 178n11, 179n12, 181

Tinker, George E., 365–366n34

Tolkien, J. R. R., 103n36, 109–110; on the eucatastrophe in fairy-story, 108–109n47

Toon, Peter, on doctrinal development, 32–33

Torrance, Thomas F., 170, 170n2

Townes, Emilie, 360; on an "ethic of justice," 371

Tozer, A. W., 138, 140

translocality, 37n93

Trinity, the, doctrine of, 48n123, 151–152, 312–313, 328; the lack of moral imperative grounded on an appeal to the inner life of the essential Trinity, 324–325; and moral reflection and deliberation, 325–327; and the New Testament accent on the imitation of Christ, 319–324; and the Old Testament accent on the imitation of God, 317–318; and the "oneness-in-distinction," 188; and perichoresis, 162, 253; social Trinitarianism, 162, 211. *See also* Trinity, the, doctrine of, and the appeal to begetting and proceeding; Trinity, the, doctrine of, and oneness and threeness

Trinity, the, doctrine of, and the appeal to begetting and proceeding: exegetical-linguistic considerations, 152–154; theological-philosophical considerations, 154–160

Trinity, the, doctrine of, and oneness and threeness: oneness (the members of the Trinity as a logically inseparable triad), 160–163; threeness (how the members of the logically inseparable triad can be distinct [metaphysical individuation]), 163–167

Trout, J. D., 93n7
Trueman, Carl R., 38n100
Tuskegee Syphilis Study, 306, 309
Twelftree, Graham H., 119, 123, 351n63

unbaptized infants, salvation of, 22–24
Urbach, E. E., 70n7
U.S. Department of Health and Human Services, "Minimum Procurement Standards," 309, 309n37
U.S. United Network for Organ Sharing, 309, 309n38

Van Aragon, Raymond J., 332n13
VanGemeren, Willem A., 273n17, 280n55
Vanhoozer, Kevin J., 39n10, 41n107, 43n112, 49n123, 206n2; on Scripture, 185–187
VanLaningham, Michael G., 84n46
Verhoef, Peter A., 73n17
Vincent of Lérins, 26, 27, 28, 48
Volf, Miroslav, 253

Wainwright, Geoffrey, 313n3
Walls, Andrew F., 39–40, 40n104, 42, 44; on "the Ephesian moment," 41
Ware, Bruce A., 214n37
Warfield, B. B., on the salvation of unbaptized infants, 23, 23–24
Warner, Rob, 336n20
Waters, Malcolm, 338
Watts, Rikki E., 279n52
Webster, John, 25, 321

Weems, Renita J., 364, 364n30
Wells, David F., 138, 206n1, 216
Wellum, Stephen J., 225n69
West, Tracie C., 360n19
Westminster Larger Catechism, Question 50, 21
Westphal, Merold, 31
Whalen, John P., 25n40
Wiles, Maurice F., 27–28, 28; on "doctrinal aims," 28
William of Rubruck, 341
Williams, Delores S., 359n16
Williams, Paul, 343n46
Williams, Rowan, 47
Wilmut, Ian, 291
Wilson, Gerald H., 265, 283n58
Wimsatt, William K., on the "intentional fallacy," 53
Wittgenstein, Ludwig, 186
Wolterstorff, Nicholas, 184–185, 186; on "deputized discourse," 185
Womanist theological ethics, 354, 356, 359, 359n16, 369–373; concern for wholeness, 360–361, 365; emphasis on the determinative nature of "experience," 372; nature and purpose of, 359–362; sources for, 362–365; twofold focus of, 362; Womanist anthropology, 367; Womanist Christology, 366–367; Womanist ecclesiology, 367–368; Womanist theology proper, 365–366
Woman's Mutual Improvement Club, 363
Woodward, Kenneth L., 351n63
Wright, Christopher J. H., 258, 260, 354

Xenophanes, 316

Yamanaka, Shinya, 291
Yandell, Keith E., 200n38, 203, 203n47, 343n46, 347n53, 348n55, 350, 350nn60–61
Yarbrough, Robert W., 60
Yarnell, Malcolm B., III, 16n3, 26; criticism of Bavinck, 36–37; criticism of Toon and McGrath, 35; on doctrinal development (believers' church theory), 35–38, 35n84, 36n90; objection of to Newman's misapplication of the biblical metaphor of growth, 29n60
Yeago, David, 46n120
Young, Edward J., 72n14
Young, Josiah U., 365, 365–366n34
Young, Richard Fox, 341n37, 343

Zenger, Erich, 273n38, 275–276, 277nn47–48

Scripture Index

Genesis
1	275n41, 279, 297
1–2	258, 278
1:2	239
1:26–27	297, 317
1:27	317
3	318
3:4, 6	294
3:15	66, 258
5:1	317
9:6	297, 308, 317
12	258
12:1–3	318
12:2	77
12:2–3	66n1
15:1–21	318
17:5	77
18:18	77
34	364n30
38	364n30
41:38–39	239

Exodus
19:5–6	66n1, 77, 319
19:6	77, 78
28:3	239
31:3–5	239
33:13	77
33:19	62
34:6	62
35:30–35	239

Leviticus
18:1–5	318
19:2	318
20:22–23	318
20:24	318

Deuteronomy
4	279
4:34	77
5:33	318n26
7:9–11	353
8:6	318n26
10:12	318n26
11:22	318n26
19:9	318n26
26:5	77
26:17	318n26
28:9–10	318
29:4	71
30:16	318n26
32:1–43	71
32:21	71, 74, 74n18
32:36–43	71

Judges
3:10–11	239
6:34	239
11:29–33	239
19	364n30

1 Samuel
16:13–14	239

2 Samuel
1	308
7:12, 16, 28f.	76n21
23:1–2	239

1 Kings
19:1–21	62
19:9, 13	62
19:11b	62

Job
26:13	239
31:15	299
32:8	239
33:4	239

Psalms
1	264, 270, 273, 276, 281
1–2	264
1:1	266, 267, 273, 277, 278
1:1–2	278
1:1, 5–6	277
1:2	268
1:5	267, 280
1:5–6	273, 278
1:6	267, 268, 274n39, 275, 278, 279, 281
2	264, 265, 269, 273, 276, 281
2:4–9	273
2:7	163
2:8	276
2:11	281
2:12	268, 281
2:12a	267

Scripture Index

2:12b	267, 273	111:1	271
3–41	281	111:7	273, 274n40
6:5	20n17	111:7b	276n46
18:25–26	267	111:10	272n34
19:1–5	274	112:1	271
22	71	113–118	271
25:10–11	268	113:1	271
25:12, 14	269	115:1	273
25:16–21	269	115:12–13, 15	280
25:22	269	115:18	271
33	275, 279	116:19	271
50:7–12	139	117:2	271, 273
51	298–299	118:1–4, 29	270
51:5	23, 299	118:3, 21	276
67:1–2, 7	66n1, 69	118:22	71
69	71	118:22–23	75
72	265, 269, 281	119	271
73	268, 269	119:75, 90	273
73:1	270	120–134	271
73:1–16	269	121	280
74	269	124:8	280
75:10	280	127–128	270
79	269	135	271, 272
80	269	135:1–3, 21	271
83	269	136	271
88	269	136:1–3	272
88:11–12	270	136:1–26	270, 272
89	265, 269, 270	137	272
89:1–2	269	138	273n35, 277
89:1–38	281	138–145	272, 277, 281
89:17	280	138:2	277
89:24	281	139	270, 299
89:38–51	269	139:15–16	299
89:49	269	143:1	273
91:4	273	143:1, 10–12	272
92:2	268, 273	144	272, 275n43
92:4	268	144–145	273n35, 275n43, 279
92:10	268	144–147	279
92:10–11	280	145	272, 272–274, 275, 275n43, 276, 276n46, 277, 280n53
92:15	268		
93	270, 273n35		
94–99	273n35	145:1–2, 5–6, 21	273n36
95–99	270	145:1–2, 6, 21	273
95:6–7	280	145:1–6, 11–12, 21	274
98:3	273	145:2, 21	274n39
100:2	149	145:7	274
100:5	270, 273	145:7–13	274
101	281	145:7, 17	273, 276
101–106	273n35	145:8–9	273
102:13, 15	69	145:9–10, 13–17	273
102:13–15	66n1	145:10	274, 280n54
103	270, 273, 276	145:10–11	274
104	276, 279	145:10, 13b, 17	274n39
104:27–30	239	145:11–21	274
104:33	273n36	145:12	274
105	271	145:13	274nn39–40, 276, 276n46
105:45	271		
106:1	270, 271	145:13b	273, 275, 276n46
107	270, 278	145:14–16	274n39
107:1	270	145:14–20	273
107:43	268	145:17	274n40
108:4	273	145:18, 20	274n39
110	273n35, 281	145:18–20	273, 278
111	271, 272	145:19	281
111–112	270	145:20	268, 274n39

145:20b	273	150:6	275, 280, 281
145:21	273, 274n39	*Proverbs*	
146	275, 275n43, 276, 276n46	8:22–23	152
146–150	264, 266, 272, 274–281, 275, 284	8:22–25	152
		14:31	293
146:1–2	273n36	16:8	295
146:3–4	277		
146:4–5	278	*Ecclesiastes*	
146:5	277, 278, 281	4:12	50
146:5–6	277, 278		
146:5, 10	277	*Isaiah*	
146:5–10	275	1:9	71
146:6	275, 280	2:1–4	79
146:6–7	274n40	2:2ff.	80
146:6–8a	277	2:2–3	68–69
146:7–8	278	6:9–10	71, 75
146:7–9	281	8:14	71
146:8	278	9:6f.	76n21
146:9	268, 278, 281	9:6–7	269, 281
146:10	277n48, 278	10:21–23	71
147	278	11	281
147:1–11	275n43	11:9	149, 150
147:1–20	277	19:21–25	69n5
147:2, 3, 6	278	27:6	86
147:2–3, 6, 12–14	278	27:9	86
147:2–7	278	27:12–13	86
147:2, 19	280n55	28:16	71
147:2–3, 6, 10–14, 19–20	279	29:10	71
147:3–6, 13–14	281	33:19–24	278
147:4, 8–9, 15–18	275	40	279
147:4–5, 8–9, 15–18	279	40–55	69, 279
147:5–12	275	40:6, 8	257
147:6	268, 279, 281	40:12–28	139
147:10–11	279	41:8–9	66n1
147:11	277, 278, 281	42:4	69n5
147:15–18	279	42:6	75
147:15, 18, 19	275	42:8	150
147:15–20	279	42:10–13	279
147:19–20	279	42:19–20	71
148	274n39, 279, 281	44:23	66n1, 279
148:1–6	279	45:8	279
148:1–13	280	45:22–23	69n5
148:1–14	275	46:13	78
148:2–13	275	48:20–21	279
148:5	279	49:6	69, 75, 259, 260
148:5–6	275	49:6–8	78
148:5, 13	275	49:7	69
148:7–12	279	49:13	279
148:13	279	51:13	279
148:14	268, 277, 280, 280nn54–55, 281	52:9–10	279
		52:13–53:12	69
149	268, 277, 280	53:1	71
149:1	280	53:2–4, 7–8	71
149:1, 5, 9	280n54, 281	54:1–3	279
149:1–9	277	55:1–3	150
149:2	280, 280n55	55:3–5	69n5
149:2, 4, 5, 9	280	55:11	187
149:4	280, 281	55:12–13	279
149:4–9	280	56:7	80
149:5	280	57:7–10	69n5
149:5, 9	280	59:20–21	86
149:6–9	280, 281	59:21–60:3, 14	79
149:9	275, 280	60	89n56
150	280	60:1–3	66n1, 69n5
		60:1–4	86

Scripture Index   395

60:3	80	9:9–10	74
62:10–12	79	10:6–12	78
63:19	75	13:7	75
65:1	72, 74	14	89n56
65:2–7	73		
65:5f.	78	*Malachi*	
66	89n56	1:11	73, 73n17
66:1	139	3:1–4:6	73

Jeremiah

3:17	69	*Matthew*	
3:18–19	78	3:11	242n9
9:23–24	149	5:16	311
22:16	293	5:43–48	319
23:5	76n21	7:14	84
23:5–6	78	8:5–13	259
24:6	78	8:11–12	75, 85
31:31–33	78	8:27	122n28
31:31–34	86, 239	10:5–6	259
31:35–40	86	10:6	70
31:36	86	12:9–10a, 13	129
33:9	69	12:38–42	121
33:31ff.	76n21	12:40	21
		13:14	71
Lamentations		13:14–15	75
3:22–24	268	14:32–33	122n28
		15:7–9	75
Ezekiel		15:21–28	259
2:2	239	15:24	70
8:3	239	16:1–4	121
20:39–42	78	16:18	242
20:42	78	17:1–13	229
34:24ff.	76n21	21:42	71, 75
36:8–12	78	22:1–14	85
36:22–26	69	22:15–20	357
36:25–27	240	22:37–40	293, 307
36:25–29	78	24:11–13	84
37:1–10	83	24:14	85
37:12–14, 20–27	78	25:31–40	74
37:21–22	78	26:31	75
37:28	69	26:56	75
39:27	69	28:19	19, 260

Daniel

7:13–14	74	*Mark*	
		1:8	242n9
Hosea		2:10	121
1:9–10	71	2:12	122n28
1:10	72	3:16–19	249n17
1:11	78	3:22–27	123
2:23	71, 72, 259	3:27	129
		5:1–20	259
Joel		8:31	121n27
2:28–32	240	9:31	121n27
		10:33–34	121n27
Amos		14:27–28	121n27
4:4–5	353		
		Luke	
Micah		1:36	299
3:8	239	1:39–40	299
4:2	80	1:41	299
		1:43	299
Haggai		1:44	299
2:9	284	1:54	70
		2:7	153
Zechariah		2:19	28
2:11	69	2:32	75
8:13, 20–23	69	3:16	240, 242n9

4:25–27 75
6:1–5 327
6:6–11 327
6:9 327
6:36 319
7:18–28 121
7:36–50 364n30
10:25–28 293
10:30–35 293
11:20 123
11:29–32 121
13:23–24 84
14:12–24 85
17:11–19 259
18:8 84
19:9–10 259
21:23–24 79
22:19 323n33
23:43 21
23:46 21
24:13 41–42
24:14–15 41
24:19–27 75
24:25 75
24:46–49 240

John
1:9–13 259
1:11 259
1:14 39, 228, 229, 284
1:31 70
1:33 242, 242n9
2:19 284
3:3 55
3:3–5 236
3:5 334
3:5–8 257–258
3:16 153
4:1–42 259
4:22 66
5:16–30 222
5:19–30 225
5:26 237n6
5:39 188
7:37–39 240
12:21 329
12:38 71
12:40 71
13:13–17 320–321
13:34 324
14–16 321
14–17 238
14:16 238
14:16–17 240
14:26 238
15 321
15:11 150
15:26 154, 238
16:7 238
16:8–11 236, 333
16:13 35
17:5 325n37
17:11, 22 253
17:17 258
17:20–26 324

17:21 253
17:24 150
19:30 21n22
20–21 229
20:19–23 261
20:22 238

Acts
1 229
1–11 259
1:4–5 241
1:5 242n9
1:8 243
1:15–26 241, 249n17
2:1–4 241, 242
2:14–36 43
2:17–18 252
2:23–32 122
2:33–34 238, 249
2:38 242
4:11 71
6:7 40
7:19 300
8:4–25 243, 260
8:26 243
8:26–40 260
8:29 243
8:30–39 243
8:40 243
9:1–9 229
9:31 37
9:40–42 129
10:34–35 260
10:44–45 242
11:15–17 242n8
11:16 242n9
11:20–21 260
12:24 40, 42
13:1–5 250
13:32–33 153
13:34 153
13:45 72
13:46–49 260
14:14 249n18
15 36
15:14 84
16:6 244
16:7 244
16:9–10 244
16:12 244
16:13–15 244
16:16–18 129, 244
16:25–34 244
17:5 72
17:24–25 140
17:25 144, 149
17:30–31 122
18:26 71
19:20 40
19:21 245
20:22–24 245
20:28 250
21:4–5 245
21:10–14 246
21:27 246n14

Scripture Index   397

21:27–36	246n14	11:25	84
21:30	246n14	11:25–26	67, 70, 79, 84n44
21:33	246n14	11:26	81, 83, 85
23:11	245n11	11:27	86
26:12–18	249n18	11:28	280n55
26:16–18	260	11:28–29	77
26:25	334	11:28–31	85
28:33	245n11	11:30–32	87n54
		11:33	42
Romans		11:34–36	139
1	87n54	12:16	254
1–8	76	16:7	249n18
1:1–4	70	16:25–26	70
1:3–4	122		
1:4	83	*1 Corinthians*	
1:5	84	2:10–16	236
1:16	75	2:14–16	334
1:19–21, 28, 32	333n15	3:1–11	241
1:21	145	3:5	249
2:12	20n17	3:10–15	251
3:1–2	75	3:16–17	252
3:3	76	4:7	141
3:8	295	4:16–17	322
3:23	23	8:6	19
4:13–22	76	9:6	249n18
5:8	22	10:11	46
5:12	298	10:31	150
5:14	298	10:31–11:1	323
5:18	83	11	314n8
6:4, 11, 13	83	11:1	317
6:5	83	11:3	313–314, 325n36
8:3	226	11:3–5	325
8:4–8	236	11:7	317
8:6	83	11:23–24	323n33
8:9	19, 238	11:29	37
8:11	236	12:3	242
8:14	258	12:7	247
8:16	236	12:11	247
8:17	284	12:13	242, 242n9
8:23	236	14	314n8
8:26–27	236	14:9, 23	300
8:28	284	14:13, 27–28	300
8:29	153	14:26–32	249
9–11	67, 74, 75–88 passim	15:3	15, 22
9:3–4	76	15:12, 13, 21, 42	83
9:4–5	77		
9:6	76	*2 Corinthians*	
9:25–26	71	1:12	251
9:27–29	71	1:22	236
9:33	71	2:16	83
10:13–15	249	3:18	236
10:16	71	4:2	251
10:19	74	5:5	236
10:20	72	8:9	325n37
11:1–6	71		
11:2	77	*Galatians*	
11:8	71	1:6–7	45
11:11	82	1:19	249n18
11:11, 14	72	2:9	249n18
11:11–16	72n11	3:16–29	76
11:12	81, 81n32, 82, 83, 84n44	5:16	254
11:12, 15	81–85	5:16–18	258
11:13–14	80	5:16–23	236
11:15	81, 81n32, 82, 83, 84n44	5:19–21	254
11:18, 20, 25	88	6:10	295

Ephesians
1:13	236
1:14	236
2:1–2	355
2:1, 5	83
2:3	355
2:10	355
2:11–21	41
2:18–22	252
4–6	355
4:1	354, 355, 373
4:1, 3	253
4:1–3	353
4:4–5	37
4:8–12	248
4:13	41, 50, 254
4:17	355
4:18	83
4:32–5:2	322
5:2, 8, 15	355
5:18	258, 355
5:18–21	254
5:19–21	255

Philippians
1	308
2:2	254
2:4	321
2:5–11	321–322, 325n37
2:6	42
2:7	229
2:16	83
2:25–30	249n18
3:10	83
3:17	323

Colossians
1:15	153
1:15–17	214
1:17	208n13, 214n39, 221, 222, 223
2:12	83

1 Thessalonians
1:1	249n18
2:6	249n18
4:16	83
5:12	249

2 Thessalonians
2:13	258
2:13–14	257
3:6–10	323
3:7	323
3:9	323

1 Timothy
1:5	251
2	314n8
2:5–6	321
3:2	250
5:17	250

2 Timothy
1:14	26
3	180
3:15	300

3:16	188, 366n37
3:16–17	60, 239

Titus
1:9	250
3:5	334
3:5–6	236

Hebrews
1:1–2	44n115, 186
1:1–5	153
1:3	153, 208n13, 214, 214n39, 221, 222, 223
2:9	284
2:14, 17	226
4:15	200, 283
5:4–6	153
5:7	153, 284
5:8	325n37
5:8–9	283
9:13–15	353
11:17	153
13:7, 17	249
13:8	18

James
1:13–15	191
1:17	141
3:9	317
5:13–15	250

1 Peter
1:2	236, 258
1:14–16	319
1:23–25	257
2:9	319
2:10	259
2:18–23	320
2:21	320
3:18–20	20
5:1–3	249
5:2	249

2 Peter
1	180
1:16–21	239
1:20–21	188

1 John
2:6	320
5:18	237n6

Jude
3	45, 169

Revelation
1:3	283
1:5	153
1:9–20	229
3:14	281
4	282n56
4:11	143
5	282n56
5:1–14	229
5:8–10	282n56
5:8–14	282n56
5:9	88, 252

5:9–10	282n56	19:1–2	282
5:11–12	282n56	19:1–7	281, 284
5:13	281, 282n56	19:2	282
5:14	282n56	19:3	282
6:10	281	19:4	282
7:9	88	19:5	282, 283
7:10–12	282n56	19:6–7	282
7:11–12	281	19:9	283
7:12	282	19:11	282, 283
10:6	281, 282	19:11–18	229
11:2	88	19:13	282
11:15–18	282n56	19:15ff.	79
11:18	79, 283	19:15, 19	88
13:3, 7, 8, 12ff.	88	19:15–21	89
14:8	79, 88	19:16	282
14:9–11	88	19:20–21	88
14:13	283	20:4	83
16:15	283	20:6	283
17:15	79	20:11ff.	80
17:15, 18	88	21–22	281
18:3	79	21:24, 26	89
18:3, 9, 23	88	21:24–26	89
19	281, 282, 283	22:7, 14	283
19:1	282	22:20	284

the

FOUNDATIONS OF EVANGELICAL THEOLOGY

series

The Foundations of Evangelical Theology series incorporates the best of exegetical, biblical, historical, and philosophical theology in order to produce an up-to-date multivolume systematic theology with contemporary application—ideal for both students and teachers of theology.

Visit crossway.org for more information.